TWAYNE'S
FILMMAKERS SERIES

Frank Beaver, Editor

PUMP 'EM FULL OF LEAD

A LOOK AT GANGSTERS ON FILM

PUMP 'EM FULL OF LEAD

A Look at Gangsters on Film

Marilyn Yaquinto

TWAYNE PUBLISHERS
An Imprint of Simon & Schuster Macmillan
New York
PRENTICE HALL INTERNATIONAL
London • Mexico City • New Delhi • Singapore • Sydney • Toronto

Twayne's Filmmakers Series

Pump 'Em Full of Lead: A Look at Gangsters on Film
Marilyn Yaquinto

Twayne Publishers
An Imprint of Simon & Schuster Macmillan
1633 Broadway
New York, NY 10019

Library of Congress Cataloging-in-Publication Data
Yaquinto, Marilyn
Pump 'em full of lead : a look at gangsters on film/Marilyn Yaquinto.
p. cm. — (Twayne's filmmakers series)
Includes bibliographical references and index.
ISBN 0-8057-3892-4 (pbk.)
1. Gangster films--History and criticism. I. Title. II. Series.
PN1995.9.G3Y37 1998
791.43'655—dc21 97-48742
CIP

This paper meets the requirements of ANSI/NISO Z39.48-1992 (Permanence of Paper).

10 9 8 7 6 5 4 3 2 1

Printed in the United States of America.

To Michael, my tireless counselor,
dedicated friend, and loving husband

CONTENTS

FOREWORD

Of all the contemporary arts, the motion picture is particularly timely and diverse as a popular-culture enterprise. This lively art form cleverly combines storytelling with photography to achieve a quintessential twentieth-century phenomenon. Individual as well as national and cultural interests have made the medium an unusually varied one for artistic expression and analysis. Films have been exploited for commercial gain, for political purposes, for experimentation, and for self-exploration. The various responses to the motion picture have given rise to different labels for both the fun and the seriousness with which the art form has been received, ranging from "the movies" to "cinema." These labels hint at both the theoretical and the sociological parameters of the film medium.

A collective art, the motion picture has nevertheless allowed individual genius to flourish in all the medium's artistic and technical areas: directing, screenwriting, cinematography, acting, editing. The medium also encompasses many genres beyond the narrative film, including documentary, animated, and avant-garde expression. The range and diversity of motion pictures suggest rich opportunities for appreciation and for study.

Twayne's Filmmakers Series examines the full panorama of motion picture history and art. Many studies are auteur oriented and elucidate the work of individual directors whose ideas and cinematic styles make the directors the authors of their films. Other studies examine film movements and genres or analyze cinema from a national perspective. The series seeks to illuminate all the many aspects of film for the film student, the scholar, and the general reader.

Frank Beaver

PREFACE

My exploration into the genre of gangster films meant first clarifying the definition of a gangster film. Second, I scrutinized hundreds of films from more than a century of moviemaking to find those that were indispensable to the genre's birth, perpetuation, and enduring popularity.

The opening chapters explore the origins and key environments that helped create the gangster genre: crowded tenements, street gangs, immigrant life, criminal "stars," and eager filmmakers. What will become apparent as one progresses through the book is that the ingredients that existed in the nineteenth century to help create and nurture criminals remain true in the late twentieth. These early chapters are vital to understanding how the genre's themes hold true and keep recurring in films even today. Only the gangster's weapon gets increasingly deadlier—not the gangster.

WHAT IS A GANGSTER FILM?

A hard definition remains elusive, yet everyone, including moviegoers, thinks he or she can easily recognize a gangster when he appears on-screen. The academic community, as well as mainstream film critics, certainly don't agree on what transforms an ordinary crime film into a gangster film. Nor do they agree if such films should be lumped together to form a genre (to cluster products similar in style, form, or content). Some argue that films should be grouped together only when they reveal the creative outlook of one artist or director (the auteur theory). In this book, I've borrowed from both approaches. I've focused on the backgrounds and work habits of individual artists when their influence was profound. However, my overall approach ultimately tilts toward reaffirming the aggregate qualities of a genre.

I also embrace the notion that filmmaking is a collaborative art form, including such unsung collaborators as the moviegoing public. Permeating gangster films are the public's economic and social worries, along with impulses that create popular culture as a whole and those that affect other art forms. The gangster genre, as a result of that blending of influences, has remarkable resilience and cultural utility when one considers that its films involve as noxious a character as the gangster. The genre has existed and evolved for nearly a century and shows no sign of losing its appeal. The genre's record of similar story lines and persistent popularity is unequaled in Hollywood history. The Western was confined to a bygone era and place, and it eventually lost its ability to adapt. But the gangster genre depends on the disturbing truth about "public enemies" and the darker side of society.

The gangster has a timeless quality, just like the sins he commits. He's been described as possessing the leftover anguish of a character from classical Greek tragedy. He's also been dubbed a twentieth century Macbeth armed with a smoking gun. Those who dabble in the social sciences have called the gangster a fitting metaphor for the battered myth of the American dream—especially among downtrodden immigrants who found that dream wanting.

WHAT'S IN A GANGSTER FILM?

To help the reader understand the common theme that connects the films covered in this book, the following is a bare-bones description of the essential ingredients that underlie most good gangster films.

A gangster, more so than other criminal types, belongs to a collective, a gang, a mob, a syndicate. That can mean a loosely gathered group such as the Dillinger gang or an organization as widespread as the Mafia. More important, though, the gangster and his cohorts think of themselves as more than a collection of professional accomplices. They tend to bond on a personal level and rely on one another as if they were extended family members.

Although the gangster film's story line includes criminal activities and "rackets," the backbone of a gangster film story is the metamorphosis of the gangster character. He will rise spectacularly and then fall horrendously until he's finally destroyed. His downfall occurs either physically, mentally (he ends up as a Corleone-type "living corpse"), or he's redeemed and transformed into something more virtuous than a gangster.

Moreover, although he's usually exterminated by outside forces (rival gangsters or law enforcement), the seeds of his destruction have already been sown within himself. He possesses a fatal flaw, and the very personal qualities that enable him to bully his way to the top ultimately destroy him. In other words, he's his own worst enemy and does himself in long before anyone else fires a shot.

The genre's best films wallow in this psychic purgatory; the worst ignore the character development and interior torment and go for the bloodletting. Although violence is an integral part of the gangster life, the best films use violence for punctuation, symbolism, historical accuracy, and indispensable shock value. But if violence is allowed to overwhelm the human drama that underpins the story, the film drifts into the territory of the "action" film, robbing the gangster of his essential tragedy.

There are also excellent foreign films and Hollywood subgenres that don't get discussed in this book, including heist films, prison films, and movies about lone stalkers and sociopaths who shun gangs and social cohesion. Foreign films usually co-opt the American gangster format and adapt it to suit the national psyche of a society other than America. Because the scope of this book traces the American genre's development and evolution, such films would be too plentiful and varied to include. And although the subgenres include a gangster in their casts, they focus more on how crimes are committed or on life after incarceration and stray too far from the genre's core values.

The gangster genre has evolved over the years—owing to fashion, morality, and the prevailing definition of what constitutes illegal and immoral activities. There's even a recognizable gangster "look," regardless of the era, that depends on an insatiable appetite for flamboyant clothes that marks him as a strutting peacock and a social misfit. Moreover, from Cagney to the boyz, screen gangsters, hoods, wise guys, and homeboys forever mistake conspicuous consumption (lavish cars and voracious materialism) as a surefire measure of success at the expense of personal growth.

The faces of the gangsters have also changed over the years, not just because movie stars shine and fade away, but because the images of real-life criminals have changed. Gangsters have nearly always come from the bottom of society and get their start in the gangs that thrive on America's meanest streets. The personnel of gangs has changed over the years to reflect the newest wave of underdogs who stir together anger and unrealized ambition to cook up the gangster persona. In a society that doesn't value these people, they find employment, stature, and abundant reward (however short-lived) in the Underworld. And after the women's movement was launched in the 1960s, a woman's finger has more often been placed on the trigger.

Not all the films included in this book are the best gangster films ever made. Some strongly affected, reflected, or stimulated the genre. Others merely demonstrate what happens when a genre gets stale and formula replaces creativity. And still others boldly delighted moviegoers despite leaving Hollywood unimpressed and uninterested.

WHY IS THE GANGSTER FILM STILL WITH US?

Perhaps the gangster keeps drawing us to the movies because we see him as a nightmare vision of our own desires and ambitions run amok. And we just can't take our eyes off him. My book asserts that we're frightened most when we believe that the screen gangster fails to understand that crime doesn't pay and threatens to roar on no matter how much lead we pump into him. The gangster has proven to be as valuable a commodity in Hollywood as the heroes invented to soothe us. For a century, we've been thrilled and mortified that no matter how many times we shoot him—with as much film stock as bullets—he keeps coming back to life. Perhaps we want to believe he's just a Hollywood invention. But deep down inside we know the screen gangster is real, even when his blood spill is make-believe.

ACKNOWLEDGMENTS

Frank Beaver for his example, inspiring scholarship, and editorial review. Mark Zadrozny for his good-natured and thoughtful guidance. Regula Noetzli for her support as my agent and for her invaluable advice as a friend and associate. The Lingemans: Sylvester, Frances, Christopher, and Michael for their love, unwavering loyalty, and generous feedback. Lorraine Jones, Michelle Arnold, Leah Gillette, and Wendy Lynn for their blind faith and never-ending words of encouragement. To friends and colleagues: Suzanne Parker for her research and public relations assistance and Philip Sherman for his candor and editing skills on the original proposal. Michael Bragdon for his scrutiny regarding the book in progress and his soothing humor regarding the writer under duress. My perennial writing coach Don Kubit for his ever-refreshing "cruelty" and sincere compassion long after classes have ended. Finally, to my student Chad Tiernan for his research contribution.

Mary Corliss and her staff at the Film Still Archives of the Museum of Modern Art for their patience and assistance in locating all the stills for this book. All the publicity stills for the films featured in this text were provided by the Museum of Modern Art/Film Stills Archives.

ILLUSTRATIONS

CHAPTER 1

Coming to America . . . and a Theater Near You

> The gang is a distemper that writes upon the generation it plagues the receipt for its own corrective. . . . [It] is the slum's counterfeit of self-esteem.
>
> —Photo-essayist Jacob Riis, 1902

"It's fixed. Cotton got in through the cellar," Jimmy Valentine whispers to his fellow gang members. Within a few scenes, the men are inside a bank, attempting to crack open its vault. Seen from a high angle shot, the safecrackers work by flashlight deep in the camera's frame. The bird's-eye view—set at an oblique angle—reveals a maze of offices in the forefront, shrouded in darkness and connected by a series of confounding doors. The commotion awakens a sleeping guard, who rushes toward the vault, forcing the thieves to scatter forward into the web of rooms. Shooting at the footsteps ahead of him, the guard fires into the darkness, smoke billowing from his gun. After tracking the thieves in a puzzling circle, the guard himself becomes trapped in one of the rooms. The bank robbers lock the doors behind them and escape through the maze unharmed—but without the loot.

This scene could be cut into any contemporary movie and be convincing. Instead, it is embedded in a silent classic, *Alias Jimmy Valentine,* of 1915. The film was based on a stage play that was in turn inspired by an O. Henry story, "A Retrieved Reformation." *Alias Jimmy Valentine* is one of the first crime films to put the crook at the heart of the story, exploring his "Underworld" and his criminal methods. It's the story of a respectable businessman who lives a double life—bank clerk Lee Randall by day, bank robber Jimmy Valentine by night—and the foiled robbery is the start of Jimmy's downfall as a thief. After leaving his monogrammed cuff link inside the bank, he flees town with his sidekick, Cotton. On the train, Jimmy meets a woman, whom he feels compelled to protect from the crude advances of Cotton. Jimmy and Cotton get into a scuffle that ends with Cotton being thrown off the back of the train. As the villain with few redeeming qualities, Cotton squeals from his deathbed to Detective Doyle. When Jimmy returns to town, he's nabbed and sent to Sing Sing. Several shots filmed inside the New York prison lend acute realism.

The girl Jimmy "saved" comes to the prison and turns out to be the lieutenant governor's daughter, Rose. The warden boasts to her of some of his inmates' skills. "Here's a man who is doing ten years for opening a safe without tools or combinations, simply by sense of touch," he says of Jimmy. But Jimmy denies that such a feat is possible. Rose, remembering his gallant gesture on the train, convinces her father that this is further proof that Jimmy is no criminal. He's pardoned, but Doyle vows to catch him again in the act. Jimmy soon reunites with his gang, which immediately plots another robbery. But Jimmy grows reluctant and wants to go straight—lured by the promise of a legitimate job offered by Rose's father.

Jimmy is seen as the bridge between Rose and her upright society and the Underworld of his former gang. Yet the criminals in their world of dingy hangouts and seedy saloons are the more fascinating characters in the film. One scene in particular is superb: After one of Jimmy's gang members gets drunk in a saloon, a diminutive waiter refuses to get him another beer. The hoodlum, wearing a hat cocked back on his head and a contemptuous smirk, bullies the waiter into fetching another drink. The scene captures the gangster's swagger and his irresistible strut. It's an absorbing display that will be spliced into nearly every gangster film to follow.

The climax of the film comes after Jimmy is working again in a bank and Rose has become his love. One day a little girl gets trapped in the vault, and the only way she can be rescued is if Jimmy cracks the safe. He does so to save the child, but Doyle is a witness and threatens to make good on his promise to take Jimmy down. In the end, however, Doyle sees that Jimmy has rebuilt his life and rehabilitated himself—with Rose at his side—and decides to let him go.

The intriguing story of *Alias Jimmy Valentine* was popular enough to foster remakes in 1920 and 1928 as well as to inspire a sequel in 1936, *The Return of Jimmy Valentine*. In the description now accompanying the Library of Congress print of the original, director Maurice Tourneur is lauded for his "mastery of space." His technique was no doubt fine-tuned in his previous roles as a book illustrator and an assistant to sculptor Auguste Rodin. Film chronicler Ephraim Katz credits Tourneur as one of the first directors to lend the criminal milieu a moody appeal. Through his pictorial sensibility and subtlety, the criminals' psychological terrain is as exciting as their movements.

Tourneur's *Alias Jimmy Valentine* was thought to be lost, as have been the vast majority of silent films. Most have disintegrated or been shamefully destroyed. Fortunately, the "found" film provides evidence that the gangster story is one of the oldest and most enduring topics in cinema—even in its youth—80 years before *Pulp Fiction*.

Catalogs for the trailblazing years of silent cinema reveal hundreds of titles of crime films, including *The Burglar* (1898), *The Kidnapper* (1903), *The Thieving Hand* (1904), *Burglar Bill* (1904), and *The Moonshiners* (1904). *The Gentlemen Highwaymen* (1905) features one of the first car chases, however crude, adding another weapon to the crime genre's arsenal.

Filmmakers working for Thomas Edison, who held the patent on the early movie cameras and projection equipment, also cranked out a crime film called *Desperate Encounter between Burglars and Police*. It was shot in 1905 in one of New York's rougher neighborhoods, the Lower East Side. That area, along with the Bowery and Hell's Kitchen, served as the location shots for many films. The insatiable demand for more one-reelers at the first movie theaters, the nickelodeons, often forced moviemakers to use what was happening while the camera was rolling as plot and neighborhood residents as actors—including local gang members. The hard-edged urban settings also gave the young genre a sense of identity strong enough to endure the more contrived landscapes of Hollywood sound stages in years to come.

The Lower East Side as an immigrant melting pot provided the backdrop for many gritty gangster stories in the decades ahead. Italian director Sergio Leone recreated New York's turn-of-the-century tenements for his 1984 epic *Once upon a Time in America*.

THROUGH IMMIGRANT EYES

Often caught in the camera's view were bona fide criminals. Organizations such as the Mafia came to the United States during the tremendous wave of immigration that lasted from 1880 to 1914, bringing in 15 million new citizens who had been born in foreign lands. The mafiosi arrived alongside their unwitting Italian and Sicilian compatriots, who numbered more than 4 million during the period. Most of these immigrants were hoping to trade the devastating poverty back home for the promise of a fresh life in a new land. The reality was that most of them found themselves in the country's most appalling slums, forming poor, overcrowded Little Italys in the major cities. Before long the Mafia had recreated the old-world terror inside the American ghettos and demanded extortion money from small shopkeepers and local businessmen. Notes stamped with a black hand and carrying a threat to kill the recipient or his family left the victim few options other than to pay up. These poor targets also brought from Italy a deep-seated distrust of authority figures and police, whom immigrants rightly estimated were often as corrupt as the criminals themselves. The Mafia's extortion rackets soon inspired enterprising moviemakers, who promptly released *The Black Hand* in 1906, with remakes in 1912 and 1913. A sequel, *The Black Hand Conspiracy,* followed in 1914.

The movies had become wildly popular, and winning ideas were often repeated to provide products for the thousands of nickelodeons, arcades, photo-kineto parlors, and vaudeville houses springing up across the country. But soon the alarm was sounded about shocking movie content. By 1909 sex and crime were the most popular themes, which for authorities were flickering back a moving picture of America that was not very flattering. In an article published in the *Review of Reviews* in 1908, an anonymous critic complained: "One's regret for such exhibitions is . . . all the thought, time and energy have been expended for the portrayal of the realism of bloodshed, crime and brutality."[1] Those who were outraged did not see film messages as being quite as dangerous as socialist propaganda, which also exposed capitalism's darker side. Nor were the moviemakers seen as fringe artists trying to tamper with tradition. On the contrary, the novice movie producers were profit-seeking businessmen keeping up with the demands of a new marketplace.

The moral minority of the era—a potent but unorganized collective called the Progressive Movement—also recognized the medium's popularity. But the Progressives wanted film exploited for education's sake. They wanted its power tapped for more than a celluloid version of burlesque or a photoplay of the tabloid press. It was the era of "causes," with campaigns to end rampant corruption, abusive child labor, and savage working conditions. Upton Sinclair's 1906 exposé *The Jungle,* which investigated Chicago's meatpacking industry, had a potent and immediate impact, prompting the passage of the Pure Food and Drug Act. The reformers' work was remarkable in getting legislation passed and for getting the authorities to examine a host of disturbing social problems. But some aspects of the multifaceted movement were about a desire to preserve traditional values. Many Progressives were nostalgic for a more genteel, nineteenth-century society that honored Victorian ideals. These activists revered a time less complicated by inventions and hordes of foreigners pouring into already plagued tenements and swelling cities. Enlightenment, though, had traditionally been accomplished through established institutions, including the schools, churches, and family elders—mediums in which the flow of information could be controlled. Even public journalism had a long-standing tradition as a pulpit, including the era's muckrakers and their push for reforms.

To be sure, the nickelodeons and peep shows were instructional, but their lack of filters—having immediate and emotional impact on their audiences—distressed the Progressives and alarmed the old guard. The immigrants were sitting in the dark, learning English from the intertitles and being dazzled by the spectacle. They were also being taught homely lessons about their new country embedded in the moving pictures. And most sensational, one-reel stories usually offered simpleminded solutions to public problems, stretching from sexy to hopelessly naive.

The audiences, though, saw the movies as the embodiment of the American dream: stories of opportunity and the rewards of individual enterprise. The consistency of the movie message in films about everyday people overcoming colossal odds helped teach a generation of new immigrants that hope didn't belong only to the upper classes. It was the promise of America made to everyone—and celebrated on the screen. (The discriminating rich, with their theater productions and other "high art" forms, shunned the nickelodeons, considering them a tasteless fad.)

An anonymous writer in the *American Movie Magazine* for July 1913 eloquently described what movies meant to these early audiences: "It is art democratic, art for the race. It is in a way a new universal language, even more elemental than music."[2]

Figures gathered as early as 1907 reveal that more than 200,000 people a day attended New York's 500 movie houses, with boys aged 10 to 14 as a group going at least twice a week.[3] Movies were pervasive, and their effects, although unknown at the time, were assumed to be powerful. Soon a barrage of groups representing clergy, educators, parents, and elected officials made the movies their business. The cries for public censorship were temporarily silenced with the formation of the National Board of Review, a group of volunteers who previewed and evaluated films to avert government interference. The board was accepted by the film industry and functioned in a semiofficial capacity until 1921.

Most moviemakers hardly viewed their products as enlightenment or propaganda—just cheap-to-produce, profitable entertainment. Bankruptcies and lawsuits kept the industry focused on itself, and it worried more about survival than offending decency. Moviemakers responded to any threats to interrupt the process of making money by caving in to complaints. At the very least, moviemakers better camouflaged the offending practice. They learned quickly to tag on a morally uplifting ending to the most titillating film about, for example, white slavery. In the final scenes, a kindly, adoptive banker would rescue the girls—a gesture meant to offset earlier scenes of scantily dressed and shackled schoolgirls.

Reformers hammered away at moviemakers for lurid storytelling but failed to be alarmed that the movies were reducing most serious issues to 10-minute soap operas. And although reformers pushed for legislation to guarantee basic human dignities in the tenements and workplaces, strikers demanding the same things were portrayed in the movies as subversives beholden to Mother Russia. These movies warned immigrants about rising too quickly in the New World. Immigrant ambition was admirable, provided it didn't upset the status quo. America's established citizens, mostly white and largely from northern Europe, had made their fortunes in the new country and had set up the established order. They weren't eager to step aside for the new arrivals. Given this, it's easy to see how the screen gangster, safecracker, burglar, or pistol-shooting outlaw, who had crawled up from the bottom of society, was so wildly popular—at least with audiences. On the other hand, the movie criminal terrified those in power, and they launched many campaigns over the next few decades to sabotage his appeal and make him conform.

The reformers, business leaders, and politicians were right to be alarmed by the moving pictures but foolish to think they could tame them. They were facing the age of "hot" media, whose visual image often overwhelms any words to the contrary. Censors soon discovered how difficult it was to expunge an idea or an overall impression within a film merely by cutting out a few frames. The underlying motif suggested by the lap dissolve or the "fade to black" remains remarkably intact, if not enhanced, in the viewer's imagination. (Radio, the "theater of the mind," would join the media family in 1922 and compound the "mass culture" picture.) Had the reformers thought of it first, they would have asked for something akin to the V chip. Newspapers (the first mass-appeal medium) were bad enough, screaming doom and sin from the front pages. But the press enjoyed constitutional protection for its role in public discourse and for the sake of the republic. The press, too, had its own spotty history. It had sullied its reputation at the turn of the century with yellow journalism. Yet most journalists, despite the occasional scandal, were well schooled in their constitutional rights. In contrast, the media's newest players, the filmmakers, were sure of nothing.

If the moving pictures were a far cry from journalism, were they art? If so, they would have had more license to provoke discussion and incite reaction—often ahead of mainstream taste. But given the level of expertise of most moviemakers at the time—many staying in business on a week-to-week basis—few aimed at artistic statement. Many often failed even to be entertaining.

With each complaint about content, movie producers searched out approved story lines from literary sources and stage plays, which were audience tested and already approved by the sensitive moralists. "From 1908 to 1914 motion pictures preached," wrote historian Lewis Jacobs. The gangster remained a tool in the movie sermons, but he was only able to menace from the sidelines. Even so, he was usually the one who captured the audience's imagination. Playwrights since Shakespeare have understood that the caliber of the story depends on the quality of the villain, with Macbeth posing as the ultimate stinker—a public enemy derived from a sixteenth-century mind.

For an America shifting from rural life to urban blight, the gangster was the ideal bogeyman to stand for everything wrong with the population's migration to the cities. In addition, immigrants continued to pour into the cities—the newest waves coming from central and southern Europe. Around 1915, more than two-thirds of New York's population were foreign-born. By 1924, xenophobia finally gripped those groups with older ties to the country, and they used their power to pass legislation to set strict limits on immigration from specific countries. A quota was set at 2 percent of the total from a country already represented in the United States as of 1890. This policy favored immigration from northern Europe and restricted it from other parts of the world. (The policy was not abolished until 1968.)

Filmmakers tried to integrate America's new diversity into their films, but the depiction of immigrants on-screen often reflected the bias and stereotypes of the larger culture: "The Mexican was caricatured as a treacherous 'greaser'; the Jew as a briber; the Negro as a cake walker, buck dancer, razor thrower; the Spaniard as a romantic, foppish lover; the Irishman as a quarrelsome beer drinker."[4] Many films after 1908 tried to offer a more sensitive portrayal of the most maligned groups. In *A Man's Man,* a Jew is shown to have "manhood, sentiments and convictions" and not just concern with thrift. The Irish, now assimilating faster than their southern and eastern European neighbors, were given a new image of "pride of heritage" in films such as *Ireland the Oppressed* and *The Colleen Brawn.*[5] However, Mexicans, Asians, Native Americans, and African-Americans were only slightly recast, because the moving pictures could not go beyond correcting the entrenched racism in the broader society. Such films were modest efforts and usually stopped insinuating the black man was a savage, making him a loyal, trusted servant instead.

Also, with America being pressured to join World War I, which had begun in Europe in 1914, many people saw the merits in rallying the nation's newest citizens around the American flag and discouraging links to old countries. The Italian, though, representing one of the largest ethnic communities, would rarely get a reprieve from a screen image as an extortionist or murderer. In part, reformist cinema couldn't alter the reality to which immigrants returned after they left the theaters. Crime-ridden streets and the existence of real-life gangsters were proof enough that the screen gangster was chillingly accurate. And the gangsters immigrants knew in Little Italy were immune to a sobering lecture on Yankee pride or the pious pleas of a pretty girl—as the movies argued. More important, the underclasses knew that real gangsters or mafiosi were more ferocious than people who steal out of desperation or fall into crime from chronic unemployment. The gangsters they knew came to America as career professionals.

CRIMINAL VÉRITÉ

Some of the most vicious gangsters in our history were immigrants, including Meyer Lansky, Dutch Schultz, Dion O'Bannion, and Lucky Luciano. Yet the most famous gangster of this century, Al Capone, took great pride in pointing out, "I'm no Italian, I was born in Brooklyn."[6] The press, though, insisted on giving his birthplace as Naples or Sicily—perhaps to make the monster less a homegrown problem. It's likely, however, that whether gangsters were born elsewhere or in American towns and cities, their parents spoke another tongue at home, as did Capone's. Most gang members who stalked the tenements weren't as prosperous as Luciano or Capone, and most rarely escaped the rotting slums they further victimized. At the very least, though, their efforts were as lucrative and stimulating as the alternatives open to them by legitimate society. Factory toil and meager street peddling weren't careers that led them out of poverty or promised upward mobility.

Despite the patriotic rhetoric, most immigrants in these neighborhoods felt impotent and increasingly removed from "the land of opportunity." The American dream often transformed into a nightmare—the New World wasn't much of an improvement over the old. The only spark of defiance that immigrants witnessed was exercised by the local gangs. Hardly a twentieth-century phenomenon, gangs in New York had been a public menace since shortly after the Revolutionary War. By the late–nineteenth century, gangs were being manned by Italian, Irish, and Jewish immigrants, who were the least respected in America's stratified society. All three groups had fled ghettos and political oppression in the old countries, and many had been members of organized gangs before leaving Europe.

Regardless of their root circumstances, these groups found their recruits on the mean streets of America. Gang leaders offered the poor boys camaraderie and the appeal of being someone who gets noticed. If for no other reason, they found a perverse respect in being feared. And time spent in a gang was an informal apprenticeship for full-fledged careers in crime after reaching adulthood. The net effect, though, was to make escaping the ghetto nearly impossible. Most gang members were sent to prison or to the morgue and didn't fare much better than their poor brethren. Still, their short but thrilling lives were often admired for a wayward dignity missing from the wretched existences of most slum people. Compared to living in quiet desperation, the gangster's pluck in exploiting his skills and rising above the miserable crowd seemed, ironically, very American.

New York's Chinatown had its brand of gangsters, who ran gambling houses and opium dens. They, like the Mafia, were camouflaged behind respectable businesses and shops and enjoyed police ambivalence at the cost of monthly protection money. Their intergang showdown, known as the Tong Wars, made front-page news around 1899.

In 1927 Herbert Asbury made a comprehensive study of New York's gangland. He claimed that the 1920s gangster was a pale comparison to his nineteenth-century forerunner, especially because the reform movement of 1914 swept in a mayor who cracked down on the city's gangs. Asbury argued that the gangs prowling the streets under the same notorious names were "merely young hoodlums who seek to take advantage of ancient reputations. . . . They [have] nothing in common with such great brawling, thieving gangs as the Dead Rabbits, Bowery Boys, the Eastmans, Gophers, and Five Pointers." He blamed the "lively imaginations of industrious journalists" for keeping the legends alive.[7] (Asbury, however, failed to note the connection between these gangs and the Prohibition gangsters who were in full swing at the time of his study. He didn't acknowledge that Prohibition had reinvigorated the gangs. Johnny Torrio, for example, was a Five Pointer who became a millionaire from bootlegging on the south side of Chicago. That territory, in his retirement, was handed over to his fellow Five Pointer and understudy Al Capone.)

Charles Dickens, in his "American Notes," thought the area rank enough to warrant mention: "Let us go on again . . . and plunge into the Five Points. . . . Poverty, wretchedness, and vice, are rife enough where we are going now . . . these narrow ways diverging to the right and left, and reeking everywhere with dirt and filth. . . . hideous tenements which take their name from robbery and murder: all that is loathsome, drooping, and decayed is here."[8]

Capone's boyhood gang was named in the early nineteenth century for the crossing of Broadway and the Bowery. The rival Eastman Gang controlled a territory that stretched from Fourteenth Street to Monroe Street, and from the Bowery to the East River—streets lined with brothels and saloons. One notorious whorehouse in the area advertised "flower girls" under the age of 16. Another, near the corner of Chatham Street (now Park Row and William Street), boasted of stabling nine girls, ranging in age from 9 to 15. During a multiday gang war around 1835, a dozen buildings were set ablaze, and five houses of prostitution were burned, "the inmates, stripped and parceled out among the gangsters."[9]

The gang members lived among the atrocious tenements, which were usually condemned by the health department but not torn down for decades because the tenants had nowhere to go. At Gotham Court, the vapors from sewer lines running underneath the building caused unusually high death rates among the trapped residents. But the sewers served the gangsters well, as they could hide their loot or themselves on the sewers' side ledges. Another infamous building was called the Old Brewery; it was so run-down that it could not function as a factory any longer but remained open as a tenement for as many as 1,000 people. The tenants were equally divided between Irish immigrants and blacks, who often married each other and sealed their expulsion from the rest of nineteenth-century society. Police estimated that a murder a night occurred inside this fortress, but few of their officers would enter the building to ferret out the killers. It was finally demolished in 1852. The most notorious tenement, though, was Mulberry Bend, situated north and slightly east of the Five Points in what is now Little Italy. Mulberry Bend became the apex for a reform movement as a symbol of the most foul hazards of the slums. The Reverend Lewis Morris Pease set

The Prohibition-era gangster Al Capone has been the chilling inspiration for hundreds of screen likenesses over the years. He continues to be the preeminent model of intoxicating power and lethal charisma. Tourists can still collect Capone memorabilia on visits to Chicago, where a 1980s eatery was named after this original Scarface. Courtesy of UPI/Corbis-Bettmann.

up a noted mission and wrote that the area's basic troubles were ignorance and poverty. He argued that the rampant vice and crime in Mulberry Bend could not be beaten unless the conditions causing them were conquered. (This idea would be echoed more than a century later as the blueprint for the Great Society of the Johnson administration, which planned to wage a war on poverty along with a war on crime. Although political approaches come and go, the tenements and the gangs tenaciously remain.)

The Dead Rabbits (slang for thugs) dressed for gang war in red-striped clothes and marked their weapons with rabbits impaled on spikes. (This was a century before the "colors" of South Central Los Angeles gangs.) The Dead Rabbits fought rival gangs such as the Bowery Boys—not to be confused with the screwball, benign boys of 1930s Hollywood. Police estimated that more than 30,000 men and boys had gang allegiances around 1850, and their intergang battles brought in the National Guard and army regiments on several occasions. During one ferocious battle, as many as 1,000 fighters met at Bayard Street, not far from the Bowery, while residents looted the shops along Mulberry and Elizabeth Streets, further aggravating the atmosphere of anarchy. According to the *New York Times,* "Brick-bats, stones and clubs were flying. . . . Wounded men lay on the sidewalks and were trampled upon." The war went on for a week, resulting in 8 dead and more than 150 men and boys wounded.[10]

While police fought the gangs, the gangs did battle for the politicians as hired thugs, including political gangsters such as Boss Tweed. The heyday of New York's Tammany Hall vice is the best known, but a similar situation at one time existed in nearly all major cities. In each, a network of accomplices extended to the police and the courts, forming a nearly impenetrable empire for racketeering.

Compared to street gangs, Tweed's mob of elected officials aimed for a more organized theft of the city treasury, using the ballot box rather than a pistol to steal and stay in power. His Common Council of 1850 was dubbed by muckraking journalists the Forty Thieves. Tweed and his cohorts linked themselves to the gangsters, though, through payoffs to keep gambling houses and brothels undisturbed. The elected officials also used gangsters to stuff the ballot boxes or beat up voters who supported opposing candidates. A famous Jewish gangster named Big Jack Zelig told a police detective what the going rates were for a hired henchman in 1902: slash on cheek with knife, $1 to $10; shot in leg, $1 to $25; shot in arm, $5 to $25; throwing a bomb, $5 to $50; murder, $10 to $100.[11]

STREET SHOOTING

Not all young gang members made crime their lifelong careers—as jail or street death was often inevitable. Some of the troubled youth grew up to become moviemakers. The mastermind behind Columbia Pictures, Harry "King" Cohn, sold stolen furs in his youth and hustled pool. Jack Warner boasts in his memoirs, "I had once been a mobster myself . . . a member of the Westlake Crossing gang in Youngstown, a teen-aged mob led by a junior Dillinger." He admits surviving "a couple of rumbles" and reveals the glamour that gangland roots lent even the personal histories of the boys who went straight.[12]

Jack Warner and his brothers were among the hundreds of young moviemakers and producers battling it out on the east coast for a stake in the new industry. They were overwhelming the Edison Company with requests for equipment. But a lack of supplies and willingness to share profits sparked an underground film industry that used contraband gear to get around the patent restrictions. Scores of moviemakers were shooting pictures from rooftops, warehouses, and back alleys—then quickly packing up the gear and going on the run to avoid having their equipment or finished films stolen. The Motion Picture Patents Company, consisting of Edison and several major players in the business, was formed in 1909 to stop the theft of equipment and available films. This company became known as "the Trust" but found its system of licensing as futile as the previous patent protection.

Adolph Zukor, who later became president of Paramount, described his days among the independent manufacturers, distributors, and exhibitors as harrowing. He said outlaws, including himself, "were fair game for the snoopers and raiders of the 'Trust.' "[13] The filmmakers' early crime stories, in fact, would have been grittier had they turned the cameras on their own brawling industry. Gangsters were hired by the renegade filmmakers to protect their operations, and the Trust sent "gangs of sluggers" to break them up. In one instance of a gang raid, the police records of 28 June 1912 describe a riot and the arrest of two men, who when asked gave their employer as Universal Studios.[14] The situation in New York became so volatile that the outlaw producers fled to the other coast, which offered year-round production possibilities as well. Hollywood as a town may already have been on the map, but as a concept, it was invented by these outlaw filmmakers around 1909. Even there, security was tight. Director Thomas Ince mounted a Civil War cannon at the studio's enclosure, "loaded to the muzzle with scrap iron, and guards with sawed-off shotguns patrolled the gates." Ince also kept a frontier model .45 caliber revolver on his hip.[15]

But New York remained a bustling film community throughout the second decade of the nineteenth century. The Biograph Film Company would benefit from its intimate view of the gang wars that rocked the Lower East Side in 1912. Newspaper headlines reported that Charles Becker, a police lieutenant who got rich collecting graft, gave the order to have gambler Herman Rosenthal gunned down at the Cafe Metropole. And Zelig was shot on a Thirteenth Street trolley car.[16] Biograph, operating out of a building just a few blocks away, on East Fourteenth Street, borrowed these street stories for an extraordinary film—*The Musketeers of Pig Alley*—often credited as the first true gangster film.

CHAPTER 2

Hollywood: America's Dream Factory

> If you steal something small you are a petty thief, but if you steal millions you are a gentleman of society.
>
> —Greek proverb

Leave it to D. W. Griffith to inspire controversy with his 1912 gangster film *The Musketeers of Pig Alley.* Perhaps because of the importance of Griffith to film history or because this film is one of the few silents to survive, *Musketeers* is extensively scrutinized for its contributions to the gangster genre.

Griffith is often called the greatest director in film history for his volume of work and his influence on others. He's also skewered for his myopic vision of morality and his manipulation of American racism. His *Birth of a Nation,* running three hours in length and costing two dollars a screening in 1915, brought praise for its dizzying artistry. The film was also called "aggressively vicious and defamatory" and "a spiritual assassination."[1] Griffith was the son of a Kentucky legislator and Confederate colonel who served under Stonewall Jackson—his family home was destroyed during the Civil War. When his father died in 1885, mounting debts finished off the family farm. The 14-year-old Griffith then moved to Louisville with his mother and sibling, joining America's migration to the cities.

Birth of a Nation chronicled the Civil War from a Southern point of view, including the South's ruin and humiliation "and the revival of the South's honor through the efforts of the Ku Klux Klan." The film, blamed for reinvigorating the Klan as a remedy for twentieth-century ills, sparked race riots in Boston. President Woodrow Wilson, a friend of the Reverend Thomas Dixon, who wrote "The Clansman," on which the movie is based, said, "It is like writing history with lightning. And my only regret is that it is all so terribly true."[2]

Before Griffith was bold enough to take on American history—using thousands of extras and California's spaciousness—he made dozens of urban dramas using New York's crowded streets and a familiar ensemble cast. Griffith was one of the loosely defined Progressives who believed that movies were uniquely suited "to bring out the truth about unjust social and economic conditions."[3] Given his upbringing, he sympathized with the urban victims and discovered the gangster as the most noxious symbol of the city's threat.

Griffith got the idea for *Musketeers* from newspaper accounts of real crime, although he omitted murder in his screen version. The opening intertitle describes the location as "New York's Other Side: The Poor." In a dingy apartment, a musician (Walter Miller) kisses his grieving Little Lady (Lillian Gish) good-bye and goes off "to improve his fortune." Alone, she is soon accosted by the Snapper Kid (Elmer Booth)—chief of the Musketeers (slang for hoodlums). They meet on the crowded street, jammed full of fruit peddlers and shabbily dressed slum residents. After she rebukes his advances, he tips his hat over one eye and winks, hinting at future trouble. He and the other musketeers hang out in a light-starved alley wedged in between the tenements where they drink, smoke, and entertain women. In the middle of one of their seedy soirees, the musician stumbles into their alley. He's inevitably hit over the head and robbed by Snapper, who then ducks into a nearby saloon to escape the law.

Meanwhile, a friend takes the Little Lady to "the gangsters' ball" to take her mind off her troubles. Snapper shows up and makes a play for her until a fight with a rival gang leader breaks out. The club owner kicks them out, leaving Snapper to plan revenge on his enemy. Griffith spends the bulk of the film building up to the inevitable "gangsters' feudal war," which displays a fury of gunfire and smoke criss-crossing Pig Alley. The musician again intrudes on the gangsters' turf and, despite his trembling, tries to grab for Snapper's gun. After Snapper shoves him against a wall, the musician flees, stealing back his wallet before getting away. The police arrive, and Snapper hits a cop in the eye before making his escape. Snapper shows up at the Little Lady's apartment and finds the musician there. Snapper ignores him, though, to brazenly invite her to go have a drink with him, threatening to strike her husband.

Director D. W. Griffith captured the gangster's milieu for his one-reel urban melodrama *The Musketeers of Pig Alley,* filmed on location on New York's Lower East Side in 1912. This scene reveals a seedy back alley soiree with loose women, buckets of beer, and dazzled children studying the gangster life.

She begs him to leave them alone, and Snapper scratches his head, confused that she prefers the scrawny musician. Snapper tidies up his suit, puffs out his chest, and asks her to take one more look. Reluctantly, he leaves but meets up with a cop outside their door. The cop is investigating the alley fight, but the couple lies to protect Snapper; he left them alone—they do the same for him. It's survival in the tenements, where the gangster prevails. Snapper arrogantly lights another of his endless cigarettes, defiantly tosses the match in the air, and leers at the cop before strutting off.

Film historian Carlos Clarens describes the lead characters as "threatened innocents cut from Victorian cardboard." But the gangster—all attitude and delectable sneer—does more than steal their money: he steals their thunder. After Griffith moved to California, he focused on Westerns and historical dramas, in which no gangster undermined his morality play. The ending of *Musketeers,* though, fits Griffith's narrative belief that a benevolent fate can intercede and remedy the plight of suffering women and children. The gangster is mysteriously struck by a sense of affection for the Little Lady that tells him she's better off with the decent fellow, but this sentiment spoils the integrity of the self-serving gangster as a character. Many modern critics also find the plot of *Musketeers* more schmaltz than journalism but praise the film's documentary-style depiction of the Lower East Side. Film scholar Tom Gunning notes: "You can almost hear and smell the close-packed, turn-of-the-century urban world. Throughout the film, Griffith and (Billy) Blitzer's images recall the New York slum photographs of Jacob Riis, which may well have supplied a direct inspiration for the film."[4]

Writer Eugene Rosow notes that Pig Alley "teems with Russian Jews." One is ever present on the sidewalk but ignorant of the criminals who stream past him on their way to saloons and side-alley fights. In *Musketeers,* according to John McCarty, Griffith hints that the gangsters are Irish. But he had a record of linking other immigrant groups to gangsterism in previous Biograph films. He showed Italians devoted to vengeance in *At the Altar* (1909). A "facinorous Sicilian profligate" hangs his victim's infant out a window in *The Cord of Life* (1909).[5] And a white slaver is made Chinese in *The Fatal Hour* (1908).

The most celebrated scene in *Musketeers* is the close-up of the Snapper Kid waiting in the garbage-strewn alley for his rival. Snapper creeps along a brick wall until he moves so close to the camera that his face fills the right half of the frame. The shot lingers while he moves his eyes to the right and then to the left, searching the alley for imminent danger before he exits right.

Musketeers left a powerful example for other filmmakers to exploit in the developing gangster genre. One such filmmaker, Raoul Walsh, who had portrayed John Wilkes Booth in Griffith's Civil War spectacle, also served as an assistant director under Griffith. When Walsh got his chance to direct in 1915, he chose a story called *The Regeneration* about a petty gangster. It's often credited as the first feature-length gangster film.

Unlike Griffith's one-reel film, Walsh's gangster story was not inspired by journalism's gore but borrowed from Broadway. Moreover, unlike Griffith, Walsh was no southern gentleman; he was a New York Irishman whose film espoused the code that "the quickest fist" ensured survival in modern society. "Ideologically at least, Walsh belonged to the next generation," wrote Clarens.

The Regeneration is a story of a Bowery gangster's struggle to accept the love and legitimate world of a compassionate socialite turned social worker. The film is a much richer story than any other to date and uses its five reels of screen time to present a gangster who embodies both admirable and illicit traits. The story was based on the stage play and autobiography of Owen Kildare—a gang leader who remade his life after meeting a "rose" among women named Marie Deering. *The Regeneration* is significant not for its theme of the reformed gangster but because it was one of the first films to trace part of his formation to his motherless childhood in the slums. That upbringing included a drunken stepfather who abused him and teen years full of unrewarding, backbreaking labor at the docks. At age 17, Owen (Rockliffe Fellowes) "still lives in a world where might is right—and where the prizes of existence go to the man who has the most daring in defying the law," reads an intertitle.

At an intimate but posh dinner party, Marie (Anna Nillson) listens intently to the new district attorney's plan to wage war on the gangster. "Really, though, they must be awfully interesting people," she interrupts. "I'd love to see one!" On a whim, Marie and her cocktail party go slumming to a Bowery saloon. While a hard-bitten, drunken woman makes a sloppy play for Owen, he studies the moves of the dainty and misplaced Marie and soon rescues her from the crude advances of another bar regular. Marie is so shocked by the world she witnesses that she dedicates her life to operating a settlement house in the district. Owen is smitten with her and drawn to her cause. After he abandons his gang, his former sidekick Skinny the Rat (William Sheer) abducts and tries to rape Marie. Police ambush Skinny's hideout, and Owen arrives, too, to rescue Marie. But she's caught by one of Skinny's bullets and mortally wounded. Skinny, who wears a creepy patch over one eye, also stabs and kills a cop. On her deathbed, Marie points to a sign that reads "Vengeance is mine, sayeth the Lord," but Owen ignores her plea and hunts down Skinny. However, instead of killing the cornered, squirming Skinny, Owen conjures up a vision of Marie that forces him to spare her killer.

Such longer, more complex films became the standard in ensuing years. Following the war, the film industry transformed itself into a mammoth business enterprise. Movie moguls built palace-style theaters, nurtured bankable stars, and produced more sophisticated feature films attracting more affluent audiences. People came to see immensely popular movie stars such as Mary Pickford and Charlie Chaplin. Chaplin's Little Tramp became a symbol of innocence the world over and united audiences despite their differences. Chaplin was one of the first media superstars by design and was astute enough to tap his own humble immigrant roots for story inspiration. In *The Immigrant* (1917), he recreated his own harrowing journey to America on a transatlantic ship, but this time for laughs.

Some directors turned to lighter themes after the war. Others delved into taboo material, including divorce, birth control, and "educational" sex dramas including *The Unborn* and *Enlighten Thy Daughter,* which dived head-on into the quagmire of the era's abortion controversy.

Postwar society was also troubled by high unemployment, and the employed suffered from horrendous conditions and poverty-level wages. According to reformers still battling for improvements, widespread alcoholism had gained a stranglehold on a war-weary America. More strident crusaders wanted to rid the country of liquor, believing a sober America would be more willing to work on its problems. Prohibition was a supply-side assault, inspired by fear of America's conquest by the urban saloon. Getting rid of a tangible symbol of a problem—like the old mammoth tenement buildings—felt like progress when few paths offered any easy answers.

DRYING OUT AND ALL THAT JAZZ

The Prohibition movement had been on the march for centuries. Colonial-era rum-running had prompted the first Prohibition in 1735, which seven years later was deemed a failed experiment and repealed. Throughout the nineteenth century, a seesaw battle over legislation occurred, with most attempts targeting retail sellers. The government further complicated the debate by adopting the Internal Revenue Act. It imposed fees and taxes on the sale and manufacture of liquor in the Union states to finance the Civil War. Thus the act created a federal dependency on the business of booze while making a mockery of rhetoric urging citizens to stay sober.

While legislation was bandied about in the civic arena, recent immigrants brought a tolerance of moderate drinking that further infuriated established "dry" Americans in the heartland. Soon, rather than point the finger at individuals and ethnic groups, prohibitionists targeted the saloon, not the drinker, as the symbol of evil. Saloons were the hotbeds of vice and the breeding ground of crime, the prohibitionists claimed.

Carry Nation, the most famous woman of the temperance fervor, was arguably the least effective. In that respect she had much in common with the exploits of the media sensation Eliot Ness, the federal agent who later earned the press's admiration for his Prohibition battles. Long before Ness smashed a barrel of beer for the press cameras, Nation had wielded her hatchet around dozens of Kansas saloons. She busted up bottles and hacked her way into the limelight followed by an army of like-minded women hell-bent on stamping out sin. Saloon keepers named drinks after her, and one hung a sign above the bar that read: "All nations welcome but Carry." The press mocked her, painting her as an embittered 50-year-old fanatic whose first husband died a hopeless drunk. Nation also blamed liquor for the mental illness of several members of her family, and she eventually died from "nervous trouble" in 1911.[6]

After the war, many suffragettes, now pushing for political power and the vote, carried forward much of the zeal they picked up during their involvement in the antiliquor women's crusade of the late 1800s. Finally, the political maneuvering and painstaking effort managed to move a constitutional amendment through the land and make prohibition of liquor the law by 1919. The Eighteenth Amendment gave the country one year to dry up. A fatal flaw in the amendment's logic, however, rooted in the eighteenth-century struggle, was to condemn only the supplier of liquor, not the drinker. This legal language was designed to avoid claims of unreasonable searches and seizures involving private citizens. The law didn't prohibit citizens from buying, using, or keeping liquor in private homes—only the seller faced criminal charges. This left a maze of loopholes that made enforcing the law, formally called the Volstead Act, a serious problem. Moreover, production of medicinal and religious liquors was still allowed, along with beer manufacturing, but the brewers had to reprocess the beer to remove its alcohol content. Because there were no enforcement dollars or manpower to ensure that the follow-up process took place, alcohol-rich beer would leave the breweries for delivery to the black market that instantly developed.

On 17 January 1920, with the great showman Billy Sunday on hand, a mock funeral was held in Virginia. Sunday shouted, "The slums will soon be only a memory. We will turn our prisons into factories and our jails into storehouses and corncribs."[7] Newspapers predicted a glut of drinking on the eve of the new law. Instead, people caused traffic jams trying to buy up all the available liquor to hoard at home. No one figured the usual law-abiding populace would disobey the Constitution. However, the middle-class American criminal was soon exposed, as the majority of Americans would break the law at some point during the next dozen years of Prohibition. Average folks took up the new indoor sport of homemade brewing, mixing poor-grade alcohol with water and flavoring, using creosote to make imitation scotch or juniper oil to approximate gin. Magazine articles and books flooded the market on how to make alcohol in teakettles, coffeepots, and washbasins for mixing up the infamous "bathtub gin." Given the chemical mixes, some drinkers became ill, went blind, or died.

But another class of criminal used Prohibition just as bankers use investment capital. The new markets reinvigorated the traditional gangs, which had begun to break apart around 1919. Many of their leaders had been hauled off to Sing Sing, and others were battered from intergang fights as well as the war. Prohibition quickly renewed employment for the gangsters. They swiftly graduated from the traditional rackets of gambling and prostitution to focus on the illegal liquor industry. Petty bootleggers gave way to organized mobs that swelled with cash—enough to add scores of cops and politicians to their payrolls.

One of the first known criminal cases occurred in Chicago less than an hour after Prohibition started. Six masked men invaded a railroad switchyard and hijacked $100,000 worth of medicinal liquor. Courts were quickly flooded with similar crimes, and even the Massachusetts delegation to the Republican National Convention was busted in Chicago that June for its liquor stock.

The colonial-era offshore methods of rum-running were resurrected to bring alcohol in, especially along the cities of the Great Lakes. By 1927 agents busted up illegal stills at a rate of more than 170,000 a year. They estimated that more than a half million people were in the business, with total sales in excess of $3 billion annually. Federal funds to stop bootlegging languished at $10 million.[8] People's sympathies were often with gangsters fleeing government agents. Thousands of sunbathers at Coney Island watched an episode between Coast Guard cutters and rumrunners, cheering on the bootleggers as their boat opened a lead on the government's.[9] The overwhelmed courts began simply to issue fines, which turned out to cost less than the licensing fees when liquor was legal. It wasn't until warring gangs of bootleggers spilled blood on the cities' streets and a man with a scar blew cigar smoke in the country's face that people demanded the end of Prohibition.

Part of the miscalculation was that Prohibition coincided with an era called the Jazz Age—a festival of excess and the reckless pursuit of feeling good. Boldness and the spirit of experimentation in topics from sex to living lavishly dominated the popular culture. Confession magazines reported the pleasure tales of the brave and bawdy. Dime novels told readers that Horatio Alger's story was not the only way to get rich in America, hinting that bootleggers were clever opportunists, not ruthless criminals. The leading ladies in these books, no matter how well-bred, were attracted to "the most foul and loathsome criminals. Many of them favor violation of marriage laws and cheapen female virtue."[10] The men in spats with cash and lethal charm offered excitement and spontaneity in a society that had just been bled of youth and optimism by an appalling war.

The film industry, too, jumped on the good times as early as 1920 and released a slew of sensation-packed romps. Frederick Lewis Allen, in *Only Yesterday,* his chronicle of the Jazz Age, notes that the movies returned many times to the same lucrative themes. Producers of one picture advertised "brilliant men, beautiful jazz babies, champagne baths, midnight revels, petting parties in the purple dawn, all ending in one terrific smashing climax that makes you gasp."

The Jazz Age was a cultural revolution that many historians compare to the tumultuous, experimental 1960s. The risk-taking spirit of the era—embodied by flagpole sitting, wing walking, and Charles Lindbergh and his daring flights—had the same kind of far-reaching effects on many aspects of people's lives, and its greatest advocates and practitioners were young people. The era unleashed potent resistance, though, from the older generation. Flappers and their Charleston dance were "an offense against womanly purity, the very fountainhead of our family and civil life," wrote a prominent Christian leader. A university president claimed that the young girls' short skirts were "born of the Devil and his angels, and are carrying the present and future generations to chaos and destruction."[11]

But the legislature had the power to do more than complain. It began a series of efforts, including one that forbade women from wearing a dress that showed "more than three inches of her throat."[12] Lawmakers also considered a ban on movies about lurid topics. In 1920 Senator Al Gore helped introduce bills to prohibit the shipment of movies that showed the acts of ex-convicts, desperadoes, bandits, train robbers, bank robbers, and outlaws.[13] Most of this type of legislation became bogged down in congressional committees and regional struggles. Still, the message was clear: the party was over.

In fact, it was a party that finally brought a government man to Hollywood long before the crusading G-man became a Hollywood character. The fateful party had been thrown by one of Hollywood's most popular stars, comedian Roscoe "Fatty" Arbuckle. A young starlet died from convulsions and a ruptured bladder following his party, and authorities blamed her death on a brutal rape. The 320-pound Arbuckle was officially charged with manslaughter, and although he was later acquitted after two hung juries, Hollywood's good times no longer rolled on unchecked. The incident incited the wrath of every preacher and moral reformer who had been waiting in the wings since 1909. They attacked Hollywood with a vengeance and forced studio moguls to take action. Their solution was the former Republican Party chairman Will Hays, whom industry leaders brought in to stem the tide of censorship legislation now gathering support in several states.

HOLLYWOOD GENIUS AND DISTORTED VILLAINS

Few films during the 1920s directly addressed the problem of Prohibition and its effects on police corruption and puppet politicians. Hollywood also didn't pass judgment on the public's weakness for speakeasies. Instead, the newly formed Hays office overseeing Hollywood allowed a sanitized bootlegger to stalk the streets of melodramas, but the tamer version still stole the show. "Rackets" became a generic term for any shady operation. To be more specific would have meant to describe drug trafficking and the flesh trade, which was forbidden, but might have done more to dampen the public's admiration for on-screen criminals. Instead, the benign and alluring image of the screen gangster supplanted all others in the public's mind, and the criminals themselves began to mimic their screen savvy.

The biggest gangster of them all, Al Capone, already a star of the front page, began creeping into movie characters as early as the mid-1920s. But Josef von Sternberg, an artist among moviemakers, brought Capone out of the shadows and put him on center stage. Sternberg was the Francis Ford Coppola of his time, lending sweep and vision rather than naked realism and squalid tenements to his criminal world. He was an auteur with a distinctive style that rivaled the comic genius of Chaplin or the allegorical chivalry of Griffith. Sternberg used this aesthetic sensibility and applied it to what's now dubbed the first "famous" gangster film, *Underworld*.

It's the story of "Bull" Weed (George Bancroft), a crime kingpin, who meets a bum on a street corner during a getaway from a holdup. Bull dubs the tramp Rolls Royce (Clive Brook) for his air of refinement underneath his downtrodden exterior. He also lets him join the gang. Rolls soon becomes the brains behind the gang's night maneuvers and the trustworthy holder of the key to the gang's hideaway. Feathers (Evelyn Brent), Bull's girl, falls for Rolls. Their love grows, but they restrain themselves out of respect for their leader. On the night of a gangland party, Buck Mulligan, a rival for Feathers, tries to grab for her and is killed by Bull. The authorities arrest Bull and sentence him to be hanged. On the evening of the execution, Rolls's scheme to free Bull goes awry, and Bull believes Rolls has double-crossed him because of Feathers. Bull escapes and goes after Rolls, who's wounded in a shoot-out with the police. Bull finds out that Rolls and Feathers were loyal to him and sees their deep love for each other. In the end, Bull gives himself up to police for their sake. The sappy story, however, is shrouded in violence and foretells the fate awaiting most gangsters for the next 50 years on celluloid.

Former reporter Ben Hecht's original script is "reworked by the director into a phantasmagoria of violence," wrote Clarens. Sternberg himself called *Underworld* "an experiment in photographic violence and montage."[14] With audiences, the film was an overnight success and soon prompted all-night screenings at New York's Paramount theater. Clarens credits Bancroft's Bull for the draw, saying that he amply possessed "the brutal bonhomie, the cunning cool" that audiences had come to expect of screen gangsters.

Before there was a screen Scarface, there was George Bancroft's Bull Weed in Josef von Sternberg's 1928 "experiment in photographic violence and montage." After the Capone-like kingpin Bull is cornered in his steel-plated hideout by police, he battles it out using a machine gun and sheer nerve.

Despite Sternberg's imprint, Hecht is given credit for the film's underlying thesis. His introduction describes "a great city in the dead of night—streets lonely, moon-flooded—buildings empty as the cliff-dwellings of a forgotten age."[15] Although Hecht accused Sternberg of bastardizing the story, Hecht won an Academy Award for the screenplay at the first outing of the Oscars in 1928.

The theme of redemption at the end of *Underworld* struck others, too, as a compromise to an otherwise great gangster tale. That such an ending was standard during the 1920s, however, doesn't alter Sternberg's genius in weaving together the visual clues that enable the story to build to a quixotic question: was Bull's reckless ride worth the deadly fall? After Bull is ambushed by police, despite his steel-plated hideout (à la Capone), a policeman poses a similar query. Bull caresses his Thompson submachine gun and smiles at the cop, admitting, "That hour was worth more to me than my whole life."[16] The idea that living fast and dying young was attractive would come to haunt the makers of gangster films. But for Sternberg's effort, the critics and the public viewers said that the film was too fantastic to harness dangerous ideas. Only realism invited censorship, whereas creating larger-than-life gangsters akin to Greek tragedy was much harder to splice out. Sternberg embedded pathos into his character, and censors found that difficult to restrain or permanently scar.

Unlike Griffith or other directors working in the California sunshine, Sternberg's sophistication was colored by his Viennese upbringing. The details of his childhood remain as ambiguous as his films, fabular and ripe with imagery. However, he dropped out of school at age 14, shortly after becoming a permanent resident of the United States. After stumbling into the film industry, Sternberg became an assistant to French director Émile Chautard before Charlie Chaplin brought Sternberg into the Hollywood fold by giving him an assignment.

Nearly dismissed from Hollywood in the late 1920s for his indulgence and directorial extravagance, Sternberg went to Germany to direct a picture. There, he met, discovered, and exploited his protégé Marlene Dietrich. After he directed her in the *The Blue Angel* (1930), a renown classic of visual erotica, both Dietrich's and Sternberg's legends were launched. But before he left Hollywood, he made another impressive crime film in 1928: *The Docks of New York.*

In the film, which tells the story of a sailor and his callous treatment of a prostitute, Sternberg exploits the "uncannily lewd detail" of close-ups. "She lustfully strokes his naked arm with indecent tattoo marks all over it, as he ripples the muscles on it for her amusement," wrote scholar Rudolph Arnheim. "This woman sees nothing of the man but power, nudity, muscle." With *The Docks of New York,* notes Andrew Sarris, "Sternberg takes his place with D. W. Griffith . . . as one of Hollywood's least condescending chroniclers of little people with big emotions." More than any other, that would become the most distinguishing element of a superb gangster film.

Sternberg's other noteworthy crime epic was *Thunderbolt* (1929), which was criticized as a reworked version of *Underworld*. Sarris calls *Thunderbolt* a "gangster fantasy" for its fanciful treatment of urban misery and the tinge of sophistry added to the criminal circumstances.

Another great auteur of the 1920s who dabbled in movie gangland was Lon Chaney. Although better known for his terrifying but plaintive monsters in *The Phantom of the Opera* (1923) and *The Hunchback of Notre Dame* (1925), Chaney made several gangster films, in which he departed from the era's routine depiction. His criminals were not chic but infused with the macabre habits of a disordered mind. He doomed his criminals, as he did most of his characters, with gruesome disfigurements and garish makeup. In *The Penalty* (1920), *Outside the Law* (1921), and *The Unholy Three*

(1925), Chaney's gangsters seem to belong more to the horror genre, in which the "man of a thousand faces" excelled. However, a gangster is the antithesis of the horror film centerpiece. By his very moniker he's a social being who must be with the "boyz" or *la famiglia* to survive. More than a simple symbol of evil, the gangster is a symbol of ambition run afoul. But Chaney's criminals are depraved—modern sociopaths, gun-toting gargoyles haunting the concrete jungle.

Typical of Chaney's criminals was a character called the Blizzard in *The Penalty*. The Blizzard's legs had been freakishly amputated when he was a young boy, forcing Chaney to portray the character with his legs bound behind him, jumping on his knees to move about. The Blizzard is the lord of the city's Underworld, or "a modern Caesar," as he calls himself. He has a grand scheme to rob the city treasury using an army of "thousands of disgruntled foreign workers."[17] At the time, this statement was a more-than-oblique insult to the impatient immigrants listening to communist pleas to redistribute America's wealth. But the driving force behind the character is revenge

With his legs bent and bound to portray a crippled, criminal madman, or a "modern Caesar," silent-screen superstar Lon Chaney created a chilling portrait of ruthlessness and depraved ambition in *The Penalty.*

for his deformity rather than politics or criminal necessity. Vengeance as a motivating factor for the Blizzard links him to every gangster that follows—down to his descendent Michael Corleone. Among regular folks, vengeance isn't an honorable quest. The Bible forbids the mortal use of revenge, and it's routinely understood throughout history to be politically incorrect and scandalous. That's exactly why the screen gangster is more interesting than other less theatrical criminals. It also explains the gangster's relentless pursuit of enemies who no longer threaten his business—only his pride. Typical of the era, though, the Blizzard undergoes surgery to remove a blood clot from his brain, and the operation restores him to decent society.[18]

In *Outside the Law,* Chaney plays a dual role: a Chinaman and "Black Mike," for whom Chaney "inculcates viciousness and strength," wrote the *New York Times* critic. The film also lives up to the genre's innate affection for using violence as the knock-

Among the personae created by the "man of a thousand faces" was a dapper but deadly gangster in *Outside the Law.* Lon Chaney's gangster look—cigarette casually tucked into his lips, a tilted hat, garish clothes, and the sidelong glance of a cornered animal—was mimicked by the hundreds of screen gangsters who followed.

out punch. The same critic notes, "Not much time is lost in this photo-drama in getting down to the business of slaughter. . . . It is almost impossible for one pair of eyes to keep track of all the killings. . . . Except for a child and an old Chinese, everybody in this picture has a pistol." And John McCarty notes that it's Chaney, not James Cagney, who sneers, "You dirty rat!" within this film.

Chaney made two other memorable gangster films in 1926. In *The Black Bird,* despite the usual crime-doesn't-pay motif, Chaney's character isn't sorry about his life of crime and continues his nefarious ways until his violent end. This defiance was daring for 1926 and would be fully exploited in a few years. Also, portending what was ahead, Chaney played a scar-faced gang leader and smuggler in *The Road to Mandalay.*[19]

According to McCarty, the essential gangster character whom we associate with the movies was created by this remarkable silent-screen star. The gangster would be finessed and modernized, but his core pathology would always resemble many of Chaney's inventions: "An undisciplined child, fascinated with the forbidden, who never grew up . . . a violent Peter Pan who justifies his every antisocial act, even murder, as debts owed to him; an innate loner, no matter how much company he keeps, and grandiose schemer determined to acquire wealth and power by the shortest route possible—who invariably sees that route through the barrel of a gun."[20]

Other talented filmmakers during the late 1920s made gangster films, but most continued to stress the gangster's remarkable rehabilitation in the end. Raoul Walsh made *Me, Gangster* (1928), originally a novel; the *New York Times* panned the ending as hokey. The finale comes down to "the good influence of Mary Regan," who persuades the gangster to return the money after he has been paroled. The critic notes that the ending may not have been Walsh's choice. "Under the guise of a moral preachment, a rather obvious and banal point is stressed for an equally obvious purpose of circumventing the scissors of the censors."

Directors working in other genres were also provoking the censors' irritation. Cecil B. DeMille made lavish religious epics using the events of the New Testament to tell dubious tales about the Bible's undercurrent of "sex, violence and spectacle." Erich von Stroheim, another Viennese immigrant, was notorious for excessive but fabulous sagas in which he pried open the gilted bedroom doors of aristocratic society. *Greed* (1924), one of the most influential films in history, was a masterpiece of one man's vision of human degradation. Another Stroheim film, *The Merry Widow* (1925), is described as an "orgiastic black comedy replete with descriptions of sadism, perversion and debauchery."[21]

Hays had been trying different approaches to restrain Hollywood since he came to his post in 1922. At the time, seven states were discussing censorship laws. At first, his interference in film production was subtle and didn't involve any direct cutting or banning. He merely insisted that movie titles be registered with his newly formed Motion Picture Producers and Distributors of America (MPPDA). The group's job was to identify potentially objectionable film scripts and discourage a bad idea long before it was put on celluloid. Then, in 1927, came "the Formula," which by 1927 became 11 "don'ts" and 26 "be carefuls." "Don'ts" included profanity, nudity, illegal drugs, sex perversion, white slavery, miscegenation (sex between whites and blacks), scenes of childbirth, display of children's sex organs, ridicule of the clergy, and willful offense to any nation, race, or creed. More directly aimed at the crime film, the "be carefuls" suggested "special care" be used when dealing with the use of firearms, arson, brutality, murder, smuggling, third-degree methods, hangings, electrocutions, sympathy for criminals, sedition, rape, lustful kissing, and the deliberate seduction of girls.

But increasing censorship cannot be blamed for the run of bad movies that are the bulk of any era's output. With or without Hays, masterpieces and artists working in the medium were few. Winning story lines even then were frequently repeated, and genre often gave way to formula. By the late 1920s, 20,000 movie houses were in operation nationwide. "The cinema was the fifth largest business in America, and only clothing and food had more basic appeal."[22] And while Hays was trying to keep on-screen gangsters in line, real ones were hopelessly out of control.

CAPONE AND OTHER ENTREPRENEURS

Alphonse Capone embodied the American dream turned on its head. He was a self-made man from the slums of Brooklyn's Navy Yard district and considered himself a businessman like any other, running a racket instead of a registered corporation. The earning power and material spoils were astonishingly similar. At the age of 26, Capone oversaw more than 1,000 employees with a payroll of more than $300,000 a week. His illiterate, immigrant father never made more than $12 a week as a barber. The younger Capone was intelligent but, having quit school at age 14, not much better educated than his father. A marine officer who witnessed the 10-year-old Capone taunting one of his recruits into a fight warned of the boy's future promise. The marine recalled thinking the military could harness the boy's misguided ferocity. "But if nothing like this will happen, the kid may drift for a few years until some wise guy picks him up and steers him around . . . and then he'll be heard from one day."[23]

Capone admired the great capitalists of the nineteenth century. Giants of industry such as Cornelius Vanderbilt, Andrew Carnegie, John D. Rockefeller, and J. P. Morgan personified success at any cost. Carnegie had used the Pinkerton security group to forcefully control worker unrest. These capitalists, often referred to as Robber Barons, used the National Guard or employed gangsters to protect their industries from unionization or competition. They did whatever it took to stay on top. So did Capone.

Like gangsters, businessmen often buy political partnerships. Railroad mogul Collis Huntington wrote to a henchman, "We should be very careful to get a U.S. Senator from California that will be disposed to use us fairly, and then have the power to help us."[24] Capone's buying favors from city hall was deemed a crime, but if done in the interest of advancing corporate concerns, this practice is neatly labeled aggressive marketing. The censors saw to it that attacks on the business community and explicit displays of systemic political corruption were cut from most movies. *The Musketeers of Pig Alley,* inspired by street gangs and their ties to corrupt city officials, included a scene in which a mysterious hand gives the Snapper Kid a wad of money. The intertitle read, "Links in the System." Eugene Rosow notes that until recently the scene was missing from most prints in circulation for the past 80 years.

Capone, like most Americans, emulated the model of the ambitious individual who rises above the crowd. As media scholar Herbert Gans puts it, "At its most basic, individualism is the pursuit of personal freedom and of personal control over the social and natural environment. It's also an ideology—a set of beliefs, values, and goals—and probably the most widely shared ideology in the U.S."[25] Whether a Carnegie, a Louis B. Mayer, or a Capone, the idea of an immigrant coming to America to find the promised land was irresistible for moviemakers and audiences alike. Economic historian William Miller, however, concluded that the usual image of American business leaders since the Civil War was quite off the mark. He noted that popular legend usually describes a "poor immigrant" or "poor farm boy" who, "fired by a passionate will to succeed," rises from obscure roots to riches, exploiting ingenuity and hard work. Miller studied 190 of America's top business leaders at the turn of the century. He found that those born poor made up only 3 percent of this group.[26] The mythical rags-to-riches story that dominated American popular culture was the exception, not the rule. The plain truth was those who had money made more money, and the poor usually stayed poor.

The 1920s, however, was about getting to "easy street," not about patient, painstaking toil to attain wealth. The bootlegger merely joined a pack already crowded with capitalists, bankers, movie moguls, and stock market speculators (who included everyday folk across America). In 1929, long before Oliver Stone put the words "greed is good" in his *Wall Street* trader's mouth, Americans were thinking it. The consumption habit of illegal hooch and goods on credit had replaced the traditional morality of "a penny saved is a penny earned." But a disaster soon occurred that brought capitalists, gangsters, movie moguls, and flappers to their knees. Beginning on Thursday, 24 October 1929, and concluding on what's known today as Black Tuesday the following week, the stock market crashed. The value of stock securities dropped by more than $26 billion in less than five days. Millionaires became penniless and suicidal overnight, and modest families lost their life savings. Most Americans were affected as the country's economy went sour. The Great Depression would make the 1930s one of the most troubled eras in American history. On-screen the gangster would live out the nation's feelings of despair—rising to the top of prosperity only to crash to the depths of community suffering. Like Christ on the cross, the gangster would die horrendous deaths of gore and symbolism for the public's benefit. America would use the gangster to purge the guilty citizen (the sheepish bootlegger or the greedy stock speculator) who lived on in every moviegoer.

CHAPTER 3

Spats, Gats, and Attitude

He's in the Big Town, doin' things in a big way. . . . This game ain't for guys that's soft!
—Caesar Enrico Bandello, *Little Caesar* (1930)

The year before the economy went into a tailspin, the film industry debuted a new invention that would make the movies, for a time, depression proof: sound. After Al Jolson uttered the first words heard on film ("Come on, Ma! Listen to this!"), Hollywood added sound to most movies by the end of 1928. It then experienced another profound metamorphosis. Audiences' wild approval of the "talking" pictures was stunning. Weekly movie attendance skyrocketed from about 57 million in 1927 to about 90 million in 1929. It continued at that level in 1930—the year most other industries began to feel the full effects of the economy's plummet.

Part of film's continued appeal was that it kept the Jazz Age alive. Like most other aspects of popular culture, the Jazz Age first invaded Hollywood in the early 1920s. The gangster seemed to personify its roar. F. Scott Fitzgerald used Arnold Rothstein, the notorious bootlegger and gambler, as the model for the character of Meyer Wolfsheim in his 1925 classic *The Great Gatsby.* Other Jazz Age books and plays made their way to the screen throughout the decade. Sound enabled the blaring reeds of popular music and the rapid tempo of street speak to rattle the movie palaces. But Hollywood's Hays office didn't welcome all novels and stage plays. Early in the decade, a review system was put in place to check whether such works were "appropriate" for the unique and volatile film medium.

However, the Hays office in the 1920s was largely disregarded, bypassed, and occasionally placated with deep cuts to a particularly flagrant film. A studio's promotions department sometimes used squabbles with the censors to help boost box office appeal. One film, *White Cargo,* prominently noted that the photoplay had been "banned by Will Hays."[1] The Underworld was portrayed as a milieu of the smart set. "The gangster was revealed as an enviable hero, quick and intelligent, refined, influential politically and powerful financially. Movies like the tabloids glorified his life, showing it full of exciting adventure, beautiful women, and plenty of money."[2] Hundreds of films showcased "speed, spice and spectacle. . . . people wanted to shock and be shocked."[3] As the Roaring Twenties progressed, gangsters were becoming scandalous, but they were not yet viewed as vicious killers.

Sound gave Warner Brothers, the studio that had introduced the new technology, a business momentum that was quickly used to bring renewed appeal to the gangster film. Now the screen clamored with popping bullets, screeching tires, and wailing police sirens. The studio spent a small fortune equipping its theaters to accept its new sound films, including its first "all-talking" film, *Lights of New York* (1928). It's a gangster yarn about two country boys who leave their hometown to set up a barbershop in New York City. They get help from two Underworld figures, who turn the business into a front for bootleg operations. The head hoodlum tries to frame one of the yokels but, with the aid of a discarded moll, gets double-crossed himself in the end. The film's prologue promised "a story of Main Street and Broadway—a story that could have been taken out of last night's newspapers."[4] But the underlying theme of country innocence versus city decadence was already a staple of the gangster film in the silent era.

Most reviewers panned the film as ordinary despite the novelty of audible action. One reason for its perfunctory result was the film's director, Bryan Foy, who would later become head of B movies, or minor productions, at Warner Brothers. The film, though, is memorable for introducing a lasting cliché: as a gangster orders a killing, he utters the phrase "take 'em for a ride." The victims are never heard from again.

The innovation of sound enriched an already vibrant genre that had been evolving since 1898. Although many film historians chart the gangster film's debut from the 1930s, it was invented before the talkies. For some critics, the genre was already getting stale. In 1928 *New York Times* reviewer Mordaunt Hall wrote of *Gang War,* "When earth's last gangster picture fades from the screen, it may, who can tell, be a relief to more than one person."

There's no doubt, though, that three films—all shot in 1930—would dramatically redefine the tired genre: *Little Caesar, The Public Enemy,* and *Scarface.* Film critic Paré Lorentz, in his 1931 review of *The Public Enemy,* was delighted that moviegoers were spared "another one of those gaudy, wine-women-and-machine-gun romances." He congratulated the writers for not focusing on "district attorneys, soft-spoken detectives, and kind-hearted ladies of leisure." Instead, he added, the public was given "a terse case history of the life and habits of a hoodlum."

The focus on the gangster at the center of the story is what set these films apart. *Underworld* had put Bull Weed in the lead but insisted he be redeemed in the end. That sabotaged his integrity as a gangster and turned him into something else. *Little Caesar, The Public Enemy,* and *Scarface* took moviegoers inside the criminal's head as well as his Underworld. This dark trio offered brutal, stark portrayals that more directly tapped the details from the life of Capone. A year after sound debuted, Capone had orchestrated his most public act of violence, the Saint Valentine's Day massacre. On 14 February 1929, Capone's men, some dressed in police uniforms, ambushed seven members of George "Bugs" Moran's gang. Capone's men lined their victims up against the wall of a Clark Street warehouse and gunned them down using submachine guns and shotguns. The blood spill capped off Chicago's escalating street wars of the late 1920s. It also brought down Chicago's mayor "Big" Bill Thompson, who had been Capone's pawn. The murders would be fresh in the minds of moviegoers who would soon see these films.

Capone's reign was rich in material and irresistible to the era's filmmakers. Moreover, a steady stream of journalists had been pouring into Hollywood to meet the script demands of the new talkies. Many of them came with vivid memories of their halcyon days with the Chicago tabloids—jammed full of Capone's exploits and killings. This new breed of screenwriter would take the gangster film back to its earliest impulses—to borrow from the street and the newspaper's front page. As modern critic Richard Corliss notes of *Scarface,* its "all-but-suffocating vitality is a kind of cinematic version of tabloid prose at its best."

The tabloids were at peak popularity by the late 1920s and had already connected with the customers of moving pictures. Newspaper circulation had nearly doubled from 1900 to 1930, owing much to the invention of the "penny" press. These cheap, mass-produced newspapers afforded nearly every American the opportunity to stay informed. The tabloids, though, were not fourth estate journalism designed to provoke public discourse. That elite press spoke to the decision makers and architects of the country's future. The tabloids aimed at concerns and recreations of everyday folks hopelessly mired in the present. In reality, the line between the two often blurred: the elite press often stooped to pandering to the sensational, and the tabloids occasionally stumbled onto something noble.

Nevertheless, the former tabloid reporters brought to Hollywood an arrogance about their journalistic license for truth telling that only moviegoers would eagerly embrace. The success of *Little Caesar, The Public Enemy,* and *Scarface,* with their raw sting of realism, would put a swift end to the classic era of the gangster genre that these pictures helped usher in.

Former newspaperman Ben Hecht, who had penned *Underworld,* was a jump ahead of his colleagues. When he had arrived in Hollywood in the mid-1920s, he had been forewarned by another former reporter, Joseph Mankiewicz, about the story spin demanded by the censors. Mankiewicz, who would win an Academy Award in 1950 for *All about Eve,* told Hecht, "In a novel a hero can lay ten girls and marry a virgin for a finish. In a movie this is not allowed. . . . The villain can lay anybody he wants, have as much fun as he wants cheating and stealing. . . . But you have to shoot him in the end."

Knowing the villain had to die didn't discourage Hecht from writing a titillating tale about the raucous life that preceded that doom. When Sternberg turned *Underworld* into something Hecht no longer recognized, Hecht tried again. His new film, *Scarface,* would no longer tiptoe about the hulk of Capone. It stole more directly the sensational aspects of Capone's criminal career and some of his personal trademarks, including his love of Italian opera and the four-inch scar on his left cheek. Like his former readers, Hecht found Capone's occupation glamorous in a society that increasingly demanded conformity and hardship. Hecht wrote, "As a newspaperman I had learned that nice people . . . loved criminals, doted on reading about their love problems as well as their sadism."[5]

Hecht's experience with Sternberg made him reluctant at first to work on *Scarface* with film producer (later famous recluse) Howard Hughes. Hecht believed that crime films compared to "real front-page stuff . . . [were] revoltingly gutless compromises."[6] Some would argue that the newspaper stories Hecht once wrote were often dubious rip-offs of police accounts. In any event, Hecht wasted no time in compromising the facts of Capone's life. His Capone—Tony Camonte—spoke with an Italian accent and lusted after his sister.

Picking up on the incestuous hint in the Armitage Trail novel on which the screenplay is based, director Howard Hawks suggested Hecht enrich the Camonte family with scandalous aspects of Italy's fifteenth-century Borgia family. The Borgias produced two popes, a military leader, and a noted patron of the arts, but their incestuous alliances and evil plots are even more memorable.

Hawks, who would later be lauded by French film scholars as a master of several film genres, had impressed Hughes with his work on *The Racket.* The 1928 film, borrowed from Broadway, was a strikingly familiar story about a gangster named Nick Scarsi who ruled Chicago (with a scar only in his name). Once on the job, Hecht, who preferred collaborating, hired other writers to flesh out the dialogue, including *Chicago Tribune* reporter Fred Palsey and W. R. Burnett.

Because the Hays office discouraged Capone as direct inspiration, Hecht, Hawks, and Hughes ran into snags from two fronts almost immediately. First, the Hays office wanted numerous changes to the film, including having Camonte turn cowardly and be hanged at the film's end. The filmmakers wanted a bloody final shoot-out. *Scarface* would battle censors for nearly two years and not be released until early 1932.

Second, Capone himself worried about how he would be portrayed on the silver screen. In his memoirs, Hecht writes that two of Capone's men came to his office holding a copy of the script—thought to be top secret. They explained that first, Capone wanted to know if the movie was about him, and second, they insisted "that nothing derogatory about the great gangster [reach] the screen." Hecht said that they came into the room "as ominously as any pair of movie gangsters, their faces set in scowls and guns bulging their coats." Hecht convinced them that the script was about other gangsters back in Chicago familiar both to him and to them. Puzzled, they asked: Why, then, is the film called *Scarface*? Hecht told them, "If we call the movie *Scarface,* everybody will want to see it, figuring it's about Al. That's part of the racket we call showmanship." If it was strictly business, it was logical to the gangsters, and they left peacefully.

THE TRAGEDY OF RICO BANDELLO

While *Scarface* languished with the censors, Warner Brothers beat Hughes to the screen. It was the right studio at the right time to help push the genre into the spotlight. Jack Warner's right-hand man, Daryl F. Zanuck, perhaps grasping the gangster's enduring appeal in the late 1920s, pushed a "headline news" policy. The studio focused on crime and corruption in stories inspired by journalism—not an original idea, but a sound one.

Warner Brothers took on an atmosphere of a newsroom with edicts on how to approach a film. "The opening shots must plunge the audience into a world of violence, tension and big city excitement, making a first reel the equivalent of a first paragraph in a front page story. . . . The actors and actresses must deliver their lines with the rapidity and ferocity of machine-gun bullets."[7]

The story chosen for journalism-turned-cinema was *Little Caesar.* It was a work of fiction by Burnett (the writer also helping to pen *Scarface*) but was permeated with the life of Capone. As a novel, the story of the Chicago Underworld had been syndicated in 82 American newspapers. Burnett explained the story's premise in the novel's preface: "Capone was King. Corruption was rampant. Big Bill Thompson, the mayor, was threatening to punch King George of England in the 'snoot.' Gangsters were shooting each other all over town."[8] One aspect of Capone inspires the character Big Boy, who embodies Capone at his zenith and lurks in the story's background. The lead figure, Rico Bandello, borrows the details of Capone's rise to the top followed by a rapid, violent fall (which did not happen to Capone). Burnett explained that Rico is a killer and a gang leader but "no monster . . . merely a little Napoleon, a little Caesar." In other words, he's a sympathetic creature out of classical tragedy.

The opening scene of *Little Caesar* shows the armed robbery of a gas station (and gunshots suggest that the attendant is killed). Afterward the criminals stop at a diner for a spaghetti dinner and furtively turn back the clock on the wall to create an alibi. Caesar Enrico Bandello (Edward G. Robinson), the squat leader of the duo, quickly reveals his ambitious character. He reads in the newspaper about the honors banquet given for gangster "Diamond" Pete Montana (Ralph Ince) and gripes to his driver Joe

Massara (Douglas Fairbanks Jr.), "He's in the Big Town, doin' things in a big way. . . . we're nobodies." Joe says that he, too, wants the trappings of the big town: the clothes, the women, the dough. But then he plans to retire from crime and go back to being a dancer. This disgusts Rico, who insists, "I figure on makin' other people dance. . . . have your own way or nothin'. Be somebody!"

After arriving in the big town at the Club Palermo—headquarters of turf mobster Sam Vettori (Stanley Fields)—Rico talks his way into a job, bragging about his skills with a gun. Vettori warns him to keep his quick fingers off the trigger: "That's old stuff. . . . This ain't the sticks."

Joe returns to dancing at the Bronze Peacock, a nightclub and gambling house backed by Vettori's rival, Little Arnie Lorch (Maurice Black). (Carlos Clarens suggests that Joe is based on George Raft, who left the fold of gangsters for a career in show business.) Vettori and his boys show up at the joint for a meeting with Montana. He has a message to deliver from Big Boy: a new crime commissioner named McClure is cracking down. "Put chains on your gorillas for the next few months," Montana orders. He also sizes up Rico and warns him to be especially careful "with that cannon of yours." But Rico is barely able to listen; he is ogling Montana's jewel-studded stickpin and ring.

Vettori plots a New Year's Eve heist of the club in Lorch's territory, but Rico picks apart the plan and tries to muscle in on his boss's realm. He's silenced, for the moment, but strong-arms Joe into acting as lookout for the heist. An alarmed Joe witnesses Rico gun down the crime commissioner, who was leaving the club after finding out it had links to the Underworld.

The story builds as Rico takes over first Vettori's territory, and then Lorch's. Lorch had tried to kill Rico in a drive-by shooting from a milk truck equipped with machine guns. A bullet only grazed Rico's arm, however. He had been on his way to buy 10 copies of the newspaper that took his picture the night before at a banquet thrown for him by his boys. He had warned Lorch as he did Vettori: "You're through. . . . you can't take it no more," Rico said, chiding Lorch for going "soft" and turning "yellow."

With each step up the gang's ladder, Rico wears finer clothes and more glittering jewelry. He obsesses over his appearance. While having his wound tended to, he uses his free hand to meticulously comb back his sleek black hair. Finally, sporting a custom-fit tuxedo, Rico gets an audience with the Big Boy (Sidney Blackmer). Rico marvels at the kingpin's home with its ornate touches of a Parisian salon. He acts like a tourist, pointing out oil paintings and lush furnishings, noting, "I bet this trick furniture set you back plenty." When Rico leaves Big Boy, he's the newly crowned "boss of the north side."

He then purchases a posh manor for himself and begins to plot his takeover of Big Boy. To help, he invites Joe to return as his underling. Rico asks, almost plaintively, "Who else have I got to give a hang about?" When Joe refuses, Rico snarls, "Nobody ever quit me. . . . you go back to that dame and it's suicide—suicide for both of ya." Joe flees to his partner and fiancée, Olga, to take her on the run with him. She refuses, arguing that there's nowhere to hide from Rico, who soon shows up flanked by his new right-hand man Otero (George E. Stone). With gun drawn, Rico creeps toward the camera until his face fills the frame, his eyes glistening with emotional torment. Otero tells Rico that it's he who's getting soft and aims his gun at Joe. Rico tries to stop him, but Joe is shot in the arm. The two gangsters flee, and the manhunt begins. Olga had called the wisecracking detective lieutenant Flaherty, who's on the gang watch, to say that Joe would turn state's evidence. Flaherty and his uniformed men

Shocked and wounded by a rival's submachine gun, Edward G. Robinson portrays the memorably vain and brutal Chicago kingpin Rico Bandello in the 1930 classic *Little Caesar.* Rico is a smallish thug with monstrous ambition and a tragic fate waiting for him in one of the genre's most influential films.

arrive just after the shooting and chase a scrambling Rico and Otero down an alley. After being shot, the loyal henchman Otero moans, "Go on, Rico, I'm done for."

Flaherty soon busts Vettori, who's hanged. But Rico remains on the lam and grows increasingly desperate. For a man who never touched liquor, he becomes a raggedy drunk sleeping in 15¢-a-night flophouses. Meanwhile Flaherty keeps his promise to root out Rico and plants a story in the newspaper that will appeal to Rico's vanity. The other resident drunks read the paper aloud, reciting the cop's indictment: "The once swaggering braggart of the Underworld wilted in the face of real danger and showed the world his cowardice." With each insult, Rico groans and writhes in physical pain as if a knife were being twisted in his gut. Rico staggers to the nearest telephone to threaten Flaherty, who has the call traced. Flaherty and his men spot the huddled hulk of Rico burrowing down a deserted, windswept street and yell for him to give himself up. Rico hides behind a billboard and continues to resist. Flaherty annihilates the sign with a machine gun, and the mortally wounded Rico falls to the ground. Flaherty promises Rico they're taking that ride to justice.

"No we ain't," moans Rico. "I told you no buzzard like you will ever put any cuffs on me." He widens his glassy eyes and lifts his voice once more to utter, "Mother of Mercy! Is this the end of Rico?" (Half the prints released used the novel's original line, "Mother of God." The other half anticipated the religious objections then brewing, explains Clarens.) The final shot captures the billboard's ironic message: it's an advertisement for the Grand Theater's new musical, starring dancers Joe and Olga.

Little Caesar was a smash hit at the box office, surpassing the receipts of Warner's two earlier gangster hits, *Lights of New York* and *The Doorway to Hell.* The *New York Daily Mirror* reported that the week the film opened, "Police reserves were summoned. . . . The crowds stormed the two box offices and the glass in two of the doors was shattered."[9]

Richard Watts, in his review for the *New York Herald Tribune,* wrote, "*Little Caesar,* by pushing into the background the usual romantic conventions of the theme and concentrating on characterization rather than on plot, emerges not only as an effective and rather chilling melodrama, but also as what is sometimes described as a Document."[10] The review was an early compliment for the film's documentary-style realism.

However, the film also retains a stagy stiffness that reveals its shyness about fully exploiting the new sound technology. Some supporting actors appear quite microphone-conscious, adding pantomime as if they were acting in a silent film. Of these landmark films, *Little Caesar* is the most antique looking, but it's made exceptional by the striking performance of Robinson.

As John McCarty notes, director Mervyn LeRoy didn't give Robinson much help. LeRoy muddied the impact of the most poignant acts of violence by using lap dissolves and was stingy with details. "As a result, the task of putting across the violence of the man and the primitive instincts that drive him falls almost entirely upon Robinson's fortunately capable shoulders," McCarty wrote. However, one strength of LeRoy's direction is dividing the film into two parts. The first is dominated by medium shots to highlight the crowded ranks of gangland battling it out. The second uses tighter shots and close-ups that focus on Rico emerging as a leader and a loner.

Robinson was already a proven screen tough when he was chosen to play Rico—his fifth gangster role in two years. He had also appeared as Nick Scarsi in *The Racket* on Broadway. For the role of Rico, LeRoy gave Robinson a cigar to make sure no doubt remained about his character's identity.

Capone was "5 feet 8 inches, 190 pounds. His nose was flat; his brows dark and shaggy, and a bullet-shaped head was supported by a short thick neck."[11] This description could pass for Robinson and made him convincing to audiences as the screen version of Capone. Robinson liked the script and said he approached the part as if he were playing Macbeth.

Robinson became synonymous with Rico. He appeared in future films to caricature him for drama's sake *(Key Largo)* or for comedy's benefit *(Brother Orchid).* He also became the all-purpose swarthy gangster of the 1930s. He reprised Chaney's role as the Chinese Underworld king Cobra Collins in a remake of *Outside the Law.* He played a Greek mobster in *Smart Money* (1931) (opposite the new star James Cagney) and made a believable Portuguese thug a year later in *Tiger Shark.*

Robinson was a Romanian immigrant, born Emmanuel Goldenberg, who grew up in New York's Lower East Side. As Clarens describes, "Robinson seemed to act by implosion, concentrating energy behind his precarious passivity, until the final, long-awaited burst. Cagney was all firecracker bounce; even in repose, he appeared to ricochet off the borders of the screen."

PUBLIC ENEMY TOM POWERS

Just six months after *Little Caesar,* Cagney's star-making vehicle *The Public Enemy* premiered. It was written by Kubec Glasmon and John Bright and earned them an Academy Award for best original story. Glasmon, a Polish émigré and licensed pharmacist, ran a soda fountain in Chicago where Bright was a part-time employee and gangsters were frequent patrons. Bright had also worked as a young reporter on the *Chicago Evening Post,* dealing in stories of the criminal underground. *The Public Enemy* was adapted from his work of fiction entitled *Beer and Blood.*

The Public Enemy begins with scenes of 1909 Chicago—its business district bustling with daily clatter and its south side neighborhoods spoiled by the nearby stockyards. Beer trucks roar down the street and contrast with the Salvation Army band's clamor to bring the neighborhood to sobriety and the Lord. Two boys about age 11 sneak a gulp of beer from a bucket outside one saloon and then are chased out of a department store for causing delinquent mayhem. Back on their turf, the rougher boy, Tom, gives the sister of his pal Matt a pair of stolen roller skates. While she clumsily scoots passed him, barely keeping her balance, Tom trips her and laughs. Matt balks, but Tom counters, "What do you care? It's only a girl." Tom is drawn to Molly but must diminish his vulnerability by turning the tables on her, making her his victim. (An omen of the future man.) Watching on the porch in stony silence is his father, dressed in part of his policeman's uniform and cap. Before Tom is beaten with a strap, he defiantly clutches his pants and sneers, "How do ya want 'em this time, up or down?" The boys return to the seedy Red Oaks Club and sell stolen watches for a half a buck each to a wiry, Fagin-like crook named Putty Nose (Murray Kinnell). He likes to entertain the boys with lewd songs on the saloon's piano.

After an intertitle announces that the year is 1915, Tom and Matt are shown still hanging around the saloon but have grown into young men portrayed by James Cagney and Edward Woods. They saunter into the back room, where pool playing and poker games keep the men busy. Putty Nose invites them to join his gang, which includes Dutch Sieberling, Bugs Healy, and Limpy Larry. Putty Nose asks Tom about his brother Mike, and Tom fires back, "That sucker! He's too busy goin' to school. He's learning how to be poor."

Putty Nose gives Tom and Matt two pistols to use that night when the gang knocks over a warehouse filled with furs. Inside, working by flashlight, Tom is startled when he stumbles onto the growling face of a stuffed bear. He instinctively fires off several shots, which alert a nearby policeman of trouble. The gang flees through the alleys, but Lumpy is shot and killed. The policeman runs into another alley, and gunshots echo off the buildings. Tom and Matt emerge from the alley, and the next camera shot shows the slain policeman on the ground, still clutching his gun. They go to Putty Nose's hideout but are sent away. Tom is furious and punches the closed door, swearing revenge on his double-crossing boss.

Tom's brother Mike (Donald Cook) enlists in the Marine Corps as America joins World War I. Scenes of pre-Prohibition frenzy follow, using actual newsreel footage and staged shots. People are jostling each other, their arms full of bottles to hoard before the midnight "dry" deadline. Paddy Ryan (Robert Emmett O'Connor), another gangster in the neighborhood, asks Tom and Matt to join his new bootlegging operation. After they pull off one job, siphoning government liquor into an empty gasoline tanker, they find themselves with a wad of cash that they quickly spend on tailor-made clothes. Arriving at a nightclub in a new sedan, sporting gloves and hats, they look like prosperity itself (notes the shooting script). At the speakeasy, they pick up two girls whose dates have passed out.

The gang expands business by joining forces with closed-down brewer Mr. Leeman and bootlegger Nails Nathan (Leslie Fenton). After Leeman tries to point out how different his motives are from those of the gangsters, Nathan deftly ends Leeman's hypocrisy. "If you're in this, you're in for the coin, same as the rest of us."

Tom and Matt begin strong-arming speakeasy owners into buying their hooch and not their competition's. In a compelling scene, Tom humiliates a bartender, first spitting beer on his face then slapping it several times. Finally, Tom opens up the man's tappers so that suds flood the floor. Tom is disgusted by the man's cowering and calls him yellow.

His brother Mike returns from the war, limping and suffering from psychological wounds as well. For Mike's welcome-home dinner, Tom and Matt put a keg in the middle of the dining table. After scowling and refusing to eat or drink, Mike bursts into a rage: "You think I'd care if it was just beer in that keg? I know what's in it. I know what you've been doing all this time. . . . where you got those clothes and those new cars. . . . You murderers! There's not only beer in that keg! There's beer and blood! Blood of men!" He follows his tirade by lifting up the keg and smashing it on the floor.

In between clenched teeth, Tom says, "You ain't changed a bit. Besides, your hands ain't so clean. You killed and liked it. You didn't get them medals for holding hands with them Germans!" Mike is left trembling, and Tom storms off to live with his moll, Kitty. But domestic life cramps his style. At the breakfast table one morning, Tom asks Kitty if there's any liquor in the house. "Not before breakfast, dear," she answers sweetly. After a nasty exchange that leaves her whimpering, Tom grabs a grapefruit half and grinds it into Kitty's face. (It's the film's most notorious scene.)

Actress Mae Clarke said that she had no idea James Cagney was going to smash a grapefruit in her face and left the set of *The Public Enemy* crying after shooting the scene. The film made Cagney a star and the gangster a symbol of the delinquent, hair-trigger male with a ready temper and a tantalizing strut.

He soon meets another woman, Gwen Allen (Jean Harlow), who intimidates him and has him acting like a schoolboy. (She's supposed to be an upper-crust party girl from Texas, but Harlow's sexual cool hints at much more.) Her control of the relationship frustrates Tom, although she finally admits her weakness for him. "You're a spoiled boy, Tommy. You want things . . . and you aren't content until you get them. Well, maybe I'm spoiled too." Dressed in a seductive, slinky dress (sans underwear, a Harlow habit), she leads him over to a chair and drapes herself across his lap. She draws his head to her breast and says, "Oh, my bashful boy. . . . You are different, Tommy. . . . it's a difference in basic character. Men that I know . . . and I've known dozens of them . . . they're so nice, so polished, so considerate. Most women like that type. I guess they're afraid of the other kind. I thought I was too . . . but you're so *strong!* You don't give, you take! Oh, Tommy! I could love you to death." With that, she forcefully kisses him before he begins to take control of the cat-and-mouse game. They're interrupted by news that Nathan has been killed in an accident with his horse. After Nathan's funeral, Tom and Matt head for the stables, where Tom shoots the horse, simply for revenge. In another act of vengeance, Tom kills Putty Nose to settle an old score. Even when Putty Nose begins begging for his life, asking Tom if he has a heart, Tom keeps a surly smirk on his face, enjoying the spectacle of fear. The camera stays on Matt, who watches the murder in stunned silence from across the room. Putty Nose has scurried over to the piano to try to soften Tom's killing mood

In *The Public Enemy,* Tom Powers (Cagney, *right*) holds a gun to his boyhood mentor Putty Nose (Murray Kinnell, *center*) while Tom's partner and lifelong friend Matt Doyle (Edward Woods) looks on with uneasy dread.

with the risqué ditties he once played for them as boys. Matt's eyes widen as the blast of gunshots is followed by the jarring sound of discordant piano keys.

With Nathan gone, a gang war breaks out. Paddy orders his gang to hole up in a hotel until he can regroup his forces. The bored men sit around playing cards, but Paddy's mistress, an "experienced" woman named Jane, takes advantage of a drunken Tom and sleeps with him. He's outraged that he's been seduced by a woman and slaps her around before fleeing the hideout, despite Paddy's warning. Matt runs after Tom, yelling, "Whadya want to run out on me for? We're together, ain't we?" Tom grins and gives Matt his customary gesture: a mocking tap on the jaw with his fist. It's his most overt sign of affection, even for his mother. Within minutes, the men are fired on, and Matt dies in the street. Tom escapes around the corner of a building and stares after his would-be killers, vowing revenge.

Tom finds a pawn shop and pretends to know nothing about the guns under the counter. He dupes the clerk into opening a gun's chamber and loading it with a few bullets. The clerk offers more bullets, noting that the gun will take up to six. Silently enjoying the inside joke, Tom answers, "Oh, this'll be enough." Quickly turning the gun on the clerk, he orders, "Stick 'em up."

In the film's climax, Tom hides in the shadows by the enemy's hideout on a rain-soaked night. He's waiting for his chance. Eventually, he creeps toward the camera with a full grin and unblinking eyes that divulge his deadly aim. With his gun drawn, he stalks into the hideout. A cavalcade of cracking bullets and tortured screams follow. Tom stumbles back out of the building and hurls the guns back through the windows before making it to the street, where he drops to his knees. After muttering, "I ain't so tough," he falls forward into the flooded gutter.

Surrounded by his mother, his brother, and Molly, Tom lies in a hospital bed. Only the center of his face is not covered by bandages. In a strained family reunion, Tom feebly apologizes for all his wrongs. Back home, Mike gets an anxious visit from Paddy, who tells him that Tom has been kidnapped from the hospital. Paddy reveals the enticing offer he made the rival gang: return Tom that evening, and Paddy would leave town and the rackets. The call comes; Tom is on his way home. Molly and a happily humming Ma Powers flit about getting his room ready, and Mike paces the floor until the doorbell stops him cold. He pulls open the front door to reveal a motionless, Tom still wrapped in bandages like a mummy and locked in a deathly gaze that looks nowhere. The body balances upright for a few seconds and then crashes face first to the floor. The last shot shows a bumping needle on a phonograph record, which has stopped playing, "I'm Forever Blowing Bubbles." The song about gaiety and frivolity bookends the film and comments on the futility of Tom's aspirations.

The original ending was not filmed: Mike steps over Tom's dead body and rushes out the door to kill his brother's murderers—his pockets stuffed with military-issue hand grenades. This ending was probably deemed an affront to the moral difference between killing as a soldier for your country and killing for revenge on the street.

The Public Enemy was shot in 26 days at a cost of $151,000 and made well over $1 million in its initial release.[12] The film tries to explain how gangsters are bred in environments and somewhat nurtured by the mean streets of the slums. A young Tom is surrounded by an unfeeling thug of a father (despite the badge), tainted mentors, and a dour, self-righteous brother. But as one critic complained, "This attempt to uncover first causes is pretty superficial and unconvincing: Tom Powers seems to have been a bad lot from the beginning."[13] Director William Wellman was known not for his character studies but for tightly constructed, unfettered narratives with well-paced action sequences.

Most critics, though, lauded the film's realism as they had *Little Caesar*'s. Watts wrote that the story "is presented simply, directly, and more in the manner of sociological document. . . . [Tom] is utterly merciless, utterly homicidal, and utterly real." Watts misses the manipulation of our sympathy for Tom when he adds, "No doubt the most impressive thing about the picture is that complete refusal to sentimentalize its central figure."[14] Tom—the persona of soon-to-be screen idol Cagney—strikes such a responsive chord that his mannerisms and sneer will be ripped off by every actor who will play a criminal in the future.

Like Robinson, Cagney had authentic street credentials; he too was raised on the rough streets of New York in a polyglot neighborhood known as Yorkville. It was full of "dialects . . . and first-generation German, Irish, Jewish, Italian, Hungarian, and Czech," in Cagney's own words. His fluid, self-assured body language can be traced to his stage work as a dancer and his youthful boxing career, which earned him runner-up status for the New York state lightweight title.

Cagney wasn't the original choice for the lead part of Tom. Edward Woods, who ended up as Matt Doyle, was slated for the lead. But Bright and Wellman pushed for Cagney, who was a newcomer but undeniably closer to Powers's core than the soft-spoken Woods. As Cagney remembers: "The director had seen *The Doorway to Hell,* and he quickly became aware of the obvious casting error. He knew at once that I could project that direct gutter quality." Cagney had played a henchman to the star Lew Ayres, whom critics charged was miscast as the screen version of Johnny Torrio, Capone's boss. Ayres came off more like a college boy than a veteran mobster. As Clarens comments, Cagney "had but to snarl and clench his fist" to make his role as the underboss fit.

Although Lon Chaney and George Bancroft sketched out the outlines of the archetype gangster, Cagney created the matinee idol gangster. (His prototype wouldn't be replaced until the genre's renaissance of the 1970s created the coolheaded, calculated repose of the Corleone dons.) Cagney would play other roles in his career and win an Academy Award in 1942 for *Yankee Doodle Dandy* about the patriotic song-and-dance man George M. Cohan. "But the images associated with Tom linger in the memory longer than any of the others."[15] Before the full star impact of *The Public Enemy* hit Cagney, Lorentz predicted, "I hope the star of *Public Enemy* gets a chance to do something besides crime movies, but I fear he will be playing one gangster after another because of his work in this production."

In an essay entitled "James Cagney and the American Hero," critic Lincoln Kirstein commented on the newfound idol, no longer the Western lawman but the "short, red-headed Irishman, quick to wrath, humorous, articulate in anger, representing not a minority in action, but the action of the American majority—the semiliterate lower middle-class." About Cagney's appealing gangster, Kirstein adds, "No one expresses more clearly in terms of pictorial action the delights of violence, the overtones of a semiconscious sadism, the tendency toward destruction, toward anarchy which is the basis of American sex appeal."[16]

SCARFACE: SHAME OF A NATION

Following the huge successes of *Little Caesar* and *The Public Enemy,* Howard Hughes's *Scarface* made its debut. The film was by then already famous for its battle with the censors. The result was a noisy premiere and immediate calls for this bolder brand of gangster movie to end.

"Of *Scarface* there has already been so much said," wrote John Mosher in his 1932 *New Yorker* review. He describes a sensational rumor that circulated, which claimed that a real corpse, "procured from some convenient morgue," was flung from a taxi during the filming of one scene.[17]

The film, ordered by censors to include *Shame of a Nation* along with *Scarface* in its title, begins with a towering perspective of tall buildings and a stormy sky. A sign announcing a stag party and a janitor cleaning up indicate that it's after hours. One of three drunken men meanders off to make a phone call. The camera pans to reveal the sinister silhouette of a man holding a gun; he whistles a tune before firing. The next camera shot reveals a dead body on the floor.

A newspaper headline screams: "Costello Slaying Starts Gang War." The editor shouts, "We'll need 40 men on this story for the next five years. This town is up for grabs. . . . They'll be shooting each other like rabbits. . . . It'll be just like war. That's it . . . war! You put that in the lead!"

Relaxing under a barber's towel is Tony Camonte (Paul Muni), whom police want to question. A close-up of a match striking a badge switches to Camonte nonchalantly lighting a cigarette. He's shoved off to the station, accompanied by his right-hand man, Guino Rinaldo (George Raft). The slick, unflappable Rinaldo has a habit of flipping and catching a coin repeatedly with one hand while his eyes look dead ahead. Tony gets released from custody on a "rid of hocus pocus," as he explains to the new boss, Johnny Lovo (Osgood Perkins). While Lovo tells Tony to expand business on the south side—making sure to stay out of the north side—Tony is distracted by the Lovo's blond mistress, Poppy (Karen Morley). Tall, slender, and decked out in a satin dressing gown, she offers Tony an icy pose and sniffs at him indifferently. On his way out, Tony asks Lovo if she's "expensive."

Tony tells Rinaldo, whom he's nicknamed L'il Boy, that "someday I'm gonna run the whole works" and talks of taking down Lovo, who has gone soft. Back at home, Tony assaults a man whom he finds kissing his sister Cesca (Ann Dvorak). He growls at her, "I don't want anybody putting their hands on you." To stop her outrage, he gives her a wad of money. The mother tries to warn her that "it's bad money" and will keep her indebted to him. But Cesca insists she can ignore him and do what she wants. "He's a-no good. . . . and now you start to be a just-a like him," warns Mrs. Camonte.

To avert a war, Lovo holds a meeting of all gang leaders in town to explain how they must organize to survive. "It'll mean twice as much dough . . . and half as much trouble." He explains how "running beer" is big business and should be run efficiently like any other. When one of the hoodlums objects to the civilized approach of affirmed territories, Tony convinces him by beating him up. "And don't interrupt the president no more," he warns.

Tony gets the job of convincing unwilling beer customers to begin ordering only from the informal bootlegging union. Close-ups of beer going down drains and a bomb being tossed into a storefront illustrate his preferred methods. Tony and Rinaldo also visit a hospital to kill off a rival they only wounded in a foray into the forbidden north side. Time advances as days of the week are machine-gunned off a calendar. Lovo is furious about the north side encroachment and warns that it will lead to gang war. Tony increasingly acts less like a dutiful employee, slowly unveiling his naked ambition. Next on his list is rival O'Hara, who's killed in the flower shop that fronts his operation.

Tony soon upgrades his lifestyle, adding a custom, bulletproof car and a new home with steel shutters on the windows. He takes Poppy there, but she insults the decor as

The lethal interior of the original screen *Scarface,* Tony Camonte (Paul Muni, *center*), is barely subdued by the pricey tuxedos he and his henchmen are posing in. To remind moviegoers of Capone's reputed love of opera, the screen Scarface and his men—packing weapons in their cummerbunds—are dressed formally to attend a highbrow theater production.

gaudy. She also describes his flashy jewelry and extravagant clothes as eyesores, including his striped lounging jacket (similar to Capone's, as photographed at his Florida estate). But she leaves no doubt that she values what the acquisitions say about his rising status.

O'Hara's successor Gaffney (Boris Karloff) prepares for war. While Poppy and Tony are sitting at a restaurant, a slow-moving fleet of black sedans pass the windows and unload torrents of bullets. An unruffled Rinaldo shoots his way into the street to retrieve a new tommy gun off a dead rival. Tony fidgets with it like a child with a new toy. Back at Lovo's place, Tony says excitedly, "Look at this, Johnny, you can carry it around like a baby. . . . Some little typewriter, eh? I'm gonna write my name all over this town with big letters. Get outta my way, Johnny, I'm gonna spit!" With his arms vibrating from the gun's action, Tony sprays the walls with a stream of bullets.

Lovo orders Tony not to avenge the O'Hara gang attack, but Tony vows, "We go after them. . . . we throw those micks up for grabs." The machine gun changes conditions on the streets, and the killing escalates. Dark, shadowy shots lit by headlights and gun blasts are coupled with a montage of gunplay, whining sirens, shattering glass, and women's screams. In a reconstruction of the Saint Valentine's Day massacre, seven men line up, and their silhouettes are obliterated amid clouds of smoke from unseen firearms.

Tony and his men shoot Gaffney at a bowling alley and then head to a nightclub, where Poppy finally chooses Tony over Lovo. She signals her switch by letting Tony light her cigarette, leaving Lovo's flame flickering in midair. Cesca is there, too, and leaves her date to approach Rinaldo, with whom she loves to flirt. She does a sultry solo dance for him, showing off her body-hugging, glittering evening gown. It has the desired effect, but Rinaldo resists because of his boss. But Tony spots her dancing with another man and races over to knock him down and drag her off. Once home, Tony's rage escalates. He slaps Cesca and tears the dress off her shoulder. She clings to her mother for protection, and Tony races onto the street and is nearly killed by a rival in a waiting sedan.

Tony and his enemies shoot it out from speeding cars that eventually crash. Tony survives and tracks down Rinaldo at one of his girlfriend's apartments to help set a trap for Lovo, whom Tony believes tried to kill him. After Lovo falls for the plan, Rinaldo kills him on Tony's orders. Tony immediately goes to collect his prize: Poppy. He shows up at her place and tells her to pack her bags.

While he hides in Florida for a month, newspaper stories report that a new reform mayor has taken over city hall. As soon as Tony arrives back in town, his tearful mother tells him Cesca is living with a man. The next shot shows Cesca playing the piano and singing a ballad for her new husband, Rinaldo, until he's pulled away by a

Tony Camonte (Paul Muni) is intrigued by the deadly possibilities of his new lethal toy that "spits"—the Thompson submachine gun. It also makes him a choice target in the erupting turf war. *Scarface* was the last and most violent of three classic films of the early 1930s that provoked a fervent moral backlash.

Tony's sister and imagined lover Cesca (Ann Dvorak) joins him for the final, bloody shoot-out with police. But his impressive arsenal is no match for police bullets, tear gas, and undaunted outrage. When Cesca is killed, Tony whimpers the gangster's most dreaded outcome: "I don't got nobody. . . . I'm all alone. . . . I'm no good by myself."

knock at the door. There stands Tony, who slowly progresses from shock to rage. A close-up catches a coin falling from Rinaldo's hand while his bride lets out a gut-wrenching scream.

Rinaldo's death kicks off a police hunt that eventually traps Tony in his secured fortress. Cesca arrives, pointing a gun at Tony, but tearfully can't shoot, telling him, "You're me and I'm you." Instead she helps him defend his fort, grabbing a rifle and smiling bravely. Through the din of sirens and gunfire, Tony discovers Cesca has been hit. He gets hysterical. "You can't leave me all alone. . . . I'm no good by myself . . . please, don't go." He keeps shrieking her name until the police throw tear gas into the place. A close-up shows him choking and his eyes watering. He cries out, "Cesca, I can't see!" and stumbles down the stairs. After police crash through the door, he pleads, "Don't shoot. . . . I don't got nobody. . . . I'm all alone." They escort him outside, where he makes a run for it, but they open fire and kill him. The camera pulls up and away from the gutter until it focuses on the flashing sign that taunted Tony, promising, "The World Is Yours."

Scarface included some of gangland's famous acts, including the death of "Big" Jim Colosimo (now Big Louie) at his Wabash Avenue nightclub, and a hospital killing borrowed from the life of Legs Diamond. The murder of Dion O'Banion (the film's O'Hara) in his north side flower shop was hauntingly familiar to the one Hecht wrote for *Underworld*.[18] (*Little Caesar* pays tribute to O'Banion's macabre 1924 funeral, in which the filmmakers mock the gangland habit of the corpse's killer sending the most elaborate flower arrangement.)

In his review of *Scarface* in the *New Yorker,* John Mosher wrote: "I should say it lacks the brilliance of acting and detail that *The Public Enemy* and *Little Caesar* both had . . . surpassing the average film of this sort only in the matter of length and in the quantity of gore."

Rosow wrote that Muni "has a bravado and a sense of humor that often make him likable and a spaghetti-savoring ethnicity that generates nostalgia for the immigrant experience."[19] However, instead of effectively imitating an Italian street thug, he often appears apish and burlesque, mugging for the camera. By the film's climax, "Camonte is almost accent-free and tuxedo-sharp—even his hairline seems to have receded from the Neanderthal brow."[20] (Convincing portrayals of Italian gangsters would have to wait for Italian American filmmakers Francis Ford Coppola and Martin Scorsese and similar actors who showed the community with candor and affection. Scorsese has described Muni's accent as "embarrassing" and derived from the "Mama Mia! school of Italian acting. . . . No one talks that way.")

When Muni is not trying to imitate an Italian, however, his portrayal of the gangster is forceful. Born Muni Weisenfreund in what is now the Ukraine, Muni trained in the Yiddish theater, which lent him the dependency on dialect, makeup, and marked body language. The Fox studio had brought him to Hollywood from Broadway to consider grooming him as the next Lon Chaney. He would win an Oscar for the title role in *The Story of Louis Pasteur* (1936), which helped him avoid being typecast as a gangster, despite his energetic performance as Camonte.

His character is made richer by the contrasting cool of George Raft, who "carved out a different dimension of the gangster character's soul."[21] The saturnine Raft had a controlled but lethal interior that would be picked up by Humphrey Bogart. Bogart was among the actors lining up to cut their dramatic teeth portraying gangsters and tough guys. This emerging Hollywood elite also included William Powell, Spencer Tracy, Gary Cooper, and Clark Gable, who had auditioned for *Little Caesar.* Even the dashing John Gilbert, who would later be paired with Greta Garbo in more sweeping films, portrayed gangster Benny Horowitz in *Four Walls* (1928)—a "product of an east side environment," as *Variety* described him.

Most actors who weren't from such gritty environments had to portray ethnic gangsters by borrowing popular stereotypes. When gang member Tony Passa in *Little Caesar* sobs to his mama, she offers him spaghetti to soothe him followed by a pitch to see the parish priest. In *Scarface* there's an organ grinder and a monkey in case the viewer misses the immigrant connection.

Filmmakers and censors grappled with how audiences would react to screen images of Italians, Jews, and the Irish, not only as gangsters but as ethnic symbols. One cut scene from *The Public Enemy* basks in ethnic slurs but is probably more of an accurate depiction of how gangsters talked to each other. In the dropped scene, Tom asks a thug named Gordon how a "polak" gets a name like Burns. Gordon answers: "Jack McGurn's a wop, Bugs Moran and Hymie Weiss are polaks, Jimmy Wells is a Jew, Al (Capone) Brown's a dago—Hell, a name ain't no indication o' what a guy is."[22] In contrast to pithy but offensive reality, a contrived scene is added to *Scarface* (not shot by Hawks) in which an overbearing newspaper publisher gives a sobering lecture on the need to "put teeth in the deportation act." He says that "gangsters don't belong in this country—half of them aren't even citizens." One of his listeners, a community leader who speaks with a heavy Italian accent, adds, "That's-a true. They bring nothing but disgrace to my people."

Previously, the films of the late 1920s named their gangsters obscure, nonethnic handles that were rugged sounding but offensive to no one: Bull Weed, Fancy Charlie, Dapper Dan Hollins, The Hawk, and Lon Chaney's Black Mike.[23] The Warners and other studio bosses, mostly immigrants themselves, understood the communal closeness of ethnic ties despite the poverty of the slums. By 1930 the studio bosses felt confident in showing the gangster's betrayal of those ties—even if doing so meant attaching their own ethnicity to the screen gangster. In a bit of prejudice of their own, however, the studio moguls usually singled out the Italian gangsters as being particularly predisposed to violence.

THE UNHOLY THREE

Contemporary critics saw these films as related and intertwined, playing off one another and each excelling and failing to live up to the genre's possibilities. They are masterpieces that hold up today because they're less about bootlegging and Capone and more about violence and timeless villainy.

In the best gangster films, including these three, violence is the gangster's calling card, but it should never take over his story. It's the story's punctuation—chiefly exploited to control pacing, inflection, and impact. The *New York Times* critic writing about Sternberg's *The Drag Net* noted that when gratuitous violence overwhelms the tale, it "teems with extravagant action, and although crooks and sleuths are polished off at frequent intervals, the result is hardly exciting. It is a picture devoid of any real dramatic quality and therefore one becomes indifferent to the wholesale massacre indulged in by the director." Noting a subtle difference, Hawks explains in 1956, "We made *Scarface* because the violence of this particular era was interesting."[24]

Because the Hays office wouldn't let blood be shown on screen, the most artistic footage in these films *is* the display of violence. It depended not on modern weaponry and ever-escalating buckets of make-believe blood but on a heavy dose of invention. The filmmakers were forced to use clever methods and symbolism to intimate pain and gore. When Rico shoots Tony Passa for running out on the gang, instead of gushing blood, he dramatically rolls down the mammoth cement steps of his church. (Coppola would borrow this for his *Godfather* finale.) The most artful film of the three, *Scarface,* introduces Tony as a shooting shadow. He also hints that he's about to kill by whistling a sextet from *Lucia di Lammermoor.* The melody's words are *Chi mi frena in tal momento?* (What restrains me in such a moment?). As Richard Corliss comments, "Obviously, nothing restrains, let alone soothes, this savage breast in such a moment. Carnage and culture go hand in hand."[25]

Hawks marks each killing with the symbol X, represented by crossed beams and shadows on walls, streets, and the backdrop of the opening credits. Tony's face is crisscrossed by a scar, and the straps of Cesca's gown are crossed. When Gaffney is killed in the bowling alley (with an X on a score sheet), the death is indicated by a lone pin that spins frantically then topples.

The details of the killings that so rankled the censors, however, were usually not the inventions of the screenwriters but real occurrences. Tom's killing of a horse is based on a true incident involving gangster Samuel "Nails" Nathan. In the real killing, however, the gangsters did it in Lincoln Park in front of horrified picnickers.

The violent screen cousin to the gangster film is the Western. But Western violence—sometimes more ruthlessly displayed than in gangster films—never caused the same furor. The context was comfortably in the past and not related to disturbing current events. The *New York Times* reviewed *Gun Smoke* (1931) and *The Public Enemy* together, calling the villains in the Western "gangsters" because of their lust for gold. And *Variety* wrote that *Little Caesar* had "enough killings herein to fill the quota for an old time cowboy-Indian thriller."

MAMAS AND WHORES

These classic films also display brutality as an everyday event that infiltrates all aspects of life. The gangster cannot control himself, so when it comes to women—whom he fears for their ability to make him vulnerable—controlling *her* is preferred. Women became a casualty of the genre and fade into images in these films—with their focus on the gangster as an alienated misfit rather than as a bad-boy Romeo. Although often overlooked in the genre, women and their power are conspicuous because of their absence. They don't seem important, yet the very choice to exclude them (and, if included, to mistreat or marginalize them) clarifies the gangsters' abnormality. They turn to their gangs as surrogate families, and their sidekicks as life partners.

In his novel, Burnett notes: "What [Rico] feared most in women . . . was . . . their ability to relax a man, to make him soft and slack. . . . He was given to short bursts of lust, and this lust once satisfied, he looked at women impersonally . . . as one looks at inanimate objects."[26] On the other hand, the moll is an acquisition. She's a status symbol dressed in expensive clothes and glittering with jewels furnished by her "sponsor." She's portrayed as an annoying leech who lacks loyalty, brains, or real ambition. As such, few moviegoers wince when she finally gets slapped around or humiliated for enjoying the spoils of crime without having taken the risks. In her boas and chewing gum, she also brilliantly exposes her thug's disguise of feigned culture camouflaging his own crude contents.

The genre represents not only the male point of view but a brutal exposé on the most misogynistic male of them all: the gangster. But to condemn the on-screen abuse of the molls and other females misses the point. Critic Bosley Crowther described the breakfast scene and Tom's malice with a grapefruit as "one of the cruelest and most startling acts ever committed on film."[27] (Crowther, though, included the film in his 1967 collection of "great" films.) Writer Molly Haskell notes that the act is "surely a cleaner and less generalized expression of hostility than rape."[28] Yet the scene is a stroke of filmic brilliance. It captures the essence of what's wrong with these people without using a heavy-handed sermon from an off-screen narrator. (The moll is so familiar that she was later brilliantly parodied by Judy Holiday in *Born Yesterday.* The comic twist: Holiday's moll had brains and dignity but was clueless about the choices open to an unmarried woman who was no longer a virgin. During the Roaring Twenties, her options were bald and few.)

Tom Powers, though, meets his match in Harlow's platinum Gwen. Her ambiguous motives and human frailty make her a rare jewel in gangster films of any era. In *Scarface,* Tony's moll Poppy is the best gangster in the film. She wisely neither loves nor is loved and treats relationships as mutually utilitarian. When Tony starts "spittin' " with his beloved tommy gun, Poppy gapes "with an ecstatic look on her face, almost as though she were enjoying the sex act."[29] By not being too greedy nor attached to anything, she's the only one who remains unscathed in the end.

The Madonna half of the gangster's Madonna-whore fixation is embodied by the sister (or other female relative) above reproach and by the peasant immigrant mother. Tony's sister Cesca is not so much a real girl as a symbol of the "wild thing" Tony cannot control or covet. She appears to have a mind of her own, but her fate is already sealed by being born a Camonte. The film insinuates that if Tony knew Rinaldo and Cesca were married, he would not have been so outraged. But Tony couldn't conceive of any man touching Cesca—even a husband.

The mother character is the most consistent of all female characters from these classics to more recent films. She's not a human mother, who would be culpable for her part in raising such a monster. At first, her saintly, unsoiled image seems to imply that the mother—derived from history's most potent images (starting with the Virgin Mary) and whom we hold responsible for the family's emotional health—is powerless. Despite her unconditional love and fierce loyalty, she cannot protect her male child from becoming a self-loathing misfit and violent destroyer of all things in his path, including most notably himself. But a closer look reveals that the gangster mother is pure metaphor. She stands for hope (especially for immigrants) and life; her son is about what is dark and deadly. The boy is born to her, but the gangster is born of the streets. He no more resembles her than he does the preferred design of the successful American male.

Before the censors ordered cuts, Hawks and Hecht had developed a much more cynical mother for Tony. They wanted to show the hypocrisy that spoils all pockets of society and combines with other forces to create the gangster. Film historian Gerald Mast notes that in an earlier version of the script, the mother lived well and uncomplainingly off Tony's criminal profits. After Cesca becomes involved with Rinaldo, the mother wires Tony to bring him back from Florida because Rinaldo is a threat to the family's financial security. As writer Richard Blake puts it: "She is fully aware of what he will do, but the murder will keep the money in the family."[30] Yet when her character is changed to an anguished, uneducated immigrant with no control over her children, Tony faces the same doom. What we lose, however, are richer insights into his character. Nuance and human scrutiny are sacrificed for clarity. In the end, Mrs. Camonte is interchangeable with Mrs. Powers (or Mrs. Corleone, for that matter). A shot later cut from *The Public Enemy* had Mrs. Powers handing Mike a glass of beer, but censors felt the scene suggested that she condoned her son's bootlegging, thus sullying her as a cherished icon. A flip-flop of the Madonna approach is used in *Little Caesar.* The mother figure is Ma Magdalena, whose very name mocks the fallen woman who befriended and nurtured Christ. And this Ma is crusty, cruel, and greedier than Rico.

Lacking meaningful family relationships, Rico, Tom, and Tony turn to their sidekicks. But the sidekicks, no matter how loyal, can never be smarter, and they fail to make the grade as gangsters. They get killed too early and in a much more mundane fashion. Worst of all, they show their weakness for traditional society: home, family, safety, a future goal. Rinaldo marries Cesca, implying that he will no longer be the ace lothario he appears to be in the story. Matt buys into convention as well and marries his moll Mamie. He also shows he's not as hardened as Tom when he's shocked at the revenge killing of Putty Nose.

GENTLEMEN OF THE PRESS

Besides family and gang members, the other supporting players in the genre are the press. They serve as the public's surrogates and eyewitnesses to the carnage. Journalism itself, the underlying source of these photoplays, often plays the Greek chorus. Montages of shots and superimposed newspaper headlines advance the story and represent the public watch over the Underworld. But the most interesting use of the press is the gangster's need to keep track of stories of his exploits—like an actor checking his reviews. In *Underworld,* the gangsters tack relevant newspaper articles about their crimes to a bulletin board.[31] In *Little Caesar,* Rico vainly buys up newspapers that feature his picture and is entrapped by an unflattering and police-planted news story.

Corliss notes, "Hecht manages both to congratulate journalism for its importance and to chastise it for its chicanery, by underlining the newspapers' complicity in promoting the underworld image."[32] One early scene shows the manipulation of the code of neutrality by an editor who wants to fuel the fear of gang war. A later scene captures an overbearing publisher who blames foreigners and the government but defends the paper's right to publish for the public's right to know. If the front page is ugly, it's not his fault. In another scene added at the censors' urging, a cop chastises an eager reporter who's after a scoop. The cop bellows, "That's the attitude of too many morons in this country. They think these big hoodlums are some sort of demigods. . . . They had some excuse for glorifying our old Western badmen. They met in the middle of the street at high noon—waited for each other to draw. But these things sneak up and shoot someone in the back and then run away."

But Camonte neatly sums up the media's meaning for a gangster: "The *News* has got-a best story. Pictures of you—and one of me, too." Once movies came along, gangsters began to watch themselves and often adjusted the reality to fit the screen image. Raft and Hawks report in their memoirs that Capone was flattered by *Scarface,* although no one dared call him that. (Capone's friends knew him by the affectionate nickname Snorky. The handle of "Scarface" was given to him by the media, and he was very touchy about it. He had earned the scars in a barroom brawl after making a crude remark to the sister of a thug with a ready knife. Capone later hired the man as a personal bodyguard.) Capone was said to have owned his own print of *Scarface.* However, he was offended by shots of Tony shoveling spaghetti in his mouth like an uncouth slob. Even so, he threw a party and invited Hawks and presented the director with a small machine gun as a special gift and sign of approval.[33]

CLASSIC AND DOOMED

These films also perfected the most thrilling symbols of the 1930s: cavernous dance palaces, speeding sedans, and pockmarked hideouts. The stark, simply lit sets hug the urban nightscape and cast a sinister glow on the shadowy streets and back alleys. They provide the ideal foil for the explosive action scenes.

Hawks took the camera on the move, experimenting with more claustrophobic framing and chiaroscuro lighting (an interplay of light and shadow) to achieve a heightened sense of intimacy. He also augmented the violent tale with humor. The comic fumbling of Tony's illiterate secretary Angelo sharpens, rather than diminishes, the terror of the surrounding violence. Angelo is inept at the simple task of answering a phone and taking messages. While the restaurant is being shot up, Angelo is straining to hear a caller on the phone, rattled by the mayhem but determined to do his job. Later in the film, his face lights up when he finally gets it right, but ironically he's in his death throes from a gunshot wound.

Another genre convention mastered in these classics is the gangster's gaudy display of material wealth. He acquires better-looking clothes, cars, women, and bedrooms with each step toward success. But screen gangsters had been snappy dressers since the 1920s. The *New York Times* review of John Gilbert's gangster notes: "[He] is so careful regarding the cut of his clothes, the selection of his necktie, the spotlessness of his linen and the combing of his hair that one would never imagine him to be a killer living on Manhattan's east side, but rather a broker with an apartment on Park Avenue." (As contemporary gang bangers have reputedly killed over a pair of Nike sneakers, coveting the right clothes is still part of the persona.)

But as the saying goes, clothes do not make the man. Nor do his riches, which cannot buy him culture. In a droll scene meant to remind the audience of Capone's love of opera, Tony and his tuxedoed bodyguards watch a performance of W. Somerset Maugham's *Rain*. Tony and his men look as out of place as mink does in a poolroom. Later, when Tony thinks about the play's outcome, he confirms his intellectual handicap and crude logic by deciding that Sadie Thompson was smart to "make hay" with the army boys and rebuke the clergyman.

Rico wants respect more than money. "Money's all right, but it ain't everything. Yeah, be somebody! Look hard at a bunch of guys and know that they'll do anything that you tell 'em." Rico doesn't understand the difference between old money and his tainted cash, even though he's given a lavish banquet befitting a Rockefeller. Tom, who never rises to become a boss like Rico and Tony, still does better than most people in his neighborhood. He acquires enough material wealth to impress others and boost his self-image. But money doesn't soothe his demons either.

Disrespect may be appalling, but being left alone is often worse than death. *Scarface* could have dispensed with the final gore and shoot-out, and even the pasted-on ending tried by censors, in which the gangster is hanged. He was already beaten when he was left alone after killing or alienating everyone who could care about or help him.

The very qualities that enable the gangster to be successful—ambition, shrewdness, audacity, and cunning—are the very traits that ruin him. These films insist their stars die, but the deaths are so spectacular and gruesome that they carry a message in themselves. These gangsters have to die so tragically because they've broken the rules by such a wide margin—a simple death doesn't even the score.

Eugene Rosow points out that the blinking signs invented by Hecht in *Underworld* and *Scarface* tell the story of the screen gangster's expanding horizons from 1928 to 1932. Bull Weed is told "the city is yours," whereas Camonte is promised "the world is yours." But Louie Costello warned Camonte: "A man-a always gotta know when he's got-a enough." Tony doesn't, which is why his death is high drama and an opera of violence. Much to the censors' horror, though, he doesn't express any genuine remorse.

More important, the deaths of Rico, Tom, and Tony fail to erase the potent image of their riveting lives. "The strongest impression is not that a gangster inevitably gets bumped off, but that there was something likable and courageous about the little rat after all."[34] Stephen Karpf goes further: "Rico was in many respects an admirable person. He bettered himself in the only way he understood."

A scene cut by censors showed Tony and Poppy yachting in Florida with wealthy society types who found Tony as amusing as a court jester. Although based on true incidents in Capone's life, the scene was judged "un-American" for indicting the movers and shakers in high society.[35] But the prologue and epilogues of *Scarface* find somebody to blame: "This picture is an indictment of gang rule in America and of the callous indifference of the government to this constantly increasing menace to the safety of our liberty. . . . The government is your government: What are *you* going to do about it?"

In the end, the viewer is blamed for being perversely fascinated with the gangster. In coming years, outraged clergy and the Hays office would remedy that. Not only would the gangster be sorry, but he would be disgraced. The censors would use the ultimate gangster insult on him: they would make him turn yellow.

CHAPTER 4

G-Men and Other Hollywood Myths

For years . . . this country tolerated racketeers and murderers because of their own hatred of Prohibition . . . but Prohibition has gone and gangsters . . . must go with it.
—District Attorney Jim Wade (William Powell), *Manhattan Melodrama,* 1934

Audience eagerness for *Little Caesar, The Public Enemy,* and *Scarface* did little to sway government or religious leaders from their belief that such films were intrinsically dangerous. These groups demanded the end of the spectacular reign of the classic screen gangster, arguing that his savage demise in the end only served to gild his legend. Throughout 1932 and 1933, the screen gangster was at his noxious best, with more productions rushed into theaters to capitalize on the success of the prototypes. Most were awash in sadistic innuendo and starred the usual battery of sleek bootleggers, scandalous flappers, and corruptible cops.

As early as 1931, though, local and state censor boards were growing as zealous in their efforts to curb the screen gangster as moviemakers were eager to escalate his appeal. A resolution by the New York State Chapter of the Knights of Columbus that year noted, "The gangster movies . . . are often brilliantly acted and directed. Their detail is conveyed with a vividness almost hypnotic."[1] This was not flattery but harsh criticism of film's tendency to create "a criminal instinct in our youth."

By the summer of 1933, Catholic bishops had had enough and formed a nationwide Legion of Decency. It began pushing for a boycott of films it condemned or found morally objectionable through its own rating system. Raymond Moley claims that within a few months, millions of people had signed the pledge to boycott (or be damned), "while Protestant and Jewish leaders praised the drive."[2] The movement seized the national media's attention and spoke through the church's news organs, which had a combined circulation of more than seven million.[3] Hays finally met with the group in June 1934 and left with an ultimatum to take deliberate action or Hollywood would suffer at the box office.

HOLLYWOOD REWRITE

Hays's decade-long effort to work from inside Hollywood had been deemed a failure. When the Hollywood moguls chose the graduate of the Presbyterian Wabash College to become their spokesman in 1922, they assumed he would be credible to the industry's critics. At the same time, they thought he would be a team player within their community. That impression stemmed from his visit to Hollywood in 1920 as the national chairman of the Republican Party. He had come to build support for his GOP candidate Warren G. Harding. Hays had already earned a reputation as a shrewd politician, and he remained unscathed even after the Harding scandals erupted. Harding's old political cronies, known as the Ohio Gang, were linked to more than $2 billion in graft and government pork. But it was the Teapot Dome scandal that did the most damage to Harding's reputation. His secretary of the interior had arranged secret oil leases with Mammoth Oil president Harry Sinclair, who had delivered a $260,000 bribe and campaign contribution to Hays.[4] Hays was never tarnished by the fiasco, which took decades to sort out.

Throughout the 1920s, Hays's piecemeal efforts to curb Hollywood excesses were tolerated by studio bosses as long as they made money. Moreover, the little nips and tucks done to a few highly publicized films each year gave the impression that Hays was doing his job, and the moralizing gadflies were kept at bay. Hays, a native of Crawfordsville, Indiana, had established two fronts of action. First, his open-door policy welcomed any civic or religious group to his office to voice a concern. Second, he installed an honor system of self-regulation, including the review board to examine plays and books slated for film treatments. But Hollywood had little respect for the reviewers, as they had few professional credentials in literary or theatrical fields. Most of them were socialites, community volunteers, and "clubwomen delegates," as Paré Lorentz dubbed them. "Can you imagine a board of nondescript women marking the works of Oscar Wilde, Fielding, Hemingway, Shakespeare even, rating them 'Good,' 'Educational,' 'Subversive to morality?' " he asked.[5] In fairness to the volunteers, most of them were mothers whose children were primary fans of screen stars, including the gangster. As concerned citizens, they were appropriate. But as critics with the power to chill free expression, they were ludicrous.

Despite the resentment of Hays within Hollywood's artistic community, the studio heads kept him on the job, figuring he was the lesser of two evils. Hays helped ward off government interference and actively worked to defeat censorship legislation, which before the boycott was the industry's most serious threat. Moreover, his meddling in government policy (using his old contacts) to provide industry protection in foreign distribution and favorable copyright laws was warmly appreciated. Hays also encouraged banks to become involved in the movie business as financial backers, and the resulting inflow of money significantly boosted the industry boom of the 1920s.

The year 1934, however, changed the uneasy alliance between Hollywood and Hays forever. The Legion and its boycott threat joined other forces already hounding the movie industry: the depression and overexposure of gangsters—real and imagined. The depression finally caught up with the movie business. Attendance dropped by half, and industry unions began pushing for standardized working conditions and fairer contracts. The cries grew louder when the studio bosses cut wages in half to cope with the deepening crisis. As labor problems persisted, the studios went to Hays again for help, this time calling on his experience in hardball politics. Hays proved his familiarity with gangsters went beyond fussing over their screen images. Hays hired Johnny Roselli as "labor conciliator" to fix the film industry's union problems.[6] Roselli later told the Kefauver congressional committee that he got the job by promising Hays he would "fight fire with fire" to ameliorate the labor troubles.[7] Gangsters had long been hired by industrialists to break strikes and bust unions. Roselli had also served as the middleman between gangsters and Harry Cohn, who desperately needed ready money to fight his brother Jack for control of Columbia Pictures. William Fox, too, used Underworld sources in his unsuccessful attempt to retain control of his company in the vigorous consolidation following the stock market crash.[8]

While Hollywood was increasingly embattled with in-house woes, the moral fury that had been building since 1909 picked the right moment to strike. When Hays left his meeting with the Legion of Decency in the summer of 1934, he agreed to an unprecedented policy of self-censorship never before levied on any form of American media. Because movies had been deemed primarily an entertainment medium, the First Amendment offered little protection. (In battling for an uncut *Scarface,* Howard Hughes tried to invoke his right to free speech, and Griffith's 1916 epic *Intolerance* had unsuccessfully pleaded for the medium of film to be considered serious expression.)

Hays soon put the Catholic activist Joseph Breen in charge of the Production Code, which had been created in 1930 but previously not enforced. The Code, written by magazine editor and Jesuit priest Daniel Lord, along with the publisher of the *Motion Picture Herald* and devout Catholic Martin Quigley, was based on the Ten Commandments.[9] Further, Breen instituted a fine of $25,000 to any picture that was produced, distributed, or exhibited without a certificate of approval.

Among its key attacks on the gangster, the Code warned that "revenge in modern times shall not be justified." Breen differentiated "evil usages of a bygone age," such as the violence and mayhem displayed in a Western. He noted that Westerns "are not subject to the same critical examination as modern ways and customs. In general, historic and older classical subjects possess a certain quality of distance and unreality."[10] Particularly regarding law enforcement characters, Breen cautioned: "The police must not be presented as incompetent, corrupt, cruel or ridiculous."[11] Not only was Breen going to discourage certain types of film treatments, but he was actively seeking to influence the story spin. As he explained, "There is no right to corrupt, but there is a duty to be decent."[12]

One could argue that if the pulpits had hammered away at Hollywood five years before—during the most roaring of the 1920s—they would have failed to make much of an impact, similar to prohibiting alcohol without first gauging the public's mood. But the bleakness of the depression had primed the public for Hollywood's new attempt at piety and repression. Besides, Camonte's bootlegging tale was nearly nostalgic by its 1932 debut anyway. Prohibition was all but officially dead. Liquor was free-flowing by the election of Franklin Roosevelt, who had made Prohibition's repeal a campaign promise. Roosevelt also soothed Americans' ears with talk of healing, optimism, and the New Deal. With the economy to repair, bootleggers no longer fascinated the public. Beaten by the long struggle, mixed reviews, and box office jitters in the wake of the Legion's condemnation, Howard Hughes withdrew all prints of *Scarface.* The film went unseen for nearly 50 years, which contributed to its reputation, compounded by the growing legend of the eccentric Hughes.

Al Capone himself was no longer concerned with the Volstead Act, as he was finally imprisoned not for its violation but for income tax evasion. In 1931 he was sentenced to 11 years but continued to run his crime empire from his jail cell. By 1934 the government dethroned him by moving him to the remote island prison of Alcatraz, off the coast of California. Capone's imprisonment at "the Rock" effectively ended his Underworld reign. (By the time he was paroled in 1939, he was already suffering from advanced syphilis, which eventually ravaged his mind and body. He died at his Miami Beach mansion in 1947.)

MELODRAMA ON DEATH ROW

Despite quelling its labor problems and averting a large-scale boycott, Hollywood was still in trouble at the box office. The industry needed help in front of the camera to keep moviegoers in the habit—despite hard times. No doubt the gangster could still be useful. Society still needed a bogeyman and a villain that audiences could love to hate. But the Hays office blocked all attempts to bring the headline-grabbing stories of John Dillinger, Bonnie and Clyde, Baby Face Nelson, and Pretty Boy Floyd to the screen—even though by 1934 they, too, were no longer menacing the public. So the gangster was put back in the supporting cast of melodramas and broad-stroke crime films that focused on plot rather than character development. Part of stripping the gangster of his potency was to blur his personal history and nefarious rise within the Underworld. His ethnic origins (other than Irish) were fudged, and knowledge about his past was simply the sum of his rap sheet.

Manhattan Melodrama (1934) was one of the first films of the new ilk, and its title said it all. (Ironically, it was the film Dillinger was supposedly watching while a government ambush waited outside the theater.) The film starred William Powell as the venerable district attorney Jim Wade and Clark Gable as his criminal nemesis "Blackie" Gallagher. Gable had tested for the part of Rico Bandello, from whom the amiable but flimsier Blackie descends. In the film, Jim and Blackie are raised together as orphans by a kindly Russian Jew, who tells the boys that America is "the land of opportunity . . . there's plenty here for everybody . . . Catholic, Protestant, Jew." A split-screen montage tracks the boys' formative years from 1904 to the Roaring Twenties, charting their different paths (without explanation): Jim grows up with his eyes glued to books and libraries, and Blackie and his sleight of hand are drawn to crap games and roulette wheels. Rather than the tarnished bootlegger, Blackie grows up to be a dapper gambler, with the vague suggestion that he dips into other rackets as well. Eventually the boyhood pals cross paths in their professional guises and have a showdown. Jim as the district attorney and then reform-minded governor is instrumental in bringing Blackie to justice. The story is enriched by a female character, Eleanor Packer (Myrna Loy), who changes from being Blackie's moll to Jim's political wife but remains torn by her affection for both men. With the return of a respectable girl to the mix, though, the gangster as we had come to know him becomes polluted. Blackie, for instance, sees how much in love Eleanor and Jim are and commits various unselfish acts to make sure they end up together. First, he kills the blackmailer threatening Jim with exposing his "soft" approach toward Blackie's crimes. Then Blackie turns down Jim's offer to commute his death sentence because it will look like preferential treatment to voters and ruin Jim's career.

Despite Blackie's buoyant charm and gutsy resolve, the screenplay (written by Joseph Mankiewicz and H. P. Garrett) asks the viewer to believe that it's Jim who's awe inspiring. As the grim district attorney enters the courtroom to plead for a murder conviction against his old chum, Blackie looks on with obvious affection for his pal Jim, whom he proudly describes as "class—it's written all over him." Rather than convince viewers of his inferiority complex (a vital gangster trait), the handsome, self-assured Blackie proves he's commendable for his humility, and for his naked understanding of his own frailty (an unlikely ability for a gangster).

Blackie is made even more attractive by Gable's portrayal. He lends the gangster a virile panache, which he would later perfect for the redeemable rogue Rhett Butler—the role that made Gable a Hollywood legend. But no actor could have made the death row scenes less saccharine. As Blackie lumbers down the hall toward his doom, he stops like a general by his troops, shaking hands, accepting a gift, and offering inane advice. He tells one fellow inmate to forgo getting his death sentence commuted. "You don't want it anyway. . . . die the way you lived, all of a sudden. Don't drag it out. Living like that don't mean a thing." When Jim visits Blackie's cell to tell him that he's calling off the execution, Blackie bellows, "If I can't live the way I want, let me die the way I want!" The syrupy stringed music and close-ups of a morose, heartsick Jim are offset by a zestful Blackie. He acts more like a gentle fairy-tale giant whose clumsy bravery will lift him from the gutter toward the promise of atonement. For Jim's boyhood friend, such behavior is a show of bravado; for a convicted killer and screen gangster, it's absurd.

The film was a Metro Goldwyn Mayer (MGM) production—the studio of musicals and high-gloss products. That's evident in Blackie, who *Variety* dubbed "too suave" for his own good. The director W. S. "Woody" Van Dyke made the far superior and lighter *The Thin Man* the same year, exploiting the best thing about *Manhattan Melodrama*—the team of Myrna Loy and William Powell.

Another problem with *Manhattan Melodrama* as a vehicle for the gangster is that the film is a one-man show, both for the gangster and for the lawman. The fraternity of the gang for either opponent is sorely missing, with one weakly developed leading lady trying to provide ballast for the skimpy duel. At one point, Jim warns Blackie, "My job means fighting you and your crowd. . . . and I've got too many guys in my gang!" We ache to see their packs on the prowl, chasing each other in black sedans and devising strategies to win the concluding battle.

LAWMEN PASS THEIR SCREEN TEST

If Hollywood wanted to exploit the gangster genre—from the law's point of view—it needed to reinstate the posse mentality. Within two years of Breen's edict to stop belittling law enforcement officers, Hollywood released a film that not only restored the lawman's forceful image but surrounded him with a fervid mob of his own. *G-Men* (1935) starred Cagney as the lead tough guy, but this time his arsenal included a badge, which greatly expanded his options for harassing his enemies. Cagney was anxious to try on other roles besides the gangster. He said he viewed his character in *G-Men* as "a step up the ladder artistically," but he admitted that he was worried about the public's reaction to his switching from criminal to crime buster. The Warner Brothers film under William Keighley's direction was an immediate success and gave the genre an extended life—despite the Code. However, as John McCarty notes, the film was probably so appealing because Cagney's lawman is "fairly indistinguishable from Tom Powers."

The opening scene takes place in an FBI training room in the future year of 1949, when the bureau marks its 25th anniversary. A sober official talks of the days when a gangster could "thumb his nose at us." Criminals could flee from justice by crossing state lines, and agents were hampered by not being allowed to carry guns. "But the bureau did have its weapons: Truth, Drive and Vitality," he adds, before introducing the story of Brick Davis—"the daddy of all FBI pictures."

The story, written by Seton Miller (who had worked on *Scarface*), begins with Brick (Cagney) pretending to sum up to the jury in an empty law office. He's bored and underused yet turns down business from crooked politicians and hoodlums who're looking for a shyster. The shady ward boss, Krantz, reminds Brick that Big Shot

McKay "didn't pick you out of the gutter and send you through college for nothing." For that, Krantz gets a punch in the nose, proving Cagney, as gangster or lawyer, comes equipped with a short fuse.

An old law school roommate turned G-man pops into Brick's office and explains that he's in town investigating gangsters who work for McKay. Then he tries to entice Brick to join him at the Justice Department. The college friend is soon killed by McKay's gang, and Brick is compelled to join the bureau to avenge his pal's death. It's classic gangster-style revenge, only this time the story puts Cagney on the right side of the law.

Before he leaves for Washington, he informs his mobster patron McKay (William Harrigan) of his plan to switch sides. He apologizes for not living up to the success that McKay's $20,000 investment in law school promised. "Nobody gets ahead fast when they play the game on the level," says Brick's affectionate sponsor. "I been in the rackets all my life. They don't pay off—except in dough," he adds, with a straight face. Yet Brick feels sheepish knowing that someday he'll have to hunt down McKay, who saves Brick the moral wrangling by announcing he's going to retire.

Once in Washington, Brick finds a rival in his trainer and later boss Jeff McCord (Robert Armstrong). The two men first spar, literally, wearing boxing gloves. Brick pretends to be clumsy with the sport but soon bests McCord with a left-right combination. Their rivalry moves to the shooting range—necessary training just in case the G-men get permission to carry firearms. Brick turns out to be a sharpshooter, a skill he attributes to having been "the marble champion of the Bronx." The final clash occurs over the affections of McCord's sister Kay (Margaret Lindsey), who represents the prize for the former street punk who finally makes the grade in legitimate society. She's classy, aloof, and quite conveniently a nurse, who cares for Brick later in the film when the bullets start popping. When he wins her, he walks away from the Underworld and the kind of women who inhabit it—molls and cabaret singers such as Jean Morgan (Ann Dvorak, who played Cesca Camonte).

The film then turns to the pursuit of the gangsters who killed Brick's friend and are responsible for the crime wave sweeping the Midwest, according to the newspaper headlines whirling through the customary montage. Because Brick knows the gangsters personally, he uses that edge to lead the hunt. More headlines advance the story and, reporting four officers killed, reenact the Kansas City Union Station massacre that involved Baby Face Nelson. The killings prompt the FBI chief to make an emotional appeal to Washington lawmakers. He howls, "Make bank robbery and kidnapping a federal crime. Make it a federal crime to kill a government agent or flee across the state line to avoid arrest, or to avoid testifying as a witness. Arm your agents and not just with revolvers. If these gangsters want to use machine guns, then give your special agents machine guns, shotguns, tear gas, everything else. This is war!"

He adds in a softer postscript: "Now, understand, I don't want to make them a group of quick trigger men. But I do want the Underworld to know that when a federal agent draws his gun, he is ready and equipped to shoot to kill with the least possible waste of bullets." That meets the genre's demand for efficient killers—badge or no badge.

The film also devotes a few scenes to the technicians who wear lab coats and look through microscopes at fingerprints and ballistics material. But the film's muscle, as in any good gangster tale, is in the violent confrontations between mobsters and agents—both sides now armed for war.

"Those guys don't like it much now that we're able to give them a dose of their own medicine," boasts McCord to his sister, failing to notice that she has started to

Still smugly hugging a submachine gun like a trusted third arm, Cagney is shooting on the law's side this time as FBI agent Brick Davis in *G-Men*—Hollywood's violent solution to the flak over violent gangsters. Davis is seen here trying to protect his boss, Jeff McCord (*left,* Robert Armstrong), for whom Brick will valiantly take a bullet before recuperating for the final showdown with the bureau's top-ranked public enemies.

sob. She's worried that the tit-for-tat macho tactics will get him killed. He scoffs and sends her home, amused that she doesn't grasp "what this is all about." It's the modern equivalent of telling her "it's a guy thing" and to butt out.

The woman in the film who does have something meaningful to do is Brick's old flame, Jean, now married to a top thug named Brad Collins (Barton MacLane). She turns informant for Brick but gets plugged full of lead by her husband for her effort. Like Blackie, though, she shows incredible pluck and self-sacrifice by risking (and losing) her life to deliver her husband to the G-men. In the course of the story, Brick also is shot by her husband but survives, saving McCord's life in the process.

The film's final blowout occurs at a Wisconsin lodge, a scene that borrows from a real melee involving Dillinger. The gangsters are holed up in retired kingpin McKay's lodge, dancing with booze-guzzling women and tormenting McKay, who's tied to a chair. When the gunfire starts, they use McKay as a human shield, and he dies in a spray of bullets, including a few from Brick's gun. The shoot-out is one of the longest and loudest in film history to 1935, with the women as well blasting away at the G-men. Ultimately, the gang is driven out of the lodge with tear gas and killed in a volley of spectacular gunfire. A particularly graphic shot shows Collins at the wheel of the getaway car as he's riddled by bullets (originating from McCord's machine gun) that pierce the windshield.

Variety wrote in its review of *G-Men:* "*Little Caesar, Scarface,* and *The Public Enemy* were more than portrayals of gangster tactics: they were biographies of curious mentalities. In the new idea of glorifying the government gunners who wipe out the killers there is no chance for that kind of character development and build-up." The crime fighter's effectiveness as an able warrior depends on the caliber of his enemy. If the criminal is lackluster, so is the crime fighter. We know nothing about Collins and feel no sense of satisfaction or remorse when he's rubbed out. On the other hand, if the gangster is vigorous and deliciously evil, he steals the film outright. (In Brian De Palma's *The Untouchables* (1987), a beefed-up version of super G-man Eliot Ness—despite a self-assured, fetching Kevin Costner—cannot keep the prurient focus off the inimitable gangster, Al Capone. Capone's brief appearances in the film, in the form of Robert De Niro, are the most sensational.)

Even in films that made sure the cop was the most intelligent character, the gangster comes off as more shrewd because he cheats or makes up his own rules to win. He's despicable but utterly compelling.

The G-man approach pleased the censors, though, and became popular with audiences, who were starved for any good shoot-'em-up to put zip back in the cheerless era. A slew of bloated crime buster sagas followed, including *Bullets or Ballots, Public Enemy's Wife,* and *Racket Busters*. For *Bullets or Ballots* (1936), *G-Men*'s director William Keighley employed Edward G. Robinson as a character who stages his own dismissal from the police force to work from inside a racket. Humphrey Bogart plays the venerable rat and henchman on the other side. Graham Greene's review notes that "All the old chivalrous situations . . . are agreeably translated into sub-machine-gun terms,"[13] making the badge more of a prop than a determining factor. (The trend toward zealous, lone lawmen who act more like Wild West sheriffs than urban police fostered a subgenre that would eventually produce the *Dirty Harry, Lethal Weapon,* and *Die Hard* series.)

Greene also blasted the G-man angle for producing "simple-minded" plots that offered "a few grim wisecracks, a bumping-off, a federal agent and a fellow's sister and romantic love." He suggested that the audience should be appalled "that the whole opening sequence of *False Faces* has already been used (whether in *G-Men, Public Hero No. 1,* or *Men without a Name* I cannot remember now): the newspaper powering off the presses, the scare headlines, the keep-calm air of the bald-headed Capitol dome, the Department of Justice, the eagle-badge in close-ups."[14]

Another problem with the flipped focus is that the crime fighter is working on the gangster's turf, which hardly suits the upstanding motives of a proper lawman—especially the revenge motive. Cagney's Brick Davis joins the Justice Department more to avenge his friend's death than out of a desire to defend the public safety. And the gangster's egocentricity is transferred to the G-man, who revels in the American ideal of individual achievement rather than team goals. Even *Little Caesar*'s Flaherty vows, "I'll get that swell-headed mug if it's the last thing I do." He relentlessly pursues Rico even after the former kingpin becomes a broken-down drunk, using police resources to settle an old score rather than focus on fresh crime. Crime fighting becomes a personal vendetta—a gangsterish tactic that cheats honor and rewards malevolence.

In most of these products, the cops become as macho as the gangsters, and aggression itself becomes the point. Violent solutions are perpetuated as appropriate, regardless of who's pulling the trigger. In fact, because the lawman is equipped with a moral license, the level of violence escalates. The Legion of Decency gave its okay to such pro-police films as *Beast of the City,* despite its being what Eugene Rosow describes as "hysterically violent."

The lawman's culpability in Prohibition as a partner in the bootlegging industry is erased as history is rewritten. But as Ben Hecht summarizes the Prohibition era, "the forces of law and order did not advance on the villains with drawn guns but with their palms out like bellboys."[15]

The real G-men of the FBI were known to be as bloody as they were portrayed on film. Some were obsessed with catching the public enemies who had captured the public's imagination. G-men often ignored due process and the honorable showdowns that were implied in their screen counterparts. Following the Lindbergh baby kidnapping in 1932, the FBI was given sweeping powers by Congress, with czarlike autonomy given to the bureau's leader, J. Edgar Hoover. He soon waged war on the kidnapper along with the host of outlaws, bandits, and gangsters swarming the headlines. He lobbied and won the right to arm his G-men to match the firepower of the criminals.

Large crime syndicates emerged in the post-Prohibition period as bootlegging profits were invested into far-flung operations. However, with the syndicates, "Hoover kept an uneasy truce. Even his power was unequal to [theirs] . . . and to attack them would be to invite a costly battle."[16] He had neutralized Capone, but Capone and his flamboyant, bloody method of doing business were already being tempered by rival mobsters—and partners. Many of them, including the Mafia, considered Capone's media show a business liability and his excess downright perilous to expansion plans. John Baxter notes that "Hoover dared not go" beyond tackling the spotlight-grabbing Capone.

Rather than wage a war he might not win against the syndicates and Mafia (which Hoover swore publicly did not exist), Hoover blamed Hollywood in 1931 for making the gangsters more of a problem than they really were. By the late 1930s, he become a Hollywood player. He appeared with his sharpshooters in the three-reel featurette *You Can't Get Away with It* and reputedly became a consultant on full-length films that made his men look good. In 1939 he supposedly wrote the screenplay that led to the four-film series *Persons in Hiding* (1939), which includes stories about Bonnie and Clyde and a thinly disguised version of Ma Barker.[17] The Hays office, of course, raised no objection to Hoover's violation of its ban on putting such notorious personalities in the movies.

CRIME WATCH

Hoover perhaps hoped the screen versions of a triumphant government and a fragmented, beaten Underworld could supplant the ugly reality. He wasn't alone in believing movies had the power to create "otherworlds." The effects of movies were an obsessive concern of the social sciences that were coming of age in the 1930s. One study asked inmates to answer questionnaires to gauge the effects of gangster films in particular. The summary concluded that "by arousing desires for 'easy money,' by inducing a spirit of bravado, toughness, and adventurousness, by fostering the daydreaming of criminal roles, by displaying techniques of crime, and by contributing to truancy, motion pictures may lead or dispose to crime."[18]

The inmates' answers make one wonder if the young men found comfort, too, in blaming moving pictures for their bad luck. "Pictures of gangsters enabled me to become one of them," noted a 20-year-old bank robber. Another prisoner, a 19-year-old safecracker, answered, "Naturally movies were the cause of my failure because I would see clothes and luxury in pictures and would try to have the same. . . . in order to have all those I had to have money, and that is why I tried to break open the safe."[19]

Another study showed that one boy's identification with Rico Bandello was so strong that he adopted the name Rico and was eventually shot and sent to prison after imitating some of Rico's crimes.[20] The study charged that movies showed young boys how to pull off certain crimes and how to use a variety of weapons. A convict credited a movie (most likely the 1929 version of *Alias Jimmy Valentine*) for demonstrating how to crack a safe.[21]

In a government-sponsored 1933 report, W. W. Charters suggested that a combination of influences including home life, peer pressure, and neighborhood surroundings contribute to the making of a juvenile delinquent. "The total effect of all these influences on the child is analogous to the total effect of an orchestra upon an audience."[22]

In the end, no study could confidently blame the movies for gangster envy. Noting the confusion, a well-respected child psychologist of the era wrote, "Mankind is always glad to find a scapegoat upon which it can project its sins. It is much less painful to accept the opinion that the motion pictures together with other new economic and social forces, are the causes of unruly conduct in children than to face the fact that the failure of family life is in large measure the most responsible agent."[23]

GANGSTERS WHO WANT TO BE GOOD

By the late 1930s, everybody seemed to agree that movies and their effects were powerful—however difficult to measure. The point for some people was to make sure those effects benefited their agenda. For some that meant not just avoiding treatments of the distasteful gangster but purposely creating a malleable gangster who could be manipulated to influence young minds. A few noteworthy gangster films that do just that were made in the late 1930s. Part of the defanging of the screen gangster was to lock him comfortably in the past. Second, he was made to serve a master other than himself and to be rehabilitated by the end of the film. As a bootlegger stuck in a bygone era, the gangster was a benign figure out of American history much like the Western outlaw, and no longer a threat to anybody but the screen's protagonist. *The Roaring Twenties* (1939), another Raoul Walsh effort, at least had the good fortune to have a superb cast, with a spitfire Cagney back in gangster spats and a brilliant wretch of an enemy behind the twitchy lip of Humphrey Bogart.

The screenplay is based on partially true accounts of "the dizzy times" of Prohibition by Mark Hellinger, whom *Variety* called a "seasoned Broadway columnist." The film is the story of two army buddies who, facing unemployment and frustration following World War I, take up careers in bootlegging. Walsh is true to his code about tough guys being admirable but skillfully shows the difference between Cagney's misguided hoodlum Eddie Bartlett and Bogart's innately vile George Halley. Trapped together in a foxhole, Eddie kills because he's fired upon. George shoots a German soldier who looks no more than 15 years old simply because killing him feels good and comments afterward, "he won't be 16." The third soldier in the foxhole—their future bootlegging partner—is Lloyd Hart (Jeffrey Lynn), who aspires to be a lawyer (and no doubt the future crusading district attorney).

The film includes a ponderous narrator who treats the story as if it were a documentary of great historical insight. He explains how in these bygone days, the bootlegger was viewed "as something of an adventurer. . . . A modern crusader who deals in bottles instead of battles." The history lesson is accompanied by the familiar montage of killings, payoffs, and flowing suds. A later montage shows how embedded breaking the law was in everyday life: freckle-faced kids in raccoon coats guzzle booze, and young women hide flasks in their garters.

Eddie falls for a sweet, displaced songbird called Jean (Priscilla Lane), who would rather be with Lloyd. Eddie's obsession with the respectable woman he can never have underpins a trademark Cagney moment. After a club owner calls Eddie a "sucker" for chasing a woman who doesn't return his affection, Eddie blows. "Don't ever say that to me again," he snaps, before snatching the cigar from the barman's mouth and smashing it back in his face. The flapper Panama (Gladys George), who loves Eddie, warns him, "You're battling out of your league, buster, you're used to traveling around . . . with dames like me." Eddie offers Jean an engagement ring, but when she stalls for an answer, he ups the ante to sway her, pledging, "Ask me for the Brooklyn Bridge. . . . if I can't buy it, I'll steal it." It's achingly obvious that he's doomed and pitiful that he doesn't understand it. Even George warns Eddie not to get mixed up with "dames [who] go for that Joe College stuff."

Eddie rises to boss status, taking over kingpin Nick Brown's territory, prompting George to accuse Eddie of acting like Napoleon. "My feelings is getting hurt," whines George, who then plots Eddie's murder. Never one to do the dirty work himself, he hires another killer and boasts, "I always say, if you got a job to do, get somebody else to do it."

Eddie survives a shoot-out involving men named Rocco and Manny and then severs his partnership with the double-crossing George. Jean runs off with Lloyd, and 1929 changes everyone's life. Eddie's downfall also picks up speed after Prohibition is repealed. Another montage shows Eddie getting arrested, and Panama bailing him out of jail. Soon he's sleeping in 15¢-a-night flophouses (like Rico at his end) and driving a cab to eke out a living. Jean—now married to Lloyd, the reform-minded district attorney—steps into the back of Eddie's cab one evening, accompanied by her four-year-old son. Jean invites the vanquished Eddie into her home, and her playful son points a toy gun at Eddie's face. The underlying message is that Eddie has been overpowered by the innocent, but more potent, force of family and virtue. The greater irony is that the well-to-do model mother sees nothing wrong with her child using a gun to greet a stranger. The assumption is that a normal, healthy boy is playing cowboys and Indians. The scene could be interpreted another way: another American male is being groomed to view the gun as an option, like any other.

After Lloyd comes home and warmly greets his old pal Eddie, Lloyd talks of his plan to go after George, who's prospering in other rackets. Eddie warns that George vowed to kill Lloyd if he ever talked about their bootlegging profits (which Lloyd has apparently invested well). Later, Jean goes looking for Eddie to ask him to intervene in the imminent showdown between Lloyd and George. Fellow cabbies tell her that Eddie is "living in the saloons" and keeping company with that "off-key canary" Panama. At first stunned by her nerve to ask him to help the man who stole her away, Eddie relents because he still carries a torch for her. The ultimate showdown is not between the lawman and the gangster but between the redeemable gangster and the lost cause. Eddie shoots George, but before George dies, he does a lot of sniveling and proves he's yellow. Eddie flees George's headquarters but is shot and mortally wounded by some of George's men. Eddie collapses on the steps of a church and rolls down them toward the gutter. It's a rekilling of Tom Powers, who never tried to make amends. Cagney's Eddie, eight years later, tries self-sacrifice so that Jean and Lloyd can be at peace. In the last scene, Panama holds Eddie's head in her lap and aptly tells the cop standing over them, "He used to be a big shot."

In his review of *The Roaring Twenties,* Graham Greene noted it was a well-worn story. And "the morality is confusing: we are explicitly told crime doesn't pay." Yet perhaps that's true only for Eddie, who didn't know when to get out of the racket. Greene dubs the happy couple the "children of light" because they "left bootlegging at the right moment," not because they realized that it was a crime. Greene saves his best compliments, though, for Bogart, whom he calls magnificent and ferocious. He adds with a wink that it's "always a pleasure to see Mr. Bogart pumped full of lead."[24]

Because many of the late-1930s films were aimed at impressionable young boys, Hollywood finally wrote them into the screenplays as characters. The most famous ensemble of scruffy boys who look up to and then admonish the gangster hero were the Dead End Kids. They appeared in several dramas before some members formed the Bowery Boys and turned their street punk act into comedy. *Angels with Dirty Faces* (1938) was the third appearance of the Dead End Kids, most of whom hailed from New York, but not necessarily the slums.

The film is the story of two boys from the tenements of the urban poor. The opening scene shows the laundry hanging on lines and wires crisscrossing alleyways and blotting out the sky at street level. The street noise is a mix of honking horns and barking street peddlers. The fiery, teenage Rocky Sullivan steals for kicks and is already headed down the wrong path. His companion, Jerry Connelly, hesitates at first, saying, "It ain't like stealing coal to keep warm."

The police bust up their crime in progress inside a freight car. The boys flee, but Jerry trips on the tracks in front of an oncoming train. Rocky aborts his getaway to come back and rescue his friend. On the run again, Rocky lags behind and gets caught by police and sent to reform school. Jerry visits Rocky in the joint just before the trial, wanting to confess his part in the crime. But Rocky tells him to keep his mouth shut and "don't be a sucker!"

A montage explains the passage of time, with newspaper headlines shouting that Rocky gets two years for petty larceny, then another three years in the state penitentiary for assault and battery. Finally, we learn that he's a grown-up bootlegger and has just been acquitted for his latest offense: murder. The adult Rocky (Cagney) has grown into the gangster persona. He sports expensive clothes, gambles at upscale clubs, displays a plumed blond on his arm, and wears the most insolent smirk as a smile.

Another montage offers the customary Jazz Age iconography: flashing exotic nightclub marquees, kicking chorus girls, tinkling glasses, and streets roaring with speeding black sedans taking out a rival speakeasy with the toss of a hand grenade. The last headline announces that Rocky is a terror sweeping the city. He's a gangster we're meant to care about, though, because he's a boy of honor who took the rap for a friend. His oily criminal associate, Jim Frazier, played handily by Bogart, is the gangster we love to hate—again.

Jerry (Pat O'Brien), now a priest in the old neighborhood, rehearses a tattered but melodic group of boys for his church choir. He grapples with another group of slum boys—hooligans he affectionately calls "the angels," portrayed by the Dead End Kids. Rocky strolls up the church's center aisle as other people walk down a midway—mildly amused but watching for pickpockets. The two men embrace and reminisce about old times. Rocky also finds an apartment in the same tenement he grew up in as a boy. He stays there for the remainder of the film, even though he becomes a partner in an upscale nightclub. On his old turf, Rocky meets Father Jerry's angels, who try to steal Rocky's wallet. He quickly turns the situation around until they figure out who the superior thug is. The kids begin to treat the former street punk who made good like a matinee idol.

One story path tracks Rocky's troubles with Frazier and another wise guy named Mac (played by the 1920s gangster icon George Bancroft). Another path centers around Rocky's relationship with the boys. He persuades them to get involved in one of Father Jerry's basketball games with other boys at the parish gym. The angels play but resort to cheating and punching to gain the advantage. Rocky, as referee, slaps them, elbows them, and pulls them by the ear whenever he spots an offense—all for the sake of keeping them in line. The lesson is that physical violence is useful, but be careful not to pick on somebody rougher than you. The priest even throws a righteous punch later in the film when he tries to rescue the boys from a pool hall. After an amused patron mocks his futile effort, Father Jerry knocks him down with a practiced right hook.

The boys are increasingly enamored with Rocky's postprison comeback. They're sold on his lifestyle, especially after he gives them a wad of cash for keeping his stolen loot safe. What the boys don't spend on cheap pin-striped suits and wise guy threads—imitating their mentor—they squander on liquor and pool hustling. However, Soapy (Billy Halop), the boys' leader, is learning from Rocky the merits of loyalty that function even in the Underworld. Soapy valiantly blocks the attempt of fellow angel Bim (Leo Gorcey) to steal some of Rocky's money while it's under their care.

The two stories converge after double crosses and plot twists involve gangsters trying to outwit each other, and Father Jerry watches helplessly as the boys creep down the same path. The final showdown occurs after the priest tells Rocky that he's going to lead a crusade to bring Rocky down—for the angels' sake. Father Jerry also returns the $10,000 cash he suspects Rocky donated anonymously toward a parish recreation center. In the process, the priest delivers the film's first sermon and pleads with Rocky, "Don't encourage them to admire you."

Father Jerry vows to go after the "corrupt officialdom" as well, but the crooked politicians remain faceless and nameless in the film. The newspapers, which have served as the film's informants, also are enlisted by the priest to step up their headline campaign against Rocky. Father Jerry gets one more chance to preach when Laury (Ann Sheridan), the "experienced" girl he saved but who's smitten with Rocky, begs Father Jerry to call off the attack. She blames Rocky's reform school years, arguing, "They made a criminal out of him."

The climactic shoot-out follows. Cops with names such as O'Flannagan corner Rocky on the roof of one of the tenements. After he ducks into the floor below, they ferret him out with tear gas. Father Jerry promises the police he can bring down Rocky alive to stand trial for the murder of Frazier (whom Rocky killed to save the priest's life). Frazier died sniveling for his life and proved himself the cowardly lowlife we suspected him to be.

While Rocky is on trial, the boys and the audience keep track of his fate by newspaper stories, in which Rocky does them proud by vowing to spit in the executioner's eye and laugh all the way to the electric chair. In the final scenes, the priest comes to ask Rocky to turn yellow before he dies to destroy the admiration of the urban angels. Cagney is superb as he reacts to the request with both dauntless piety and dazzling defiance. The exchange between Rocky and a sniping guard just before Father Jerry enters Rocky's cell is a jewel. Rocky is stretched out on his bunk like a vacationer on a chaise longue. The guard sarcastically asks Rocky if he enjoyed his last

Returning as "public enemy" Rocky Sullivan, Cagney pairs up with Pat O'Brien in *Angels with Dirty Faces* as boyhood pals who took different paths in life: Rocky sank deeper into the murky Underworld, and O'Brien's priest found a saving grace from those same mean streets. Despite the gun pointed at him, the priest is in control, leading Rocky toward a warmed-up electric chair.

meal. With studied cool and a full bite of Cagney sneer, Rocky compliments the dinner but returns the sarcasm with the complaint: "the meat was kinda burnt. I don't like burnt meat, do you?" Without waiting for an answer, he forcefully flicks a glowing cigarette into the guard's face. With minutes left to his life, Rocky offers nothing but routine contempt to his miserable end. The guard snarls, "I'm gonna tell the electrician to give it to you slow and easy, wiseguy."

In the hands of another actor, the gangster's enduring bravado followed by the primitive grace he displays in obeying the priest's request would have been pure camp. But Cagney manages to show that the same man, at least on-screen, is convincingly capable of both. Equally, O'Brien lends Father Jerry subtlety, humor, and a veiled potency. As he accompanies his friend down the shadowy hall to the death chamber, the lighting neatly highlights his pristine, starched collar and Rocky's defiant face. Rocky strides toward his doom with that signature bounce in his step, walking toward and past the camera with an unblinking, dead-eye stare and a crooked smile that reads, "You go to hell." (Unlike Blackie's odd pretense behind Gable's toothy grin, Cagney's expression signals that he may be scared but never intimidated.) The camera cuts to the shadow on the wall as Rocky is taken to the chair. His shadow writhes as he whimpers and pleads for his life. A close-up of Father Jerry shows him lowering his eyes, and a tear falls from one. Then the lightbulb over his left shoulder dims, indicating by the drain on the lights that a fatal charge has surged through Rocky's body.

The last scene shows the boys reading the newspaper story that reports Rocky was "a yellow rat" in death. Father Jerry joins them at their hideout and stands on the staircase, showered in streamers of light coming from above. As the choir starts in, the boys climb the stairs after the padre, up and out of the camera's view—headed for the light.

Cagney, though, said he worked hard to leave some doubt as to whether Rocky actually has "a seizure of fear." He explained, "I've actually had little kids come up to me on the street and ask, 'Didya do it for the father, huh?' . . . I played it with deliberate ambiguity so that the spectator can take the choice." But Michael Curtiz, a gifted and willful director (soon of *Casablanca* fame), may have decided the lasting impression by making the shot of Rocky's resolute and committed smirk the last shot of Cagney we see.

Variety tagged the story "thoroughly hokey" but raved about Cagney and O'Brien as an "irresistible team." They ended up making eight films together as congenial but fierce rivals. In private life, they were rumored to be part of the friendship circle called the "Irish mafia" that hung out together in Hollywood.

MYTHS AND DEAD-END DREAMS

Because the classic gangsters of *Little Caesar, The Public Enemy,* and *Scarface* were just as mythic and contorted as the late 1930s gangsters, no one had any right to accuse the later characters of being sorry comparisons. In their way, they were just as brilliantly crafted—aided by the extraordinary skill of Cagney and Bogart. If the stories were lame, it wasn't their fault.

But the screen gangster ceased to retain much connection to his real-life counterpart—leaving only the myth to endure on-screen. According to the famed scholar Joseph Campbell, myths are useful cultural stories that societies use to define and solve problems that don't lend themselves to rational solutions. More fitting, he calls myths "public dreams." The screen gangster was no longer about the mundane facts of routine crime or particular faces, even Capone's scarred one. He was about profound fear and deep-seated flaws that spoil America's best intentions. As Robert Warshow explains, the gangster "is what we want to be and what we are afraid we may become."[25]

But the gangster and his on-screen world had become far removed from the street—where moviemakers first found him. His urban turf had evolved into something surreal, and *Dead End* (1937) is the zenith of that approach. The film's gangster, in fact, "Baby Face" Martin (the third-billed Bogart) joins his mother (Marjorie Main) as a contrived metaphor—being less about what's human and more about a warped social by-product. Yet Bogart gives his synthetic character a sense of defiled ambition. In place of revealing dialogue, Baby Face divulges the troubled core of the wounded man-boy through studied silence and a paralyzing stare.

Dead End's main story tracks the lives of out-of-work architect Dave Connell (Joel McCrea), who's struggling with hope and the rotting milieu around him. His love interest (but not until the end) is Drina Gordon (Sylvia Sidney), who talks of getting a bump on the head by a cop while walking a picket line. She's battling to stop workplace abuse despite the employer's depression leverage and to keep her little brother Tommy (Billy Halop) from becoming a full-fledged hoodlum. Tommy is already the leader of a slum gang, played by the Dead End Kids. The film was their debut performance and reprises their stage roles in the play that made them famous.

Gangster Baby Face Martin weaves in and out of the story and brings everyone else's woes out of the darkened corners of the crowded ghetto. In fact, the environment is the film's real star. It, too, was borrowed from Sidney Kingsley's hit stage play (adapted for the screen by Lillian Hellman), which featured claustrophobic settings of riverfront tenements, where most of the story takes place. Rather than take advantage of the expanded horizons of film, the characters are purposely confined in a gray, breathless environment stripped of sunlight and nature—despite the presence of the river. It's hopelessly polluted but used regularly by the boys for swimming and taken for granted like the rest of the neighborhood's insults.

For obvious conflict involving the story's lead characters is the walled-off residence of a rich family adjacent to the slums. From the moment we see the snotty rich boy emerge through the manned gate, we know it's only a matter of time before the Dead End Kids rough him up. His father (and brother to Judge Griswold) nabs Tommy for the crime but gets stabbed in the struggle. While Tommy goes into hiding for the knifing, Dave, too, has a run-in with the rich people. Before he realizes he loves and admires Drina, he tries to woo the exclusive crowd's party girl, Kay. But she clings to her loveless relationship with a rich man and chooses to be "kept" rather than be poor again. Kay is made less flagrant than her stage version, as is Baby Face's old girlfriend Francey (Clair Trevor, who earned an Oscar for supporting actress). Francey is sup-

Left, Baby Face Martin (Humphrey Bogart) offers the roughneck slum boys some pointers on winning a gang fight. Martin is slick and scared and can't seem to stay away from the old neighborhood despite being a hunted killer. *Dead End* made stars of the Dead End Kids, but Bogart remained the stock villain, always snarling at lead characters from a shadowy corner.

posed to be ravaged by syphilis from being a prostitute, but that's obscured in the film. Her tight black dress glittering in broad daylight, though, informs on her anyway.

Throughout the film, Baby Face and his sidekick Hunk (Allen Jenkins) lurk around the waterfront, watching the subplots like the rest of us. Baby Face has had plastic surgery (inspired by Dillinger's attempts at surgical disguise) to make him unrecognizable to police and his old neighborhood. He has returned to visit his Ma and to retrieve Francey and perhaps settle down and give up his criminal life. "I'm getting sick of what I can pay for," he tells Hunk. After he finds out about Francey's ailment, he sends her away with a wad of cash but remains visibly shaken by the encounter.

In Baby Face's initial encounter with Dave—society's demolition man against the hopeful architect—Bogart displays his best gangster chops. Dave stops him from teaching the boys how to win a rumble by cheating and then recognizes Baby Face from their youth, despite the surgery. He also recalls what the newspapers have been reporting about Baby Face's eight murders. "You been reading about me in the papers, huh?" Baby Face asks proudly. Then he bursts out laughing at Dave's unemployment and his dream to escape the slums to get what he desires. "I got mine," he snarls. "I took it. Look!" He points to his custom-made silk suit and brags about the women he's known. When Dave asks Baby Face if he's ever scared as a hunted man, he displays the gangster's relaxed fatalism: "Me? What of? You can't live forever." Baby Face's reunion with his mother is grim. She recoils at the sight of him and calls him "a butcher." He's hurt deeply, and his tormented expression betrays the vicious words that warn her, "I killed a guy for looking at me the way you are now."

In the end, Tommy is sent to reform school for the knifing and to stop "the little gangster before he can do more harm." And Baby Face's strange plot to kidnap the rich boy for a ransom ends when Dave, having borrowed Hunk's gun, shoots and kills the gangster. Dave reluctantly collects a reward for Baby Face's killing and, after getting together with Drina, vows to use the money to get Tommy legal help to avoid reform school. Reform school, they argue, is what turned Baby Face from a street punk into a professional killer.

The visually taunting film was directed by William Wyler—a German immigrant who would make three Oscar-winning films in the years ahead, including the poignant war drama, *Mrs. Miniver. Dead End* was nominated for best picture of 1937, which was an honor no gangster film had ever earned before.

"But what we remember is the gangster," wrote Graham Greene. Bogart's character is the film's charisma and "the ruthless sentimentalist . . . up against the truth," adds Greene. "He and the children drive virtue into a rather dim corner." It would be Bogart—having spent most of the 1930s in the shadows—who would reinvent the gangster as the 1940s opened. He would lend the character texture and mercurial torment that would go beyond dead ends and yellow rats.

CHAPTER 5

Slide into Darkness

> You may catch lead any minute, Roy. What you need is a fast young filly you can keep moving with. You know what Johnny Dillinger said about guys like you and him. . . . He said you were just rushing toward death!
>
> —Doc Banton to Roy Earle in *High Sierra*

At the close of the 1930s, Humphrey Bogart was poised for stardom. He had first gained attention for playing the outlaw gangster Duke Mantee in Robert E. Sherwood's stage play *The Petrified Forest.* When the story came to Hollywood in 1936, the play's star, Leslie Howard, fought for Bogart to reprise his role as Duke (Warner Brothers wanted to cast proven commodity Edward G. Robinson). In Duke, Bogart took the mythic antihero and gave him a precarious mix of worthy and corrupt components—sometimes at odds within the same moment of action. Bogart finessed that quality in the next decade and expanded the scope of his criminals' plausible behavior. His heroes, too, were hybrids and possessed an engaging tinge of warped virtue.

Unlike Cagney and Robinson, Bogart wasn't born into the immigrant enclaves of the urban ghetto. And he didn't learn his tough-guy pose from the streets. His father was a well-to-do Manhattan physician, and his mother a renowned illustrator. Bogart was schooled in academies and prepped for an Ivy League future before he opted for the navy. While he was a soldier, an injury severed a nerve in his upper lip, leaving it paralyzed and his speech hampered by a now famous lisp. He then drifted into acting—first appearing on the stage in the 1920s as the sleek, youthful, "tennis, anyone?" type, to use Bogart's words. He also made an early trek to Hollywood, playing similar parts before returning in 1936 as Duke, which won him a Warner Brothers contract.

On the surface, the story line of *The Petrified Forest* explores an extraordinary, action-packed day at a family-owned diner and gas station in the middle of the Arizona desert. The desolate centerpiece draws several transient people who become snared in Duke's desperate attempt to remain alive and free. He holds them hostage while he waits for the rest of his gang. The story is anything but its surface description, though. Each character speaks for a particular community in poetic muse far too thoughtful for people trapped in a dismal eatery and at the mercy of a vicious killer. Allen Eyles notes that seen today, the film "is something of a creaking curiosity."[1] However improbable, the enlightened exchanges are still fascinating, largely due to the fine performances of the cast. In particular, the dialogue centers around the concerns of the erudite but penniless writer Alan Squire, played by the film's (and the stage play's) star Leslie Howard, and the cafe owner's daughter Gabby, an arty idealist played by a wistful Bette Davis.

The film's opening scene shows the forlorn desert, with drifting tumbleweeds and a howling wind. Remarks about depression conditions betray the customary image of the hopeful, limitless Wild West. As one workman describes his task there in the 1930s, "We're not pioneering—we're repairing."

Gabby is young, lonely, and stifled by the barren environment. She was born in France but was taken to Arizona by her American father, who had been a soldier. (He still wears a uniform as part of a vigilante group that battles trumped-up enemies in the desert.) Gabby wants to return to her mother's homeland to find optimism and thoughtful expression. Her grandpa Maple is stuck in the mythic West of old—where he was once shot at by Billy the Kid. He relishes the tale and has warped it with time to keep the newcomers entertained. Gabby argues that the environment is crammed not with folklore and ghosts of adventure but with "trees (that) turn to stone" in the petrified forest.

Alan intrudes on the family's isolation and quickly captures Gabby's imagination. A writer who has been to her native France, he unleashes her frustrated ambitions. Born in "the year Victoria died," Alan explains how he's a member of that "vanishing race" of intellectuals who're being displaced by the "new order" of industrial might. The depression is perhaps Mother Nature's revenge, he suggests, on the people who traded artisans for laborers.

He has lived on the Riviera as a gigolo, he confesses, waiting for the "artist to emerge" or for "something to believe in . . . worth living and dying for." By the time Alan finishes his dinner—which Gabby provides on the house—she becomes his cause célèbre. "Perhaps you're a genius. Perhaps it's my mission to introduce you to posterity," he proposes.

Interrupting their ballet of words is a wealthy couple whose chauffeur-driven car has been hijacked by the outlaw. Media reports of his crimes have been tantalizing the outpost from the film's start. Duke Mantee (Humphrey Bogart) and his gang finally overrun the diner, much to the delight of grandpa Maple (Charley Grapewin). He hails Duke: "a real old-time desperado." The beefy footballer and garage mechanic Boze (Dick Foran) argues that Duke is nothing "but a gangster and a rat." The old man counters, "Gangsters is foreigners. . . . he's an American." At one point Boze tries to be a hero, and Duke shoots him in the hand to shut him up.

Most of the day the characters bask in a sepia-tone pose amid the rustic surroundings while Duke peers out of sinister shadows that engulf his face and exaggerate his scowl. The group carries on its ponderous exchanges while Duke guards a sawed-off shotgun on his lap. The gun is a reminder to his engrossed captives that he's clenched in a more base fight for survival.

The banker's wife tells Gabby not to settle for less than her dreams—not to repeat her mistake by marrying "this pillar of the mortgage trust" and lose her soul. Duke interrupts their talk about tarnished dreams, grumbling, "I spend most of my time since I grew up in jail. It looks like I spend the rest of my life dead."

Then Alan devises a morbid scheme to turn his dire circumstances and Duke's doom into Gabby's hope: he proposes that Duke shoot him so that his life insurance policy will buy Gabby her freedom. "Living, I'm worth nothing to her—dead I can buy her . . . golden vineyards . . . dancing in the streets."

Once Alan discovers that Duke is holed up in the diner to wait for his girl Doris, he aims for Duke's romantic core. He describes Duke as "one of the last great apostles

Humphrey Bogart *(center)* as Duke Mantee, flanked by two of his gang members, portrays a Dillinger-like outlaw in *The Petrified Forest.* Duke becomes both a scourge and a moral irritant to a diner full of hostages who get to know and fear him.

of rugged individualism." Like Duke, Alan says that he, too, is a misplaced relic condemned to extinction, but the literary mood is shattered when another gang member bursts into the café to tell Duke that the police have nabbed Doris and she has snitched on the gang's whereabouts.

Duke is broken by the news and grows more frantic by the moment. Alan pleads, "You want revenge, well, don't do it. Don't betray yourself—run for the border and take your illusions with you. They're going to get you anyway." Wearing a tormented expression that became one of Bogart's acting trademarks, Duke's eyes reveal a wounding betrayal and fear of imminent doom. But Alan keeps hammering away. "You're obsolete like me. . . . you got to die. So die for freedom. That's worth it—not for something so cheap and unsatisfactory as revenge."

A shoot-out with police follows, but Alan keeps challenging Duke to shoot him amid the chaos. Agitated and about to flee, Duke obliges the suicidal writer, who dies in Gabby's arms from one of Duke's bullets. (Two endings were shot; the alternate kept Alan alive, but preview screenings proved the death a more fitting ending.)[2]

Soon the diners learn that Duke has been killed by police. As Alan predicted, both were destined to die in the petrified forest—"the graveyard of the civilization that is shot from under us—the world of outmoded ideas."

Graham Greene, in a review for *Spectator,* faults the story's obsession with "ideas being expressed—significant *cosmic* ideas" as if "the Whole of Life is symbolized in the

Arizona filling-station." Rather, he insists, the film's moral "ought to be implicit in every action," not belabored in every word. He accuses the film of being "a canned play," using a "too pasteboard desert [and] stunted cardboard studio trees." He places no blame on the direction of Archie Mayo, who was better adept at action thrillers such as *The Doorway to Hell.* But Greene commends Bogart's Duke—the "sad simian killer"—as the salvageable element in the overwrought story.

Twenty years later, Bogart commented on Duke's effectiveness, noting, "Nobody could take their eyes off Duke because they were never sure when he was going to shoot up the place."[3]

Shortly after *The Petrified Forest,* Warner Brothers put Bogart in a pin-striped suit and had him sneer as a supporting player in the 1930s gangster fest. Most of the 28 roles Bogart played between 1936 and 1940 were in B productions or as the lead gangster's nemesis—including five pairings with Edward G. Robinson alone. During this period, Duke's emotional reach and inner confusion were flattened into the sociopath with little mystique, the perfected killer with no conscience. Not until *Dead End* did Bogart's talent for lethal ambiguity emerge, giving his gangster a pitiful scourge beneath that shopworn veneer.

Finally, Bogart resurrected Duke's enigmatic appeal for the criminal character that helped make him a major star in 1941. Like Duke, Roy "Mad Dog" Earle in *High Sierra* possessed the harrowed sense of a desperado with his back to the wall. He's unwillingly thrust into the vortex of action—attention he would rather avoid. Cagney's bad boys, despite their untidy flashes of temper, gained our sympathy because they were emotional heaps flaunting their ambitions and their flaws. They were pitiable for trying to apply their crude, contaminated talents to the success formula. But one never knew for certain what Bogart's characters were thinking. His slow, deliberate speech and rich nonverbal cues pointed to competing motives. As such, Bogart helped move the gangster beyond the rat-a-tat ferocity (and trite stereotype) of the Roaring Twenties hoodlum. Roy Earle is more isolated, despite the enduring presence of accomplices. And although the gang remains a criminal necessity, it no longer represents his pseudofamily. Neither Duke nor Roy enjoy running with the pack or leaning on others for support. (This sullen, urban-wolf quality is at the core of Bogart's noir characters that dominate the 1940s.)

Becoming an anomaly even among criminals is the overriding theme of *High Sierra.* As Carlos Clarens comments, Raoul Walsh, who had given the 1920s gangster spiritual redemption, now focused on a tale of "the gangster's personal alienation." Jack Shadoian notes that *High Sierra* was made during the "tense and energetic perspective of 1941 [when] the Dillinger era of folk-hero bank robbers" was being viewed with embroidered nostalgia. As with *The Petrified Forest,* the lesson of *High Sierra* is that "life used to be lived with poetry, loyalty, codes of honor." And Roy, as a "vestige of the era, is consciously made into an aristocrat"—the name Roy derived from the French word for king *(roi),* and Earle from the ranks of nobility.[4]

In *High Sierra,* from the minute the opening credits appear—huge letters rolling up toward a great, invisible zenith—one is aware that the story is going to be grand and expressive. The establishing shots show a prison pardon being signed, followed by barred, clanging doors being unlocked. Outside the prison gate a car waits for Roy (Bogart) who tells the driver he must first make "sure grass is still green." He takes a stroll through a nearby park, taking in the leaves, the music of singing birds, and giggling children, and he looks skyward with wonder. Near his feet, a newspaper headline shouts, "Roy Earle, Famous Indiana Bank Robber, Wins Pardon!"

Roy is driven to a meeting with a crooked cop named Jake Kranmer (Barton MacLane) who has instructions for Roy from Big Mac—the man who arranged

Roy's pardon. On the road alone headed for California, Roy pulls off the highway in Indiana to visit his boyhood farm. A farmer, who first fears that Roy is a foreclosing banker, laments about the pond being "fished out" and ruined (like the rest of the Midwest landscape during the depression). Once the farmer recognizes Roy as the famous bandit, Roy cuts his reminiscing short. Back on the road, he meets some country folk who had to abandon their bankrupt Ohio farm and, like Roy, head for California to start a new life. They take to each other, although the family doesn't know his real identity. The old man describes Roy and himself as "old-timers . . . [who] both believe in fair dealing."

Roy is visibly impressed by the majestic scenery of the Sierra Mountains and is unaware that he's staring at his destiny. He arrives at the resort near Tropico Springs (supposed to be Palm Springs). It's "the richest little town in the world," according to Jake Kranmer. As Roy arrives at Shaw's Camp outside town as instructed by Big Mac, he's greeted by his two assigned accomplices, Red (Arthur Kennedy) and Babe (Alan Curtis), along with a woman named Marie Garson (top-billed Ida Lupino). They gush over the honor of being able to hook up with such a famous crook. But Roy has no use for the praise and is leery of the "dame," whom he orders sent back to the "dime-a-dance joint" where she came from. Together the group is supposed to knock over the resort's safe, where the rich patrons store their "rocks" and jewelry.

After failing to arouse a sense of camaraderie with the cool but pensive Roy, Babe complains to Red and Marie, "You can have your Roy Earle. . . . he don't look like much to me. . . . He may be a powerhouse to some people but he's a blowed-out fuse to me." But Marie is drawn to Roy's tight-lipped composure, which the two men mistake for a hallmark of someone passed his prime. She knows that it camouflages a seasoned force to be reckoned with. "I bet he's plenty tough. Get out of line and you'll see," she argues.

Soon the two "jitterbugs," as Roy calls Babe and Red, start fighting over who's giving the orders and finally over Marie, just as Roy feared. But her deference to him and her candid plea not to be sent back to a life that she's trying to rise above softens Roy's stand. He agrees to let her stay for a few more days to see what pans out. Within that time, he ends up defending her after she receives a black eye from Babe.

Roy is compelled to protect any wounded or downtrodden creature and comes to the aid of the underdogs and the handicapped who stumble onto his path. This trait makes him wholly compassionate and appealing, despite his profession. Roy takes pity on the mongrel dog Pard and points a gun in Babe's face for torturing the animal. He remains loyal to the dying kingpin Big Mac amid the crippled integrity of a new breed of criminals, and he befriends an amiable but persecuted black man. Most telling, Roy pays for the expensive surgery to correct the clubfoot of the country folks' Velma (Joan Leslie), whom he covets for being decent and who reminds him of his own homespun roots. All these folks will pay him back by contributing to his doom. Roy even remarks on his soft spot when he agrees to let Marie play a role in the heist and totes the dog along as well. He gripes in mock disgust, "Of all the 14-cent saps—starting out on a caper with a woman and a dog!"

However, during a meeting with the hotel employee and accomplice for the planned heist, Roy displays his enduring ability to instill palpable fear in anyone who threatens him. The hotel clerk, Louis Mendoza (Cornel Wilde), "assumes a superior air and is very proud of his tiny moustache and patent-leather hair," explains the shooting script. Roy doubts Mendoza's mettle and tells a war story from his celebrated past that explains how he gets even with anyone who gets the "shakes" and rats him out to "a bunch of coppers." While Roy fondles a .45, Red and Babe gape, Marie smiles, and Mendoza laughs skittishly.

The heist ends badly when Mendoza and the two small-timers panic, flee, and crack up their getaway car, leaving only Mendoza alive and able to squeal to the police. Roy and Marie drive off in another vehicle after Roy kills a cop (who fired on Roy first). Roy manages to keep his composure, though, and successfully steals the glittering contents of the hotel's strongbox. The couple heads for Big Mac (Donald MacBride) for instructions on fencing the jewels for a $10,000 cut of the haul. (Roy also makes sure that Marie is promised a cut for taking part in the caper.) However, Roy finds his boss dead and the cop Kranmer demanding the caper's booty, worth half a million dollars. With a stare described in the script "as hard as flint," Roy guns down Kranmer in a gun duel but gets shot himself in the exchange.

Doc Banton (whom the story insinuates is a skilled but discredited doctor now called Mr. Parker) mends Roy as best he can and advises him to leave town and "blow fast." But, true to his soft spot, Roy, Marie, and Pard stop along the way to see Velma take her first steps following her surgery. The visit is heartbreaking for Roy because Velma's smug, divorced lover from Ohio has come to claim her as his own. Worse, she has transformed into a rude young woman in high heels, more concerned with Scotch than gratitude.

Before leaving Velma, her drunken boyfriend tries to pay Roy for the operation, but Roy pushes him away in disgust. Velma shouts, "You're just jealous, and mean 'cause I don't want you—'cause I never wanted you!" This finally cures Roy of his infatuation with Velma. Even before the visit, Roy told Doc that it was Marie who had won his trust, if not his love, as a "dame that can stand the gaff." Roy gives Marie one of the stolen diamonds to seal their bond before they take the jewels to the fence. But he still hasn't been paid in cash for the crime. Staying in motels has been using up whatever money there was, prompting Roy to hold up a gas station. His worsening gunshot wound is also hampering his escape.

Meanwhile, newspaper headlines report that there's a $10,000 reward for the resort gunman, who's soon identified as Roy. The papers also reveal that Roy is traveling with a woman named Marie and a mutt named Pard. They dub Roy "Mad Dog" and declare him "America's New Public Enemy No. 1."

He snarls about "those newspaper rats" and predicts a frenzied manhunt by police. "Brother, when they hang that Number One tag on you, they shoot first and argue afterwards." Marie begs for them to head east and flee, but Roy wants to wait for his money. We also suspect he knows that if she remains in hiding with him, she will be killed. In a touching scene, he hides the dog in a basket, kisses Marie tenderly, and puts them both on a bus out of town. He promises to catch up with them the next night.

Roy is soon recognized and drives frantically out of town amid chattering radio reports and wailing police sirens. A montage of speeding cars, maps, and dispatch announcers is shown while Roy leads the police on a climb into the Sierra Mountains. Roy looks increasingly diminished against the imposing backdrop as he scrambles toward his dead end. Armed with a shotgun, Roy abandons the car and begins to scale the rock ledges. The police bail out of their cars along with scores of spectators and print and radio reporters—all feeding off the unfolding melodrama. Marie, too, abandons her bus and arrives at the scene. Her tears convince one reporter that she's Roy's companion. Once she's exposed, a cop orders her to call out to Roy to surrender peacefully. She refuses, lamenting, "He's gonna die anyway. . . . he'd rather it was this way."

Roy shouts defiantly back at the police while scribbling out a note about Marie's innocence. Then Pard's barking catches him by surprise and lets him know that Marie is down below. He begins frantically calling out her name and straining to see her in

The soon-to-be-famous Bogart enigma: the hardened criminal but honorable tough guy Roy Earle in Raoul Walsh's *High Sierra*, the 1941 film that made Bogart a major star. His role was also a harbinger of the crusty, trench-coated private dicks of film noir that would make Bogart a legend.

the crowd. This exposes him to a police sniper, who easily picks off Roy with a high-powered rifle and a telescope sight.

While staring down at a dead Roy, a reporter smirks and says, "Big shot Earle . . . look at him lying there. Ain't much now." Marie hovers over his body and sobs while Pard licks his hand. Before being led away, Marie asks the reporter what it means to "crash out"—a phrase Roy often mumbled during his nightmares.

"It means he's free," the puzzled reporter answers. She looks up tearfully, repeating the word "free" several times with relish. Flanked by police, she then strides toward the camera until her tear-stained face fills the frame and the visual becomes a blur.

Bosley Crowther, in his *New York Times* review, called *High Sierra* "truly magnificent, that's all." The film about the "twilight of the American gangster" was told, he wrote, "in a solemn Wagnerian mood . . . giving that titanic figure a send-off befitting a first-string god." *Time* magazine, too, congratulated the film's "sensitive delineation" of the gangster character.

Earle's story captures the gangster's fall, not his rise. "But by falling the hero rises. He does not die . . . in a gutter, but nobly, at the foot of a mountain, and his death is equated with freedom. Having transcended the world and the judgments of morality, the classic gangster has achieved the best he could have hoped for."[5] Crowther noted of the film's ending, "It's a wonder the American flag wasn't wrapped around his broken corpse." The film, written by W. R. Burnett and John Huston, was the epitaph of the classic gangster. Roy was a product of the depression and had become obsolete; he belonged to a bygone era and was snuffed out like so many family farms along the Ohio Plains—reduced to the sorrowful tag of "the dust bowl." The film also suggested that the edges of many of America's most beloved myths were fraying—most notably, the goal to pursue money and success at any cost.

ROBIN HOOD AND THE AMERICAN OUTLAWS

By the mid 1930s (the timing of *High Sierra*), the darkest days of the depression were gripping every corner store and main street in America. Unofficial estimates put unemployment at one-third of the country's workers. Even the conservative *Fortune* magazine reported that about 25 million people were in dire need and possibly starving. In factory cities of the Midwest, where as much as 80 percent of the workforce was idle, employment riots broke out.[6] In this climate, big-city gangsters joined east coast bankers and Wall Street investors in seeming more greedy than admirable. Soon the American castles of the Robber Barons no longer inspired wonder—merely contempt.

A select senate committee revealed the nasty deals of numerous Wall Street bankers. Senator Burton Wheeler of Montana suggested that "the best way to restore confidence in the banks would be to take these crooked presidents out of the banks and treat them the same way we treated Al Capone when he failed to pay his income tax."[7] (But only Capone's tale continues to be resurrected; the sagas of Wall Street bottom feeders are rarely turned into fodder for movies.)

For most of their public careers, the Robber Barons had acted like gangsters. Even during the early years of the depression, they spent obscene amounts of money on lavish living while other men stood in bread lines. As the public grew increasingly poor, the Robber Barons transformed themselves into Robin Hoods and embarked on vigorous campaigns of philanthropy. They became generous both to respond sincerely to the needs of their hard-hit countrymen and to curb the creeping socialism of Roosevelt and other economic "fixers." Carnegie, for example, once a tightfisted capitalist known for ruthless business proficiency, became the name behind generous endowments and a famous performing hall. Capone, too, discovered the public relations value of charity (before he was locked away) with soup kitchens in Chicago that reputedly cost him $1,000 a week to operate.

Products of popular culture, such as the comic strip *Little Orphan Annie,* in which Annie is rescued by the generous Daddy Warbucks, also reworked the image of the successful capitalist. The trend was reminiscent of Progressive thinking, in which a benevolent upper class is preferable to "foreign" socialism. However, as in the second decade of the century, benevolence did little to investigate the systemic problems of orphans or the poverty behind America's brush with Skid Row.

The Robin Hood theme was also echoed in the journalistic accounts of real-life outlaws, including "Pretty Boy" Floyd, Bonnie and Clyde, and Roy Earle's inspiration, John Dillinger. Given the era, "the list of evil organizations had dwindled primarily to banks, and the criminals who became heroes were exclusively bank robbers."[8] Their favorite targets were in rural locales where banks were small and unprotected.

Like all great gangster films, *High Sierra* borrowed from journalism and the legend of a real-life crook. In the introduction to the published script, Douglas Gomery notes that Roy is written as a sympathetic "Robin Hood figure of the Great Depression."[9]

Dillinger, arguably the best-known bank robber of the twentieth century, earned his notoriety through a career that lasted only from June 1933 to July 1934. After Dillinger deserted the navy in 1923, he was arrested a year later in his native Indiana for robbing a store. He served a harsh nine-year sentence, which many claimed hardened him as a criminal. (Even the man he robbed wrote the parole board to ask for a reduced sentence.) After his release in the heart of the depression, the 30-year-old Dillinger soon became a bank robber for the sensational year that roused the nation's curiosity.

Dillinger first made the front page as a small-time bank robber who was not yet the leader of his gang. The Indiana state police got the idea of creating jealousy within the gang (to help it self-destruct) by telling the newspapers that Dillinger was the gang's mastermind. The local press also described him sympathetically as an "honest farmer" and a once-promising baseball player. Soon he caught the eye of the national press, including the *New York Times,* which described him as "true to the old frontier types" such as Jesse James, whom Dillinger openly admired. *Time* magazine did a four-page spread on Dillinger, linking him to both James and Robin Hood.[10] An article in the *Chicago Tribune* noted that during one of Dillinger's robberies, a bank customer began to back away from money just cashed from a check. Dillinger intervened and said, "You go ahead and pick it up. We don't want your money. Just the bank's."[11]

Press stories noted other bandits' thoughtfulness for burning mortgages while fleeing bank robberies. The press and the people dubbed these new rural criminals outlaws rather than gangsters, even though bank robbers, too, work in gangs. Webster's defines the term *outlaw* as "a person excluded from the benefit of protection of the law." That has a much different connotation than the word *gangster,* which reeks of "foreign" connections and urban slums. Also, an outlaw is linked with the rich ancestry of the American Wild West, which celebrates such American individualism and pluck. Indeed, the 1930s outlaws were viewed as heroic among families who were suffering from swift foreclosures and homelessness. For those who had to watch as their homesteads were repossessed by banks, the marauding outlaws often appeared as daring "avengers of injustice."[12]

Rural angst had begun in the 1920s as farm acreage decreased for the first time in American history. The twenties may have been the prosperity decade for urban residents but "just meant hard times for farm people." The depression, then, merely accelerated a downslide already in motion. By the mid-1930s, 1 out of 10 farms was forcibly sold at foreclosure auctions, and some farmers resorted to violence themselves to stop the sales.[13] But the overall response of most farmers was similar to that of hungry folks in the cities—a prevailing apathy and a focus on survival.

The government had no social net in place to handle the national emergency. And it had no muscle or political will to force private capital to come to the rescue. (For as many capitalists who became philanthropists, so many more did nothing but use depressed prices to consolidate and shore up fortunes.)

In reality, the notorious bank robbers were more concerned with "filling their pockets than in promoting social justice."[14] Yet they supplemented the media picture by writing to the newspapers and providing their own folksy anecdotes. Bonnie and Clyde supplied the press with poems and pictures as well. "This arrogance was their downfall. Left to compete solely with the state police, most of them would have lived for years, but their growing popularity encouraged the Federal authorities to intervene."[15]

Dillinger became Hoover's obsession, and the outlaw was finally declared the preeminent public enemy. In a subtle display of scorn, Hoover provided his G-men with a cardboard likeness of Dillinger to use for target practice. Dillinger had earned Hoover's wrath by staging several daring escapes from local jails whenever he was arrested. For one jailbreak, Dillinger reportedly used a wooden gun disguised with shoe polish. What made the incident more aggravating for Hoover was the press photos of local police posing with Dillinger while he was in their custody. He even used the unwitting sheriff's squad car to make his escape.

The government finally enlisted the help of a brothel owner to entrap Dillinger. They promised to cancel her deportation papers and pay her the $15,000 reward money if she agreed to set Dillinger up for arrest. (Anna Sage, the so-called Lady in Red, was later deported to Romania anyway despite her cooperation and received only a fraction of the reward money.)

Once Dillinger emerged from the Biograph Theater with the Lady in Red, federal agents gunned him down in a nearby alley. Immediately afterward, people began swarming around his body, dipping pieces of clothing and straw hats into his blood. After his body was put on display at the Cook County morgue, 15,000 curiosity seekers came to ogle the slain bank robber and ripening legend. Hoover, too, made Dillinger immortal by compiling artifacts and displaying them in a mini-museum outside his office in Washington.

Another celebrated bank robber was Charles "Pretty Boy" Floyd, whom the press depicted as an Oklahoman who turned to crime out of desperation to support his family after their farm was destroyed. His moniker, like Capone's, was invented by media folklore. Floyd was also frequently called the "sagebrush Robin Hood."[16]

Adding to the folk hero status of these bandits was their violent, premature deaths. Rather than capture the outlaws and bring them to trial, federal agents killed them. The authorities, perhaps, didn't want to risk intense scrutiny of their evidence—or be stonewalled by sympathetic juries.

Floyd became public enemy number one following the Union Station massacre in Kansas City (showcased in Hollywood's *G-Men*). Floyd was accused of murdering the federal agents who died at the train station and was aggressively hunted and killed in a farm field in October 1934. Yet Floyd claimed to his dying breath that he had nothing to do with the massacre. In hindsight, most historians side with Floyd. (Myths about overzealous authorities killing the wrong man have persisted about other famous outlaws, including Billy the Kid, Butch Cassidy, as well as Dillinger.)

Balladeer and political satirist Woody Guthrie captured Floyd's popularity in a song called "The Ballad of Pretty Boy Floyd." Its lyrics note, "You say that I'm an outlaw / You say that I'm a thief / Well here's a Christmas dinner for the families on relief."[17] Floyd was further immortalized in John Steinbeck's classic *The Grapes of Wrath*.[18] (The novel, about a beaten farmer searching for dignity in the withered dust bowl, was brought to the screen starring a doe-eyed Henry Fonda in 1939. It was a rare Hollywood effort to talk about the depression—although the depression was nearly neutralized by then.)

GANGSTERS TURN PATRIOTS

As the troubled 1930s drew to a close, America faced new threats from abroad as the world marched closer to another full-scale war. Yet the movies largely maintained their commitment to escapist cinema. Perhaps studio heads such as Louis B. Mayer (one of the richest men in America) were not eager to fan the flames of the grumbling masses. Dudley Nichols, president of the Screen Writers Guild, described the pressure on writers to conform to a distinctive moral, political, or business point of view in a radio speech given in January 1939. He noted, "Hollywood, in its fear of losing profits by making enemies, in its mad desire to appease the prejudices of every group, has submitted to an ever-tightening censorship under which it becomes impossible to deal [honestly] with reality."[19]

The Japanese attack on Pearl Harbor in 1941 finally broke Hollywood's trance. The industry quickly reinvested in new villains to replace the worn-out gangsters. Soon the furtive Jap was introduced, and then the fascist Nazi. They soon became the consummate threats to America's domestic peace.

Hollywood's version of World War II, however, drafted the hackneyed gangster along with every other able-bodied character in the land. His chilling gifts for mayhem and his efficiency as a hired assassin were deftly exploited. Unfortunately, he was no more realistic than the uniformed soldiers that marched on-screen. Khaki-clad, helmeted men were shown taking back the European countryside with Superman aplomb and few tools outside a tear-stained bazooka and a wind-whipped American flag. The truth was that the effort to defeat Hitler's Third Reich took deliberate, painstaking strategy and body bags full of mortal will. Instead, most wartime films—including those enlisting gangsters—reduced most blood-soaked battles to chaste struggles about democratic dreams and retrieved manhood. German soldiers were rarely shown as ordinary citizens who had grown pregnant with power—a truth that would have been more chilling with its familiar link to human history. Rather, Nazis were depicted on-screen as freakish murderers who acted intrinsically nasty—a view that shamefully reduced their crimes against mankind into shockworn comic book pulp. (The same fate would soon overtake screen gangsters.)

As Stuart Kaminsky comments, "The Depression had ended and fear of the Axis had replaced fear of hunger." Films in which the gangster goes to war include Alan Ladd's *Lucky Jordan* (1942), in which his character (a con man and Mob killer) joins the army to infiltrate a Nazi spy ring. Bogart appeared in the "Runyonesque comedy" *All through the Night,* in which his Alfred "Gloves" Donahue and his gang of fellow gamblers get snared in the "Washington racket" of fighting foreign saboteurs and securing democracy abroad. Such wartime roles for Bogart—including his most famous as Rick Blaine in *Casablanca* (1942)—enabled him to shed his menacing gangster mantle and become the reluctant hero who's merely stained by a questionable past and shadowed by unsavory associates.

GANGSTERS IN THE SHADOWS

As Bogart's Roy Earle signaled the end of the classic gangster, his film noir characters pointed to the future of the crime film for the 1940s. *Film noir* is a French phrase meaning dark cinema and describes a mood or attitude in filmmaking rather than a genre. Noir describes a particular mise-en-scène that focuses on unusual placement of human figures in a frame, stark and meaningful lighting, and irregular views—all meant to heighten the sense of "dislocation, danger, and mystery" playing upon the viewer's expectations.[20]

Much of noir's source material came from pulp fiction, detective stories, and a myriad of clever whodunits. (The term *pulp* was first given to the industry because it mass-produced sensational subject matter on cheap, rough paper.) Screenplays borrowed from the fiction works of Dashiell Hammett, Raymond Chandler, and Ross Macdonald, among others. Many of the hard-boiled writers behind noir began by publishing stories in pulp magazines such as *Dime Detective* and *Detective Fiction Weekly*.[21] Their plots thrive on deductive reasoning and cool logic, although this is somewhat diminished in the film versions. In fact, the screen plots are often hopelessly byzantine and difficult to follow. But film noir was obsessed with mood and innuendo, making sinister intentions more essential than a coherent plot. Robert Sklar describes noir as a "sense of people trapped—trapped in webs of paranoia and fear, unable to tell guilt from innocence, true identity from false. . . . In the end, evil is exposed, though often just barely, and the survival of good remains troubled and ambiguous."[22]

Filmmakers who used the noir approach weren't aware they were developing a distinctive style. It wasn't given the collective label until French film scholars and filmmakers of the 1950s noticed a uniqueness and haunting quality to American crime films of the 1940s. The French found these films' bleakness a blast of fresh realism—however highly stylized—for a Hollywood better known as "the dream factory." However, most American audiences who saw these films in the 1940s shared *Life* magazine's dismay at "Hollywood's profound postwar affection for morbid drama."[23]

For his part, Bogart lent his smoldering, self-reliant pose to characters who still worked in professions loosely linked to crime: private detectives and dubious businessmen. However, they never lost the biographical misprint marked on his screen persona and earned through dozens of gangster roles. From the sardonic private eye Sam Spade in *The Maltese Falcon* (a George Raft reject, as was Roy Earle) to the brooding Rick Blaine, Bogart played characters who're sullied by violent impulses. Yet they eventually scrape by the marker that separates the good guys from the rogues. Spade warns an acquaintance, "Don't be so sure I'm as crooked as I seem to be."

In addition to the superb *Falcon,* Bogart also appeared in two of Howard Hawks's famed noir thrillers: *To Have and Have Not* (1945), loosely based on an Ernest Hemingway story, and *The Big Sleep* (1946), borrowed from Raymond Chandler's Philip Marlowe, "the knight of the mean streets."[24] During the Bogart revival of the 1970s, the *New Yorker* described Bogart's Spade as a "mixture of avarice and honor, sexuality and fear." The description suits any great screen gangster as well.

John Huston, who directed *The Maltese Falcon,* was a major force behind many Bogart successes. Bogart won his only Oscar in Huston's *The African Queen* in 1951, with Bogart playing against type as a slovenly boat captain who falls for a bossy English spinster (Katherine Hepburn) after they endure a harrowing journey together. Huston came to screenwriting (including *High Sierra*) after stints as a boxer, a Mexican cavalry officer, and a journalist. (He was fired as a reporter, though, for his "casual treatment" of the facts.)[25] In another collaboration with Bogart, *The Treasure of Sierra Madre* (1948), Huston won Oscars for screenwriting and directing.

In yet another collaboration, *Key Largo* (1948), Huston put Bogart on the captive side of the hostage crisis that Bogart had created in *The Petrified Forest.* This time the gangster competes with a hurricane in terrorizing Bogart's Frank McCloud and the family of his dead army pal. Johnny Rocco (Edward G. Robinson) and his gang take over the Key Largo hotel that the family owns while they wait for a counterfeit fortune to finance Rocco's criminal comeback. Rocco's men kill the local sheriff at the hotel and blame the murder on local Indians. Worrying about his safety, though, Rocco forces Frank to take him and his hoodlums by boat to an island off Cuba. But Frank finally sheds his aversion to risk his neck and becomes a hero by overpowering and killing Rocco and his men aboard the boat. Frank had backed down earlier when challenged by Rocco in front of his pal's widow Nora (Lauren Bacall) and her father-in-law James Temple (Lionel Barrymore). She called Frank a coward. He snapped back, "Me die to rid the world of Johnny Rocco? No thanks!" As Eyles notes, though, Frank's words "fail to shake one's confidence in Bogart . . . he bides his time as any sensible figure would in the circumstances." Macho tactics will get them killed. Instead Frank uses intelligence and fine-tuned instinct to outsmart Rocco.

For Rocco, Robinson delightfully rips off the legacy he himself created 18 years earlier with Rico Bandello. At one point, alluding to the similar Caesar-like stature of Rocco in his heyday, Frank sarcastically notes, "He was more than a king; he was an emperor." Along with his men, Rocco is joined by his drunken, used-up moll (veteran genre player Claire Trevor, Bogart's old flame from *Dead End*). In a brilliant scene, Rocco forces her to sing for the group to earn the alcohol her body trembles for. She delicately navigates through a tune with scant dignity and even less vocal skill. In the end, Rocco sadistically refuses her the drink because he didn't like the performance. We suspect he also wants to punish her for no longer being young—or captivated by his every need. Trevor won another Academy Award for her portrayal of this fading songbird, who proves she still knows right from wrong when she finally turns on Rocco.

Bogart portrays his familiar and successful persona of the loner turned community hero, but it's Robinson as the vicious gangster who steals the film. By the time he appears on-screen, anticipation for his entrance is palpable. And as Eugene Rosow emphasizes, "The opening shot of gangster Johnny Rocco in his bath with a cigar is the epitome of the gangster at ease." The dominance of Rocco in the story leads Eyles to call *Key Largo* "just another gangster film, despite the attempts to gain greater significance."[26]

BROTHERS GRIM

Noir was well suited to police action dramas such as *T-Men* (1947) and dozens of thrillers and detective films, but it found a perfect marriage in the gangster genre, which already possessed a somber quality and a dark, seductive charm. When applied to the gangster film, however, the noir approach obscures the difference between good and evil. In an about-face from the late 1930s, noir enables the cops, victims, district attorneys, and eyewitnesses to share the criminal's operating philosophy and his pliable morality.

This approach contorts the classic premise and makes the gangster less grand and less obvious. Noir forsakes the tragic elements of the gangster's motives: he's not following a predestined path to resolute doom; he's suffering from the same nagging malaise of pessimism that afflicts the rest of the characters. In the genre's classic era, the gangster was "a figure of vitality and enterprise . . . a celebration of self-assertiveness . . . [whereas] the *noir* hero wants mostly to be left alone."[27]

Bogart was the poster boy of the noir blended character, but he sidelined his pure gangster character in the process. A more consummate example of noir influence on a gangster film without destroying its essential conviction is the 1948 film *Force of Evil:* a story of two brothers who rise from the slums to occupy different ranks within the Underworld. Although Joe and Leo Morse are both involved in the rackets, it's the younger Joe who's ambitious, cocky, and classically doomed. The film opens with a shot of Wall Street and the voice of Joe (John Garfield). He tells us that he's a lawyer for the numbers racket and proudly explains that "tomorrow," America's birthday, the

Fourth of July, "I intended to make my first million dollars—an exciting day in any man's life."

Gambling brings an "annual income to cheap crooks and racketeers [of] over 100 million dollars," Joe explains. "It seemed a shame for so much good money to go to waste in other people's pockets." The youthful, good-looking attorney works for the former bootlegger and reigning numbers kingpin Ben Tucker. The shooting script describes Tucker as "a big man going fat, but still handsome and strong with easy power." As Tucker's "clever little lawyer," Joe has a plan to make his boss's numbers game legal and even more profitable. But the newspaper headlines warn: "Prosecutor opens drive on million dollar swindle."

Further, Joe's 50-year-old brother Leo will be wiped out by the scheme. The plan is to fix the number 776, which perversely exploits the public's optimism for heavily betting that patriotic number as a shortcut to American wealth. When the number hits, the 20 or 30 small numbers banks in the city (including Leo's) will be busted, leaving Tucker's operation with a monopoly on the racket.

Tucker is suspicious, however, of Joe's soft spot for his brother. "I can't risk $200,000 for sentimental reasons. Don't worry about your brother, Joe. . . . He won't die of heart failure as long as he remembers he has a rich brother."

Against orders, Joe goes to warn his brother—whom he hasn't seen in years. He offers him the chance to join the monopoly as one of the remaining banks. Joe finds Leo "gray with worry, plump, explosive with fear and anger." He's working at his "cheap desk in the three-room cold water flat."[28] Leo (Thomas Gomez) rejects his brother's tip and resents the interference in his "respectable" business. "I'm an honest man, not a gangster," Leo snarls.

The hypocrisy infuriates Joe, who calls his brother "a small man" who thinks if he stays poor it makes him less of a crook. "I've come to take you out of this airshaft . . . [to] put you in a real office in a real business to pay you back for everything," Joe shouts. "You're my older brother," he adds, racked by anguish as much as anger. Leo describes the sacrifices he made to enable Joe to go to law school. "I wanted to be the lawyer and could have been if I'd have thrown you out of the house when our parents died," Leo bellows. "I worked for you like a fool, I gave you everything . . . and I owe it to the whole world because . . . of what you are, a crook, and a cheat, and a gangster!"

Joe arranges a raid on his brother's operation to ensure that his brother will have to ask for his help and accept his offer to survive. Meanwhile, a disgruntled bookkeeper who works for Leo is enticed by Tucker's old beer rival Ficco to help spoil the fix. Also, the district attorney has planted a wiretap that promises to break down the conspiracy. In one last attempt to look out for Joe, Leo tries to stop his employee and the snitch Bauer. Leo argues that it will be Bauer's fault when Joe becomes "a butcher" and is forced to kill Bauer to protect his plan. "I'll kill you with my own hands rather than let you put the mark of Cain on my brother," Leo vows. Bauer sets up a meeting with Ficco anyway, which leads to his death and Leo's disappearance.

Joe senses that he's losing control and is next on the hit list. He empties out the safe and broods about lost opportunities in a nightclub with his girlfriend Doris (Beatrice Pearson). She works for Leo and is struggling with her loyalty to Leo and his tenacious hold on moral boundaries and her attraction to Joe and his spoiled ambition. While drowning his sorrows, Joe delivers one of the best explanations of a gangster's internal torment. After Doris asks him when things began to go wrong, he moans, "The day I was born. . . . You don't know what it is to have real fear in you. You don't know what it is to wake in the morning, go to sleep every night and eat your lunch, and read the papers, and hear the horns blowing in the streets and all the time wherever you are, whatever you're doing, whatever you're seeing . . . you're afraid in your heart. Is that what life is?" Then he notices a newspaper headline that abruptly ends his tirade: "Tucker-Ficco War! 1 Dead. 1 Kidnapped. Leo Morse snatched; bookkeeper slain."

Joe bolts out of the nightclub and barges in on Tucker. He suspects that Tucker knows what happened to Leo, whom Joe fears is dead. Ficco is now working for Tucker and wants Joe killed as well. But Tucker insists such killings are sloppy and unnecessary. Joe is appalled by the new partnership and gets Ficco to admit he ordered Leo's murder. A scuffle ensues, with shots fired and a table lamp knocked over, leaving Tucker's study shrouded in darkness. The three men scramble in the blackness, trying to outwit each other and to stay alive.

The scene is a superior example of the noir style and a masterpiece of cinematic suspense. According to the shooting script, "A bulk of shadow inches along the floor towards the door. The tiniest knife edge of light seeps through the door edge, and this figure begins to obscure it." Ficco watches, raising his gun, ready to fire at the first glimpse of a body. "The figure is at the door. It raises a cautious hand to the knob, and then infinitely careful, soundless, turns the knob. Shots flame out of Ficco's gun. The figure at the door trembles and then slumps to the floor. The door, touched slightly, slowly starts to open admitting a thin but widening corridor of light across the blackness from the lighted balcony outside. Ficco begins to rise, tense, the light from the door disclosing him, revealing him fully, slowly. A shot is fired. Ficco is hit. A gun fires two more shots. Ficco turns to look, surprised. Two more shots and he slumps. . . . A foot comes in and kicks the gun away. The feet go to the desk and stop at the phone on the floor. A hand comes down and picks up the phone, raises it to the face of Joe Morse."

Knowing the phone is tapped by the DA's office, Joe promises to meet with the police in an hour. Joe and Doris then search the viaduct, where as expected they find Leo's body. As Joe stands over his dead brother, he explains in voice-over that he feels as if he helped kill him. Doris leads Joe away, and his last voice-over confirms that he's turning himself over to the police. Despite this conclusion, the film is not a tale of classic redemption. It remains a nagging exposé of the seductive nature of the criminal Underworld for men such as Joe who're enterprising but flawed by a pathetic ability to subvert their own gifts. The film's end implies that Joe will rejoin society and even become law-abiding, perhaps marry Doris and settle down. But he can never earn his dead brother's respect or forgiveness—which was what he craved all along to become whole.

Martin Scorsese, a master director working in the modern gangster genre, battled to preserve *Force of Evil* in the early 1990s. He wanted Abraham Polonsky's script and directorial effort given its due respect and renewed acclaim. In the introduction to the videotape edition, Scorsese speaks to the film's influence on his work of the 1970s and 1980s. He first saw the film at age 13 and "was overwhelmed by its writing, its direction, its use of music, and its acting."

The film was dismissed by American critics as a "routine gangster drama," adds Scorsese. *Variety* had noted that its "poetic, almost allegorical, interpretation keeps intruding on the tougher elements of the plot." In particular, *Variety*'s critic wanted more details on the numbers racket and less fraternal wrangling. In contrast, Scorsese lauds the film's richness of characterization—not its re-creation of crime details or killing sprees. He recalls a British critic who exclaimed, "My God, it's written in blank verse." Scorsese adds, "Its poetry creates a hyper-reality. . . . for me, the poetry culminates in the graceful and tormented presence of John Garfield. His face becomes a landscape of moral conflicts." Scorsese suggests that *Force of Evil* belongs in the ranks of the genre's most exceptional films because "The moral drama has almost a mythic scale. It displays a corrupted world collapsing from within."[29]

Noir and its flair for ambiguity wouldn't last. But the interesting characters of noir, many inspired by classic gangsters, provided some abstraction and surrealism during the genre's big sleep of the 1940s. Besides, noir didn't exclusively showcase gangsters, and its style wasn't always suitable for gangland's most coveted ingredients: calculated action, blunt violence, and ferocious noise. In the fog of noir, the gangster was difficult to pick out. In a postwar society increasingly looking for black-and-white boundaries, some folks wanted him to return to being obvious, inadequate, and easy to exterminate.

CHAPTER 6

Gangsters and Other Alien Threats

> It ain't like waiting for some human being who wants to kill you. . . . Cody ain't human. Plug him full of lead and he still comes at ya.
>
> —Verna (Virginia Mayo), speaking about her husband Cody (James Cagney) in *White Heat,* 1949

Noir lived on in the late 1940s and early 1950s with several gifted directors, including Alfred Hitchcock, Orson Welles, Stanley Kubrick, and the German-born Fritz Lang. They continued to explore the more claustrophobic and domestic aspects of crime. Guest starring in the noir thrillers and private eye yarns, the gangster was kept alive. But as a full-fledged character in a starring role, his appearances were sporadic and lonely.

One such intrusion on the gangster-as-star hiatus was Cagney's ferocious Cody Jarrett in the 1949 release *White Heat.* Cagney had spent most of the 1940s in musicals or battling America's enemies abroad. But at age 50, Cagney returned to the Underworld with a new excuse for committing mayhem: mental illness.

The film tracks the inner workings of Cody and his gang, which includes his wife Verna and his mother, for whom the police describe his "fierce, psychopathic devotion." Ma Jarrett (Margaret Wycherly) is her son's criminal manager and is modeled after the real-life legend Ma Barker. After a botched train robbery ends in murder, Cody tries cleverly to outwit the law by pleading guilty to a lesser crime (which he did not commit) to avoid facing the electric chair on the more serious charges for which he's hunted. While in prison, he meets an undercover G-man who befriends him and then infiltrates his gang.

The male rival to Cody within his band is Big Ed (Steve Cochran), whose name comes from his "big ideas," snarls Cody, ever keeping a suspicious eye on his burly lieutenant. Ed is a stock character, dressed in the gangster "uniform" of dark shirt and light-colored tie, and is much too obvious about his aim to replace Cody as gang leader and steal his wife as well.

But Big Ed is no match for Cody, even though Cody is often crippled by mental fits. These attacks leave him reeling and moaning from what he describes as the "red-hot buzz saw" in his head. One of the film's more startling scenes shows a sedate Cody eating prison food in the mess hall until he finds out about his mother's death. Within moments he's reduced to scrambling madness, groping at his temples for relief from the terrorizing forces in his mind. He's finally subdued and straitjacketed. The police tell us that Cody's lunacy began in childhood as a way to get his mother's attention and then evolved into a real ailment. And authorities are being urged to work fast to bring Cody to justice before he becomes "a raving maniac" like his father.

The police and federal authorities in the story are as stiff and robotic as usual. The exception is the undercover agent Fallon (Edmund O'Brien). He acts and thinks like a criminal to earn Cody's trust, rubbing Cody's head during one of his mental attacks and listening to Cody's intimate ravings about his mother. The agent, however, doesn't blink when he betrays Cody at the end of the film. Rather than introduce a complex G-man caught in the inner circle of a gang, Fallon's motives remain nothing more than an abstract belief in crime fighting. The character's simplicity keeps him dull and diminished next to Cagney's stretch from mama's boy to butcher.

Cody's wife Verna, (Virginia Mayo), is a loathsome creature who switches allegiances with the wind. She clutches her mink coat as if it's in danger of being snatched away, has a villain's arch in her Revlon brows, and nimbly spits out her gum before kissing. But Verna has the sharpest survival skills of anyone in the gang. She possesses a clarity of purpose when it comes to allegiances: who has the dough? After Cody "crashes out" of prison, he comes after Verna and Ed for betraying him. While Ed explains why he must stay and face Cody like a man, Verna wisely explains the merits of going on the run. Only after Ed promises to tell Cody that it was she who shot his mother in the back does Verna stay. Once Cody shows up, though, Verna tearfully convinces him that Ed did the dirty work, which gets Ed promptly killed. Verna then unflinchingly retakes her post at Cody's side as accomplice and lover. It's not that Cody trusts Verna, but for him a woman's artifice is less lethal than a rival's ambition.

The revamped gang, with Fallon replacing Ed, plans its biggest heist to date—ripping off the payroll of a chemical plant. (Cody's racket until now has been vaguely defined as stealing federal money and reselling it for a profit on the European black market.) But Fallon finally reemerges as a cop, and the factory becomes a death trap for the gang. Ma Jarrett's oft-repeated advice to Cody to get to the "top of the world" becomes his epitaph. Like Roy Earle, Cody chooses to die on his own terms. As scores of police kill off his gang members running for cover, Cody defiantly climbs to the top of the metal fortress of pipes, catwalks, and holding tanks.

Trapped at the apex and groping for shelter, Cody keeps chuckling like a madman. Fallon fires at him with a rifle and pierces his body with bullets, but Cody keeps going. After pumping more shots into his target, Fallon asks in exasperation, "What's holding him up?"

A cackling Cody starts shooting at the tanks around him, setting off explosions. Finally, he lifts his face toward the sky—his manic face a moonscape of flickering shadows. He musters up his remaining energy and bellows, "Made it, Ma, top o' the world!" The next shot shows an immense mushroom cloud accompanied by the fierce racket of successive blasts as the chemical tanks blow their contents into the sky.

Through smoke and flying debris, Fallon asserts to his bureau chief, "Cody Jarrett finally got to the top of the world and it blew right up in his face." Fallon's insipid remark does little to tilt the story toward a testament to the law's awesome power. Instead, the apocalyptic ending perversely celebrates Cody's monstrous will and his grotesque death.

Jack Shadoian credits veteran gangster director Raoul Walsh for *White Heat*'s "hard, clear outlines [that] bang along with a sledgehammer force and the tenacity of a power drill."[1] Shadoian also notes that Max Steiner's musical score "represents the

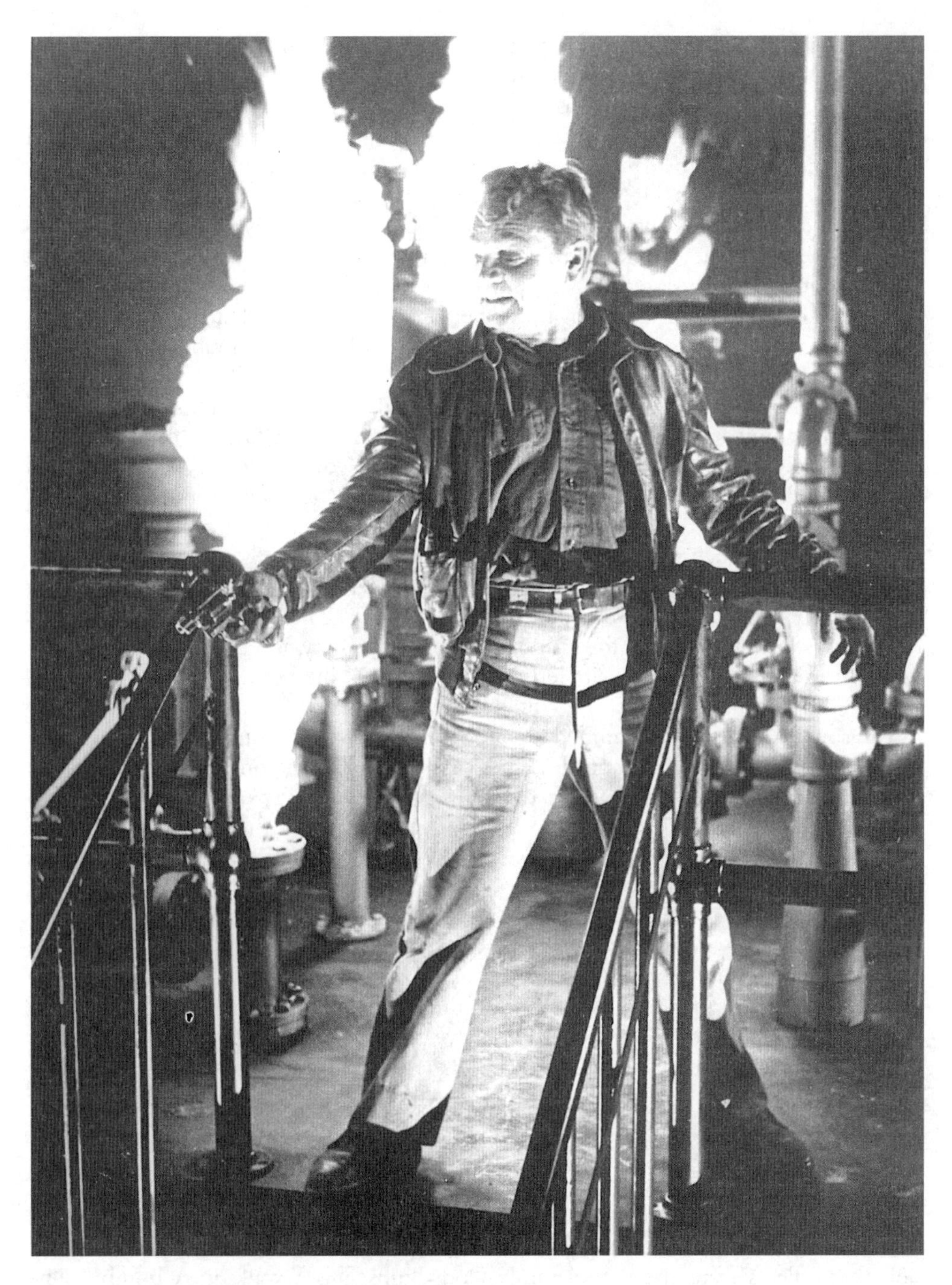

Cagney returns to gangland in 1949 as Cody Jarrett in Raoul Walsh's *White Heat*. The mentally tormented but ever-defiant character chooses to blow himself up rather than give in to swarming lawmen. This ending was still interpreted by genre fans as a gangster in control of his own gruesome fate rather than a suicide brought on by panic.

beginnings of modern assaults upon the ear."[2] The film concludes with a shattering tonal finale that matches the factory fireworks.

In the original script, Jarrett was intended to be a violent man with little explanation for his brutality. It was Cagney, however, who decided that Jarrett should be a psychopath.[3] And Cagney put his usual charismatic stamp on the character's virility, too, despite his 50 years. He shows his female companion—portrayed by the comely, 29-year-old Mayo—his customary snootful of abuse along with much sexual aggression. In one scene, the drunken Verna jumps on the furniture like a spoiled child and eagerly plots what they should do with the loot from the heist. Cody quietly watches her with a devilish smile and then hoists her onto his back, so that she straddles him like a child on a piggyback ride. After he playfully orders her to grab the half-empty liquor bottle, he carries her off to a bedroom.

Cagney also offers his trademark swipe at candid violence when a hostage locked in a trunk complains that it's "stuffy" inside. Cody stops gnawing on a piece of chicken long enough to shout back, "Hold on, I'll give you a little air." Then he shoots the trunk full of holes. Scenes like this prompted the *New York Times* to note, "Mr. Cagney achieves the fascination of a bull-fighter at work, deftly engaged in the business of doing violence with economy and grace."

Cagney would create one more memorable gangster in the coming years as Martin "The Gimp" Snyder in *Love Me or Leave Me* (1956). The role earned Cagney an Academy Award nomination for his portrayal of a crotchety, aging bully of a hoodlum who's further besieged by a crippled leg. He sponsors the young aspiring nightclub singer Ruth Etting (Doris Day), who was a famed 1920s torch singer before her career soured and she succumbed to alcoholism. Snyder strong-arms people into accepting her and instills a gratitude in her that's tainted with contempt. Day plays the torn songbird with brilliant shadings that exude both her guilty obligation to the man who helped her realize her ambitions and her distaste for the expected payback. There's a young rival for her affections, but it's Cagney's emotional distress that keeps us absorbed in the story.

Cagney's character senses her martyred affection like a bloodhound. He rejects his weakness for her by unduly abusing her, much as Tom Powers did with the women in his life. Old or young, Cagney's characters are born of human contradictions and are still likable even though they sin. As the quintessential tough guy, he continued to infuse his gangsters with defiance and resolve that were ignorant of age. A Cagney gangster would be a menace until the day he died—either from a bullet or old age.

MONSTER GANGSTERS

White Heat was released only four years after the U.S. military dropped the atomic bomb on Hiroshima. The timing prompts Shadoian to note, "It is not just the conclusion that reflects fears about the bomb, Cody himself is a walking A-bomb."[4] The atomic bomb had ended World War II and forced a commendable peace. But its ability to kill nearly 100,000 people within the flash of a few seconds left a haunting legacy that spoiled the braggadocio of victory and left Americans sick with worry. A year later, Winston Churchill described an "iron curtain" to define the Soviet empire and characterize the emerging Cold War.

Once the Soviets detonated their own atomic bomb in 1949—the year *White Heat* premiered—worry turned to paranoia. Also in that year, China was lost to the communists, and spy trials were nurturing homegrown fears. In 1952, during the darkest days of the Korean War, anxiety intensified with the unveiling of the hydrogen bomb. The H-bomb had 10 times the capacity for destruction of the atomic bomb. The guided missile—a device controlled by radar—was also introduced in 1952, further muddying the connection between war and human discretion.

The twin fears of nuclear annihilation and communism spilled over into many aspects of American society, including the political arena. Not since the "Red Scare" following World War I had so many American citizens been fingered as enemies of the state. This time not just immigrants were suspects; anyone could be accused and ruined by the suggestion alone. From 1947 to 1954, Senator Joe McCarthy waged a vicious hunt for closeted communists, looking for "reds" hiding in the State Department but also influencing Hollywood products. Considering Hollywood's eager role in wartime propaganda and its sheepish acceptance of self-censorship, many historians argue that Hollywood was attacked because it was easy pickings. Hollywood had proved before to be a convenient target. (Once the hysteria subsided, few concluded that Hollywood had ever been a hotbed of communism or a tangible threat to national security.)

At first, Bogart and others fought back by forming the Committee for the First Amendment. They attended the testimonies of the infamous "Hollywood Ten" before the House Un-American Activities Committee. But Bogart, too, eventually denounced the effort because it gave the appearance that he was defending communism rather than supporting the battle for political openness. Like others, he also feared being unemployed.[5] Among the victims who were put out of work was *Force of Evil*'s director Abraham Polonsky. He wouldn't direct another Hollywood film for 21 years.

Hollywood, as one barometer of our nation's psyche during the Cold War, invented monsters that were linked to nuclear accidents and staged invasions by extraterrestrials. Science fiction films were teeming with alien invaders, mutant creatures, giant flies, rampaging reptiles, and oozing blobs. Once the Soviet satellite Sputnik was launched, an exuberant race to conquer space fueled more alien fantasies—and nightmares.

Hollywood also began to transform noir's delicate suspense into sloppy anguish bulging on-screen with distemper. In the years just ahead Hollywood would begin to pump out dozens of crime films "about every freakish calamity and human nastiness the mind can conjure short of the supernatural."[6] Gangsters were no longer creations of the Underworld but creatures from another world. They became gruesome exaggerations with Cagneyesque poses but with motives more akin to Lon Chaney's frightful sociopaths. They were completely distilled from ethnicity, families, or neighborhoods—and simply invented for programmed violence and shock value. The comfort for the viewer comes from being able to kill these stray monsters in our midst, aberrations rather than common social by-products. The late-1930s films had already begun to neutralize the effects of crime's connection to social status and poverty. The lead gangster had been offset by a priest, cop, or brother who grew up on the same mean streets, thereby downplaying the environmental factors. Cagney's Cody Jarrett is the epitome of the gangster as damaged goods. Other loony gangsters flourished in the second-string roles that still employed the gangster. He also appeared in crime subgenres, including prison stories focusing on convicts and heist films investigating how key crimes are planned and executed, such as Huston's superb *The Asphalt Jungle*.

Most of the these Cold War hoodlums are already fully developed by the time they arrive on-screen. There's no further evolution into evil. Consequently, there's little

Dressed in the recognizable gangster "uniform" of light tie and dark ensemble, Richard Widmark *(left)* offers a memorable debut performance as the sadistic, giggling thug Tommy Udo, who terrifies the ex-con turned informant Nick Bianco (Victor Mature) in the noir thriller *Kiss of Death.*

mystery or thrill left in tracking their moves. The only new wrinkle is *how* they kill. In the convict-centered drama *Brute Force* (1947), the gruesome deed is done with blowtorches. In *Kiss of Death* (1947), Richard Widmark as thug Tommy Udo shoves a victim's mother, still confined to her wheelchair, down a flight of stairs. Carlos Clarens describes Udo as "given to giggles and gurgling" while he contemplates how to make his victims suffer longer. Lee Marvin, playing mobster Vince Stone in director Fritz Lang's *The Big Heat* (1953), throws a pot of scalding coffee and permanently disfigures his girlfriend's face. (The film also includes a barfly who's beaten and tortured with cigarette burns, along with a cop's wife who is obliterated by a bomb, prompting Colin McArthur to note that the film is "particularly horrifying" to women and surpasses most gangster films for misogyny.) However, when *The Big Heat* leans on its noir principles and indicts everyone with criminal tendencies, the film is an engaging story about obsessive behavior and a sense of hopelessness.

Another Widmark film, *The Street with No Name,* was a loose remake of *G-Men* by the same director, William Keighley. Despite its opening endorsement by J. Edgar Hoover about a "vigilant" America battling crime, the moment Widmark makes his entrance as the stylish crook, wearing a silk scarf and munching on an apple, "the pic-

Lee Marvin portrays the dressed-up punk Vince Stone in Fritz Lang's acclaimed noir story *The Big Heat*. But Stone's attire cannot cloak his viciousness toward women and would-be enemies. Gloria Grahame portrays the wisecracking moll he roughs up here. Later Stone will scar her face with boiling-hot coffee.

ture was his," notes Clarens. Yet, keeping with the era, the gangster is also a hypochondriac who lives in fear of drafts and gets neurotic relief from staging sadistic rows with his girlfriend.

The gangster characters in most of these films are the most memorable because of their comic zeal. Moviegoers watched them for the same reasons they gawk at circus sideshows: morbid curiosity. But these characters stretched parody beyond the limits of credulity and severely strained the audience's appetite for imitation. Another stock character in most of these films is the cop or DA who delivers the same stale sermon announcing the public's demand to stamp out crime. (The public rarely vows to give up its vices, though, which could also cripple the rackets.) For a change, the sermon in *The Big Heat* comes from the foreign-born crime kingpin Lagana. He warns, "Things are changing in this country—never get the people steamed up. They start doin' things. Grand juries. Election investigations. Deportation hearings."

RETREADS, RIP-OFFS, AND COMIC RELIEF

A fresh approach would have been to investigate the most chilling, authentic crime fighter of the era—the government in its search for spies. The few films that brought up the subject did so from the government's point of view—to nobody's surprise. *Pickup on South Street* (1953) used the gangsters as patriotic henchmen. This role was reminiscent of their role in wartime films: they looked like gangsters but acted like obedient soldiers. Because accusing the G-men of acting like grand inquisitors was too risky—given the repressive climate—few fresh story lines came forward to reinvigorate the genre. Hollywood had to look in its own files to resurrect old gangster stories and remake them. *The Racket* was among those exhumed. Once a controversial play banned in Chicago for its on-target indictments of political corruption, the film version debuted in 1928. (The New York censors, though, cut out the scene of a state official being bribed.)[7]

The film had presented Nick Scarsi as a Capone clone with recognizable links to ethnicity and the head of a particular criminal empire: bootlegging. In the 1951 remake, the gangster's name is changed to the bland Nick Scanlon, who battles an inflated cop portrayed by Robert Mitchum. His McQuigg is as rancorous as any hoodlum. He and the film are so sanctimonious that you can't help but root for Robert Ryan's wisecracking Scanlon to win—despite the looming odds.

Hollywood also began borrowing from the upstart entertainment medium: television. Successful programs such as *Dragnet* and *The Untouchables* eventually inspired *The FBI Story* (1959) and a film conglomeration of Eliot Ness's TV exploits. Ironically, it wasn't called *The Untouchables* but named after the film character with greater box office appeal—Eliot Ness's criminal nemesis Capone. When transferred to the big screen, the story was called *The Scarface Mob.*

But the box office draw of these crime stories proved to be out of favor no matter how modernized, graphic, or patriotic—and no matter from whose point of view. Some audiences may have reveled in their comic book catharsis, but most moviegoers spent the early Cold War years with their eyes glued to spectacle and lighthearted fare. Unlike the trend of "art" films trickling in from Europe that embraced realism, most gangster and G-men products were B productions lacking in artistic merit, critical acclaim, or major audience appeal.

The gulf between what critics regarded as quality films and the crowd pleasers was wide. Although *White Heat* may have impressed critics, Cody Jarrett didn't have the box office draw of Tom Powers. In 1949 the public was more enthralled with *Jolson Sings Again* and *I Was a Male War Bride.* A critics' pick for 1953 was *The Big Heat,* yet moviegoers that year favored *The Robe,* which may have been attractive because it was the first CinemaScope film presented to the public.[8]

Movie attendance had declined since its peak of 100 million moviegoers in 1946,[9] and Hollywood would never again dominate America's entertainment dollars. Moreover, the government aggravated the industry's woes in 1949 by forcing studios to give up their lucrative exhibition monopoly. They had to reorganize profit margins around the remaining production and distribution operations. Rather than dabble in dramatic experiments to bring audiences back (as European cinema was doing), Hollywood turned to gimmicks and technical innovations: 3-D, Vista-Vision, stereophonic sound, along with CinemaScope.

WHAT'S IN A NAME?

Some of the dazzling foreign films did more than draw discerning audiences—they also challenged American censorship. A ban on Roberto Rossellini's *The Miracle* was taken to the United States Supreme Court, which finally ruled that such bans were an unconstitutional abridgment of free speech. Further, the Court concluded in its 1952 decision, "it cannot be doubted that motion pictures are a significant medium for the communication of ideas."[10] Much of the Production Code was still in place at the production level, but subsequent challenges continued to weaken its enforcement.

Encouraged by the slight opening the censorship battles provided, Hollywood began reintroducing more graphic crime and sex into films of the mid-1950s in hopes of luring audiences away from their televisions. For the most part, Hollywood wasted the liberal license to further gild the glossy spectacles rather than use the more tolerant climate to foster innovation. With remakes exhausted and in no mood for fearless creativity, gangster filmmakers again turned to the genre's richest source material for renewal: journalism. Unfortunately, this time Hollywood stole from the newsroom morgues rather than the front pages.

Dillinger was an early forerunner of the famous dead-gangster biographies that would populate the screens of the late 1950s. Even in its 1945 debut, *Dillinger* removed all depression context and portrayed Dillinger as a common thief plucked from obscurity rather than a criminal sensation that dazzled the public. Despite the documentary-like approach with a listless narrator, the film focused on events rather than on characterization. It ignored the nuances and influences of Dillinger's youth, prison experience, and depression timing.

The film begins with a contemporary theater audience watching newsreel footage of Dillinger's "bloody trail." On hand is Dillinger's father, who tells the titillated crowd about John's "normal" rural Indiana boyhood and his plans to go to the city to become a "big broker." The film then flashes back to 1933. John Dillinger (Lawrence Tierney) is sitting in a seedy bar with a tawdry blond who's demanding John buy her another drink. Short of cash, he slips next door to a grocer and robs the store of $7.20. He's nabbed and imprisoned with a white-collar criminal named Specs Green (Edmund Lowe). Green impresses John because he embezzled the tidy sum of $70,000 and reads *Bank Digest* in his cell.

Nothing explains John's wise-guy arrogance or his toughness, yet at the same time, he shows deference to "Mr. Green." He even vows to help Green escape after he gets paroled. John makes good on his pledge, and a montage reveals Green's escape along with a coterie of men who recognize Green as their leader. Another montage shows the gang robbing shops and planning a more complicated heist. But the ambitious and trigger-happy John makes Green nervous. The story is a classic gangster plot, except we don't know why John went through the trouble to get Green out of prison only to overthrow him, which John does shortly after the bank robbery.

He borrows the classic gangster's need for revenge, but this time the impetus is pretty flimsy. He returns to the seedy bar to kill the bartender who had refused to give him and his moll a drink. The killing is the most creative scene in the film, though, as the barman is mauled by John with the jagged end of a broken beer mug. As the scene progresses, the bar's piano player signals the impending gore with an increasingly loud and thundering boogie tune. At the moment of the assault, which occurs off camera, the piano player is shown frantically banging on the keys to match the violent act.

The film includes some accurate episodes from Dillinger's real biography: hiding in a Midwest lodge, heading west and hitting banks throughout the plains states, and escaping from jail using a wooden gun. But the screen Dillinger speaks with a Brooklyn accent, which reflects the actor's roots but betrays the Indiana-bred Dillinger. At one point, Tierney complains, "this toothache's moider" and later vows "to get guys with noive" for his comeback.

When John is finally mowed down in an alley outside the theater, his death is not only anticlimactic but deadeningly dull. A cop lifts John's wallet and finds $7.20—the exact amount of money that first sent him to prison. With this bit of invented drama, irony mutates into shameless corn.

However, the film made money for its independent filmmakers, Frank and Maurice King. They had bought the rights to stock footage, which make up almost one-third of the film, borrowing scenes from numerous 1930s films, including car chases, gun battles, and Fritz Lang's superb footage of an armored-car heist from *You Only Live Once.* "From the sheer corner-cutting, the genre had been distilled to its essence . . . skill divorced from heroics, mayhem without a cause."[11]

Dillinger's picked-over story would be resurrected again by Nick Adams in *Young Dillinger* (1965), with the added burden of running from the law with his pregnant teenage wife in tow. (Not until the gangster renaissance began in the 1970s would a candid version be put on-screen with a surly but convincing Warren Oates in the lead role.)

Dillinger would have enjoyed the films of his life, if tales of his vanity and weakness for publicity are true. That was part of the problem with most of the outlaws of the early 1930s: they loved drawing attention to themselves. But urban criminals, including Capone, had always looked on the rural gangsters as "small-time thieves, thrillseekers, and freaks."[12] In the eyes of emerging syndicate criminals, outlaws such as Dillinger, Floyd, Ma Barker, George "Machine Gun" Kelly, Lester Gillis ("Baby Face" Nelson), along with Bonnie and Clyde, used violence sloppily and dangerously provoked the authorities. That's precisely why they were perfect choices for Hollywood makeovers: they were colorful and safely dead and made the authorities look efficient. When made into movies, though, their stories were drab and mechanical. This approach was the crime, considering the genre, the personae, and the excuse for delectable deviance their lives provided.

Pretty Boy Floyd was given screen time—and John Ericson's face—in a 1960 B production of the same name. The *New York Herald Tribune* noted, "Early in the film, an effort is made to explore the causes of Floyd's behavior. Commendable as this may be, the attempt at social analysis and authenticity is not sustained. Soon the screenplay descends into stereotyped violence."[13] John Baxter notes that Ericson's Floyd is portrayed as "a narcissistic killer lacking both Guthrie's folk-hero charisma and the real Floyd's resilience and skill." (A heavy emphasis on Floyd's fictional good looks and youthful charm would bring Fabian Forte and Martin Sheen to the role in the 1970s.)[14]

The Untouchables of television also introduced the public to a colorful band of New York mobsters who were rivals and colleagues of Capone. Legs Diamond and Dutch Schultz were both protégés of Arnold Rothstein—the recognized boss before the organized syndicates formed in the 1930s. "Like many other such screen chronicles, *Portrait of a Mobster* [with Vic Morrow as Dutch Schultz] disguised its paltry budget behind a smoke-screen of violence." Another critic noticed its familiarity, complaining, "It seems to have been lifted intact from previous Warner epics."[15]

Other biopics of the late 1950s include *The Rise and Fall of Legs Diamond, Machine Gun Kelly, King of the Roaring Twenties: The Story of Arnold Rothstein,* and *Baby Face Nelson* with Mickey Rooney in the title role. The last film (directed by Don Siegel, of *Dirty Harry* fame) chronicles Nelson's trigger-happy reputation and his brief membership in Dillinger's gang. Eugene Rosow notes that Rooney's "intense portrayal" captures "a psychotic character who becomes progressively crazier throughout the story." The film has no historical accuracy, though, and ends with Nelson's girlfriend having to shoot and kill him after he vows to murder several children. Mickey Rooney also earned praise for his performance of Rothstein's childhood friend Johnny Burke in the Rothstein biography.

In Legs Diamond's story, the reviewers called Ray Danton's mobster "a natty, glittering personality." But *Variety* blasted Warner Brothers for trying to "recapture its pre-war gangster image" with such a lackluster movie.

In one of the worst biographies, *Machine Gun Kelly* (1958), Charles Bronson offers a schizophrenic portrayal of a hotheaded hoodlum who's in love with his tommy gun and scared of his wife. True to director Roger Corman's vociferous style, Kelly is shown to be more deranged than brutal and has little in common with the real-life gangster. The screen Kelly has irrational fears of tattoos, caskets, and ceremonial relics. And given the era's outlandish reach for unusual methods of killing and maiming, Kelly uses a captive jungle cat to gnaw and claw his victims apart. In the end, his wife Flo (Susan Cabot), who has been the brains of the outfit, reduces Kelly to a sniveling coward. "I gave you a backbone," she shouts, "I could use you and make you do anything I wanted you to do." He whimpers back, "Don't shame me, Flo. . . . I never wanted any of it. . . . I didn't want to be public enemy number one!"

Finally, the biopics got around to chronicling the biggest gangster of them all: Al Capone. The 1959 production *Al Capone* stars an ignitable Rod Steiger in the title role that many gangster watchers had eagerly awaited. However, like *Dillinger,* the film is sluggishly chronological and lacking in insights. It tracks Capone's life from his arrival in Chicago, where he came to work for gangster Johnny Torrio as a bodyguard. Capone soon becomes Torrio's right-hand man and then his successor, topping his former mentor in criminal reach and riches.

The dialogue is more profuse than previous stories that borrow Capone's life, but Steiger often substitutes shouting for acting to portray Capone as a crazed killer. (Capone was indeed a killer but also a shrewd, stalwart businessman who ran a multimillion-dollar enterprise.) Reaching near burlesque effect at one point, Steiger bellows at his men through a mouthful of food: "Stop yellin' . . . you got no manners!" In another instance, when he's informed that the Saint Valentine's Day massacre has been successfully executed, he throws back his head and lets out a peal of diabolical laughter that's pure vaudeville.

The film mimics the classic *Scarface* more than it qualifies as a minted original. As the *New York Times* critic noted, the "brand new movie doesn't come up with anything new. . . . It isn't the devastating critique we might expect after all these years." The film merely wallows in the genre's icons: a rising gangster being fitted for a custom suit, a gum-snapping moll, period decor, flowing suds, flickering crossfire, exploding storefronts, and cigar-spoiled smiles.

For *Scarface,* Howard Hawks lent murder artistic articulation because on-screen blood was forbidden. The violence in *Al Capone,* given the advanced date, is illogically sanitized—especially while Steiger is playing for exaggerated threat. Gangsters are shot but die without blood or holes in their clothing where bullets would have penetrated. The first time we see blood, in fact, is at the film's end when Capone is beaten up by fellow inmates at Alcatraz.

Left, Rod Steiger stars in the long overdue but disappointing film debut of Capone—stripped of the usual censor-induced disguises. Here, Capone puts a choke hold on a reporter (Martin Balsam) who double-crosses the kingpin despite being on his payroll. *Al Capone* was among the string of churlish late-1950s films about dead gangsters.

The one fairly fresh inclusion by director Richard Wilson is the indictment of the Chicago reporter who was on Capone's payroll. The incident is based on facts about journalist Jack Lingle, who was killed in a LaSalle Street subway station by Capone's men. Martin Balsam as the serpentine journalist is the best bit in the film.

Once the seal on Capone's file was broken, though, screen adaptations about Capone and some of his henchmen kept reappearing—and continue to do so. One of the more authentic Capones was crafted by Ben Gazzara in Roger Corman's 1975 *Capone,* although as *Variety* pointed out, "It's hard to shoehorn developed drama between machine gun bullets." Other Capones (before De Niro's consummate match in 1987) include Neville Brand against Robert Stack's Eliot Ness in *The Scarface Mob* and a convincing Jason Robards in Corman's near tongue-in-cheek nostalgic gore-fest *The St. Valentine's Day Massacre* (1967).

Most of these Capone biographies, as well as the other biopics, focus on career highlights rather than craft a full-bodied approach to the man and his myth. (A notable exception was Ray Sharkey's 1989 portrayal, which is told in flashbacks with Capone as an enfeebled patient in a wheelchair trying to investigate the significance of his life.) Rather than use the modern license to investigate character pathology, including a gangster's familiarity with pimping, drug trafficking, and brutal jailhouses, only his violent deeds get a fresh outing.

Hollywood ravaged the once vital genre until finally formula took over and in some cases further transmuted into musical comedy. Comic gangsters, though, had first appeared in the silent era. During the classic heyday, Edward G. Robinson was a frequent spoofer of his own creation Rico Bandello. Bogart, too, created a funny gangster in 1955 with *We're No Angels* (remade in 1989 by De Niro). And George Raft pulled off the greatest parody yet when he recreated his trademark coin-flipping nonchalance in the comedy *Some Like It Hot* (1959).

But the film version of Damon Runyon's *Guys and Dolls* in 1955 finally had gangsters singing and dancing; it was the most benign image left to be presented. It's probably no coincidence that the stage play about the Roaring Twenties was finally put on the big screen toward the end of the 1950s, with little changed to reflect the modern era. In contrast, *West Side Story,* using contemporary gang members who sing and frolic in between rumbles, had a somber tone in 1961—its underlying theme too fresh and real to be droll.

SYNDICATE STARS

Genuine gangsters, on the other hand, were increasingly difficult to ignore. And few would have considered them amusing. They had been thriving since Prohibition in far-flung syndicates that reached markets around the world like multinational corporations. However, in the initial postwar climate, Hoover had held fast to his claim that the syndicate, Mob, or Mafia did not exist. Instead he focused on spies and threats to national security. His high-profile arrests of the era included Alger Hiss and the Rosenbergs, who were ultimately executed for espionage. Hoover also fed McCarthy a steady supply of thick files on Americans who had no criminal records but were considered subversives nonetheless. Hoover's denial of the Mob, however, was finally eroded by Senator Estes Kefauver.

Kefauver, a "liberal" southern Democrat who had aspirations for the White House, chaired a committee that sought to investigate organized crime and held hearings in 14 cities starting in March 1951. The hearings were televised nationally and created a media sensation as dozens of colorful mobsters were subpoenaed to testify, including the reputed racketeering kingpin Frank Costello. He was the heir to Lucky Luciano's throne, the undisputed "boss of bosses" in the post-Prohibition Underworld. The hoodlums fascinated the public with their lingo and their denials about being a part of an astonishing web of organized theft, prostitution, gambling, and labor racketeering. During Kefauver's hearings in New York City, 70 percent of the televisions (which were by then in 51 percent of American homes) were tuned in. That was twice the ratings of the World Series televised the previous fall. *Life* noted, "All along the television cable . . . [people] had suddenly gone indoors. . . . There in eerie half-light, looking at millions of small frosty screens, people sat as if charmed."[16]

Kefauver had made some impact on Hollywood, though. The proof came when he was asked to play a bit part in *The Enforcer,* which exploited the syndicate theme.[17] The film starred Humphrey Bogart—not as one of the newly unveiled syndicate boys—but as the immutable DA who hunts them down. It was a tired plot, and Bogart, however effective, was underused. The syndicate was just another flavor on the menu of sidelined criminals to order up for a story. The starring role was still largely reserved for cops and victims.

In 1955 Bogart discovered which character was better suited to his legacy and asked to be in the new film *The Desperate Hours.* The story tracks three escaped convicts who hold a suburban family hostage. The lead jailbird had been portrayed on Broadway by the bright new star Marlon Brando. Director William Wyler recalled that when he spoke to Bogart about the film, he assumed Bogart was looking to play the terrorized father—a character closer to his age. "Christ, no," Bogart argued. "Play that dull part? I want the gangster." They rewrote the part, but Bogart's biographer points out that having an older, cynical hoodlum "sapped the gutsy vitality" from the story. It lost a key subplot about the young gangster's hatred for his father, which had previously supplied a prickly tension to the standoff between thug and family man. (In 1990 the film was remade with Mickey Rourke in the lead, with just as lousy results.)

Not until Bogart resurrected his memorable Duke Mantee in 1955 did he find a fitting swan song for his gangster persona near the end of his career. (He died of throat cancer in 1957.) Acknowledging the new powerful medium of television, Bogart agreed to resurrect *The Petrified Forest* as a teleplay. Henry Fonda portrayed Alan Squire and Bogart's wife Lauren Bacall portrayed Gabby. Bogart admitted that he brought Duke back for pure nostalgia. "It's really an easy role. All I had to do was just sit there in the corner and look tough."[18]

Bogart's famed role of Roy Earle was also resurrected in 1955, but not by Bogart. It was halfheartedly repeated as *I Died a Thousand Times* with Jack Palance as Earle. As James Parish and Michael Pitts note, "Hollywood . . . just cannot seem to leave a good thing alone."

Finally, Bogart's syndicate-theme film, *The Enforcer,* was reshuffled in 1960 under the title *Murder, Inc.* In this version, the cops are DAs, and the victims include a nightclub dancer and her out-of-work musician husband. He's snared into Mob service because of a debt that's rapidly expanding with the "juice," or interest, owed. But, as usual, the *New York Times* noticed that the gangster character was the film's highlight. Newcomer Peter Falk as the hired killer Abe Reles gives an "amusingly vicious performance," notes the review. Falk is electrifying when "the water suddenly freezes in his eyes and he whips an icepick from his pocket and starts punching holes in someone's ribs."

Reles and other professional assassins were supervised as a distinctive group called Murder, Incorporated, in the 1930s by mobsters Louis (Lepke) Buchalter and Albert Anastasia. These killers-for-hire were made available to any of the major crime brokers in New York. The film, which has a subplot in which Reles rapes the musician's wife, provides a more arresting portrait of a killer's mind than had been seen onscreen for years.

Lepke himself is highlighted in *New York Confidential* (1955), which presents corporate-looking mobsters living normal lives except that their business is murder. Not until the modern era's *Lepke* (1974)—with Tony Curtis exaggerating the mobster's Jewishness—did Hollywood focus on Lepke's surrender to columnist Walter Winchell. Winchell, a close friend of Hoover, had arranged Lepke's voluntary arrest on federal charges. If he did, he was told that he would avoid being tried for murder under the jurisdiction of New York's crusading prosecutor Thomas Dewey. But the government reneged on the deal and tried Lepke in a New York court, which sent him to the electric chair.

As for the labor racketeering exposed by Kefauver's and other crime commissions, Hollywood kept its customary silence. Unions had been and remain as tricky for Hollywood's factories as they are for the rest of corporate America. In the 1950s, they were also considered for many critics a socialist invention that was only a short leap away from full-blown communism. (The struggling unions finally banded together in the mid-1950s to shore up their strength and formed the potent collective, the AFL-CIO. By the end of the 1950s, though, the teamsters were tossed out of the alliance on charges of persistent Mob influence.)

On the Waterfront (1954) is the exception and an extraordinary film for any age. It uses the syndicate theme as a rich backdrop to show off its storytelling muscle about lives forever altered by violent events. For a tale about mobsters, it is also a bittersweet chronicle of the redemptive powers of love and the leftover cobwebs of forfeited dreams. The film also benefited from having Marlon Brando and director Elia Kazan working together again as a team. Their first collaboration was in 1951 for Tennessee Williams's *A Streetcar Named Desire*. The upstart Brando mesmerized audiences as Stanley Kowalski and helped indoctrinate Hollywood to a revolutionary new approach to acting called "the Method." In this technique, an actor attempts to embody the traits of the person being portrayed rather than merely learning lines and pretending to project a character's persona. (Brando had been nominated for an Oscar for his Kowalski but lost to the old school's Humphrey Bogart.)

On the Waterfront is the story of Terry Malloy (Brando): a talented boxer turned reluctant bum then enlightened street warrior and finally modern urban hero. Each transformation is linked to his association with mobsters, including his older brother Charlie, whom one of his victims calls "a butcher in a camel hair coat."

Terry's promising boxing career is soured after he takes a dive at the Mob's request to pay off on a bet. He then resorts to running errands for the mobsters, who also serve as corrupt union bosses. The chief mobster and union leader is played by Lee J. Cobb as Johnny Friendly, whose real name is Michael Scilia. The other notable gangster in the film is Terry's brother Charlie (Rod Steiger) who's Friendly's right-hand man. After Terry admonishes Charlie for helping turn him into a bum, Charlie looks out for Terry but ironically gets himself killed trying to warn Terry to look out for himself. Charlie warned Terry not to talk to the Waterfront Crime Commission, which is investigating the Mob's corruption of the longshoremen's union.

As in *Angels with Dirty Faces,* the symbol of restoration is a gutsy priest named Father Barry (Karl Malden). He urges Terry and the other dockworkers (mostly Irish and Italian) to fight the corruption and take back their union and their lives. Terry is also pulled back toward the light by Edie Doyle (Eva Marie Saint), the sister of dockworker Joey Doyle. Terry had "set up" Joey to get punished for talking to the crime investigators, but Joey was pushed off a building and killed instead.

Unlike *Dead End*'s surreal environment, which had been created on a soundstage, *On the Waterfront* was shot on location on New York's waterfront. The gray soot, moaning freighters, and rooftop pigeon coops lend the film authenticity and equip a genre starved for realism with endless choices for the future. However, Kazan's other choices were criticized in *Sight and Sound* by director Lindsay Anderson. He said that the film gives no explanation for Friendly's power outside of personal charisma, making his Mob bosses invisible and irrelevant. Kazan, the son of Greek immigrants, was an artist who saw himself as "a working-class radical," wrote journalist David Halberstam. "He had no use for the conventions of American life." But Kazan—with the new American rebel Brando in front of his lens—chose to focus on the individual's struggle with personal alienation and triumph rather than on the labor struggle. The Mob and the union difficulties were the excuse for the characters to make moral choices; they were not the point of his film.

Unlike its soft investigation of syndicate politics, *On the Waterfront* was lauded for its gutsy display of bloodstained violence—given the still active censorship. Brutal battles with baseball bats and a dead Charlie hanging off a hook in an alley gave the film a grisly feel. The film also provides a brief glimpse into the youthful gangs that feed the Mob's adult ranks. Terry is a hero to boys who wear the Golden Warriors jackets until he starts talking to crime investigators.

A bloodied Terry Malloy (Marlon Brando), longshoreman and Mob enforcer, debuted a new type of brooding, vulnerable thug in *On the Waterfront*. Malloy and other early Brando characters presaged the youthful confusion and impulses that would accompany rock 'n' roll and Elvis Presley—the musical equivalent of Brando and his devotee James Dean.

The priest convinces Terry not to fight Johnny "like a hoodlum down here in the jungle." After he talks Terry out of using a gun to avenge his brother's death, the priest convinces Terry to stand up to Friendly with nothing more than conviction and a court of law. The film, thankfully, doesn't end in a dull courtroom, though. Like any great gangster film, it concludes with a violent showdown on the streets. Accompanied by Father Barry and Edie Doyle (who has become Terry's girlfriend), Terry challenges Friendly. But Friendly cowardly orders his boys to beat up Terry then stands by to watch the pummeling. Dozens of dockworkers whom Friendly controls look on helplessly but become increasingly sickened by the beating. One worker remarks, "That boy fights like he used to." The longshoremen ultimately refuse to work for Friendly unless Terry (who's blackballed from the union's work list) gets to work. Battered into a bloody pulp, Terry gets up from the pavement, with the priest's urging, and leads the men to the ship waiting to be unloaded. In the process, they walk past a barking Friendly and his idled goons.

Linking the film with its great gangster ancestors, the *New Yorker* review noted, "The sort of galvanic movie we used to get when Warner Brothers were riding herd on Al Capone."[19]

Noting the fresh take Brando brought to the gangster character, James Neibaur wrote, "Malloy is powerful and brutal, as well as sensitive, caring, and vulnerable. This diversity presents a more honest male image and thus creates a newer, more detailed example of screen toughness."[20] The role of the beleaguered but intense punk "who couldda been a contender" won Marlon Brando the Oscar this time. When he moans, "I couldda had class, been something more than a bum, which is what I am," he could have been speaking for any gangster since the start of the genre. But in 1953—after more than a dozen years of largely plastic, predictable thugs—Brando had reinvented the screen antihero. Although he had finally earned the respect of traditional Hollywood, Brando and his vulnerable machismo would have a profound impact on the next generation of actors, filmmakers, and consumers of movies.

"If Garfield was the virile young counterpart to Bogart's middle-aged tough guy . . . Brando's screen image was one of the child and the adult wrestling for control. Brando was capable of exhibiting strong macho bravado while through the same character displaying the inarticulate, mumbling insecurities of the awkward postadolescent male who feels trapped by the suppressive society that was America of the fifties."[21] His costar Eva Marie Saint described his demeanor throughout the film's production as "an open wound." And his biographer David Downing noted, "On screen he was opening up more than himself or a single character—he was laying bare an age."[22]

The age Brando was exposing was one beginning to question its values. In his now cultish role as Johnny in *The Wild One* (1953), Brando personified cool and signaled the coming of the counterculture. His Johnny is a leather-clad member of a motorcycle gang wandering the country instead of living in the suburbs. When asked by a "sensible" teenage girl what he's rebelling against, he asks her, "Whaddya got?" His flippant response exposed a general restlessness rather than any specific gripe that could be easily placated. Other rebels picked up Brando's lead, including James Dean, who openly worshipped Brando and his moody posturing. Dean, too, would be nurtured by Kazan. These rebels without a cause were the first popular symbols of the era's youthful rebellion—at least in the movies. For most Americans, this brave new world, or counterculture, would be as menacing to the public peace as any Underworld—and a lot harder to contain.

CHAPTER 7

The Sad Ballad of Bonnie and Clyde

> Some day they'll go down together.
> They'll bury them side by side;
> To few it'll be grief—
> To the law a relief—
> But it's death for Bonnie and Clyde.
>
> —Bonnie Parker, "The Story of Bonnie and Clyde," 1934

As the 1950s lumbered along, the spirit of rebellion and the stirrings of a counterculture kept gathering momentum. On one front were the bohemians and Beats of the postwar period: intellectuals, artists, and the "swinging group of new American men intent on joy." That's how Jack Kerouac explained the offbeat inhabitants of Greenwich Village (once including Marlon Brando) to the suspicious "establishment" in 1959. Kerouac had become the unofficial spokesman for the Beats by writing—and living—*On the Road*. His now classic novel aptly captures the disillusionment of postwar America, urging the pursuit of the unbounded and the unrehearsed. Kerouac traced the term *Beat* to the word *beatific*—its expression meant to counter the staleness of a society increasingly hung up on conformity and resentful of self-expression. Soon a columnist coined the word "beatniks," and they grew in fame as goateed artists and musicians who spouted poetry and wore sunglasses at night.

By the mid-1950s, rock 'n' roll presented another front shouting about restlessness and discontent. As much as Allen Ginsberg's Beat poem "Howl" assailed traditional sensibilities, Little Richard's wail in "Tutti Frutti" assaulted mainstream senses. The Beats had embraced the Negro's jazz for their musical core, and rock 'n' roll built on blues rhythms, blending them with other influences to create a revolution in music. Like the Beat movement, rock 'n' roll had political overtones—encouraging races to mix and tap each other's cultures. However, society was increasingly agitated over the Supreme Court's 1954 order to desegregate. A civil rights storm was gathering that threatened to alter centuries of racial separatism.

It was the white, southern-bred Elvis Presley who became the first musical artist to do for rock 'n' roll what Brando accomplished at the box office: bring about popular acceptance. Although Presley first frightened the established sectors with his black man's growl and swiveling hips, he soon proved to be more ambitious than rebellious. Like Brando, Presley eventually went Hollywood and became hard to distinguish from other matinee idols. Brando and Presley may have been tamed, but the impulses that spawned them continued to grow more fierce.

Hollywood discovered the emerging youth market in the late 1950s but depicted beatniks and rock 'n' roll followers as juvenile delinquents and kooky threats to adolescent minds. Even when teenage angst was featured, it was seen as a craze to be tolerated. In the end, the films ultimately reiterated more traditional values.

Like any other crossroad in American history, a combination of forces changed society in the 1950s. However, change didn't seem tangible and irreversible until the 1960s. Many historians trace the violent end of the nation's innocence to the assassination of the young President Kennedy in 1963. Soon afterward, the escalation of the war in Vietnam further aggravated the nervous temperament of the era. Vietnam galvanized disparate groups over a common gripe: those who merely wanted to question authority suddenly became political bedfellows with those who advocated counterrevolution.

By the mid 1960s, the Beats and other original counterculture thinkers evolved into the next generation of social activists, including Bob Dylan, a disciple of folk philosopher Woody Guthrie. Dylan's message in 1965 prophetically warned that "The Times They Are a Changin'." His message and much of his protest music quickly got him labeled an anarchist, but mainstream commentators also described him as an astute poet who wrote "weirdly compelling songs."

It was an era of explosive action for black power, gay and lesbian rights, the women's movement, the plight of Native Americans, the battle to save the environment, experiments in Eastern religions, drugs, sex, and the comeback of Marxist philosophy. Just as the teasing lyric of John Lennon's song "Revolution" noted, "You say you want a revolution? Oh, yeah . . . we all want to change the world." By the so-called Summer of Love of 1967—the same summer that the urban ghettos went up in flames—love-ins were mandatory events for anyone trying to stay hip. For a subculture populated by flower children and hippies, these "happenings" were an open celebration of an alternative lifestyle.

Nineteen sixty-seven was a watershed year for America and for America's dream factory. For most of the 1960s, Hollywood had occupied itself with farce and escapist cinema, doing its best to ignore the growing melee outside the theaters. However, Hollywood released two films in 1967 that signaled that times were changing for filmmakers as well: *The Graduate* and *Bonnie and Clyde.* In particular, *Bonnie and Clyde* touched off a social and cultural brawl. It used the gangster genre's best conventions and a story from the 1930s to comment on the tumult of the 1960s. In particular, the element that most reflected *Bonnie and Clyde*'s modern release date was Bonnie. Perhaps influenced by the clamorous women's movement, Bonnie became a full-fledged partner in crime and the audience's surrogate within the gang.

But the character and essence of Bonnie Parker had appeared on-screen before. She had a rich cinematic legacy that revealed as much about past irritants as Dunaway's Bonnie disclosed about the late 1960s. Previous Bonnies had frequently matched the concerns of the times in which they had debuted. Over the years, she had been a depression *frau,* a noir home wrecker, and a grisly aberration bred of Cold War neurosis.

DEADLY IS THE FEMALE

Women gangsters have been around since the genre's start—breaking up the monotony of the men's club and giving the flashy molls some screen company. In the 1920s, molls were occasionally promoted to lady mobsters, channeling their newfound aggressiveness onto traditionally masculine turf. (After all, Amelia Earhart made headlines in the 1920s as the daredevil aviatrix who was as bold as the male fliers.)

In the classic period, *Madame Racketeer* (1932) featured a con woman who marries rich to get her hands on a fortune but is easily exposed and packed off to jail. She's a classic gold digger with a twist: a maternal impulse to provide money for her daughters, who may not find homes during the depression. The superb *Blondie Johnson* (1933), starring Joan Blondell, is another woman's depression choice between acting as her boss's mistress to keep her job or becoming a gangster. She chooses crime and prospers handsomely in the rackets, wearing trousers and barking orders at men.[1] The film differs from the usual approach by showing the choice to become a hoodlum was hers. She wasn't seduced into the life by a boyfriend; nor is she restricted to being a "hostess" (a screen euphemism for prostitute).

Even Warner Brothers' publicity teased that Blondell was getting even for all the molls she had endured. It advertised: "She's been slapped and cheated . . . but throughout the string of pictures in which she has appeared, a man has dominated her. . . . As Blondie Johnson Joan not only refuses to allow the male to govern her, but she rules that species with a hand of iron."[2]

Unfortunately, as the screen morality of the 1930s dictated, Blondie reforms before the curtain goes up, admitting her love for a man and vowing to live a normal life. Unlike her male counterparts, Blondie doesn't go to jail or the electric chair but is

Blondie Johnson stars Joan Blondell as a criminal boss who finally comes to her senses and gives up the gangster life for the love of a good man named Curley (Chester Morris). Despite the sappy 1933 ending, the plucky Blondie is the ancestor of all gun-toting female gangsters who followed.

sent back home to be conquered by domesticity. Like *Little Caesar* and *The Public Enemy,* the ending does little to erase the image of a gun-toting, able-minded gangster, though. This one just happened to have a higher voice.

In Fritz Lang's superb film *You Only Live Once* (1937)—loosely based on Bonnie and Clyde's legend—Joan (Sylvia Sidney) is a loyal wife but a reluctant accomplice. The film is a wholly sympathetic portrayal of the infamous couple but heavily distorts the truth to accomplish the task. Eddie Taylor (Henry Fonda) is a petty thief who gets embroiled in a bank robbery and murder, for which he's framed and sent to prison. When a friendly priest approaches Eddie with news of a pardon, he panics and accidentally shoots the priest. Then Eddie escapes from prison and goes on the lam with Joan. She's forced to have a baby in the woods but leaves the nameless infant with her sister to stay with the fugitive Eddie. Eventually she commits crime herself. Near the Canadian border, the two are finally ambushed and gunned down by police. The film stresses the isolation of the couple and their star-crossed fate—like a depression-era Romeo and Juliet—rather than focusing on the gang mentality, which the genre prefers.

"The screenplay hits hard, its social criticism giving dimension to the study of two hounded, lost souls."[3] The film even points out a deformity surrounding capital punishment, as Eddie's electrocution is postponed until he undergoes a transfusion to save his life. But in a scene more typical of the film's delicate moments of meaning, Eddie brings the pregnant Joan a can of milk, which is leaking profusely after being shot up in a gun battle with police.

The early 1940s offered a few uninspired gangster stories with women in the lead roles. In *Lady Scarface* (1941), Judith Anderson portrays a gang leader named Slade who masterminds several spectacular robberies and murders. But her impulse toward crime is rooted in her Chaney-like rancor for having a repulsively scarred face. Rather than explore her character, the film tracks the cop's effort to hunt her down and his relationship with his girlfriend. Another entry was *Lady Gangster* (1942), with Faye Emerson, that tells the tale of a small-town girl who moves to the big city and falls in with the wrong crowd. But the film never lives up to its title.

The debut of film noir provided a veritable outbreak of cunning criminal women with malignant motives and fiendish talents. The sirens and fearsome black widows became the most visible "gangsters" within these gothic stories. These women pose the most chilling threats to male protagonists who become their unfortunate lovers, unwitting accomplices, and frequent victims. Whereas most of the films of the classic era largely ignored women, noir comes to see them as the most fearsome predators, aggressively blaming them for the spread of evil. Increasingly, women were shown to be armed and dangerous—a quirk even the hard-boiled Poppy in *Scarface* was never permitted. She only got the orgasmic thrill of watching her man "spit" with a machine gun.

A noir version that included a Bonnie-like character was Nicholas Ray's much acclaimed *They Live by Night* (1948). But Cathy O'Donnell's character, Keechie, is pushed to the sidelines so that the film can focus on the Clyde-like Bowie (Farley Granger)—"the unlucky hounded man, who, given half a chance, might have gone legitimate."[4] After he consorts with hardened bank robbers, he ultimately becomes the most hunted fugitive among them. The film is based on the best-seller *Thieves like Us,* by Edward Anderson, which used Bonnie and Clyde's legend for inspiration.

A better example of a noir Bonnie appeared in *Gun Crazy* (1950)—originally titled *Deadly Is the Female.* The film, however, takes its title more seriously than it does the causes of Laurie Starr's gun fetish. After Peggy Cummins's character hooks up with Bart (John Dall)—another sharpshooter like herself—they marry and go on a crime spree that eventually gets them hunted and killed. She has no past, although she's responsible for their escalating crime. However, the film traces his evolution from reform school to armed robbery and highlights his preference to wound whereas she aims to kill.

Other spotty roles reflected the radical change that finally spoiled noir, as the femmes fatales of Raymond Chandler are reduced to the crude bimbos of Mickey Spillane, "for whom women counted as little more than animals," notes David Halberstam.

Among the biopics that invaded screens of the late 1950s, Bonnie finally moved into the spotlight with *The Bonnie Parker Story* (1958). Unfortunately, the film shows her as just another loony without a cause—a mutant mobster with few human shadings. This Bonnie (Dorothy Provine) sprays her enemies with a vibrating tommy gun and becomes so skilled at planning and executing bank jobs that when Chuck Darrow (a thinly disguised Buck Barrow) is killed, she takes over as gang leader. His brother Guy (Clyde), her spineless lover, does little more than sheepishly accept the power transfer.[5] As John McCarty puts it, "Provine's cigar-smoking, pistol packing Bonnie is clearly the deadlier of the male/female duo—an attractive blond package on the outside but a hardened killer beneath." Eventually the Texas Rangers set a trap for her, killing her and her gang in their car. McCarty calls the film "an exciting, fast-paced little production with a nice hard edge." It was modestly successful and was released as part of a double bill with the other churlish biopic from American International Pictures, *Machine Gun Kelly*.

By 1967, when a new Bonnie was unveiled, Hollywood and audiences were ready for the full-blooded but nuanced character that Faye Dunaway brought to the screen. This version was pieced together by first-time screenwriters David Newman and Robert Benton from newspaper accounts, police reports, biographies, and bittersweet family memoirs. Benton was born in 1932 in the same Texas region that the notorious couple called home, and he absorbed the vivid tales that lingered after they died (when he was two years old). Dunaway's Bonnie becomes a timely blend of fresh bits of reality and highly stylized doses of mythology. And like all superb Hollywood gangsters before her, Dunaway's memorable Bonnie is also a matter of blessed timing.

By 1967 some of the essential tenets of the women's movement had been absorbed by popular culture. By then "the feminine mystique" was the target. That was how Betty Friedan, one of the founding mothers of the women's movement, had described the phenomenon that afflicted a generation of women hemmed in by the 1950s. Once women had been hustled out of the postwar factories (losing the independence that being Rosie the Riveter had brought them), they were urged to focus on getting married and raising families. They were also encouraged to be strangely mercurial, breathy, and tentative—equal parts Donna Reed, Marilyn Monroe, and Doris Day. This model supplanted the capable career women embodied by Katharine Hepburn and Bette Davis a generation earlier. Rejection of conformity brought harsh punishment. (Peggy Cummins is shot by her screen husband before police get to her.) Other forms of discipline included social banishment, as revealed in the runaway best-seller of 1956, *Peyton Place.* The women who defied the social order—either through promiscuity or careerism—became victims of cruel gossip and public ostracism. Halberstam notes that the novel's staggering success pointed to a truth straining the seams of a tight-jacketed society.

But by 1967 enough people were primed and ready to accept Bonnie as a precarious mix of honor and greed—the same attributes that realistically create male gang-

Dorothy Provine stars as the female half of the infamous depression-era bank-robbing couple in *The Bonnie Parker Story.* The 1958 film offers one of the genre's rare female leads but turns her into a cartoonish sexpot who knows how to work men and machine guns with equal aplomb.

sters. Depending on one's age, politics, or imagination, the new braless Bonnie was either an uppity hillbilly who failed to grasp her limitations or a dust bowl Joan of Arc. Her reception may also have represented a backlash against the women's movement, as we're finally given the spectacle of a maverick female being annihilated by bullets for a finale. (The death of Bonnie-like characters had always been daintily tended to off-screen and never graphically depicted, but equality brought Bonnie a death as bloodstained as Clyde's.) Although the real Bonnie had been so bloodied more than 40 years earlier, the moviegoing public had been considered unready to witness her death until 1967. Its modern showing, although a step closer to historical accuracy, was quickly labeled a festering symptom of 1960s violence and a symbol of the breakdown of traditional women's roles. Bonnie remains an interesting character for any age, but cropping up again in 1967—in the midst of the cultural fray—her story was considered groundbreaking.

CLASSIC OUTLAWS IN THE AGE OF AQUARIUS

The 1967 version of Bonnie and Clyde's saga opens with a credits sequence featuring family photos of the real couple and ending with black-and-white shots of Beatty and Dunaway with recaps of their characters' lives before they meet. The stark pictures remind us that they're familiar, folksy, and already ill-fated. The first scene shows an extreme close-up of lipstick going on the sensuous mouth of Bonnie Parker (Dunaway). Naked, she sprawls across her bed and looks bored and restless. (She is filmed through the bars of the bed to heighten the sense of confinement.) Still nude, she stands at the window and notices a young man fiddling with her mama's car. She yells out, and when he looks up, she notices his fashionable suit and charming grin. She races down to the street, hastily buttoning up her dress, and begins flirting with him as they walk down main street. After he tells her that he's an ex-convict, she eagerly asks him what armed robbery "feels like." When he wavers, she calls him "a faker." To get back her interest, he shows her his gun, which she strokes sensually. After she challenges his "guts" to use it, he disappears to rob the local grocer. Returning in a stolen car, he invites her to escape with him. As they exchange names, the banjo music kicks in, and their adventure toward infamy begins. As Clyde (Warren Beatty) speeds out of town, Bonnie is mauling him with kisses, forcing him to veer off into a field and push her away. "I ain't much of a lover boy," he tells a humiliated Bonnie. But he keeps her piqued by giving her a choice: a dismal future in West Texas as a waitress or an unpredictable, reckless adventure with him.

While at target practice in the yard of an abandoned farmhouse, they're startled by the farmer who used to own it before it was repossessed. His family waits by the roadside in a car loaded down with their worldly belongings. Clyde instinctively shoots up the bank's foreclosure sign and invites the farmer to take a shot. The farmer hands his black helper the gun to take aim. When Clyde finally introduces himself and Bonnie, he proudly proclaims, "We rob banks!"

Soon a nervous Clyde rushes into a bank to hold it up, leaving Bonnie in the car. The bank is deserted except for a listless man who dryly tells Clyde that it was shut down by the government three weeks ago and the money is gone. A frustrated Clyde then shoots up the bank's windows for simple revenge and shouts at a wildly amused Bonnie, "We got $1.98 and you're laughing!"

At the next confrontation, a more desperate Clyde waves a gun around at a grocer while two bags are stuffed with food and supplies. Then, from behind, a butcher attacks Clyde with a meat cleaver. Clyde wounds the old man, wrestles free, and flees. Stunned, he shouts at Bonnie, "Why'd he try to kill me? I didn't want to hurt him!" Soon the bandaged butcher identifies Clyde, picking out his mug shot from police files.

At a run-down gas station, they meet a slow-witted attendant named C. W. Moss (Michael J. Pollard), whom they recruit as their driver and mechanic. This time Bonnie describes them as bank robbers. Rather than recoil in fear, C. W.—a veteran of reform schools—grins and joins them.

At their next job, an armed Bonnie joins Clyde for the bank holdup, leaving C. W. in the getaway car. Clyde announces the stickup so quietly that nobody reacts at first. Then he grows more confident and takes control. They flee the bank with a bag full of money, but an inexperienced C. W. has parallel-parked the car and wastes time maneuvering out of the space. Amid alarms and shouting witnesses, a panicked Clyde shoots a man who jumps onto the car's running board. A close-up shows the man shot through the eye.

While hiding out in a movie theater, Clyde berates C. W. for leading him to kill a man; Bonnie remains engrossed in the glossy musical on-screen. Back in their motel room, she's humming the film's song, "We're in the Money," puffing on a cigarette, and trying on jewelry. A worried Clyde sits her down and explains that he's known to police, but she can still flee unharmed. She vows to stay with him, and they start to make love. In an earlier scene, Clyde pretended to be asleep to avoid Bonnie's ideas about intimacy. Ultimately, he cannot go through with it, rejects her, and buries his face in the pillow. "At least I ain't a liar. I told you I wasn't no lover boy," he hollers. She smiles to signal that it's all right; there's more to their union than physical attraction.

Soon Clyde's older brother Buck (Gene Hackman) and his prudish wife Blanche (Estelle Parsons) arrive on the scene. The couples take photographs of each other, and Bonnie grabs a gun and poses by the car with one of Clyde's cigars jammed in her mouth. Blanche keeps carping at their shenanigans. With Buck and Blanche along, the group heads for Missouri, where nobody is looking for Clyde. On the road, the lead car contains a jovial Clyde and a talkative Buck telling a funny story. The women are locked in silence in the car behind them. The two couples, along with C. W., rent a house, but soon Bonnie demands of Clyde, "Don't you ever just want to be alone with me?" Fearing a request for lovemaking, Clyde runs off complaining of hunger. When groceries are delivered to the house, an abrupt Bonnie makes the delivery boy suspicious.

Later, while everyone is listening to one of Bonnie's poems, Clyde interrupts when he spots police coming up the driveway. The men and Bonnie go on the offensive, shooting out the windows with shotguns, submachine guns, and handguns. The hysterical Blanche, along with her yapping dog, runs into the yard trotting in a circle with her hands in the air and shrieking. Buck shoots a policeman before Clyde gets everyone in the car and plows through the police jam. Finding the ranting Blanche on the street about a block away, they pull her into the car.

There's bedlam inside the car as it careens out of town. Bonnie is ferociously bellowing at Blanche. Blanche starts begging Buck to go home, but he explains that he killed a man and is in too deep to go back. She resumes her wailing, and Bonnie cuts loose again, prompting Clyde to scream at Bonnie to shut up. She makes him stop the car, and the two stalk off into a field to have a row. She wants to dump Buck and Blanche, but Clyde insists that they're family and they stay. "You're just like your brother . . . a big, ignorant, uneducated hillbilly. Except the only special thing about you is your peculiar ideas about lovemaking, which is no lovemaking at all," she complains. They quickly regret their remarks, and the getaway resumes.

Back on the road, they laugh as they read in the newspaper about their exploits. Clyde's mood darkens, however, when the papers give the Barrow gang credit for bank robberies in New Mexico, Chicago, and Indiana—places he and Bonnie have never been. While they're stopped on a dirt road, a Texas Ranger confronts the group. Clyde, who had walked off, sneaks up from behind and shoots near the lawman to startle him. Ranger Frank Hamer (Denver Pyle) is soon tied up, and the angry Clyde vows to kill him to discourage other bounty-hunting lawmen. But Bonnie gets the idea to take Hamer's picture and send it to the newspapers. She says the snapshots will show Hamer "with the Barrow gang . . . and all of us just as friendly as pie." She drapes herself on him while holding a gun, and Clyde plays with his badge and tells him how ordinary folks are protecting them. "You're supposed to be protecting them from us and they protecting us from you. That don't make sense, do it?" Clyde asks, chuckling.

Warren Beatty's Clyde Barrow and Faye Dunaway's Bonnie Parker take aim at the genre and the soothing notion that gangsters are monsters invented by the movies. Beatty and Dunaway startlingly portray them as "jus' folks" who become deadly by chance rather than heartless choice.

Bonnie poses for another shot, this time kissing Hamer on the mouth. His eyes widen and darken with fury then he spits in her face. She backs away, horrified, while Clyde goes berserk. After Buck and C. W. calm Clyde down, they put the still-bound Hamer in a boat and float him out into the middle of a nearby stream.

The next bank robbery reveals a more polished performance and a controlled Clyde, announcing, "This is the Barrow gang." He stops to ask one man, "Is that your money or the bank's?" After the answer, Clyde says soothingly, "You keep it then." Moss is outside as a lookout, and Blanche waits uneasily in the backseat. When the alarm sounds, Bonnie, Clyde, and Buck flee, although Clyde shoots and wounds a guard along the way. Amid the familiar banjo boogie, the Barrow gang are chased out of town by two cars that exchange gunfire with the gang.

Meanwhile, droll scenes are edited into the chase sequence showing witnesses later getting their pictures taken and revealing their harrowing experiences. One cop describes what it was like "staring square into the face of death." The farmer whom Clyde refused to rob says earnestly, "They did right by me. And I'm bringing me and Mrs. Flowers to their funeral."

At the Oklahoma border, Clyde zooms over the state line, and the police turn back, unable to continue the pursuit. In the middle of a meadow, Clyde divvies up the money, noting, "Ain't much is it? Well, times is hard." He gives everybody an equal share, except Blanche, who soon demands a cut of her own. "I earned my share. I coulda gotten killed same as everybody. And I'm wanted by the law same as everybody." When Clyde relents and gives her money, Bonnie storms off. She tells Clyde that if he's going to start spreading money among kinfolk, her family could use some.

Next the gang steals another car from a farmhouse where a couple is necking on the front porch. The young man and his girlfriend jump into her car to chase after the thieves. With flimsy conviction to tear "those punks" apart when he catches them, the young man is easily talked into turning around. When he does, a playful Clyde turns and stalks them. (The real Clyde said of the incident, "We'd been chased so much, it was a new experience to start chasing someone else.")

A frightened Eugene Grizzard (Gene Wilder) and Thelma Davis (Evans Evans) are forced off the road and put in the gang's new ride. Bonnie tells them, "Don't be scared. You're just folks, just like us." Soon they're laughing at Buck's story and sharing take-out food with the gang. Eugene gushes, "You're grand hosts." But once he reveals he's an undertaker, Bonnie's face tightens, and she orders the couple dumped by the side of the road.

Bonnie soon runs off, leaving a frantic Clyde running up and down a cornfield looking for her. He finds her and tries to soothe her, but she cries out, "I wanna see my mama!" In a wistful scene seemingly shot through gauze for a surreal, nostalgic effect, dozens of members of the Parker clan gather in a field for a picnic. They show Bonnie the scrapbook full of the couple's exploits, but her mother maintains a forlorn silence. When asked about future plans, Clyde grins and says, "At this point, we ain't headed to nowhere. We just runnin' from." When he tries to reassure Bonnie's mother that they intend to settle down close to home, she speaks with a frankness that startles them. "You best keep runnin', Clyde Barrow, and you know it." Then she bids her "baby" good-bye, leaving Bonnie stricken and mute.

Back on the road, the group settles in for the night in motel cabins, and C. W. and Blanche go into town for food. A patron notices a gun jammed in C. W.'s pants and notifies the sheriff. In the middle of the night, the cops knock on Buck and Blanche's cabin door, prompting Blanche to cover Buck's mouth and shout, "They're next door!" Soon the motel entrance is crawling with police and a military tank. They begin shooting into Bonnie and Clyde's room, and the battle begins. Bonnie shoots a machine gun out the window, and C. W. reaches for a grenade.

Hiding behind a mattress, Buck and Blanche try to cross the yard, but Buck is shot in the head. Finally, the group blasts their way to the white sedan, and Clyde races past the police armada. Inside the car, chaos and panic are mixed with wails and spattered blood. Clyde keeps a stony silence, his sweaty face and dead-eye stare focused on the road.

In a field lit only by headlights, C. W. studies the rambling, deranged Buck lying on the ground and tells Clyde, "Half his head's blown off." Blanche's eyes have been cut by flying glass when bullets shattered the car's windows. On the next morning, the war begins anew, and their makeshift campsite is besieged by gunfire. This time Clyde is shot in the arm, and they're forced to bail out of the car. Clyde, Bonnie, and C. W. crawl into the woods, leaving the car an open target for the frenzied posse, who keep firing upon it. The gunmen whoop like movie Indians and shout with delight until the car explodes into flames. Blanche, who stays at Buck's side, keeps begging him, "Daddy, don't die!" He lies in a bloody heap as the posse keeps plugging shots into him.

As Clyde, Bonnie, and C. W. wade through a nearby river, Bonnie is shot in the shoulder. Clyde carries her to the opposite bank and then goes to search for a car to steal. They drive until daybreak, when they come to a colony of homeless people liv-

Bonnie (Faye Dunaway) is shot in the shoulder as she and C. W. (Michael J. Pollard, left) and Clyde (Warren Beatty) flee another assault by zealous lawmen. Bonnie is humanized and glamorized in the 1967 *Bonnie and Clyde,* a film as much about social ostracism in vexing times as it was about the slain Texas couple.

ing near a pond. C. W. is at the wheel and a bloodied and badly wounded Bonnie and Clyde are slumped over each other in the backseat. C. W. asks the strangers, "Spare us some drinking water?" A crowd gathers around to stare until a few recognize the notorious couple. A shabbily dressed man brings C. W. water, and another reaches through the window to touch Clyde and confirm that the legend is made of flesh.

C. W. takes them to his father's homestead. Daddy Moss (Dub Taylor) agrees to help nurse Bonnie and Clyde back to health but in private slaps his son for bringing them home. While Bonnie and Clyde regain their strength, Hamer, the Texas Ranger, visits Blanche in the prison hospital. Both her eyes are bandaged, so that she can't recognize him from the taunting episode. He tricks her into identifying C. W., who has been the unknown gang member until now.

In a melancholy scene, Bonnie reads her latest poem to Clyde, entitled, "The Story of Bonnie and Clyde." She says that she's going to send the ode (that ends with their deaths) to the press. Rather than be mortified, Clyde smiles and says with wonder, "You told my story! You made me somebody they gonna remember!" They start to make love and this time succeed. He tells her he wants to marry her, and she asks if they could start anew, would he do things differently? "First off, I wouldn't live in the same state we do our jobs," he says matter-of-factly. Bonnie turns away in disappointment, realizing that Clyde is doomed to be a thug, and she is, too, as long as she remains with him.

Meanwhile, C. W.'s father secretly meets with Hamer and then tells his son about the deal he has cut if C. W. betrays Bonnie and Clyde to the law. The always meek C. W. at first tries to defend the couple but is bullied by his father into doing what he's told. As planned, C. W. goes into town with Bonnie and Clyde and disappears inside a store. Bonnie goes looking for him while an unwitting sheriff pulls up next to Clyde. Clyde backs the car out and goes after Bonnie, calling out, "Gladys Jean" to signal trouble. As they speed off, C. W. grins from behind a curtained window at their escape.

On the road out of town, while casually munching on a pear, Clyde notices Daddy Moss flagging them down and standing by his disabled truck. As Clyde steps out of the car, the editing cuts quicken. A flock of birds flutters out of the trees, and Moss dives under the truck. Quick close-ups of Bonnie and Clyde show them exchange mournful looks; they understand the moment's meaning. Framed by a medium shot that shows Clyde standing not far from the open driver's side door and Bonnie seated in the passenger side, a fusillade of bullets unload into their bodies and their white sedan. The barrage lasts for 35 seconds. Bonnie's body rocks from the dozens of rounds penetrating her torso, and Clyde gyrates gently on the ground in slow motion. Soon his body rolls over in the dirt, and Bonnie's slumps out of the car, her hair brushing the ground. The camera lingers as they lay in their death poses, motionless and silent. Then a half dozen men pop up from the heavy brush across the road, still clutching their firearms, and creep across the road to assess the damage. The last camera shot is seen through the car window with a bullet hole smack in the center of the frame. In silence, Hamer and his gunmen gather to stare at their victims before the scene fades to black and the film ends.

POSTMORTEM ON *BONNIE AND CLYDE*

On its release, *Bonnie and Clyde* was immediately vilified by most major critics and enthusiastically embraced by young moviegoers. The ruckus ultimately spilled over into popular music, fashion, and dinner conversations. The film grossed more than $20 million in its first year—impressive for the time.[6] Its success prompted one observer to note, "this sleeper blew up Hollywood like an atomic bomb."[7] *Time* magazine put the film, which it deemed a "cult phenomenon," on its front cover—the first film ever to earn the spot.[8] Among the condemnations, the film was lambasted for putting pretty people in the title roles of gruesome gangsters and for contorting history. A war among critics battled over whether the film was a landmark piece of contemporary art or an abomination of Hollywood excess.

Bosley Crowther of the *New York Times* called the film "a cheap piece of bold-faced slapstick that treats the hideous depredations of that sleazy, moronic pair as though they were as full of fun and frolic as the jazz-age cut-ups in *Thoroughly Modern Millie.*" Andrew Sarris fired back, accusing Crowther of using the newspaper's pulpit for a "personal vendetta" rooted in his fear of a breakdown of law and order, particularly among young people.[9] Page Cook wrote, "There is evil in the tone of the writing, acting and direction of this film, the calculated effect of which is to incite in the young the delusion that armed robbery and murder are mere 'happenings.' "[10]

On the other side, the *New Yorker*'s Pauline Kael lauded the film's artistry and unconventionalism, noting it "put the sting back into death." She viewed it as a welcome reverse of Hollywood's obsession with spoof that had dominated the screens of recent years. She compared it to *The Public Enemy,* which also unnerved audiences when it reminded us that "we don't need to pretend we're interested only in the falsely accused." Such films have appeal, she claims, because they tell a truth about crime's connection to all of us; the dirty little secret that we're attracted to crime, whether or not we ever break the law. "The gleam in Cagney's eye told its own story," adds Kael, and we kept our eyes on Cagney, despite the moral browbeating in 1931 that told us to look away.

Arguably the film's most surprising defender was the Reverend Anthony Schillaci of the National Catholic Office for Motion Pictures (formerly the Legion of Decency). He wrote, "The banality of their evil, compounded of boredom and meaningless lives, inhuman landscapes and the social disorder of the Depression, makes Bonnie and Clyde tragic folk heroes with whom we can identify. They are not brilliant plotters who mastermind fascinating robberies, nor are they powerful rulers of a worldwide conspiracy. Simple Americans of their age, they careen through their career of violence, partial victims of sensational journalism, totally the prey of their own innocence." He even thought "their death is one in which the avengers emerge even guiltier than their victims."[11] His group highly recommended the film.

But Charles Thomas Samuels pointed to Siegfried Kracauer's book *From Caligari to Hitler,* which links movies with a nation's mentality—a sort of "national fever chart." Samuels wrote, "In the thirties in Germany, the disease was authoritarianism; in the sixties in America, it is anarchy." He accuses *Bonnie and Clyde* of further encouraging such chaos.[12] Even so, he noted, "Those who riot against conditions in the Negro ghetto or the war in Vietnam can claim precisely the moral validation for their acts which the Barrow Gang so conspicuously lacks."[13]

Although the film's ending has become famous for portraying the bloody ambush of Bonnie and Clyde, it shows the least blood flow in the film. Its fame owes more to its extraordinary direction and inventive editing. The final scene took three days to shoot with four cameras and two weeks to edit. The number of bullets reportedly used on the real couple vary from as few as 167 to sensational claims of 1,000.[14] Hamer insisted they tried to fire back. Other witnesses say the officers started firing the moment the couple was in shooting range.

Carlos Clarens notes that the slow-motion killing had been used before, most notably in Don Siegel's *The Killers* (1964). But Penn used it to orchestrate an entire siege on a man's body rather than just a fleeting glimpse of one bullet's momentary damage. "I wanted the two kinds of death: Clyde's to be rather like a ballet, and Bonnie's to have the physical shock," Penn explains.[15] "We were trying to change the character of death, to make their deaths more legendary than real."

In reality Bonnie and Clyde's death was certainly gruesome—among the most chilling aspects was the fascination of ordinary folks with the couple's fate. The coroner said that when he arrived at the field two hours after the killing, Bonnie's dress was nearly cut off her back along with most of her hair. The crowds were picking up the empty shells as keepsakes; some were reportedly digging the casings out of nearby trees. Bonnie's mother was told by a man who had been at the scene that he had to stop someone from trying to cut off Clyde's ear to preserve in alcohol.

Emma Parker recalls that the Arcadia, Louisiana, undertaker's parlor was a back room in a furniture store. Curiosity seekers had busted out the plate glass windows and were filing past the naked corpses. The undertaker told her that he had to squirt embalming fluid at the crowds to keep them back. As people did for Dillinger and Floyd, tens of thousands came to both funerals—held on opposite ends of Dallas.

She also believes the law wanted to kill the couple rather than capture them alive. Emma said "the kids" came to see their families nearly every night in the months preceding their deaths. "All the law needed to do was to watch our houses. . . . But, who am I to tell the police how they could have captured my daughter and Clyde? They got them in the end."[16]

The fascination with Bonnie and Clyde, dead or alive, notes Penn, is rooted in America's fascination with violence. "We're living in a society of violence. . . . I find myself forced to explain it . . . gangsters were all-powerful when I was young; I went to war at eighteen years of age, then there was Korea, and now Vietnam."[17]

LEGEND OR WHITE LIES?

The most illogical criticism was of the film's artistic license in mixing fact with legend, because gangster films have rarely had anything to do with historical accuracy. Samuels accused the lead characters of being unrealistically sympathetic whereas their foes were overtly sinister. Hamer is shown with a "devilish mustache and, in the death scene, wears a black shirt," in contrast to Bonnie's white dress.[18] (In reality she was wearing a red dress when she was killed.) No doubt Hamer had been enhanced with qualities of G-man Melvin Purvis, who relentlessly pursued Dillinger and Pretty Boy Floyd. Fellow lawmen accused Purvis of shooting first and figuring out the justification later. (Purvis committed suicide in 1960, using the same gun he had used on Floyd.)[19] Although the real Barrow gang never met and taunted Hamer, the couple was notorious for kidnapping cops and taking them for joyrides before releasing them unharmed—sometimes with travel money to get back home.

The filmmakers omitted the horrible accident that crushed and burned Bonnie's leg near the end of her life—some would argue to guard the image of a pretty, unscathed female antihero. If the film had delved into this episode, however, Bonnie and Clyde would have appeared even more compassionate. When Clyde crashed their car, it rolled over, burst into flames, and pinned Bonnie's leg underneath. She could not be taken to a hospital (for she would have been arrested), although Clyde was convinced she was going to die. He moved Bonnie to a remote cabin, where he stayed by her bedside and painstakingly nursed her back to health. His sister Nell Barrow recalls that Clyde, who idolized Jesse James and Hollywood cowboys as a child, "the desperado who had already killed three men, broke down and sobbed like a little boy." Moreover, it was seven months before Bonnie could walk without crutches, despite press stories of her running in and out of banks all over the Midwest.

As for the criticism that Beatty's Clyde was not nearly as vicious as the press accounts, the filmmakers chose to go with the family's version of a young man who possessed a fatal charm and little respect for the law and pulled the trigger with ease once he convinced himself he was cornered. As a teenager, his first run-in with police was for speeding. Rather than stop, he fled the scene. He told Nell, prophetically, "I hate rows. . . . It's easier to run away." Once he had killed a man, he described his feelings to Nell. "I . . . felt—sick inside—sick and cold and weak—and a sort of dull wishing that I'd never been born." That Clyde was deftly captured by Beatty and remains a more disturbing portrait than an exaggerated assassin because his Clyde is utterly real and clearly imaginable.

Moreover, Penn explains, "We weren't making a documentary, any more than Shakespeare was writing documentaries in his Chronicle plays. To some extent we did romanticize—but so, inevitably, does any storyteller. . . . We do not purport to tell the exact truth, but we do tell a truth."[20]

There are many versions of truth when it comes to Bonnie and Clyde, as they join the bloated sagas of outlaws dating back to Jessie James. Some records purport that Bonnie and Clyde killed as many as 17 people, of which 8 were law enforcement officers. The numbers are hard to verify because the outlaws were never tried for any crimes and were on occasion blamed for unsolved murders out of convenience, as happened to Pretty Boy Floyd. Penn said that he was after their legend and the "mythic aspects of their lives" because of what the story says about our society then and now. "The fact is when Bonnie and Clyde were killed, they were regarded as enormous folk heroes by many people. . . . To dismiss them simply as killers, or pariahs, would be inaccurate. Because they were folk heroes, it's necessary to examine the times to see *why* they should be folk heroes. The times were out of joint. . . . A time creates its own myths and heroes. If the heroes are less than admirable, that is a clue to the times."[21]

Embellishing the depression context for modern audiences, Penn had the farmer and his black helper interrupt Bonnie's target practice. The Okie camp of the homeless was added as "a sort of homage" to *The Grapes of Wrath* (by director John Ford, whom Penn admired).[22] Another contrived scene is the "cat fight" between Blanche and Bonnie, which underpins the group's internal strife and petty problems. The scene is also a bit hostile to women—reflecting the lingering stereotype that they're problematic, emotionally troublesome, and lousy team players.

The writers also dropped some historical figures for simplicity, and others were blended together to simplify the story and add coherence.[23] C. W. Moss, for example, was a composite of several Barrow gang members, including Raymond Hamilton and two teenagers—D. W. Jones and Henry Methvin (whose father betrayed the couple in exchange for his son being spared prosecution). All the men were rumored to be lovers of both Bonnie and Clyde, but no proof exists to back up the claims. The original draft of the script had the couple and C. W. involved in a ménage à trois. In the final draft, however, Clyde is made temporarily impotent, and the sexual dysfunction of the others is muddied so that this provocative element wouldn't overtake the story.

Also in the original script, Bonnie was "more of a wise-cracking flapper," whom Penn later softened and probably brought closer to the real woman.[24] Along with her sentimental poetry, Bonnie wrote gushing love letters to Clyde while he was in prison. At one point, she asked if they could move away from Dallas, where he was branded, and try to be plain folks. "Sugar, you could go somewhere else and get you a job and work," wrote Bonnie. "I want you to be a man, honey, and not a thug."

Further evidence that the real Bonnie was more akin to Dunaway's moody child-woman is the story of Bonnie's deterioration near the end. Clyde had told Emma that Bonnie had started drinking. He told Nell, "I let her have at it about once a week because the poor kid's nerves can't stand the strain. She's not built for this sort of thing." Clyde also said that Bonnie's passion for babies was getting out of hand. Nell recalled, "She was always wanting to 'borrow' some woman's baby for a few days, and . . . he had his hands full with her sometimes when she'd get lonesome . . . for home. She'd sight a baby in some little town and begin to beg for the privilege of borrowing it till she got over the blues."

The most sentimental side of Dunaway's Bonnie was her dreadful homesickness for her mama. Even after the 16-year-old Bonnie married Roy Thornton, the couple soon moved back in with her mother. Eventually, Bonnie asked Roy to leave because he was "a roaming husband with a roaming mind," to use Bonnie's words. She never officially divorced Thornton, though.

Dunaway also could relate to Bonnie's hunger to get out of a sleepy Texas town. Dunaway was raised in rural Florida, which she found stifling. "I understood this kind of hunger, this kind of desperation. . . . I wanted to get out of the South, and I wanted to go places."[25] Dunaway called Bonnie "my soulmate. . . . There was a real kind of fierceness I'd seen in Bonnie that I recognized in myself." The role earned Dunaway an Oscar nomination and shot her to stardom overnight.

Beatty also earned an Oscar nomination and was the bankable name on the marquee, having already earned movie star status in the studio system. (The film was nominated for 10 Oscars, winning for cinematography and for Parsons in her best supporting role.) Beatty originally wanted to cast his former girlfriend Leslie Caron as Bonnie. He and Penn also considered Natalie Wood, Carol Lynley, and Tuesday Weld. Weld nearly played the role but had to decline after becoming pregnant. Beatty even pitched his sister Shirley MacLaine, but Penn fought for Dunaway. She had just finished two films, *The Happening* and *Hurry Sundown,* neither of which had yet been released.

EVERYTHING OLD IS NEW AGAIN

Part of Dunaway's success with Bonnie owes a debt to the fashion craze that her costumes set off. Critics noted, though, that although her clothes were period accurate—the work of costumer Theadora Van Runkle—Bonnie's hair and makeup were conspicuously 1967. Perhaps this was done to heighten her contemporary appeal rather than preserve Bonnie as a relic from the past. (Also, the real Bonnie was a brunette, but the myth about her being "Clyde's yellow-haired accomplice" dated back to press stories from 1933. Provine also had played her as a blond.)

Within months of the film's debut, berets became the rage and maxiskirts became as popular as miniskirts. By the year's end, Dunaway in full Bonnie regalia had graced three national magazine covers. Even the French film goddess Brigitte Bardot dressed up like Dunaway's Bonnie on New Year's Eve and crooned the chart-topping song "The Ballad of Bonnie and Clyde" for French television.

The hit single belonged to British pop artist Georgie Fame and ended in a barrage of machine gun sounds, for which the song was banned in several countries. Even New York radio ran a cleaned-up version that omitted the gunfire. The movie's theme song, "Foggy Mountain Breakdown," by bluegrass artists Earl Flatt and Lester Scruggs, made the top-ten list, reaching number one in England. Country star Merle Haggard also had a hit song that focused on Bonnie, lamenting, "Some said that Clyde made her life a shame / But the legend made Bonnie the head of the game."[26] Folksinger Susan Brodie wrote a more bittersweet "Bonnie's Song" that asked, "What would you do if we could walk out of here / If we could be free?" Even mainstream crooner Mel Torme penned "A Day in the Life of Bonnie and Clyde," which focused on Bonnie's flirtation with a man during a bank holdup. The strangest of all was a talking recording by Bonnie's sister Billie Jean Parker. It was entitled "The Truth about Bonnie and Clyde" and offered a "special bonus": a picture of the notorious duo "suitable for framing."

The *New York Times* noted, "Bad-man ballads are as old in world folklore as bad men. But this rash of recordings to be inspired by a film 34 years after the death of the principals involved may be without precedent in the recording industry, or, perhaps even more remarkably, the motion-picture industry."[27]

In London, the film broke all box office records, and one reporter noted that the film "captured the rollicking dream-life-cum-reality of thousands of young Britons. . . . There is an unmistakable affinity between the euphoria of L.S.D. and the kick Bonnie and Clyde get from robbing banks."[28] One British exhibitor went a step further and rereleased *Dillinger* and *Al Capone* on a double bill to tap the renewed appeal of films about public enemies.[29]

As Robert Sklar comments: "It was as if audiences understood better than either the distributor or the critics the emotional power of the film's anarchic individualism, its depiction of the awesome force of violent authority, its stereotyped but skillful evocation of past movies and past time."

"In a sense they were avant-garde stylists," said screenwriter Newman. "If Bonnie and Clyde had been alive in '65 they would have become two of Andy Warhol's superstars." When someone asked him in 1973 why the film had been such a success, he said he and Benton apparently "hit society's nerve." People speculated that the film was "*really* about Vietnam . . . *really* about Lee Harvey Oswald, *really* about police brutality. . . . After a while we began to say, 'Well, if you think so,' because its impact goes way beyond all of us."[30]

Newman and Benton came to screenwriting after successful careers as magazine writers, which in part fueled the disdain of some critics for their work. They weren't Hollywood regulars but hipsters who were accused of pandering to whatever was faddish in the pop culture. They're given credit for inventing *Esquire*'s "What's In and What's Out" and Dubious Achievement Awards. After *Bonnie and Clyde* (the screenplay earned them an Academy Award nomination), the two teamed up for several more projects, including *Superman*. Then Newman's career petered out, and Benton went on to win Oscars for both writing and directing *Kramer vs. Kramer* in 1979 and acclaim for *Places in the Heart* in 1984.

A NEW FILM GENERATION

The old guard of Hollywood was dazed and confused by the success of *Bonnie and Clyde*. Penn had predicted that old Hollywood was undergoing a drastic change—if not its death—as early as 1963. He said in part McCarthyism had seriously wounded Hollywood's creative soul. "The big companies got scared, made crazy films."[31] Penn said he admired Elia Kazan, though, who had done superb work in the otherwise stilted 1950s. He called Kazan the greatest director of actors, especially those from the Actors Studio such as Brando, whom Penn directed in *The Chase* (1966).

Penn first earned acclaim as a director for Broadway and then for television dramas. He first focused on an outlaw legend in his 1957 film *The Left-Handed Gun,* about Billy the Kid. But he lent it the grandeur of the gangster's mentality rather than retrace the steps of the standard Western. He admits he intended to locate through Billy's legend "the deep myths of Greek tragedy." His most mainstream Hollywood film was *The Miracle Worker* (1962), which garnered Penn an Oscar nomination and earned awards for Anne Bancroft and Patty Duke.

By 1968, after *Bonnie and Clyde* had made its impact, Penn observed that his predictions for Hollywood were on target. "The men who direct the studios [now] are young. . . . that makes a big difference. It was very difficult before, when there were those old kings, to talk to them about modern life. . . . Their values were from another time. . . . Hollywood studios are now only places where you get technical equipment. . . . Hollywood as a 'place' no longer exists.' "[32]

The National Society of Film Critics even asked in a 1968 survey: Are we standing on the brink of a radically different film age? Penn made a further contribution to that end a year later with the offbeat *Alice's Restaurant,* starring Woody Guthrie's son,

Arlo. Penn also took a fresh look at the enduring myths of American Indians and the Wild West in *Little Big Man* in 1970.

Although Penn earned auteurlike praise for *Bonnie and Clyde*'s final form, he credits Newman and Benton for the film's core. Robert Towne (who later won an Oscar for his *Chinatown* screenplay) also worked on the script while the film was in production. Like most films, though, *Bonnie and Clyde* is a collaborative effort and owes a debt to the genre's body of work to date. But another source was reflected in this film that was new to American cinema: French New Wave. New Wave is a label to describe the collective of French films that had poured into American "art" theaters of the early 1960s. The French, though, acknowledge that their original influence was the American gangster films of the 1930s and 1940s. What was bold about the new French hybrid was the pioneering visual style characterized as cinema verité. It consisted of jump cuts, hand-held cameras, irregular tracking shots, staccato and often illogical editing, and improvisational dialogue—all contributing to a feel of captured spontaneity and realism.

In *Shoot the Piano Player,* Francois Truffaut "shifted abruptly from gangsters to Chaplinesque comedy to romantic melodrama."[33] Jean-Luc Godard's *Breathless* has been described as "an odd mix of gangster movie and screwball comedy."[34] The story centers around "a downbeat, existentialist version of the American archetype, the Good Bad boy."[35] To show the links to the enduring gangster genre, the character Michel Poiccard pays his respects to a promotional poster of Bogart.

The scenes in *Bonnie and Clyde* that pay homage to French influence are the mishmash of film speeds, the distorted photography for the family reunion, and the extreme close-ups of Bonnie's lips to open the film (rather than the customary establishing shot of the town or Bonnie's room to orient the viewer). Even Dunaway said she played Bonnie with a touch of Jeanne Moreau, whom she admired in Louis Malle's *The Lovers.*

In fact, before Penn was involved, Newman and Benton first approached Truffaut to direct. When he declined, they asked Godard. Both directors had other commitments, but Truffaut told his friend Beatty about the project. Beatty then bought the rights to the script and went to work as a first-time film producer.

An actor as producer, a script by two unknowns, and a search for a foreign director were further proof that filmmaking by the late 1960s was a new enterprise. Even though the studio system had disintegrated, it seemed more than a coincidence that Warner Brothers—the veteran gangster film workshop for decades—was the distributor for *Bonnie and Clyde.* Jack Warner, however, no longer had his customary ironfisted control. Penn edited the film in New York with his associate Dede Allen to further sidestep studio interference.

Like the all-encompassing studio, the Production Code, too, had faded away. It was replaced by the new G-man in town, Jack Valenti, a former presidential assistant to Lyndon Johnson. When Valenti became the new president of the Motion Picture Association of America, he instilled a new rating system, which is still with us today in modified form.

IMITATION OF LIFE OR REALISTIC ART?

Within a year of *Bonnie and Clyde* real-life violence made the film's screen blood look contrived. As the war in Vietnam continued to mushroom and antiwar sentiments reached an equally theatrical pitch, bloodshed was a nightly news event. Then came the assassinations of Bobby Kennedy and Martin Luther King as well as the street rioting outside the Democratic National Convention in Chicago. It must have looked as if no amount of screen violence could ever seem like overkill to a public feeding off a daily diet of carnage.

Yet some still blamed the movies. During Bobby Kennedy's funeral, broadcast journalist Eric Sevareid took a swipe at *Bonnie and Clyde,* saying Penn's film made heroes out of killers. His point, perhaps, given the context in which he was speaking, was that somehow screen violence was abetting a climate in which assassinations and violence were becoming commonplace. It was a feeble attempt to explain the rupture in American society and did little to explain why everyone felt under siege.

As *Newsweek* reviewer Joseph Morgenstern said in his second review of *Bonnie and Clyde* (his first noted the film's "essential ugliness"), "Violent movies are an inevitable consequence of violent life. They may also transmit the violence virus, but they do not breed it any more than the Los Angeles television stations caused Watts to riot." He also warned, though, "that violence begets violence in life and engenders confusion in art."

By 1969 director Sam Peckinpah gave us *The Wild Bunch,* supposedly a Western about a bygone era, but the slaughter on-screen was as fresh as anything ever filmed before. As James Monaco notes, "Slow-motion death in a hail of bullets soon became a cliché." And within a few years, Richard Corliss connected Peckinpah and Don Siegel (*Dirty Harry*) with a battalion of action directors who "embraced the balletics of violence so rigorously (if not pathologically) that Arthur Penn's meticulously constructed sequence can now be charged with siring an entire subgenre." It was now possible to make an action film without having to borrow the conventions of the gangster genre, which demands characterization, motive, and public meaning. It was also the dawning of movies aptly titled "exploitation" films, which seized on a trend for quick profit but gave scant thought to artistic merit.

In Bonnie's wake, even female gangsters were made more fierce. Roger Corman's *Bloody Mama* (1970) takes the genre's Madonna and transforms her into a demented matriarch who takes her sons on crime sprees and foments incest and drug abuse. The film brutalized the real Ma Barker, who had inspired several films over the years, starting with J. Edgar Hoover's didactic *Queen of the Mob* (1940). Ma Jarrett in *White Heat* was another look-alike, and during the run of biopics, *Ma Barker's Killer Brood* (1962) presented a far-fetched story in which Barker joins Dillinger, Baby Face Nelson, and Machine Gun Kelly for an all-star gang. Regrettably, a movie about the real Ma Barker would be savage enough without hypertilting the facts. The creepier truth was that Ma Barker "was a God-fearing woman named Arizona Clark Barker who took her four boys to church every Sunday and taught them how to kill and steal during the week."[36]

An advertisement for Corman's film quotes Ma Barker saying, "The family that slays together stays together." It also shows Mama—the campy Shelley Winters—sporting a cigar, a Capone-like grin, and a tommy gun. The future gangster superstar Robert De Niro portrays Lloyd, one of her four sons.

"Corman was obviously fashioning a grotesque amalgam of Dogpatch and the Manson gang while keeping his distance from the facts," notes Clarens. *Bloody Mama* was halfway through production when the Manson murders became public—another example of atrocity amid the daily news feed. *Bloody Mama* was not so much an example of where the genre was headed as it was an evolution of Corman's raucous style that traces the "King of Schlock" back to the 1950s.

Other than stepped-up bloodletting, Robert Ray claims that after 1968 the industry made films that bounced in theme between "irony and nostalgia." The products were often more "corrected" genre films, including *Butch Cassidy and the Sundance Kid,* which made the Western more meaningful for "hip," educated audiences who were too jaded to sit through *High Noon.* Ray points to Robert Altman as a contemporary of Penn who "made a whole career out of such films, working almost exclusively within standard genres whose conventions he discredited." *M*A*S*H* (1970) was Altman's contorted war movie (about Korea but really for audiences strangling on Vietnam). His *Thieves like Us* (1974) paid homage to the gangster film, blending the 1948 story with Penn's version, and adding his own touches. *Esquire*'s John Simon, though, accused Altman of ripping off *Bonnie and Clyde,* from which his film "is almost servilely derived." However, other critics noted his effort to take the story in a different direction. He had bled the characters of the genre's pathology; there's no darkness revealed about his Bowie (David Carradine) and Keechie (Shelley Duvall), only the social desolation that surrounds them. As Colin Westerbeck wrote, "Altman's thieves really *are* like us. It is not the Law or some special Fate that overwhelms them, but the sheer picayunishness of living that afflicts us all."[37] This approach makes for a thoughtful art film but fails as a gangster film, which is the structure Altman borrowed. He strains the visual story to elevate the emptiness of depression-era Mississippi at the expense of defining his tender characters. When they get chewed up in the genre's customary violence, rather than coming off as profoundly victimized, their fate seems empty and finessed because we don't know them very well.

Such experiments and the fusion of the era's impulses were providing endless possibilities for the gangster genre to explore in the future. *Bonnie and Clyde* remains a signpost of the modern era that's still unfolding. When audiences first saw the film, as William J. Free puts it, "We recognize the subject—a gangster film—but the values presented on the screen are so different from our stereotyped expectations that we see the subjects in a new light." The film enabled the genre to use violence in a more literal manner—not just for the punctuation, but also to explore the brutality of violence itself.

Soon several young filmmakers would blend Hollywood mythology, French New Wave methods, and American realism to restore the screen gangster to his mighty throne—a titular pharaoh for the new Babylon. The redrafted gangster would become a seductive, tortured character whom audiences could no longer resist—and Hollywood could not refuse.

CHAPTER 8

Blood Brothers: Scorsese and Coppola

> I refused to be a fool, dancing on a string held by all those big shots. I don't apologize—that's my life—but I thought that . . . when it was your time . . . that you would be the one to hold the strings. Senator Corleone. Governor Corleone.
>
> —Don Corleone (Marlon Brando) to his son, *The Godfather,* 1972

As the studio system gave way to independent filmmakers, Hollywood was transformed from the assembly lines of the "dream factory" to the art of the deal. Studio moguls were replaced by agents and producers, who became the new kingmakers in town. Directors—who had become as expendable as screenwriters—made a comeback as auteurs in the 1970s. While the deal makers scrounged around for financiers and bankable stars, several star directors emerged who would lend films a signature motif. Martin Scorsese and Francis Ford Coppola were among them.

Both men were products of film schools. A relatively new concept in the industry, film schools not only provided formal training in a host of cinematic techniques but exposed students to the rich collection of films that chart moviemaking's evolution. Budding filmmakers were able to review the imagination and politics of film throughout the history of the art form, searching for patterns and signs of lasting wit. Students also perused genres for their essential qualities, conventions, and surviving utility. For the gangster genre, the rise of Scorsese and Coppola to prominence was good news, for they appeared obsessed with the amoral mystique and timeless appeal of gangsters. What these directors have brought to the genre is original insight, contemporary relevance, and fresh blood. Their gangsters are authentic and from streets we know we could locate on a map.

Both men are also Italian Americans. Their gangster films explore the strength and comfort of that ethnicity while revealing the often distorted outlook their culture has of the American dream. Scorsese is a Sicilian American raised in New York's Little Italy. With the boyhood nickname "Marty Pills"—for a reliance on medications for asthma and pleurisy—he was not one of the street toughs. "The only way I was able to defend myself was to be able to *take* punishment," Scorsese recalled.[1]

His frailty kept him mostly indoors and glued to the television, and he grew especially fond of old movies. His father also took him uptown to see the classic films being showcased at the Museum of Modern Art. At an early age, though, he began drawing storyboards and designing productions from his own imagination.

Catholicism was also an early obsession. Schooled by Irish nuns who stressed the religion's residue of remorse, Scorsese left for the seminary at age 13, fully expecting to become a priest. He quit after discovering girls and rock 'n' roll and rejecting the narrow margins of the church's dogma. After entering Greenwich Village's New York University in the early 1960s, he began soaking up the atmosphere of the "beatnik coffeehouses," notes Les Keyser. Scorsese earned a master's degree in 1966, stayed on as an instructor, and continued his tutelage with Haig Manoogian, the author of a classic textbook that influenced a generation of young filmmakers. Manoogian stressed "individuality and artistry" as the real "life blood" of American filmmaking.[2] Scorsese was "mesmerized by this new gospel of personal filmmaking . . . [and] realized that his Italian heritage, his Catholic faith, his rock-and-roll music, and his inner turmoil could all be synthesized on screen."[3]

Keyser describes Scorsese's award-winning 1964 student film *It's Not Just You, Murray,* as his "first full-fledged attempt to recall his childhood in Little Italy and to balance the values of family, church, and tradition against the materialism, deception, and violence of the Mafia."[4] The film is the story of a gunman whose career begins in 1922, "featuring a glittering universe of fast cars, fancy guns, champagne bubbles, and dancing girls."[5] Much of *Murray* was filmed in Scorsese's parents' apartment, with incidents borrowed from stories about the family's brush with local mafiosi. Scorsese remembers the neighborhood as being infested with wise guys, of whom his father advised him to be respectful, aloof, and closemouthed.

Scorsese describes *Murray* as an homage to classic films, including Raoul Walsh's *The Roaring Twenties.* "*Murray* recalls the Warner Bros. films of the late thirties, early forties," Scorsese explains. "But within that structure I used actual stories about the neighborhood . . . intermixed with . . . the gangster filmmaking tradition [and] a touch of Fellini, whom I was very much influenced by at the time."[6]

His next project focused on the counterculture mood of the era. He went off to Max Yasgur's farm as an assistant director (and principal editor) for a film about the three-day extravaganza known as Woodstock. (The film won the Oscar for best documentary in 1970.) Then Scorsese lent NYU's film equipment and labs to a group of activist students filmmakers who were chronicling the student demonstrations of that year. Following Nixon's decision to bomb Cambodia and the killing of four Kent State students, Scorsese got involved in the antiwar movement and helped make what became *Street Scenes* in 1970. The film ends in the middle of an argument because he ran out of film. But he left it that way because it seemed appropriate. "Nobody knew what to do, neither radicals nor conservatives," to solve the political standoff, he remembered.[7]

Finally, Roger Corman—the polar opposite to Manoogian's filmmaking philosophy—gave Scorsese the job of directing the sequel to *Bloody Mama,* called *Boxcar Bertha.* The film is a *Bonnie and Clyde* offshoot about two petty thieves during depression times. Corman told Scorsese: "Every fifteen pages it has to have nudity, a little violence here and a little action there, otherwise you can do what you want with it."[8] As Keyser notes, "With mind-numbing regularity there are plane crashes, stickups, fistfights, episodes of torture, and finally the film's *piece de resistance,* a crucifixion so daring in its execution and so horrible in its effect that Jeffrey Lyons . . . declared it 'should have been cut.' "[9]

The film that put Scorsese on the genre's map is *Mean Streets,* which he cowrote with Mardik Martin. With its home movie feel, Scorsese explains, "*Mean Streets* was my attempt to put myself and my old friends on the screen, to show how we grew up, how we lived, what the whole way of life was like in Little Italy."[10] (Scorsese was forced to film much of the film in Los Angeles, though, because shooting in New York was too costly for his meager budget.)

Mean Streets tracks a few days in the life of Charlie (Harvey Keitel), a small-time hood in Little Italy whose uncle Giovanni (Cesare Danova) is in the Mob. Giovanni dangles the prospect of giving Charlie a restaurant to run—after it's confiscated from the present owner, who can no longer make his "loan" payments. The soul of the story, though, is Charlie's obsession with wanting to make amends for his accumulated sins. But Charlie believes that "you don't make up for your sins in church; you do it in the streets." The symbols of Catholicism contaminate his petty wise-guy existence. As a self-ordained priest on his turf, he pinches his fingers over a mixed drink in a bar as if holding a host. And he occasionally sticks his fingers into open flames or holds them over matches to imagine the fires of hell. But as he sees it, "You don't fuck around with the infinite."

He also believes that the self-destructive Johnny Boy (Robert De Niro) has been sent by God to test his moral conviction. Johnny Boy owes money all over the neighborhood, but one loan shark and friend named Michael (Richard Romanus) is running out of patience. Charlie tries to pacify Michael, who's more concerned with looking like a "jerk off" for letting Johnny Boy stall. Charlie explains that he's sticking his neck out for Johnny Boy because Charlie wants to bring the example of Saint Francis to the modern street world. As a product of that battered environment and its codes of survival, though, Charlie and his efforts are doomed. As his girlfriend Teresa (Amy Robinson) notes, "St. Francis didn't run numbers."

Part of his failure is his own confusion, particularly when it comes to Teresa, who's Johnny Boy's cousin. Charlie can't make a commitment and move into an apartment with her outside the neighborhood, but neither can he give her up. Giovanni warns Charlie to stay away from her and the "half-crazy" Johnny, noting that the whole family has problems. Although Teresa is the most well-adjusted person in the film, she has epilepsy, or as Giovanni puts it, "She's sick in the head." If she can't occupy the pedestal, then she's cast aside, or at least undervalued; if not the Madonna, then the whore. Half joking one day, Charlie calls her a "cunt" and then quickly apologizes. He's ashamed of having sex with her in secret but continues to want her. He even guiltily confesses about a dream he has in which they're making love and he ejaculates blood.

After Charlie arranges one last meeting between Johnny Boy and Michael, his plan falls apart, and more brutal street justice takes over. Charlie had given Johnny Boy $30 to offer Michael as a good faith effort on a $2,000 debt. While waiting for Michael at their pal Tony's topless bar—the boys' sanctuary—Johnny Boy squanders all but $10 buying drinks. When Michael arrives, he's already angry, but Johnny Boy taunts him further, scoffing, "You're the only jerk-off around here that I can borrow money from without paying it back."

Johnny Boy puts Michael off with a gun, but Charlie decides they need to disappear for a while. He borrows Tony's car, picks up Teresa, and the three cruise the streets. They have nowhere to hide, however, and Michael and his accomplice (actually Scorsese) find them and start shooting into Tony's car. A bullet hits Johnny Boy in the neck, and another wounds Charlie's arm. Charlie finally crashes the car and ends up on his knees in the street as a final act of penance. Teresa's bloodied hand twitches through the broken windshield, and Johnny Boy gushes blood and wanders down the street until put into a rescue vehicle. When Charlie first appealed to God about atoning for his sins, he complained (in a voice-over supplied by Scorsese), "We play by your rules, don't we?" In the end, Charlie fails to save Johnny Boy and sabotages his

Harvey Keitel portrays a low-level gangster named Charlie who ends up bloody and on his knees as real-world penance for his sins in Martin Scorsese's groundbreaking film *Mean Streets*. The film established Keitel, Scorsese, and costar Robert De Niro as authentic genre regulars who were closer to the street than the Hollywood factory.

own future as a hoodlum and street savior. Charlie is the tragedy because he can't understand nor overcome what he is; and this failure keeps him hopelessly mired in his dead-end neighborhood. "Johnny Boy is the only one . . . who is his own man; he is the true hero, while Charlie . . . is the director's worst vision of himself," Pauline Kael notes. It's the Scorsese character, after all, who does the shooting. Charlie has picked a lost cause to save, and his failure to save Johnny Boy reinforces Charlie's conclusion that he's the loser he thinks he is. When Charlie's plan to manage Johnny Boy starts unraveling, it's Johnny Boy who points out, "You got what you wanted."

Johnny Boy plays no such games. He's pathetically aware of his fate, which is why he acts crazy. He shoots up the neighborhood from a rooftop because "it's dead," he tells Charlie. Shooting gives him a thrill, and what more harm can it do to the beaten tenements?

Rather than show the Mob as a closeted community that tries to remain invisible to most of America, Scorsese shows how much a part of the landscape organized crime was in Little Italy—as familiar as the garbage, the sirens, and the smell of peppers and sausage. But his glimpses show organized crime's bottom rungs: the street punks, Mafia soldiers, bag men, and petty extortionists like Michael. On one occasion, Tony and Michael scam two teenagers out of a lousy $20, which they use to take Charlie and the gang to the movies. Scorsese captures this kind of day-to-day pilfering superbly. His wise guys lack glamour, act macho while struggling to be men, and act brave when deep down they're scared as hell.

Scorsese's street warriors get in spontaneous, near-comic brawls in pool halls and bars, antagonize women who cross their path, and make grumbling attempts to protect their turf from outsiders, including blacks and Puerto Ricans. But Scorsese's street fellows thrive on the example of neighborhood guys who have made it—who have earned respect at least as successful criminals. It was that lottery-like long shot that kept their hopes alive and kept them from channeling their energies into less grandiose (albeit more legal and mundane) approaches to getting ahead.

WORRIED ABOUT THE MOB

The neighborhood guys "who made it," the Uncle Giovannis, were nearly always members of the Mob. In the 1950s, despite J. Edgar Hoover's long-standing denial, the government finally admitted that the Mob existed. Their exploits proved to be titillating television fare during the Kefauver hearings—later buttressed by the testimony of Mafia soldier-turned-rat Joseph Valachi at congressional hearings in 1962. (His story became the 1972 film *The Valachi Papers*.) These public disclosures traced the history of the Mob's reigning kingpins back to Prohibition—when fortunes were made and extensive organized-crime syndicates were bankrolled. Salvatore "Lucky" Luciano (a Five Pointer who grew up on Little Italy's Mott Street) consolidated a post-Prohibition Underworld. He organized it under a corporate-like commission of family bosses who voted and approved business beneficial to everyone's interests.

One reason the government feigned ignorance was that it didn't want to explain why known mobsters such as Luciano—the *capo di tutti capi* (the boss of bosses)—had been tapped to help fight the war in Europe. As Giovanni in *Mean Streets* notes, politicians use criminals when it suits their interests. He explains to Charlie how Luciano was asked by the government to take "care of the docks" during the war and assist the U.S. Navy. From his jail cell, Luciano ordered the waterfront unions to cooperate with the military and also urged the Sicilian Mafia to aid the Allied effort. Unlike the old wartime movies that showed mobsters fighting out of patriotism, these mobsters wanted a payback. After the war, the government turned a blind eye to mobsters' criminal exploits unless they needlessly provoked headlines.

During Thomas Dewey's years as a crusading district attorney, he busted Luciano for running a prostitution racket. History has proven that Dewey framed Luciano to get the conviction because he was unable to get the insulated Luciano on more serious crimes, including murder. However, because of Luciano's "special services" during the war, he was paroled and thrown out of the country in 1946 after serving only 9 years of his 30- to 50-year sentence. Dewey—then the governor of New York—had arranged the deal. As many news reports noted, the government gave the Mafia a break. By merely deporting Luciano, the government had ensured that his thorny presence was no longer a problem for the American justice system, but he was free to run his criminal empire from Naples, including his American interests. The Italian government frequently complained, but to little avail. (This saga is aptly showcased in *Lucky Luciano*—a 1973 Italian-French film with Rod Steiger as a Genovese-style black marketeer and Luciano accomplice.)

Genovese, who later became boss of one of New York's five Mafia families, did his tour of duty on Italian soil. He was an official translator on Allied military bases and ran an extensive black market that the U.S. military blissfully ignored.

Once the government hearings were over, though, most Americans assumed that the Mob had been conquered or was at least keeping a low profile. (Hoover turned to his new enemies of the state—antiwar protesters.) The mobsters who were thriving such as Genovese and Carlo Gambino (another New York Mafia boss) lived understated lives, cloaking themselves as decent citizens with modest homes and strong memberships in local charities. As Raymond Moley put it, the reason the Mob is so hard to stop "is that it looks like normal life."[11]

The smattering of syndicate films of the 1950s and 1960s rarely put the mafiosi at the center of the story. Films such as the first-rate *Underworld USA* lean on a thriller plot with suspense-style action. Like most Mob films of its era, *Underworld USA* failed to probe its characters' mixed motives or investigate the seeds of their criminal behavior—including those that might be related to Italian American households. Another example is *The Brothers Rico* (1957), starring frequent Hollywood gangster Richard Conte as a former Mob accountant who's drawn back into the life while trying to keep his younger brother out of the rackets and alive. This film focused on Conte's struggle to stay straight more than on life within the Mob. In 1968, however, the breakthrough film *The Brotherhood* told the story of Mafia boss Don Francesco. The story's core is the troubled relationship between Francesco and his younger brother Vincent. Vincent is a newly minted lawyer who's hesitant to join the family business, but once he gets involved, he argues with Francesco (or Frank) on how to modernize it. Eventually Vincent is ordered by the Mob's commission to hit Frank, with whom he exchanges "the kiss of death" before shooting. (Mario Puzo claimed the film was pirated from early galleys of *The Godfather*—which Paramount Pictures had recently bought.) The film garnered decent reviews, including one from the *New York Times,* which called *The Brotherhood* "a blunt, square, and sentimental Mafia movie." It had a competent director in Martin Ritt and the star power of Kirk Douglas, who also served as producer. But the film was a box office failure. Part of the problem was Douglas's unconvincing depiction of an Italian don. Douglas portrays Frank as mawkish and foolishly hot tempered. He also mistakes shouting and waving his arms about for Italian communication, which is a worn-out stereotype already put on screen by Muni and Steiger.

The Brotherhood left Paramount in no hurry to rush Puzo's book into production. However, when the novel stayed on the best-seller list (ultimately for 67 weeks), Paramount was compelled to develop its property. (Puzo's name remained with the film's title credits, which also display the book's cover art of a puppeteer with strings dangling from his grip.) Paramount first envisioned a low-budget gangster film put in contemporary times to avoid the cost of a period film. The studio also hired newcomer Coppola, whom it figured had not had time to cultivate an expensive appetite for production.

Puzo, although he had never written a screenplay, was hired to adapt his book for the screen. Most original authors are rarely given the job because they're viewed as unwilling or unskilled at reworking their material for a different medium. Puzo first earned critical acclaim for his 1965 novel *The Fortunate Pilgrim,* about Italian immigrants told from the mother's point of view. But his next book proposal was rejected except for the Mafia intrigues it mentioned. He expanded that material into *The Godfather.* Part of his novel's ultimate success—with stories borrowed from the real Mafia history—was its sense of peeking into a world rarely unveiled. (Puzo surprised many *Godfather* fans when he told the *Washington Post* that Vito's quiet mastery and ingrained faith in family were inspired by Puzo's mother and not a real-life Mafia don. "Whenever the Godfather opened his mouth, in my own mind I heard the voice of my mother," Puzo said.) In the end, Puzo's book contained enough literary merit to impress top-flight critics and enough pulp to draw mass readers. *The Godfather* ultimately sold 10 million copies.

Raised in the slums of New York's Hell's Kitchen, Puzo grew tired of the popular clichés "of lovable Italians, singing Italians, happy-go-lucky Italians. I wondered where the hell the moviemakers and storywriters got all their ideas from."[12] The truth he wanted to tell is one that darkens the image of Italian Americans but is no less real. It deals with their brethren (however small a percentage) who are assassins and professional mobsters. These mafiosi corrupt the culture's penchant for elaborate codes of honor and its weakness for vendettas. The "silence" that Scorsese was told to maintain about the Mafia in his neighborhood ultimately interferes with the ability of many Italian Americans to get out from under pernicious stereotypes that keep them guilty by association.

Keyser said of Scorsese, "To understand his art, one must consider the culture of Elizabeth and Mulberry streets" (the comment also applies to Puzo). Keyser points to Richard Gambino's study *Blood of My Blood,* which describes the problem for Italian immigrants, especially peasants, based on the rigid hierarchy of values they bring to America. First, there's loyalty to family, or "blood of my blood." Then comes allegiance to other Italians. However, non-Italians remain outsiders who don't merit respect.

Just as the FBI tried to ignore the Mob, Italian immigrants tried to ignore the Mafia. Puzo was joined by another *paisan* who thought the time was ripe to reveal Italianism as a source of pride but also a subculture with a persistent criminal element. Coppola, though, first thought Puzo's book was "pretty cheap stuff." After studying it more closely, however, he began to see it "as a story of a king and three sons . . . a classic noble family. . . . It could just as well be about the Kennedys or the Rothschilds. . . . It is about power and the succession of power."

Coppola understood the power of the Italian family. He grew up in a "warm, loving, and active environment, replete with upheavals, shouting, and passion," recalled his sister Talia Shire. Their father was a classical musician who kept his family close to him despite a nomadic existence traveling with orchestras and theatrical productions. But his father's unrequited dream to be a renown composer dominated the family's outlook. When absorbed by Francis, that dream became his insatiable desire to be an artist with a taste for high drama.

Like Scorsese, Coppola was a sickly child, afflicted with polio and missing the playtime afforded most healthy children. But the social isolation led to a fertile imagination that was drawn to inventing theater and film productions. "I did a lot of work with puppets, and was given a 16 mm film projector," Coppola remembered. "I was fascinated with synchronizing sound and movies." By age eight, he was matching soundtracks to his family's home movies and went into commerce staging exhibitions of them.[13] He, too, had a nickname, as a techno geek called "Science," who preferred gadgets and inventions to sports and girls.

At Hofstra College (now University), he focused on theater productions and became president of the drama society, guiding productions with fellow students such as James Caan. After entering UCLA's film school, Coppola became its star pupil. But the gifted Coppola was also a pragmatist and soon found work directing soft-core "nudies"—despite the disdain of his "purist" classmates. Like Scorsese, Coppola came under the influence of Roger Corman, who considered Coppola his "all-purpose guy." In one instance, when Corman needed a soundman, Coppola claimed to be one then crammed all night to learn how to become one. On Corman's watch, Coppola wrote and directed the low-budget horror film *Dementia 13,* which gave few hints of the filmmaker to come.

Coppola also became a contracted screenwriter, which eventually netted him his first Oscar for cowriting *Patton.* Coppola made his own "youth market" movie, *You're a Big Boy Now* (1967), which brought him moderate acclaim and an invitation to do major films, including *The Rain People* (with Shirley Knight, James Caan, and Robert Duvall) and *Finian's Rainbow* (with Fred Astaire and Petula Clark). Both films showed wisps of Coppola's ability to create both intimacy and pageantry, but they were box office failures—mostly criticized for being dazzling in spots but derivative on the whole.

By the time Paramount offered him *The Godfather,* the studio figured he had been humbled by his spotty record thus far. But the 31-year-old director had already proved to be an outlaw in Hollywood by moving to San Francisco, where he helped establish an alternative movie studio (with George Lucas, among others) whose goal was to be as sensitive to art as to commerce. The employees were called "the family."

Coppola reworked Puzo's script, cutting out the novel's more lurid material about the Corleone mistress with gynecological problems and reducing the role of crooner Johnny Fontane (a Frank Sinatra doppelgänger). Coppola invited Robert Towne (another Corman graduate) to write a scene while the film was in production; Towne's addition captures the peculiar generation gap between the reigning don and his successor, but also the unspoken bond between father and son.

Given that the Vietnam war was still raging and the collateral damage to America's self-image in the early 1970s, like Penn with *Bonnie and Clyde,* Coppola knew his film was also a commentary on the rupture in American society. The film's opening line is spoken by the undertaker Bonasera, who states emphatically, "I believe in America." Then he promptly asks the don to direct violence to overcome the flaws of the American justice system.

"I feel that the Mafia is an incredible metaphor for this country," explains Coppola. "Basically, both the Mafia and America feel they are benevolent organizations. Both the Mafia and America have their hands stained with blood from what it is necessary to do to protect their power and interests."[14]

Fortunately, Coppola honored the strengths and limitations of the gangster genre. Rather than aim for zeitgeist, he made what he termed "an authentic . . . film about gangsters who were Italian, how they lived, how they behaved, the way they treated their families, celebrated their rituals." Like all great gangster films before it, *The Godfather* was multilayered and didactic for those who notice. It was also richly entertaining and narcotically violent for those who like movies with stylish punch. It proves why the gangster film can occasionally rise to the level of art—with this one being of the genre's most magnificent examples.

THE GODFATHER—THE MOVIE

The film tells the tale of the powerful Corleone "family" and its struggle to stay intact as a criminal organization as well as a collection of blood relatives. It opens with a lavish wedding and ends with a courtly baptism. Each celebration is violated by violence and betrayal. The film is a tale of contrasts and the consistent matching of emotional and visual opposites. Murky, somber interiors with characters' eye sockets shrouded in darkness and swarthy men who seem monstrous are juxtaposed with white wedding gowns, rainbow-hued gardens, and the sun-washed starkness of Sicily. While grown-

The Godfather. Vito Corleone (Marlon Brando, *second from left*) and his heirs *(left to right):* Michael (Al Pacino), Santino (James Caan), and Fredo (John Cazale). The men pose at the lavish wedding of the only Corleone daughter. The loner Michael will end up the sole survivor and the crime family's boss in Francis Ford Coppola's masterpiece, which has been hailed as the genre's high-water mark.

ups whisper death threats and order men to kill, children giggle and wives serve heaping bowls of pasta. The life of *la famiglia* and its rituals seems everlasting. So do its lies.

Interrupting the opening wedding scenes is a grim business meeting between the bride's father, Vito Corleone (Marlon Brando), and a man who asks that his daughter's brutal beating be avenged. A Sicilian tradition directs that Vito cannot refuse any request on his daughter's wedding day.

But Vito asks Bonasera why he first went to the police. "You were afraid to be in my debt. . . . You found paradise in America . . . made a good living. Police protected you and there were courts of law. So you didn't need a friend like me. But now you come to me and you say, 'Don Corleone, give me justice.' " After the man grovels, the don agrees to do "the favor." But it may have to be reciprocated someday, he warns.

While other guests feast, sing with the orchestra, dance the tarantella, and gulp red wine, Mafia leader Barzini (Richard Conte) assaults a photographer for taking his picture, and the eldest Corleone son, Santino (James Caan), spits on an FBI badge held out by an agent as identification outside the estate's front gates. Santino, called Sonny, also takes a bridesmaid named Lucy Mancini up to an empty bedroom, where their stand-up sex act has her slamming up against the door.

Vito refuses to take the family portrait until his youngest son, Michael, arrives. When Michael (Al Pacino) makes his entrance, dressed in uniform and adorned with medals as a war hero, he's accompanied by Kay Adams (Diane Keaton), a WASP New Englander in a bright red frock and hat. Soon Michael tells the story behind the ominous hulk she's ogling. "His name is Luca Brasi," Michael says and explains Luca's part in Johnny Fontane's career. The famous crooner (Al Martino) has just arrived and is delighting shrieking females with a love song. Michael says that Luca helped the don make a bandleader "an offer he couldn't refuse." Luca held a gun to the man's head while the don "assured him either his signature or his brains would be on the contract." (In the original script, Michael also tells of Luca's battles with Capone's men.) While Kay gapes over her plate of lasagna, Michael reassures her, "That's my family, Kay. It's not me." Michael also explains how the fair-haired Tom Hagen (Robert Duvall) became his adopted brother: when Sonny was a kid, he brought the orphan Tom home to the Corleones, who raised him as one of their own.

The tone and style abruptly change for the next sequence, in which Tom—who's quickly on his way to becoming the don's *consiglieri*—arrives in the plastic world of Hollywood. (*Consiglieri* is a Mafia term for the family's key business advisor.) Tom has been sent to deal with Woltz, a studio czar who has refused the don's godson Johnny a contract in Woltz's new movie. It's "a very religious, sacred, close relationship" among the Italian people, Tom explains to Woltz (John Marley). Tom also hints he could make union problems "disappear." But Woltz is angry that Johnny spoiled one of his protégés and made him look ridiculous. After Woltz shows Tom his mansion's prize amenities, including a $600,000 stallion named Khartoum, he refuses the don's request. When Tom warns against that, Woltz raves about not letting Tom's "dago, guinea, wop, greaseball" associates push him around. Tom, ever composed, stops chewing his dinner and politely leaves. The next morning, in one of the film's most famous and horrific scenes, Woltz wakes up to find his pajamas covered in blood. He frantically searches the bedclothes until he discovers he's in bed with Khartoum's severed head.

After the Corleones meet with a mobster named Sollozzo, better known as the Turk for his Turkish drug connections, an attempt is made to assassinate the don. Sollozzo (Al Lettieri) had offered Vito a 30 percent return for a $1 million investment in a drug partnership. But Sollozzo really wanted to tap into the don's connections—"those politicians you carry in your pocket like so many nickels and dimes." Before the meeting, Tom advised the family that "narcotics is the thing of the future," and if the Corleones don't corner the market, the other Mafia families will and use the profits and power to come after the Corleones. But the don warned that officials on his payroll "wouldn't be friendly very long if they knew my business was drugs instead of gambling, which they regard as a harmless vice."

Sonny tipped his hand at the meeting and showed interest, which gave Sollozzo the idea to kill the don and work with Sonny. Sollozzo and his backer, Bruno Tattaglia (Tony Giorgio), first garrot Luca, then kidnap Tom, and finally order an ambush of the don while he's buying fruit from a street vendor in Little Italy. His other son, the fragile misfit Fredo, weeps while his father lays in the street, bleeding from five gunshot wounds.

Michael has remained outside the family business but now begins to be drawn into the fold. While enjoying Manhattan's Christmas ambience with Kay, he's devasted by a newspaper headline that reports his father's murder. He rushes home and finds the homestead transformed into Sonny's war room. Armed men patrol the gates, and the hotheaded Sonny and his *caporegimes* (captains) plot their revenge. Listening to the roster of men to be murdered, Michael asks with quiet disgust, "You gonna kill all those guys?"

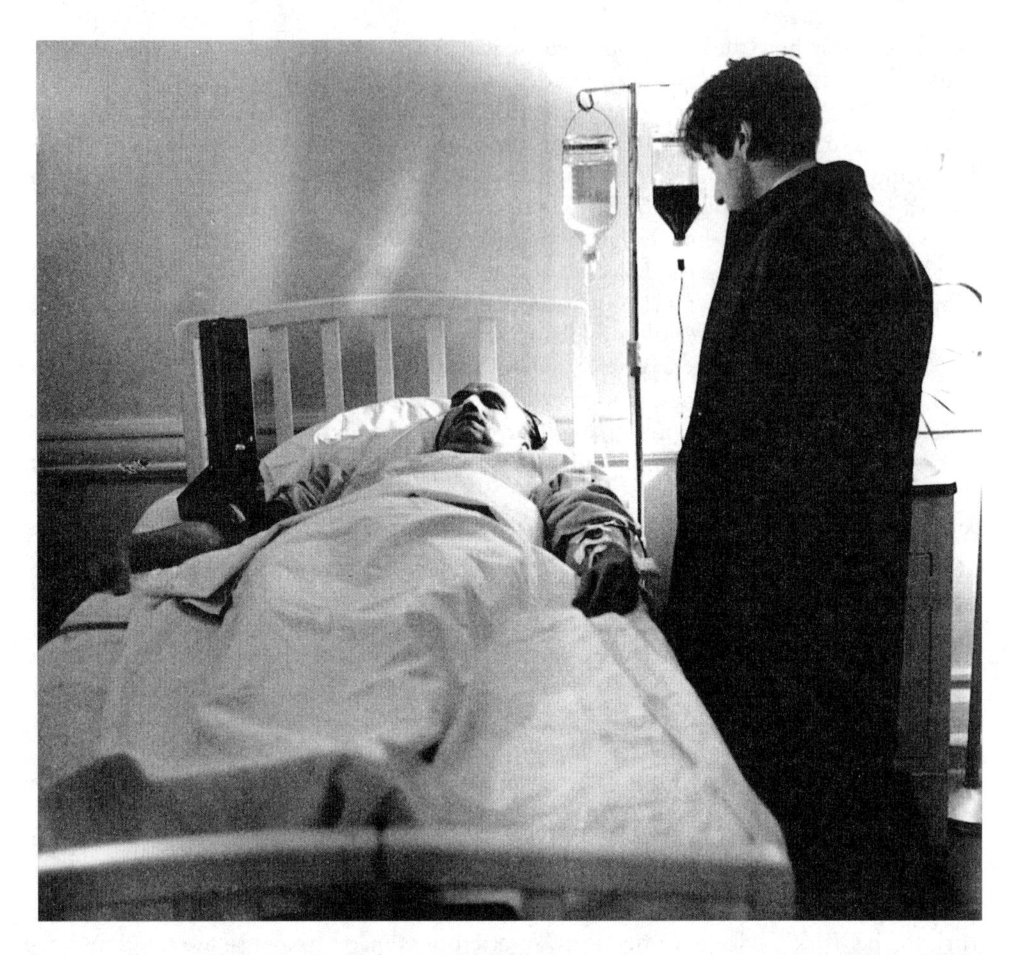

In a turning point in *The Godfather,* Michael (Pacino) whispers to a sickly, bullet-torn Vito (Brando) about sticking by his father and battling his enemies. The scene is unusually restrained for a gangster film, deftly displaying Coppola's mastery of quiet, composed drama pitted against the genre's more conventional screen violence.

Once released, Tom tries to barter a truce between Sonny and Sollozzo to avoid a full-scale war between the Mafia families. It's 1945, warns Tom, "Nobody wants bloodshed anymore." Sonny accuses Tom of not wanting revenge because he's not a real son to the don. Sonny quickly apologizes, but the insult remains a sore spot between the two men. Mafia rules maintain that a *consiglieri* or other family power broker should be another Sicilian.

During dinner with Kay, Michael is quiet and evasive. He mutters, "I don't want you to get involved." Afterward he goes to see his father at the hospital but finds the place deserted. His father's bodyguards have been sent away, and Michael knows that his father is vulnerable to attack. The hospital sequence, which ends with Michael telling the don, "I'm with you now," changes Michael from "civilian" to family player. Rather than panic as Sonny fears, Michael takes control. He warns the nurse that men are coming to kill his father, whom she helps move—tubes and monitors attached—out of the room. He then enlists the help of Enzo the baker, who unwittingly arrives with flowers to pay his respects. Michael and Enzo stand outside the hospital entrance pretending to have guns to scare off the assassins, who eventually drive on when they see the entrance guarded. Enzo is rattled by the close call with the killers, and his hands shake as he tries to light a cigarette. But Michael is steady, projecting a cool tolerance for danger that was previously cloaked.

The Turk's bodyguard, a corrupt police captain named McCluskey (Sterling Hayden) arrives and ends up breaking Michael's jaw. In the next scene, in the family library, Michael makes the formal leap into the family trade. First, he sits quietly in the background, listening to Tom and Sonny fight over strategy. Sonny brags about the "hundred button men on the street," referring to the soldiers who carry out the killing. Michael finally speaks, slowly outlining a calculated scenario that ends with him murdering Sollozzo and the police captain. After a long silence, the other men burst into laughter. They're amused not only at who's suggesting the double homicide but that one of the victims should be a cop. The fallout from killing a cop is too dangerous, Tom warns, fearing that the family would be an outcast within the Underworld.

"Whadya gonna do, nice college boy? Didn't wanna get mixed up in the family business—now you wanna gun down a police captain," Sonny says, mocking Michael's plan. "Whadya think this is, the army where you shoot 'em a mile away? You gotta get up close like this . . . badabing! You blow their brains all over your nice Ivy League suit."

Michael remains unruffled. He soon convinces them that feeding a story to the reporters on their payroll about a "crooked cop who got mixed up in the rackets and got what was coming to him" will deflect the fallout.

Michael's murder of Sollozzo and McCluskey in the restaurant is a taut orchestration of anxiety, anticipation, and swift violence. After the blood of Michael's victims mixes with sumptuous food and purplish wine, Michael flees looking both stunned and deliberate.

When Vito is brought home from the hospital, he learns that Michael murdered his enemies and is now hiding in Sicily. The Sicilian sequence shows Michael roaming the idyllic countryside with two armed bodyguards, eventually visiting the village where his father was born: Corleone. It became the family name when Vito arrived in America. Interspersed between Michael's courtship of a *signorina* named Apollonia are ferocious episodes involving Sonny and Connie back home. Connie's husband, Carlo, angry that he's been shut out of the family business, stages a cruel row with Connie to entrap Sonny. Sonny has come to his beaten sister's aid before, savagely thrashing Carlo on the street while his goons kept the crowds back. But Connie (Talia Shire) had begged Sonny not to seek revenge, shrieking that the fight was her fault. This time, taunted by Carlo's mistresses and his abuse, a very pregnant Connie performs an orgy of destruction in her own home, smashing china and glass and waving a butcher knife at Carlo. He knocks the knife away, corners her in the bathroom, and beats her with a belt. Afterward Connie calls Sonny, who drives off without bodyguards and becomes trapped at a deserted Long Island tollbooth, where he's mowed down by a waiting squad of machine gunners.

Meanwhile, in Sicily, Michael marries Apollonia (whom Molly Haskell dubs his "tribal soul mate"). The elegant peasant wedding captures the stony austerity of the bombed-out village, where all the men have died from vendettas and the ravages of World War II. Michael patiently abides by the village customs and treats Apollonia with tenderness. However, shortly after their nuptials, she's blown up by a car bomb meant for him.

In the wake of Sonny's death, Vito orders Tom to call a meeting of the heads of the five families. "This war stops now!" he proclaims. In an opulent boardroom fit for any corporate power broker in America, Vito ensures Michael's safe return from Sicily in exchange for his political links to launch the interfamily drug business. But Vito warns, "I believe this drug business is going to destroy us in years to come." One of the other Mob bosses assures Don Vito that the drug trade will be kept "respectable" and not targeted at children. "In my city, we would keep the traffic in the dark areas. The coloreds. They're animals anyway, so let them lose their souls."

After Michael has been back a year, he goes to see Kay outside the school where she teaches. Wearing a black fedora and overcoat, Michael looks like a spider against the warm, muted tones of the New Hampshire autumn. He explains that he's working for his ailing father, and she reminds him that he vowed never to get involved. Michael argues that his father is no different than other powerful men, likening Vito to a senator or president. Kay tells him how naive he sounds, noting that such leaders "don't have men killed." He stares for a moment (most audiences laughed out loud) and explains that his father's way of doing business is over. "In five years the Corleone family is going to be completely legitimate," he adds. "Trust me. That's all I can tell you about my business."

She's seduced by the memory of an idealistic Michael and his caressing, intimate words that now reassure her: "What's important is that we have each other, that we have a life together, that we have children." She finally climbs into the back of his black limousine and becomes a Corleone.

Eventually taking a seat behind his father's regal desk, Michael seems agitated and frosty as he listens to Tessio (Abe Vigoda) and Clemenza (Richard Castellano) complain bitterly to Vito about other families eating into their territories. They also are hinting that Michael is too inexperienced to run the family. "Do you have faith in my judgment? Do I have your loyalty?" Vito asks them, tearing himself away from feeding his fish. "Then be a friend to Michael and do what he says." But Michael, in his pricey three-piece suit, doesn't have his father's tact or ability to subdue people. Rather than reassure his *capi,* Michael tells them little about his plans. He also abruptly fires Tom as *consiglieri* but keeps him on as family lawyer.

Soon Michael goes to Las Vegas, where Fredo was sent to lay low during the street wars. Fredo has changed from the meek, invisible Corleone son to a garish dresser who barks at bellboys to act tough. Neither camouflages his basic docility or self-loathing. As such, he has become a lackey for mobster Moe Greene (Alex Rocco), whom Michael has come to strong-arm into selling his casino to the Corleone family. First, Michael gets Fontane to agree to perform regularly at the new Corleone casino. Then, despite Fredo's earnest effort to impress Michael Vegas-style with glitzy women and free-flowing booze, Michael orders Fredo's party dismantled. When the legendary Greene (a Bugsy Siegel match) finally makes his splashy entrance, Michael quickly slices through the small talk and demands that Moe answer for slapping Fredo around in public. Moe bellows back, "He was banging cocktail waitresses two at a time!" After Michael pushes for a buyout price on the casino, Moe storms off, leaving Fredo to scold Michael for being disrespectful. Michael is barely able to contain his rage and further humiliates Fredo by ordering him never to take sides against the family again.

As Vito putters around his garden sipping wine, he and Michael go over the plan to wrestle back power for the Corleones, in particular, from the Barzini family. In between tender musings between father and son about the family legacy, they plot Michael's next move. Later, while Vito is playing the monster for his grandson's amusement, he has a heart attack and drops dead in his vegetable garden.

At Vito's funeral, Michael recalls his father's advice that the capo who approaches him with a Barzini meeting will be the traitor, who turns out to be Tessio. Michael also explains to Tom at the funeral that he plans to meet with the heads of the five families after the baptism of Connie's baby; he has agreed to become a godfather.

The film's finale has become one of the most celebrated in the history of the cinema. Playing on the contrasting structure, the last sequence juxtaposes the rituals of the baptism with the preparations of Michael's henchmen to massacre his enemies. In one scene, the priest dabbles ointment on the infant's lips while the face of a Corleone soldier is smeared with shaving cream before his appointment to kill. As the sequence progresses, the baby moves from peaceful slumber to frantic wailing, the organ from melodic tones to frenzied noise, with Michael answering the priest's query: "Do you renounce Satan?"

As Michael answers his vows, each boss of the five families is summarily executed. Barzini is shot and rolls down the steps (as in *Little Caesar* and *The Roaring Twenties).* Moe Greene is shot in the eye, another boss is blasted at close range by Clemenza's shotgun, a revolving door becomes a cage for another victim, and the remaining kingpin is riddled with bullets alongside a naked and equally bloodied woman. Moreover, Michael orders Tessio and Carlo killed as revenge for their betrayals. Carlo is garroted by Clemenza; and realizing he's about to die, Tessio tells Tom, "Tell Mike it was only business. I always liked him."

In the last sequence, a hysterical Connie bursts into Michael's office and howls about the massacre, which included her husband. "Want to know how many men he had killed?" Connie shrieks at a confused Kay. "Read the papers. . . . That's your husband."

The final scene in *The Godfather,* in which Michael (Pacino) assumes irrefutable power over the shored-up crime family. The gentle kiss to his hand from Clemenza (Richard Costellano) belies the horrendous bloodshed Michael has orchestrated to command such respect and earn such a Mafia honor.

Michael is anxious about Connie's hysterics. He tries to put his arms around her, but she quickly pulls away and wails more ferociously than before. Michael avoids Kay's eyes and nervously paces around his office. She keeps asking if Connie's accusations are true until he shouts a reminder that she's not to ask about his business. Soon he quiets himself and permits her to ask him "just this once." Fearfully, she repeats her question, and Michael looks her straight in the eye and utters a convincing "no." Her face relaxes and they embrace. After she leaves to fix them a drink, remaining out of focus in the front of the frame, Michael is in the background surrounded by his underlings, including his father's workhorse Clemenza. Clemenza then kisses Michael's hand and calls him "Don Corleone." Just as the door is about to shut on Kay's view, the last shot shows her face flushed with dread as she comprehends the unfolding ritual.

SO YOU WANT TO BE A MAFIOSO?

While the film was in production, two fronts threatened to interfere with its completion: the Mafia and the Italian-American Civil Rights League. The league was the brainchild of Joseph Colombo, who was earnest about its charitable goals and its push to stop the defamation of Italian Americans at the movies—especially the Mafia stereotypes. Unfortunately, he was the wrong man for the job. In reality he was the head of New York's Colombo crime family and under indictment for running a syndicate, income tax evasion, larceny, and conspiracy. No one was sure whether to blame the league or the Mafia for the bomb threats that occurred during filming. Eventually producer Al Ruddy met with Colombo and negotiated a deal to stop the harassment of film production. Ruddy agreed that the word *Mafia* would never be uttered onscreen, and a portion of the film's premier ticket sales would go to charity. Columbo in turn secured the Mafia's cooperation, and production problems disappeared and unions become friendly again. Real mobsters then became frequent guests on the set, serving as extras. In fact, Caan was often spotted with known mafiosi. It was enough to prompt the *New York Times*' Nicholas Pileggi (who would later cowrite *GoodFellas*) to note that Caan had "absorbed so many of their mannerisms that undercover agents thought for a while that he was just another rising young button in the Mob."

Because life and art often mimic each other, before filming of *The Godfather* was finished, Colombo was gunned down by Mob assassins just a few feet from the Gulf and Western headquarters—the entity that owns Paramount. Shortly after the film's premiere, mobster Joey Gallo was killed in a Little Italy gang war that many claimed capped off a decade of Mafia turf battles. Moreover, the FBI claims that the film prompted Mafia soldiers to start kissing hands and referring to their bosses as godfathers—a practice that Puzo had dreamed up. John Gotti's underboss and infamous government rat, Sammy "The Bull" Gravano, told ABC's Diane Sawyer in 1997, "I love *The Godfather*. I thought that was the best interpretation of our life that I've ever seen." It was a great plug for the film, just rereleased for its silver anniversary.

Audiences reacted favorably, too, helping *The Godfather* earn $1 million a day in its initial release. It soon became the biggest box office success in film history to date. Historian Arthur Schlesinger noted, "There is no doubt that *The Godfather* is the cultural phenomenon of the season."[15] Jeffrey Chown observed, "This film touched American's collective unconscious. It appeared during a phase when 1960s activism and rebellion was just beginning to turn to the cynicism and self-interest of the 1970s."[16]

Like previous gangster films, Coppola's film was condemned for excessive violence. He credited Arthur Penn's work in *Bonnie and Clyde* for inspiring the scene of Sonny's massacre and argued that most of the violence depicted came from real life. Most critics, however, assumed the film's amplified violence was in keeping with the film's epic scope. *Time* noted, "*The Godfather* is a movie that seems to have everything—warmth, violence, nostalgia, the charisma of Marlon Brando in one of his finest performances, and the dynastic sweep of an Italian-American *Gone with the Wind*." The *New York Times* was impressed with how the film "describes a sorrowful American Dream." But Pauline Kael said it best, noting *The Godfather* was "the greatest gangster picture ever made."

Brando became a media darling all over again. The fuss prompted one Paramount executive to acknowledge that Brando's masterful portrayal of Don Vito "reminded the film community that Brando really is a legend . . . one of the great actors in the history of the cinema."[17] Puzo had envisioned Brando as Vito when he wrote the novel. When he heard that Danny Thomas was going to buy Paramount to get the role, Puzo recalled, "That got me scared." Coppola insisted on casting Brando but had to wage a war to get him. Brando's awesome talent, when on target, was never in question, but most studio executives complained that he was unreliable and difficult on the set. All agreed, though, the role needed "the greatest actor in the world" because Vito must emote quiet, dignified power and possess a commanding charisma to anchor the story (yet he appears on-screen for only one-third of the film).

In a remarkable 16-millimeter screen test, despite Brando wearing a kimono and sporting a ponytail, then stuffing Kleenex in his jowls to make him seem older, Vito emerged. Brando earned an Oscar as best actor but did not disappoint his critics, either. He sent Sacheen Littlefeather to the ceremony to reject his award as a protest against the treatment of American Indians in Hollywood. That night, the film also won Oscars for best picture and for the Puzo-Coppola screenplay. Oscar history also was made when three of the film's stars competed for best supporting actor—Caan, Duvall, and Pacino. (Joel Grey won for *Cabaret,* which went home with most of the night's awards.)

Duvall and Caan—alumni of Coppola's early films—had landed their roles fairly easily. (De Niro had auditioned for Sonny, but Coppola called his "electrifying" audition too intense for a character who's also a doting older brother.) But Michael—the most pivotal role in the film—had been difficult to fill. The casting search in general was called the biggest since *Gone with the Wind,* according to the producer, with trying to find Michael equated to looking for Scarlett O'Hara. Because Michael was to be an "outsider," some pushed for a more "all-American" type. Ryan O'Neal was considered, coming off the huge hit *Love Story,* as well as Warren Beatty and Robert Redford. But Coppola wanted the unknown Pacino and fought for him as he had for Brando. "I thought you should see the mark of Sicily on the face of the character," Coppola explained, aptly describing the ancestry and look of Pacino.

Pacino screen-tested several times for the part with decreasing effectiveness. Even after he was hired by Coppola's sheer force of will, the first few days' work left studio executives doubtful about his screen charisma. They complained that he looked "dull," recalls Pacino, who assumed he would soon be fired. (Coppola, too, was plagued by nightmares about being sacked, hearing rumors that the studio had already contacted Elia Kazan to finish the film. On top of casting wars, Coppola had fought to make the film a more expensive period piece and later insisted the studio find money to let him shoot on location in Sicily.)

In the end, Coppola's instincts were right, and Pacino's acting abilities proved extraordinary. His controlled but smoldering portrayal of Michael was penetrating and haunting. Even Brando noted Pacino's "intense, brooding quality." Through Pacino, Michael evolved from a sweet loner to a merciless despot—making the transformation in subtle behavioral ways. He also effectively invented a new gangster prototype for the modern era. Pacino's Michael and his cool, calculated pose supplanted the Cagney-style gangster that had endured since the 1930s (which Caan paid homage to as Sonny).

Pacino was raised in the tough South Bronx and dropped out of Manhattan's High School for the Performing Arts at age 17 to work menial jobs until he could afford acting school. After his study at Lee Strasberg's Actors Studio (the workshop of the young Brando)—Pacino won kudos and a Tony for his work on Broadway. But it was his potent performance as a heroin addict in the film *Panic in Needle Park* (1971) that got him noticed by Coppola.

When audiences cheered for Michael's well-choreographed hits of revenge, however, Coppola said he was shocked. "I was disturbed that people thought I had romanticized Michael, when I felt I had presented him as a monster."[18] However, it's easy to understand Michael's appeal: he had been a brave soldier, a stricken widower, a loyal son to his father, and a shark at business with a no-nonsense style of dealing with competitors. That last reason—and its bloody demonstration—grabbed us the most. It also makes us feel the most guilty for getting such a vicarious thrill out of Michael's revenge.

Coppola further failed to recognize that given the era, the Corleones were confirming that "Americanization is a failure," as Edward Rothstein of the *New York Times* commented. Michael retains his ethnicity and still beats a white-bread America that looks down on him. The film embraces the genre's timeless obsession with the underdog. First, we like him because he wins. Second, the American system he beats is one that deserves a pummeling—at least it seemed that way to many people in 1972.

BECOMING BIGGER THAN U.S. STEEL

When Paramount started clamoring for a sequel, Coppola suggested Scorsese. "The idea of a sequel seemed horrible to me," Coppola recalled. "It sounded like a tacky spin-off." Then the studio offered him a lot of money and complete creative control.

"I had to write the script . . . in three months and then go right into preproduction. . . . I was making a $13 million movie as if it were a Roger Corman picture."[19] Of the follow-up story, Coppola explains, "I didn't want to go the easy way, which would be just to continue the story of Michael. . . . I decided to make a film about a man obsessed with his father's success on the eve of his own failure."

The sequel takes the theme of contrasts to new heights—juxtaposing not only violence with family devotion but one era with another. The film switches back and forth between Vito's humble life in Little Italy in the early 1900s to Michael's new-world success in the 1950s. The two plots comment on the escalating corruption of gangsters as well as their connection to modern-day America.

The sequences that involve a nostalgic look back at the young Vito are filmed in rich sepia tones that accentuate their historical perspective (with period costumes created by Theadora Van Runkle of *Bonnie and Clyde* fame). Vito is easily able to dominate the Italian universe created within America, whereas Michael, *la famiglia*'s new patriarch, seems out of place in the western frontier of Nevada and the carnival colors of Havana's nightlife.

The plot of the 200-minute film—also coauthored by Puzo and Coppola—focuses on betrayals as well. But it's often difficult to know who's forsaking whom and why. In the end, Michael's goal, as in Part I, is to avenge his enemies and maintain control over his domain. Young Vito's struggle is to gain power despite starting out a disadvantaged immigrant hemmed in by poverty. He eventually blends Sicilian customs with American opportunity and becomes a crime czar. Michael, on the other hand, is threatened by forces his father never had to deal with: the loss of family and deteriorating respect for traditions. Mama Corleone (Morgana King), the heart of *la famiglia* but its most unwitting member, tries to soothe Michael by explaining that he can never lose family. "Times are changing," he laments.

The film opens with the last scene of Part I, in which Michael is revered as the new Godfather. The story shifts abruptly to Sicily circa 1901. The nine-year-old Vito accompanies his mother to his father, Antonio's, funeral. His brother, Paolo, is soon gunned down by his father's murderer—the local Mafia chieftain, Don Ciccio. Ciccio refuses to heed the widow's pleas to spare her remaining son, the "weak, dumb-witted" Vito. Ciccio says Vito will "come for revenge" when he becomes a man. (After becoming an American Mafia boss, Vito returns to Sicily to kill Ciccio personally.) Hearing Ciccio's refusal, his mother puts a knife to his throat and orders her son to run for his life. She's killed before Vito's eyes, but the townspeople hide him despite warnings of Mafia reprisals. He's soon smuggled out of the country and arrives at Ellis Island, where his name is mistakenly changed from Vito Andolini from Corleone,

Poignant, heartwarming scenes in which a hauntingly quiet nine-year-old Vito (Oreste Baldini) arrives alone at a bustling, chaotic Ellis Island. In *The Godfather Part II,* the young Sicilian immigrant and his offspring will conquer the New World and subvert the American dream to attain criminal riches.

Sicily, to Vito Corleone. He also is quarantined for three months for smallpox. The quiet boy takes each setback with quiet resignation and unblemished innocence. In the last shot in the sequence, he sits alone in his sparse room at the hospital, humming to himself and looking out the window at the shores of America—now just a river away.

As a grown man with a wife and son, Vito (Robert De Niro) works at Abbandando Grosseria. But a series of events start him down a different path. First, he loses his meager job because the grocer is forced to hire the nephew of the Black Hand—the local extortionist named Fanucci who makes everyone in the neighborhood pay protection money. After meeting Clemenza (Bruno Kirby), Vito learns the tricks of stealing to gain material wealth and clout. When Fanucci approaches them for a cut of their profits, Clemenza and his associate Tessio agree to pay, but newcomer Vito votes no. He instructs them to give him the money, ask no questions, and trust him to "make him an offer he don't refuse." He stalks Fanucci during the San Gennaro festival in Little Italy and shoots him three times, the last time with the gun's barrel jammed in the blackmailer's mouth. Completely composed, Vito then joins his wife and three sons on their brownstone stoop for the rest of the festival. As Vito's reputation in the "import business" continues to grow, so does his prestige in the neighborhood.

The opening sequence for the modern era is the Holy Communion of Vito's grandson Anthony in Lake Tahoe in 1958. In addition to showing many familiar faces, the sequence also introduces new players: Pentangeli, an old-timer who worked for Vito; Hyman Roth, the legendary Jewish mobster from Miami (inspired by Luciano's

Like criminal immigrants before him, Vito (De Niro) soon abandons such dead-end jobs as being a grocer in Little Italy. Instead he earns his Underworld fortune blending old-world Mafia with American opportunism. His import business remains in Little Italy in *The Godfather Part II* flashback scenes, but the maturing Vito uses the business as a front for illegal rackets.

associate Meyer Lansky); Johnny Ola, Roth's "Sicilian messenger boy"; and a U.S. senator named Geary.

At the Communion party, Pentangeli (Michael Gazzo) demands that Michael stop the Rosato brothers' encroachment on his New York territories. He complains that the Rosatos recruit "spicks . . . niggers . . . do violence in their grandmothers' neighborhoods" and ignore the gambling business until they have spent themselves on drugs and whores. Michael says that the Rosatos remain unharmed because they answer to Roth, with whom Michael is working on a deal.

"Then you'll give your loyalty to a Jew before your own blood?" sneers Pentangeli. Michael reminds him that Vito worked with Roth, but Pentangeli warns, "Your father did business with Hyman Roth. Your father respected Hyman Roth. Your father never trusted Hyman Roth."

Also at the Communion party, Geary (G. D. Spradlin) accepts a handsome endowment check from the Corleones, which he pronounces in its American patois in public. In private, the name rolls off his tongue as if he's cursing in Italian. Michael wants the senator to help him with the gaming license on a new casino that the Corleone family wants to take over. But Geary tries to extort money from Michael instead.

GEARY: I intend to squeeze you. I don't like your kind of people. I don't like to see you come out to this clean country . . . your oily hair and dressed up in those silk suits and you try to pass yourselves off as decent Americans. I'll do business with you but . . . I despise your masquerade, the dishonest way you pose yourself . . . yourself and your whole fucking family.

MICHAEL: Senator, we're both part of the same hypocrisy. But never think it applies to my family.

Geary is later caught with a bloodied, dead prostitute at one of Fredo's brothels. When Tom shows up and offers the shamed, shocked senator the Corleones' help, he's permanently drawn into their service. Although Geary was a willing partner in the sex games with the prostitute—with whom he had played the bondage game before—he can't remember how she was murdered. The circumstances point to a Corleone frame as Tom assures Geary that the woman had no family. "It'll be like she never existed. All that's left is our friendship."

Besides the legal gaming license, Michael must deal with Roth, who's the casino's true owner along with a partner. Roth, however, gives Michael approval to oust the partner and remain in business with him. As the plot unfolds, however, Roth double-crosses Michael several times while pretending to be his mentor. "He acts like I'm his son, his successor, but he thinks he's going to live forever," Michael remarks. "He wants me out."

The first time Roth tries to have Michael killed is in his bedroom at the Nevada homestead, "where my wife sleeps . . . where my children come to play with their toys." Michael is led to believe that Pentangeli attempted the murder for revenge. At first Michael believes this theory but ultimately realizes that Roth set him up. Later, while Michael and Roth are in Cuba working on a deal that will make them "bigger than U.S. Steel," Roth tries again. He first wants the Corleone's $2 million investment, but Michael is stalling for time and sends his henchman to kill Roth first. While in the act of smothering Roth in his hospital bed, however, Michael's man is mysteriously shot by Cuban soldiers. Part of Michael's reluctance to consummate the deal is his astute observations about Castro's unfolding revolution, which threatens the entire structure of Cuba's gambling kingdom.

When Fredo arrives in Cuba with the Corleone money, he's dressed in a white suit with black shirt and a coordinating hat, looking every inch the pimp. Fredo also is on hand to perform his specialty—arranging entertainment for Michael's business associates, including Geary. But Fredo resents being treated like an errand boy. Michael finds out how deep Fredo's outrage goes when he learns that Fredo is the one who betrayed him and nearly got him killed in his bedroom. Fredo lies when he's introduced to Ola, pretending they never met. But when the group moves their party to a sleazy club to watch a live sex act, Fredo boisterously recalls how Ola first took him there. Michael hears the gaffe and fills in the rest. During Havana's colorful New Year's Eve celebration, he tells Fredo he has arranged to flee and has a plane waiting to take them both away. Then he forcefully grabs Fredo, kisses him on the mouth (the kiss of death) and hisses, "I know it was you Fredo. You broke my heart."

Fredo had tried to confess his betrayal to Michael earlier when the two shared a drink at a Cuban bistro. Fredo admitted that he had been mad at Michael when he was "stepped over" so that Michael could head the family. Fredo also regrets not marrying a woman like Kay, instead of the showgirl Deanna—whom Michael's men frequently have to subdue. At the Communion party, a drunken Deanna had to be dragged off the dance floor while yelling, "Never marry a wop. They treat their wives like shit."

Back in Nevada, Fredo, who disappeared in Cuba, is found and brought to Michael. He explains how he was lured with the promise of a deal of his own, not a hand-me-down from Michael. But he swears he knew nothing about a hit. Michael banishes Fredo, telling him that he's no longer a brother or a friend. But during the interrogation, Fredo divulges a useful item: Roth has a Senate lawyer on his payroll and has arranged for Michael to be exposed before a congressional committee investigating organized crime. At the hearing, a nervous Geary gets a former family soldier to admit that he never took orders directly from Michael and that the godfather claims are speculation. But prosecutors have a star witness who worked under Michael with no "buffers": Pentangeli. The Corleones believed Pentangeli had been killed by the Rosato brothers on Roth's orders, but Pentangeli survived the attack and was told Michael ordered the hit. When nabbed by the feds, Pentangeli agreed to testify against the Corleones out of revenge.

While in Washington, Kay announces she's leaving Michael. When he tries to sweet-talk her back into the fold, she plays her trump card, revealing that she didn't have a recent miscarriage as he believes, but had an abortion. "Like our marriage!" she shouts. "Something that is unholy . . . evil." With bitter relish, she explains how she refused to "bring another one of your sons into this world. . . . I had it killed because . . . this Sicilian thing" must end. Michael strikes her and leaves her cowering in fear. He assumes custody of their children, Anthony and Mary, and allows Kay to visit only when he's not home.

Connie is put in charge of Michael's children. Connie was shown at the film's start as a party girl and a lousy mother. She arrived at the Communion with the blond gigolo Merle (Troy Donahue) in tow. She came for money to marry him and leave for Europe, although Michael pointed out that "the ink on your divorce isn't dry yet." Then he lectured, "You see your children on weekends. . . . you fly around the world with men . . . who treat you like a whore." But later in the film, she comes to him on her knees, whispering, "I'd like to stay close to home right now if it's all right." She admits that she did things to harm herself because she was mad at him but now realizes he was just being strong like Papa and taking care of business.

When Mama Corleone dies, the last obstacle is removed for Michael's final sweep of revenge. He had vowed to spare Fredo while she was alive, but at the funeral, hugging Fredo at Connie's insistence, Michael glares at his henchman and signals Fredo's murder. Michael also orders Roth be shot. Roth is trying to flee Castro's Cuba and go to Israel but is refused entry, as in every country he tries to bribe for a resident's permit. And although Roth has only six months to live, Michael wants him assassinated at the Miami airport. Tom asks Michael, "Is it worth it? You won. . . . you wanna wipe everybody out?" Michael says, barely above a whisper, "Just my enemies."

He has distanced himself from Tom as well. When Michael had left for Cuba, he affectionately called Tom "his brother." He also appointed Tom the acting don in his absence, noting Fredo has "a good heart . . . but he's weak. And he's stupid. And this is life and death." Tom wept that day, moved by Michael's love and trust. As the story comes to a close, Tom asks, "Why do you hurt me? I've always been loyal to you."

To save Michael the trouble of murder, Pentangeli kills himself. First, he gets "amnesia" during the government hearings when he spots his older brother from

Michael (Pacino) stares coldly at his henchman and gives the order to kill Fredo (John Cazale), whose head Michael gently presses to his chest in a gesture of brotherly love. Pacino found the sequel's hardened Michael more difficult to portray. His character's metamorphosis degenerates from the original film's invading darkness to Part II's finale of Michael as a remorseless, dying soul.

Sicily seated next to Michael. The message: your family will be killed if you testify. Tom visits Pentangeli in prison, and they discuss how traitors were handled during the Roman empire (the structural model for the Mafia). If they committed suicide, their families were taken care of for life by the Roman regime. Pentangeli explains how they took a bath, "opened their veins and bled to death," prefiguring his own demise.

Michael once again settles the family business, but this time the victory leaves him totally isolated. A final flashback shows the day when the Japanese bombed Pearl Harbor and Michael enlisted in the Marines. It was also Vito's birthday. While the children wait to surprise their father, Sonny tells Michael that soldiers are saps "because they risk their lives for strangers. . . . your country ain't your blood." Michael answers derisively, "That's Pop talking," implying that his allegiance is to America and not to an antiquated code from the Old Country. Michael is ultimately left alone in the room—as he is in life. He never felt he belonged to the family nor wanted any part of its criminal business. Yet after a dozen years, he has become its leader and the most ruthless of them all. The last scene shows Michael, still wearing a wedding ring—another hollow symbol of his pose as a family man. He's sitting alone outdoors as winter overtakes the Nevada landscape. The film ends with an extreme close-up—Michael's eyes now dark and desolate.

HOW DO YOU LIKE MICHAEL NOW?

Coppola said at one point in the production of Part II that he realized he had created two movies. His friend and director George Lucas told him, "Throw one away. . . . it doesn't work." But Coppola had a hunch that if he could make it work "it could be fantastic." (The story of young Vito was in Puzo's novel, but Michael's downfall was fresh material and largely attributed to Coppola's pen.)

The dual theme worked well enough to earn the film the best picture Oscar again and be labeled by several critics as superior to the original *Godfather.* Pauline Kael wrote, "It is an epic about the seeds of destruction that the immigrants brought to the new land, with Sicilians, WASPs, and Jews separate socially but joined together in crime and political bribery. This is a bicentennial picture that doesn't insult the intelligence."

But as Vincent Canby notes, "This beautifully made, intermittently exciting film never pulls us once and for all into its own world." The sequel is more ambitious but also less sentimental about its characters, and this distance makes it less intoxicating. But the film also represents a brave attempt by Coppola to tamper with his art rather than merely repeat a formula. Nominated for 11 Oscars, including three of its stars for best supporting actor again, the film earned Oscars for direction, screenplay, art direction, and musical score. De Niro won for his supporting role, which he delivered nearly entirely in Sicilian. He beat out fellow nominee and acting mentor Lee Strasberg, who had been suggested for Roth by Pacino, another former student. Although Strasberg had never been in a film before, Coppola rightly believed that the actor could be a "wily, introverted wizard" to confound and match the ripened Michael.

Kael praised Coppola in particular, writing, "The sensibility at work in this film is that of a major artist." Richard Schickel of *Time* also gave Coppola heaps of credit, noting that he made a "richly, detailed, intelligent film that uses overorganized crime as a metaphor to comment on the coldness and corruption of an overorganized modern world."[20]

Others thought that without Brando, the story's heart was gone. Molly Haskell wrote in the *Village Voice,* "The characters are not only not mythic—they are not even very interesting."[21] Some noted that the Communion scene that opens the film had none of the radiance and authenticity of the wedding that opened the original. Coppola claimed that was exactly his point—to show the loss of ethnic identity and to rob the family of its soul. Coppola recalls, "This time, I really set out to . . . punish Michael. . . . Yet . . . in the way that I think most profound—from the inside. . . . At the end he is prematurely old, almost syphilitic, like Dorian Gray. I don't think anyone in the theater can envy him."

But, like the original film, Part II struck a nerve with American audiences, who made the film a box office hit. Nixon had just been disgraced by Watergate, leaving the American presidency horribly disfigured. Audiences may have equated the failure of the Corleones' political high jinks as a fitting, cynical commentary on power politics of any kind. Besides, Michael may have been stripped of his allure, but Vito had lovingly recreated images about the Ellis Island experience. It further boosted the ongoing fad for Americans to take an interest in their backgrounds and trace their roots.

Coppola's endings, particular in Part II, also effectively retooled the genre's longstanding tradition that the gangster must be killed in the end to fulfill his tragic destiny. Coppola gave us the gangster's "afterlife" in mortal form: his body keeps functioning, but his humanity has died. "Michael Corleone, having beaten everyone, is sitting there alone, a living corpse."[22]

Coppola vowed never to make another sequel. "Give me a minor chord, Nino," he told his composer while working on scoring the last scene for Part II. Then Coppola added, "Just so there will never be a Part III, give me one more bong." Afterward Coppola sighed and said, "It's over." (Sixteen years later, someone would make Coppola another offer he couldn't refuse, and the bewitching Corleone saga would go on.)

THE TWIN PEAKS OF MOVIE GANGLAND

Despite the conventions of the genre and the similar cultural backgrounds of Scorsese and Coppola, the two directors have carved out distinctive approaches from which today's gangster has descended. Scorsese showed us that "Violence is a form of expression. . . . its how people live."[23] For De Niro's Johnny Boy (and later his Travis Bickle and Jake LaMotta, among his Scorsese characters), violence is endemic and spontaneous. Johnny Boy blows up a mailbox for kicks, and lurking underneath the gangsters' constant ribbing of one another is potential confrontation. In contrast, Coppola's masterful dons and *capi* use violence to expand business, maintain control, avenge a death, or send a harsh message. Careless displays are not their style; they're bad for business.

For Scorsese, being Italian is not nearly as vital as religious shaping or as influential as the neighborhood. For Coppola, being Catholic is not nearly as profound as being Italian. But both men understand the interdependence of these factors within their culture, and their movies are in a way the presentation of what happens when the mix produces hypocrisy and sin. Coppola explained that being Italian "helped enormously" in making *The Godfather,* including the lush depiction of Catholic rituals. "I knew the details [and] I've almost never seen a movie that gave any real sense of what it was like to be an Italian American."

For Part II, Coppola put his conscience into the story's political digs, but he admits, "my heart was really in the Little Italy sequences." Although their visuals might seem literally transcribed from the historical photographs of Jacob Riis, Coppola's portrait of such condensed humanity is ripe with sentimentality and the lush symbols of a more earnest, culturally rich past. In fact, he was criticized for portraying young Vito as more of an Italian Robin Hood of the quaint Lower East Side than the slum thug he is in Puzo's novel. As Roger Ebert notes, "The Don seems more like a precinct captain than a gangster, intervening on behalf of a poor widow who is being evicted from her apartment."

Part of Coppola's mythmaking is his assumption that these characters, despite their pathology, are capable of unselfish love. Not only are Vito and Michael nurturing and patient fathers, but neither of them displays any desire for women other than their wives. As Vito puts it, "A man who doesn't spend time with his family can never be a real man." He wins our affection for his devotion to family, "not as a Scarface in flashy suits and monogrammed shirts."[24] For Scorsese's characters, however, their capacity for love has deteriorated along with the neighborhood. Their families are fragmented, and what relationships they have lack intimacy and genuine affection. The hoodlums lack respect for each other, and at the core of their alliances is mutual suspicion.

Each director exploits the cinematic tools he has at his disposal—music, lighting, camera work, and editing—to suit his unique style. Coppola uses "scored" music to complement mood and dramatic action. *The Godfather* score, by Frederico Fellini's composer, Nino Rota, is among the most memorable in cinema history, "laced with intricate melody, Italian-tinged passages, and hauntingly tragic themes."[25] The music ensures continuity within a self-contained and artificially created environment. Scorsese achieves the opposite effect. He encourages the "contamination" of popular songs, just as other outside forces hassle and soothe his characters. As Johnny Boy strides in slow motion down the length of the bar with a woman on each arm, "Jumpin' Jack Flash" by the Rolling Stones tells his tale. Eric Clapton's guitar adds screaming energy to Charlie's frantic street cruising. These hoods worship at the altar of rock 'n' roll, and they approach the bar's jukebox—stocked with oldies—as if it were a shrine. Meanwhile, the old-world uncle indulges in Italian opera, comfortably transfixed by the past and keeping American noise tuned out.

Coppola's camera work is carefully composed and visually stunning. His director of photography, Gordon Willis, composed a "tableau format," in which the camera frames scenes so that they look like paintings. *The Godfather* contains a beauty that the cinema had been losing as movies increasingly absorbed the influence of television's flatness (in part due to videotape).

In contrast to Coppola's interplay of light and dark, *Mean Streets* seizes the nightscape with headlights and shadowy alleys. Indoor shots of the bar are washed in red, giving it the look of a brothel—or a hell. Scorsese borrows the urgency of television news with a jumpy, handheld camera that crowds his characters. As Johnny Boy runs through the streets, the camera stalks him, bumping and dodging through traffic with him.

Most distinguishing, Coppola's mobsters keep reaching for the globe and seeking Herculean accomplices to share the blame for their corruption: human greed, cultural pollution, unchecked capitalism, and permanent vice. Scorsese, on the other hand, dredges up few excuses for his unromantic street punks to blame for their hard luck. What molds a gangster is not Scorsese's concern. He merely provides an eye witness account of common hoods going about the day-to-day vandalism of society.

The 1980s would prove fertile ground for gangsterism—both on and off the screen. Other directors would join the frenzy, but they would toil on the turf that Coppola and Scorsese had already staked out. They, too, continued to perfect their screen gangsters: Coppola's dons kept feeding their titanic greed, trying to pull the heavens into their hell, and Scorsese's petty hoods worried about losing their lifestyles along with their blood.

CHAPTER 9

Gorging on Gangsters

> You don't have the guts to be what you want to be. You need people like me so you can point your fuckin' finger and say, "That's the . . . bad guy!"
>
> —Tony Montana (Al Pacino), *Scarface,* 1983

With the arrival of the 1980s came another epic story about American gangsters and one of the genre's most distinguished films. But *Once upon a Time in America* wasn't the brainchild of an Italian American director investigating the degeneration of Italian American gangsters. Sergio Leone, a native of Rome, was old-world Italian, and his film gangsters were new-world Jews. Leone was already famous in America for inventing the "spaghetti Western." The best of Leone's Westerns starred Clint Eastwood as the Man with No Name and were praised for being stylish, ironic, and unflinchingly violent. So was his new gangster film.

Leone had admired the American cinema even while working for his father, a pioneering filmmaker in Italy. He then worked for other Italian directors in the 1940s before becoming an assistant to several American masters, including William Wyler and Raoul Walsh.[1]

Leone's 1984 film, *Once upon a Time in America,* is the tale of a gang of Jewish gangsters from New York's Lower East Side. Spanning five decades, the film tracks their humble beginnings as petty thieves and their success as bootleggers and finally reveals the disintegration of two of them into callous old men. The story primarily focuses on the gang's leader, Max (James Woods), and his soul mate, Noodles (Robert De Niro). The other two principal gang members, Patsy (James Hayden) and Cockeye (William Forsythe), are killed in the 1930s.

As British critic Damian Cannon notes, the plot and characters are revealed through a complex maze of "flash-backs, flash-forwards, dreams and memories." The film opens in the 1930s with the cold-blooded killing of a woman and the savage beating of Fat Moe (Larry Rapp) in an effort to find Noodles. He's stretched out and blissfully stoned at a nearby opium den. After the initial spurts of violence set the tone, the film then shifts down and requires close attention to quiet nuance, behavioral clues, and visual rhythm.

The young bootlegger Noodles goes looking for the $1 million supposedly hidden at a railroad station locker, where his gang (now dead) kept their combined earnings. But the money is missing. The next scene puts him in 1968 as a displaced nobody living under an assumed name. He's intrigued by a notice addressed to his real name—David Aronson—from a synagogue regarding the grave sites of Max, Patsy, and Cockeye. He visits the mausoleum and finds another key to the station locker, where he finds a briefcase filled with money. Confused and curious, Noodles returns to the old neighborhood to question Fat Moe, who now runs a seedy diner in the same spot his parents had their thriving kosher restaurant in the 1920s. Noodles then has a flashback that returns him to that era.

As a teenage boy in the tenements, Noodles is disconnected from an unhappy family and obsessed with Fat Moe's sister Deborah. (We know that she grows up to become a famous dancer.) As a young girl, practicing her pirouettes in the back room of the family restaurant, she shares Noodles's love but despises his street life. "He'll always be a two-bit punk so he'll never be my beloved," Deborah laments, referring to Noodles's work for a neighborhood thug named Bugsy.

Noodles soon meets Max—a brash, intense kid who has just moved from the Bronx—when they both try to roll the same drunk. After a beat cop steals their booty, they catch him having sex with the underage prostitute Peggy and blackmail him into cooperation. Peggy also introduces Max and Noodles to quick, passionless sex. As their friendship grows, Max becomes jealous of Deborah or anyone who distracts Noodles from their partnership. Max is cunning and ambitious, convincing Noodles that a Jewish holiday—when the stores are deserted—is the ideal time to steal. Max's audacity also gets them severely beaten by Bugsy, who views Max and his gang as competition.

In Sergio Leone's epic *Once upon a Time in America,* the ambitious young street hoodlums—dressed in grown-up 1920s fashions—agree to pool their criminal profits and behave like blood brothers. They believe their gang will provide the rewards otherwise denied by their slum environment. The gang, though, will turn into another cauldron of misery for boys who become men.

As soon as the boys make money, they buy flashy grown-up suits to announce their arrival. But Bugsy and the cops keep the harassment up. In a stunning scene that blends haunting slum scenery and gutter warfare, a clash in the streets ends with the youngest gang member, Dominic, dying from a gunshot in the back. He's smaller than the others and couldn't run as fast. Noodles grieves over his body then retaliates in a stabbing frenzy that kills another boy and a cop. Noodles is sent away for a dozen years, robbing him of whatever youth he had left. When he's released from prison, he's withdrawn, privately battered, and emotionally ruined.

Noodles is released in time, though, to reap the rewards of the gang's Prohibition success and its speakeasy. They also find work with an Italian gangster who pays them to rip off a jeweler. While the others go about collecting diamonds, Noodles grabs Carol (Tuesday Weld), who set up their heist, and brutally sodomizes her—an act that stuns even Max. Max then masterminds the group's double cross of the Italian mobster to keep the diamonds and the money. Another racket for them is union infiltration as well as its flip side: beating up union organizers and other "socialist assholes" for factory owners.

After a corrupt police chief named Aiello (Danny Aiello) gets mixed up in the union deals, his weakness for a male child (after four daughters) prompts the gang to switch babies in the hospital nursery to terrorize him into cooperating. (They never do return the right baby.)

Carol, the woman Noodles raped, strolls into the speakeasy one day seeking participants for a gang bang and later ends up as Max's girlfriend. Noodles opts out of the initial group sex, rejecting her now that she's the aggressor. Instead he pursues his childhood sweetheart, Deborah (now Elizabeth McGovern). He reveals a deep longing for her and the different life she could offer him. In a gorgeous scene, Noodles reserves an entire seaside restaurant as grand as a hotel ballroom with a full orchestra to try to court her. But sadly, she says, although she will always love him, her destiny is the theater. He gets instantly sullen. On their way home in the back of a limousine, she kisses him tenderly, but Noodles defiles the moment and turns her rejection into another rape.

Afterward he goes to the opium den for solace. When he returns to the gang, Max is furious that Noodles has been chasing Deborah and neglecting business. "Fuckin' broads do not get in the way," Max shouts, brutally denigrating Carol to prove his point. Max is also peeved at Noodles's increasing reluctance to get into more sophisticated rackets. Noodles balks when Max gets them involved with a corrupt politician named Sharkey. "You still think like some schmuck in the streets," Max complains. "You'll carry that stink of the streets with you your whole life."

Max—whose father "died in a nut house"—becomes enraged when Noodles accuses him of being more crazy than ambitious. When Max cooks up a scheme to rip off the Federal Reserve ("it's a dream I've had all my life"), Carol and Noodles conclude that Max is suicidal and will bring them all down. Torn and intimidated, Noodles tips off the cops; the job is botched, and a bomb fire kills Max, Patsy, and Cockeye.

In a flash-forward to 1968, Noodles accepts an invitation from a business tycoon and prominent politician named Bailey at his swanky Long Island mansion. Noodles not only finds Deborah there but learns she's Bailey's mistress. Bailey had told the press he came to America "as a starving immigrant to make a lot of money," Deborah explains. Bailey turns out to be Max, who didn't die in the explosion 35 years ago. He reinvented himself, stole the gang's money, and pulled Deborah into his lie. Max is now under indictment, and his kingdom is on the brink of collapse. He put payment in the locker and brought Noodles out of hiding to perform one last contract: to kill him and put him out of his magnificent, dressed-up misery.

With the powerhouse party for the Bailey Foundation buzzing outside Max's office door (with a Catholic cardinal in attendance), Max urges Noodles, "You do it. You're the only person I can accept it from." Max explains that it's his way of paying Noodles back for taking his money and his girl and letting him torture himself for years thinking he killed his friends.

Noodles, finally realizing that Max has manipulated him his whole life, refuses. "I have a story also. . . . it's a little simpler than yours," he says, like a sibling who has been living in another's shadow. Noodles leaves but stops across the street from the estate's gated entrance long enough to spot Max staring at him. Max is standing stoically in the middle of the road, waiting for the truck roaring toward him. A shot of the garbage truck grinding up refuse off the street hints that Max has become part of its ripe compost.

Noodles finally realizes that he has squandered a lifetime believing in loyalty and friendship with a man who lacked a soul. The last shot shows the younger Noodles in the womb of his favorite opium den. Reclining and staring at the ceiling, he breaks into an irrational grin—a smile of utopian numbness, a rarity coaxed from a man who knew little joy.

The film is a treasure not only because it revels in the genre's conventions but because it tampers with the basic story line and introduces another option. Rather than focus on the rise of the kingpin, the film follows the path of the associate who has a bird's-eye view of unbridled ambition but lacks the natural audacity himself. Noodles was not destined to be a successful gangster, but tragically he was enough of a gangster to have rotted out his humanity. His story is more poignant and complex because he has been abused by two worlds—Max's and Deborah's—and is locked out of both.

Leone's original film, at three hours and 47 minutes, was initially butchered to just over two hours for theater release. When later restored to its full length, the film earned resounding critical acclaim. The film is a vision, however, of a European looking at immigrant life in America. The film is titanic in scope but doesn't have the organic quality of an eyewitness account. It lacks the clear-eyed naïveté of someone inside the culture.

Part of Leone's wisdom, well earned by age 63, was knowing that after the two *Godfather* films, among others, the genre had enjoyed its renaissance. He didn't need to re-create a gritty, turn-of-the-century Lower East Side; Coppola had carved a superb one into our memories in *The Godfather Part II.* Leone's version, then, contains streets too wide and too clean to be real. Yet they suit his imposing portrait rather than detract from it. Moreover, Leone knows we no longer see the speakeasy (his is as regal as the Waldorf Astoria) as a symbol of sexual energy or criminal frenzy. It has become hackneyed. Thus his 1930s milieu looks more like an old-world tapestry that's threadbare but has grown more elegant with age.

After *Once upon a Time in America,* no one should have attempted to make another gangster film about the 1930s without unearthing a startling new discovery. Leone's gangster saga (his last film, as it turns out) was the Last Supper for classic-era gangsters.

Pauline Kael admired the film, which she said obsessed Leone for 10 years before he started production. But she, too, notes how it strays from realism when it aims for high art. "Leone doesn't have enough interest in the real world to make the gang's dealings with bigger mobs and its union tie-ins even halfway intelligible," Kael wrote. "Leone's vision of Jewish gangsters is a joke. As a friend of mine put it, 'It wasn't just that you never had the feeling that they were Jewish—you never had the feeling that they were anything.' " She also faults the casting of Elizabeth McGovern as Deborah, who "looks dispirited. . . . she's so bad you feel sorry for her." Because she's unconvincing as Noodles's path toward salvation, his wrenching regret over losing her falls short. Essentially, Kael concurs, the film is "kitsch aestheticized by someone who loves it and sees it as the poetry of the masses."

THE ROARING EIGHTIES

Leone's view of Noodles in a 1968 milieu lacked contemporary context, except for the Beatles' *Yesterday* crooning in the background. Moreover, coming out in 1983, the film failed to tap into the nervous system of American society at the time—a necessary linkage for a gangster film to connect with its audience. And America in the 1980s was about excess, not Leone's undertow of elegance. At least that was the impression that leaked through most of the era's popular-culture products, including the movies.

The "Brat Pack" of young directors of the 1970s, Brian De Palma and Michael Cimino (along with Coppola, Scorsese, Spielberg, and Lucas) had matured. In the 1980s, De Palma and Cimino presented their versions of modern gangsters. Unfortunately, their efforts were as self-indulgent and reckless as the times.

The era's extravagant spirit prompted columnists and analysts to dub it the Roaring Eighties. The stock market, as in the Roaring Twenties, was the promised land, the destination for the nation's best and brightest. Wars on foreign soil or the Peace Corps—with its two-decade anthem to serve America or develop the world—were no longer preoccupations of the young. The focus now was on homegrown interests, private ambitions, and flaunting any success the moment it was earned. It was the decade of the yuppie—the young urban professional as wolf—who wanted a hard body by Fonda, a BMW in the driveway, and his MTV.

Oliver Stone's prickly film *Wall Street* (1987) aptly captured the core goals of the eighties, with its leveraged buyouts, junk bonds, and motif of "greed is good." In this film about financial brokers and their lousy ethics was the best gangster to stalk the screen in years: Gordon Gekko. His suits were not pin-striped but Giorgio Armani. But Gekko wasn't an ambitious immigrant who cheats because he thinks he's an outsider. Rather, Gekko was as American as Michael Milkin or Charles Keating—men who have everything but want more.

Gekko was a nightmare vision of ambition run amok and a well-dressed ugliness that reflected the nation's ravenous appetite for instant gratification. However, as in other eras, few movies investigated such men as public villains. Even journalism had trouble keeping track of the savings and loan debacle, brought about in part by deregulation, cynical moneygrubbing, and a roller-coaster economy. The S&L bailout would cost taxpayers roughly $500 billion.

However, the Mafia bosses, Columbian drug lords, and the occasional overdosed celebrity continued to snatch the headlines. No better story surfaced than the tale of Underworld trouble as old dons died and new regimes took over. Mafia families were designed to operate just below the public's consciousness. But that era ended when Carlo Gambino, the boss of New York's most powerful family, died in 1976. Gambino had lived in a modest row house in a quiet Brooklyn neighborhood with a loyal wife he coveted and few flashes of the millions he earned. In keeping with the times, a battle ensued to succeed him, pitting a Wall Street impresario against an aspiring yuppie.

Gambino's appointed successor was his cousin and brother-in-law Paul Castellano. The Castellano family had arranged for the 19-year-old Gambino to be smuggled to American shores and join its New York operation in 1921. Castellano had also been a close adviser to Gambino and proved himself ruthless enough for the top job. A few short years after Connie became a widow in *The Godfather,* Castellano contracted a hit on his son-in-law for abusing his pregnant daughter—also named Connie.

But Castellano was a new kind of don. He dressed like a banker and had a diversified portfolio of investments along with healthy, legitimate business entities (wholesale meats among them). He also enjoyed a handsome cut from the Gambino family rackets, including construction bid rigging, extortion, union infiltration, gambling, and murder for hire. In an era of escalating greed, Castellano's Wall Street aura reminded everyone that he had never paid his Mob dues on the street, and his *caporegimes* also figured that he wasn't giving family operations his full attention. Among the disgruntled troops was John Gotti—a rising star with street punk credentials and colossal ambition. The war for power was launched, and Mario Puzo couldn't have written the outcome any better.

Castellano had told his mistress (and FBI informant) that "people like me die in the street," and there he died just before Christmas 1985 after leaving a Manhattan steak house. Mob watchers then eagerly waited to see who would emerge as the new don. The *capi* vote was soon obvious when Gotti began wearing $2,000 Briani suits. He also stood in the middle of Mulberry Street in Little Italy accepting deferential kisses from a stream of Mafia hoods who came to pay their respects. His audacity and movie star delusions helped make Gotti the most fascinating gangster since Al Capone. Gotti ended up with nearly the same fate. (After he was arrested several times on racketeering charges but set free, the press dubbed him the Teflon Don. He graced magazine covers, and fans cheered him each time he emerged from the courthouse victorious. In 1992, though, he was finally convicted, aided by the extensive testimony of Gravano, his former underboss. Gotti was sentenced to essentially 100 years in jail, where he now languishes.)

ANOTHER GANGSTER FRESH OFF THE BOAT

The 1980s saw a new crop of immigrant criminals arrive on American shores looking for Underworld opportunities. Among them was Tony Montana, the lead character in *Scarface*—an updated version of the classic Howard Hawks film. Tony comes by boat after Castro opens up Mariel Harbor and invites Cubans to flee to the United States, which welcomes them as survivors of communism. As the film's prologue reads: "It soon became evident that Castro was forcing the boat owners to carry back with them not only their relatives, but the dregs of his jails. Of the 125,000 refugees that landed in Florida, an estimated 25,000 had criminal records."

Scarface was another Oliver Stone script steeped in political intrigue and able to exploit the knee-jerk excess of the era and the genre. Stone used a skeleton of the original Ben Hecht story and expanded it to indict the Reagan drug war. The film suggests that the war on drugs had much the same effect that Prohibition did in the 1920s: it helped feed a rollicking black market getting rich off the enduring desire for banned substances. This time it's not alcohol but illicit drugs, which Americans continue to snort, smoke, and shoot up at record levels.

As bootlegging once did for the ambitious but uneducated Tony Camonte, the drug trade provides employment for his descendent Tony Montana, who quickly rises to become a rich, powerful drug lord. At the time of Montana's story, the political strategy was to keep drugs illegal, stop the flow breaching U.S. borders, and tell the citizenry to "Just say no."

Part of the gangster's timeless appeal is that he gets to spout theories we try to ignore. As Tony puts it, "It's the fucking bankers, the politicians. . . . they're the ones who want to make coke illegal so they can make the fucking money and . . . get the fucking votes. . . . They're the bad guys!"

As the film opens, U.S. officials interrogate Tony (Al Pacino), suspecting that he's a criminal who sneaked into the country among the refugees. He speaks fluent English, which he tells them he learned from watching gangster movies with Bogart and Cagney. If the scar on his cheek doesn't signal that Tony is trouble, his heart-shaped tattoo embellished with a pitchfork does, for as the officials suspect, it's the mark of an assassin. Tony is shipped off to a detention camp as an undesirable. There he's joined by his associates, Angel (Pepe Serna), and Manolo "Manny" Ray (the updated Raft character, played by Cuban American Steven Bauer). A Cuban businessman arranges their green cards in exchange for their murder of a former Castro collaborator who once tortured the businessman's brother. The victim is also among the refugees. "I would kill a communist for fun," Tony says. "But for a green card I carve him up real nice."

Tony does and settles in the United States. But he soon loses patience with his American life as a dishwasher—a menial job for someone with such criminal talent. He soon finds work with the local crime network, which earns him $500 a hit. His price goes up to $5,000 for one afternoon's work when the sharklike mobster Omar (F. Murray Abraham) instructs Tony and his cohorts to pick up two kilos of cocaine from Colombian traffickers. Tony then meets with the Colombian connection, Hector, in a motel room. Hector pushes Tony for the money, assuring him the drugs "are close by" for transfer. Tony wants to see the drugs first, swearing that the money, too, is "close by." Hector's female accomplice Marta aims a shotgun, and the room fills up with other armed Colombians. Marta turns up the volume on the TV (ironically showing a cop show) to drown out the sound of Hector's chain saw revving up in the bathroom. Hector and his men put choke chains on Tony and Angel and string them up in the shower. Hector gruesomely tortures Angel—his grim weapon growling and whining until Angel dies and is hauled away. But Hector's chain saw conks out—the engine clogged with blood and flesh—before they get to Tony.

Manny, who has been standing watch on the street and absorbed by passing bikinis, finally bursts into the room with a chattering Uzi, and any Colombians left standing scatter about the motel grounds as they return fire. Tony finds Hector on the street and shoots him in the forehead. Then he phones Omar to tell him that he's keeping the "buy" money and the cocaine for his trouble.

Tony finally visits his estranged family. They live in a modest home kept going by his mother's work as a seamstress in a Florida factory. She doesn't believe him when to explain his cash roll, he says that he's a "political organizer" for an anti-Castro group. Not only is she worried that he'll snare her daughter Gina into his corrupt world, but she's concerned over his unnatural affection for his sister. After calling him a bum and an animal, she throws him out. The subplot follows the original film's suggestion of incest along with Tony's head-banging ability to keep suitors away from his sister. Gina (Mary Elizabeth Mastrantonio) also can't resist flirting with Manny, who wants her but resists, fearful of Tony's rage. Tony eventually draws her into his world, buying her a lavish beauty salon (she's a beautician) and introducing her to Miami's nightlife.

Tony's rise within the Underworld accelerates after he meets Omar's boss, Frank Lopez (Robert Loggia), a mobster who runs one of Florida's top drug distribution

Tony Montana (Pacino) visits his Cuban immigrant mother (Miriam Colon) and sister (Mary Elizabeth Mastrantonio) shortly after arriving in America. Rather than toil in a factory as his mama does, Tony makes his fortune in the Miami drug trade. Brian De Palma's *Scarface,* a remake of the 1932 classic, updates the immigrant angle by making a Latino the modern social underdog.

outfits. Omar (dressed in the gangster outfit: white suit and dark shirt) keeps a suspicious, jealous eye on Tony while Tony ogles Lopez's smart-mouthed girlfriend, Elvira (the new Poppy, played by Michelle Pfeiffer).

Lopez offers Tony two lines of advice: "Don't ever underestimate the other guy's greed . . . and don't get high on your own supplies." Tony, doomed to ignore both, puffs on a fat cigar and grins at Lopez, whom he concludes "is soft." When Manny asks Tony what he's after, he shouts, "I want what's coming to me . . . the world . . . and everything in it."

Unlike Manny, who chases every woman in his path, Tony has marked Elvira as his own. But Elvira wants nothing to do with Tony, whom she figures "just got off the banana boat." Tony has a plan to win her, though. "In this country you gotta make the money first. Then when you get the money, you get the power. Then when you get the power, you get the woman," he tells Manny. "That's why you gotta make your own moves."

Those moves include being more than Lopez's messenger boy when Tony and Omar go to Bolivia. Omar has been sent to talk with a cocaine factory owner named Sosa (Paul Shenar), who's looking for an American distributor. Tony begins negotiating a new deal directly with Sosa, who's impressed by Tony's potential. Sosa dismisses Omar and has him killed by hanging him out a helicopter with a rope around his neck. (Sosa tells Tony that he's certain Omar was a government informant.) Sosa also warns Tony never to double-cross him. Espousing his peculiar, self-styled code of honor, Tony vows, "I never fucked anybody over who din have it comin'."

Lopez is upset that Tony agreed to accept 150 kilos of cocaine each month. Tony argues, "You can't lose money, no way. We make $75 million on this deal. . . . The time has come to expand." Lopez reminds Tony whose operation it is and warns him that Sosa is a snake. "Remember, I told you when you started, the guys who last in this business are the guys who fly straight . . . low key . . . quiet," Lopez says. "And the guys who want it all . . . they don't last."

No longer trusting Tony, Lopez goes on the attack. He sends a crooked cop to squeeze Tony for monthly protection money and has him ambushed in a nightclub. Tony escapes, figures out it was Lopez who set him up, and plots revenge with Manny's help. He sets a trap for Lopez (as in the original film), and he and Manny kill Lopez and the corrupt cop.

With Lopez dead, Tony goes to collect his prize: Elvira. She asks few questions and packs her things as ordered. Tony once told her, "With the right woman, there ain't no stopping me. I could go right to the top." After a vulgarly lavish wedding, they move into a mansion decorated in garish contrasts of deep red, black, and white and embellished with ornate gold trim. His office is equipped with six monitors and a leather throne for a chair, adorned with his initials scrolled in gold. Between two massive staircases that curve up toward the second floor is a fountain with statues holding up a globe emblazoned with the message: "The World Is Yours." (Tony first saw it flashing on the side of the Goodyear blimp and borrowed it for his personal motto.)

Tony's success in the cocaine trade escalates quickly. So does his personal use of coke. He's making so much money that his American banker tells him the price to launder the cash must be hiked also. "The IRS is coming down heavy on South Florida," the smug, Waspish moneylender complains.

Soaking in his gargantuan, solid-gold tub with bubbles and a cigar (reminiscent of Rocco in *Key Largo*), Tony raves at a TV commentator who argues against legalizing drugs as a way to stop the spiraling drug trade. Elvira wearily listens to his tirade before shouting, "You're an immigrant spick millionaire who can't stop talking about money." He bellows that she's a hypocrite for not working for the money she spends, wasting her life snorting cocaine and lying on her back waiting for him like a common whore. Eventually Elvira leaves him after a nasty exchange in a restaurant where he loudly complains about her being a junkie, adding, "I can't even have a kid with her—her womb is so polluted."

Tony is finally caught trying to launder $1.3 million that he can't explain earning. After newspaper headlines report that he's out on $5 million bail, his oily lawyer warns him that he may go to prison for tax evasion. Tony vows, "I'm not going back in any cage."

At a meeting with Sosa in Bolivia, Tony is presented with a deal by compromised Bolivian and U.S. officials: his legal troubles will disappear if he helps kill a UN delegate who has vowed to expose Sosa's drug cartel and its multigovernment connections. Tony agrees but welches when the deal collides with his self-styled honor code. As he chauffeurs the Bolivian assassin around New York, Tony comes unglued when the plan to bomb the victim's car means killing the man's wife and child. Even more reprehensible in Tony's view is that the killer won't "look 'em in the eye" when he kills. Tony sneers, "You gotta hide with that shit," referring to a remote control device that triggers the bomb. Just as the switch is to be flicked, an agitated Tony shoots the assassin instead.

When Tony arrives back in Florida, his mother is panicked that Gina is missing. Manny is gone as well. Tony arrives at Gina's new posh place in Coconut Grove, and

Manny answers the door in his robe. Tony pumps several bullets into him before Gina can explain that they were just married. A dazed Tony, numbed from the killing and the nonstop flow of coke, orders his men to grab his hysterical sister and put her in his white Rolls Royce.

Looking disheveled in a rumpled pin-striped suit, Tony prepares for war with Sosa—most of it to be waged inside Tony's gaudy palace. While his enemies begin crawling over the estate walls and ambushing his soldiers, a frazzled Gina comes into his office, half dressed, and dares him to have sex with her as he has always fantasized. Looking comatose, with his nose blotted with coke powder, Tony tries to appease her, but she takes aim with the gun she has hidden at her side. One of Sosa's men crashes through the window and kills Gina. Tony is jolted out of his stupor and quickly avenges her. Amid the roar of gunfire outside his office, he lays his head on her shoulder and sobs, begging her to smile for him. He kisses her cheek and tells her lifeless body to "wait here."

After taking in another snootful of cocaine, Tony loads himself down with an arsenal of weaponry, including a grenade launcher. He bursts through his office door and, shooting from the balcony, kills a half dozen men who are scrambling around the main floor. But more keep coming, their guns hammering away at him. Amid the deafening assault, De Palma's quick close-ups blend with slow-motion shots that show rolling, tumbling bodies littering the steps and floor. Tony roars boastfully, "I'm still standing!" while groping for more ammunition and jerking from another volley of bullets ripping into his body. Finally, one of Sosa's men creeps up behind him and

Tony (Pacino) becomes a coked-up, torqued-out killing machine in the outrageous finale of *Scarface*. The film had a profound impact on young filmmakers. Tony had ignored the age-old wisdom never to "get high on your own supplies." The real Scarface, Al Capone, ignored such advice and contracted syphilis sampling his own supplies; in his case, prostitutes at his own brothels.

shoots him at close range, sending Tony's body flying off the balcony and into the fountain. The camera pans up from his shredded torso and past the globe that promised him the world. Then the screen displays the message: "This film is dedicated to Howard Hawks and Ben Hecht."

DE PALMA WASTES THE GANGSTER

Following the death of Howard Hughes, film prints of his locked-away masterpiece *Scarface* began circulating and stirring up interest in a remake. Producer Martin Bregman hired Oliver Stone to write the screenplay and then brought Brian De Palma on board. Originally set to direct was Syndey Lumet (*Serpico, Network*), but Bregman decided that De Palma's provocative style was more in tune with the material.

De Palma was another Italian American filmmaker who attended film school for training and broke into the business as a Corman protégé. As a boy, De Palma saw himself as the voyeur within his family, watching everyone else prosper and earn praise. "My father was the great doctor, my mother was the opera singer, my oldest brother the genius, my older brother the artist—what did that leave me?"[2]

Like Coppola, De Palma was somewhat of a nerd. "I was one of those science types who was always up in his room," he recalled.[3] He attended Columbia University, where he started as a physics major but soon discovered theater arts and ultimately film. He earned minor acclaim in the late 1960s with several low-budget comedies (a few with the then-unknown De Niro). Gene Siskel describes these early films as focused on Vietnam, social protest, and radical chic. But soon De Palma's work earned him the mantle of the "poor man's Hitchcock."[4] His special talents were a "stylish handling of rather garish . . . thrillers," Ephraim Katz notes. De Palma, too, credits French New Wave as an influence. He even aspired to be "the American Godard."[5]

De Palma's smart, voyeuristic style first emerged in horror films such as *Sisters* (1973), for which Hitchcock's musical collaborator Bernard Herrmann was hired. Music from *Psycho* and *Vertigo* was also used in the film. Then came the precocious *Carrie* (1976), based on Stephen King's novel about telekinetic power, and buckets of pig's blood as prom night surprises. In the early 1980s, De Palma practically invented a new subgenre best described as horror noir, blending the stalking qualities of a thriller, the plotting nuances of suspense, and the bloodletting of a slasher film. Two prime examples are *Dressed to Kill* (1980) and *Body Double* (1984). Regarding the former, *Halliwell's Film Guide* noted, "Occasionally brilliant, generally nasty suspenser clearly derived from many viewings of *Psycho*." The guide sees Hitchcock again in *Body Double* but this time blended with "semi-porn" touches.

For better or worse, though, *Scarface* is the film De Palma will be remembered for, if only for its fight with the censors (mostly for the chain saw scene). Cuban Americans protested the criminal pall that the film cast on their community, and most critics attacked its over-the-top approach and the deluge of coke, cuss words, and bullet holes. Karen Jaehne wrote in *Cineaste,* "De Palma's violence does not seek stylistic excuses or social justification: because his vision eschews elegance in favor of exaggeration." Critic Pauline Kael noted that the story seems gutted: "Tony is just starting to learn the ropes, and then, sated with wealth and dope, he's moldy." David Chute wrote in *Film Comment* that "we need to see . . . how, exactly, did this crass, pushy, vulgar little creep harness his personality and pull in so much dough."

And despite the suggestion that he blends into Miami's Little Havana on his arrival, there's little about Tony to suggest a Cuban persona—outside Pacino's passable accent.

Only his mother shows signs of genuine roots, but like the 1932 film, Mama Montana is written in clichéd shorthand; she reveals few clues about her son's deviance.

Pacino also seems to be either shouting at a level equal with his tour de force performance in *Dog Day Afternoon* or in a cocaine stupor. Kael noted, "After a while, Pacino is a lump at the center of the movie. . . . This is a . . . picture with a star whose imagination seems impaired . . . without internal contradictions or shading." Then, she added, there's the "*White Heat* finale," in which "he gets more vital as he's pumped full of lead."

Film historian Frank Beaver notes, "*Scarface* is shallow precisely because Stone is unable to project himself into any kind of otherness. *Midnight Express* works because it's told from the protagonist's [point of view]. *Scarface* fails for the same reason."[6] (Stone had won an Oscar for his *Midnight Express* screenplay.) Laurent Bouzereau claims that Stone "felt quite frustrated by De Palma's approach to his screenplay. The director made the scenes longer than they had originally been written by Stone. In consequence, the script had to be cut by at least thirty pages—mostly scenes that involved character development."[7]

Others pointed out that De Palma's excess suited the era. David Ansen of *Newsweek* wrote, "It's a grand, shallow, decadent entertainment which, like all good Hollywood gangster movies delivers the punch and counterpunch of glamour and disgust." Roger Ebert called the film "a wonderful portrait of a real louse," giving the film an enthusiastic thumbs-up. Although the film barely broke even at the box office, several young filmmakers were devouring it, taking it apart, studying it, and would soon try to mimic it.

MANHANDLING NESS AND THE UNTOUCHABLES

De Palma was never a media darling like Coppola. And he had become a target of feminists ever since Angie Dickinson's character was slashed to death for adultery and *Body Double* had a female murdered with a ghastly use of a power drill. He also irked critics for not making films about likable characters—misogynists or otherwise. With *The Untouchables,* his 1987 film, he found several likable characters: a veteran cop, a brave police cadet, a nerdy but alert accountant, and a natty Capone assassin. Unfortunately, they weren't the focus of the film. The exhausted legends of Eliot Ness and his rival Al Capone were its main thrust. Capone is wisely reduced to an "extended cameo," enabling him to hover over the story without stealing it. But Ness is at its heart, and he can't sustain the show; the film drags whenever he's put at center stage.

Worse yet, the film's overall tone is borrowed from the 1950s TV series, which was already an aberration of the classic era G-men pictures. The TV show had been based on Ness's book *The Untouchables,* written by journalist Oscar Fraley. He had overheard Ness telling war stories in a bar and was soon invited by Ness to write his memoirs. The TV show expanded the material to include Ness battling public enemies from Dutch Schultz to Legs Diamond—gangsters Ness had never met. In reality, Ness raided Capone's operations and pestered the kingpin like a fly buzzing around a bear's head. His most memorable moment was parading Capone's seized beer trucks up Michigan Avenue in front of Capone's headquarters to rub it in. Ness and his Untouchables did find incriminating ledgers during a raid and turned them over to accountants, who nailed Capone. (Ness's raids, the ledgers, and getting Capone's bookkeeper to testify about them are included in the film.)

Eliot Ness's real band of incorruptible bootlegging battlers was reduced to three formidable associates in *The Untouchables.* Ness (Kevin Costner) is flanked left to right by Andy Garcia, Sean Connery, and Charles Martin Smith. In this box office hit but flawed film, De Palma makes everyone interesting except Ness.

David Mamet, who's best known for his Pulitzer prize–winning play *Glengarry Glen Ross,* takes further liberties with the screenplay. One serious misstep, though, is having Ness push Capone's henchman Frank Nitti off a building in a fit of revenge. This scene, in which Ness becomes corrupted to nab the corrupted, flagrantly robs the story of its "good versus evil" claim, which Mamet touted in interviews. (Nitti actually shot himself in 1943 after being indicted for extortion and mail fraud.)[8]

Mamet acknowledges that Ness has become as contorted and tired a figure as Capone. "That's why I made up this story about a sort of Eastern sheriff who comes West and meets a cowboy who teaches him a few tricks." De Palma himself said, "I never saw it as a gangster movie. I saw it more like a *Magnificent Seven,*" the distinguished 1960s Western.[9] Those comments in part explain why *The Untouchables* makes a flawed gangster film. It's not disappointing because it embroiders myths. Nor is it contrary to the genre to have Ness resort to gangsterish tactics. Both treatments are as old as the tommy gun. The film's failure is modeling Ness after the monotone, stone-faced Ness as Robert Stack played him on TV—surely with his tongue in his cheek. Kevin Costner doesn't stand a chance to make his atavistic Boy Scout stand tall against updated, stepped-up violence and a robust Capone, who's now allowed to spew four-letter expletives and use a baseball bat to settle employee problems (the scene is based on fact). Even Costner said that his first instinct was to tinker with the role and bring some crosscurrents to the character. "He's not the sharpest," noted Costner of Mamet's Ness. But Costner played him straight as urged by the filmmakers. Later, after his performance was panned for being wooden, Costner said of his initial doubts, "I was right."

The scenes that sparkle in the film, though, are those involving Jimmy Malone (Sean Connery), the veteran "cowboy" cop. During a secret meeting in a church (at Connery's suggestion), Malone gives Ness some advice on how to beat Capone. "He pulls a knife, you pull a gun. He sends one of yours to the hospital, you send one of his to the morgue. That's the Chicago way." Aside from the tainted morality, Malone is the film's emotional anchor and comes off as an authentic Irish cop, brogue and all. He also mentors the young police cadet George Stone, whose real name is Guiseppe Petri. (Actor Andy Garcia is a Cuban American.) George Stone obscures his heritage because the image of Italians has been so ravaged by Capone. Malone justifies that shame when he later chides a corrupt police lieutenant for running "with the dagos." Stone has his shining moment in the film's climactic shoot-out when he expertly picks off a killer despite his having a hostage draped across him. Even the short-lived, bespectacled accountant neatly portrayed by Charles Martin Smith has fun shooting bad guys instead of checking ledger columns. On the other side of the law, Billy Drago as Nitti is a superb supporting player, and the warm whites of his Armani suits against the sleek black sedans are an authentic reminder of the genre's best stuff. (Armani furnished the film's wardrobe.)

The action scenes have De Palma's fingerprints on them, though. A superb sequence takes the assassin's point of view as he creeps through Malone's apartment, meandering down its narrow halls until he eventually splashes Malone's blood on the walls. The more celebrated crowd pleaser is the well-choreographed shoot-out in Union Station. In this scene, De Palma pays tribute to film pioneer Sergei Eisenstein and his classic *The Battleship Potemkin.* Recalling Eisenstein's famous sequence, De Palma uses the station's enormous staircase to re-create the hugging drama of a baby carriage tumbling down the steps while caught in threatening crossfire. But rather than elongate time and maximize the moment's impact through intricate editing as Eisenstein did, De Palma shoots the scene in "pretentious overuse of slow motion," as critic Dave Kehr wrote, and plenty of Peckinpahish spurts of blood. Slow motion is key, though, to capturing the playful toss of a gun from Stone to Ness, who work in tandem like a shortstop and a second baseman.

The film falls apart in the Ness-Capone face-offs. Weighing in against Costner is the ferocious, bloated-for-the part De Niro, who gained 30 pounds to make Capone swell back to life. And he does so at the expense of heaving Costner off the screen. (Bob Hoskins was let go and paid $200,000 when De Niro decided at the last moment he wanted the role.) De Palma even opens the film with Capone in his milieu, mistakenly priming the audience for his ribald magnificence to return. Meanwhile, we have to endure Ness's insipid, heavy-handed scenes as a family man, equipped with a proletarian brown-bag lunch and dull sermons about injustice. His naïveté is astonishing when he's shocked that his first raid is spoiled by a tip-off from cops on Capone's payroll. Any newsboy on the street could have clued him in. (The real Ness—vain but not stupid—grew up in Chicago and knew the extent of Capone's network. Mamet, another Chicago native, should have known better.)

In the two nose-to-nose matchups between Ness and Capone, the inequity is downright embarrassing, especially when Ness taunts Capone to step outside and fight him as if they were two teenagers at a rowdy sock hop. "You want to fight, you and me, right here?" mewls Ness to a Capone flanked by a half dozen armed men. De Palma, too, seems to have realized that the moment was more funny than poignant and inserts a comic interplay. As Ness digs into his suit coat to unholster his gun, Capone's thugs snap, click, and aim their weapons back at him.

After the film's courtroom finale (never a good place to end a gangster movie), Ness can't resist one more poke at Capone. He trots across the courtroom, sticks his chin out, and announces, "Never stop fighting till the fighting's done." It's too bad, since the film is already a fable, that De Palma didn't let Capone punch Ness for such a silly scrap of dialogue.

Ness (Costner, *right*) taunts Capone (De Niro, *left*) in the courtroom finale of *The Untouchables*—a deflating place to end a gangster film, especially one featuring De Niro's fat and flamboyant Capone.

Even more frivolous is De Palma's lone female character in the film: Ness's wife (so nondescript that she's listed in the credits as such). After De Palma had been picked on about his female characters, he told the *New York Times,* "If you put a woman in peril [now], you're into a political issue of violence against women. . . . I think it's unfair." He demonstrates his ire by turning Mrs. Ness into a mannequin who has no blood to spill. She's about as necessary to the story as another fedora. Her presence only makes women seem trivial—a worse screen fate than being iced by a thug. He could have dispensed with their ersatz family moments and intimated her utility with the lovely note she leaves in Eliot's lunch that tells him she's proud of him and draws a heartfelt smile from Ness.

(Even Mrs. Montana, the slinky, smart-mouthed Elvira, was a failed De Palma stand-in and untrue to the genre. It's highly unlikely Elvira could have offered that much lip to the hair-trigger Tony and not have gotten smacked. Michelle Pfeiffer portrayed an Elvira clone in the 1988 dark comedy *Married to the Mob,* but this time her character is as vulnerably alive as she is tough talking.)

The Untouchables was a box office triumph despite its flaws. But some critics noted its sleight of hand. *Commonweal*'s Tom O'Brien called the film "exquisite-looking schlock." However, putting the auteur theory in play, it would have been interesting if De Palma had made the Capone-Ness story without Mamet's retrograde script. Capone died insane, and Ness ended his career supervising the fight against venereal disease on U.S. military bases—ripe ingredients for De Palma's usually cynical but stylish approach. As Robert Stack described Ness, "There's a touch of strangeness to him. Nobody could declare war on Capone and be found normal."[10] Tapping the complex motives of such a man—still admired for refusing bribes—would have made a more absorbing film.

If his gangster films to date had left the impression De Palma didn't understand the genre, then his 1986 comedy film, *Wise Guys,* proved he understood gangsters' core paranoia. Gene Siskel called the lead characters "the Laurel and Hardy" of the local Mafia, but De Palma has some affection for them—or at least a healthy curiosity about their warped lifestyles. As Roger Ebert wrote in his review, "Laughter doesn't come out of formula, or stupidity, or the manipulation of things that worked in other films. It comes out of characters and performances, out of people who have some measure of reality, and whole dilemmas we can share." De Palma finally gives us flesh-and-blood gangsters—if sadly only for laughs.

MICHAEL CIMINO AT HELL'S GATE

Like Leone, Michael Cimino likes to construct moving poetry and ravishing scenes of meaningful drama. However, unlike Leone, Cimino has no respect for the gangster genre in which he occasionally works. He's another young Italian American film-maker who showed remarkable promise in the 1970s. He attended Yale University, where he earned a fine arts degree, and worked on Madison Avenue making commercials before discovering film. His reputation has been largely based on the 1979 multi-Oscar film *The Deer Hunter,* starring Robert De Niro, John Cazale (who had played Fredo Corleone in *The Godfather*), and Christopher Walken (who netted an Academy Award). The film was only Cimino's second major project and became an archetypal film for revealing Vietnam-era rage at the root of domestic confusion and defiled hope. Cimino then made several missteps that badly damaged his reputation, which is still in recovery.

First came his extravagant flop *Heaven's Gate,* which has become synonymous with Hollywood disaster as much as Watergate is linked to political misconduct. Most critics skewered the film as tedious and recklessly self-indulgent. It cost $44 million to make and nearly put MGM and United Artists out of business, earning back only $7.7 million.[11] Then his 1985 gangster film *Year of the Dragon* came to be mockingly called "Hell's Gate" or the "Chinese *Godfather.*"[12] It tells the story of a Polish American police captain (and Vietnam vet) named Stanley White (Mickey Rourke), who's "the most decorated cop" in New York. His new assignment is to stop the gang violence erupting in Chinatown (White claims to have eradicated the Colombians from Queens). But he soon expands his mission to dismantling the secret crime societies known as the Chinese Triads, with roots in America dating back to the Tongs and their nineteenth-century turf battles. His rancor for Asian-Americans, as he broods about Vietnam, intensifies his quest. But the department wants him to lay off the crime syndicate, considering their long-standing "arrangement."

His opponent is an ambitious gangster name Joey Tai (John Lone), whom the media label "the unofficial mayor of Chinatown." He engineers his takeover of the Triads and aims to expand their control of the heroin trade—including ending their partnership with the Italian Mafia. As White's efforts make an impact, Tai retaliates by killing White's estranged wife and sending three thugs over to gang-rape his Chinese American girlfriend, Tracy Tzu (Ariane). As a TV reporter, Tzu had been instrumental in pressuring the Chinese syndicate through exposés and news leaks provided by White. The film ends with a duel between White and Tai at the docks, where Tai has gone to meet a drug shipment. But Tai kills himself to save face—using White's gun.

Most critics flayed the film and accused Cimino and Oliver Stone—who adapted the script from Robert Daley's novel—of adding immigrant stereotypes as a shortcut to storytelling. Chinese American activists picketed the film and staged protests. But actor John Lone, a native of Hong Kong, claimed the Triads were behind the protests.

In the film (but not the novel), White's girlfriend is Chinese American, and White is Polish American with a new surname. His self-mocking jokes about being a "stupid Pollack . . . a peasant" are perhaps meant to balance the disparaging remarks about Asians. One ethnic jab is simply opaque. After Tai attempts to bribe him, White declares, "I'm not an Italian. I'm a Pollack and I can't be bought."

In another tirade, while telling Tracy how he hated her before they even met, he says her most detestable feature is her occupation—she's one of the "vampires" who's "killing America." Then he asks if he can have sex with her. When she declines, he proceeds anyway, forcing her into submission and committing what appears to be rape. Many also found Tzu's nurturing of the racist White a sensational manipulation of her character to lend him dimension but rob her of dignity. His relationships with his estranged wife and Tzu chew up screen time but fail to provide much insight into his character. Their encounters lack detail and genuine affection.

Another fatal flaw is weaving Vietnam angst into the story, where it seems strained and trivialized as a result. The subplot that could have been strengthened for a better movie is the crumbling relationship between the Italian Mafia and the Chinese Triads. It provides a rare glimpse into a clash of cultures that has authenticity and narrative promise. As Little Italy continues to deteriorate, its neighbor, Chinatown, continues to expand. Storefronts and cafés boasting the tricolored Italian flag fill the air with pungent odors of garlic and olive oil but stare across Canal Street at skinned ducks hanging in windows and Chinese lettering adorning doors and street signs. In the film, as the Chinese try to move into Mafia-controlled rackets, one store owner warns, "You come across Canal Street and start throwing your weight around here?! You l'il chink scumbag, you're gonna end up with a wire around your fuckin' neck." At a meeting with the elders—his "honorable uncles"—Tai complains that the Italians "still treat us like junior partners. Behind our backs they call us yellow niggers." Tai also has new competition among the Vietnamese, who want to muscle in on the gambling rackets.

The Stone-Cimino script reveals how both communities distrust the American justice system and would rather settle their disputes privately. Early on, Tai explains how, like the Sicilians, the Chinese shopkeepers pay protection money and have done so for 1,000 years. White shouts back, "You think gambling, extortion, corruption are kosher because they're 1,000 years old? . . . This is America you're living in."

Cimino, though, is a visual stylist of the highest order. As Stanley Kauffmann noted, Cimino has a "vivid sense of swirl and motion."[13] *Year of the Dragon* contains long shots of perplexing beauty along with claustrophobic scenes of jarring violence and ear-assaulting street chaos. A Chinese funeral parade down Mott Street—with the participants dressed in white with black accents—is stunning. For texture, Cimino adds his near-trademark swirling smoke and mist engulfing his characters and adding mystique.

But Cimino seems itching to turn the film into a Western. (Kinder reviews of *Heaven's Gate* noted his talent and appetite for big sky shots and breathtaking panoramas.) But the out-of-place Western motif pops up in *Year of the Dragon* as police mention the "wild west show" shoot-out at the Shanghai Palace, and White declares himself the "new marshal in town" at his first meeting with Tzu.

Cimino's next crack at a gangster film took the Western motif one step further, adding herds of horses and pounds of swirling dust. The story didn't take place in the American West, though, but focused on Sicilian bandits. Using Steve Shagan's screenplay of Mario Puzo's novel *The Sicilian,* Cimino had all the right ingredients to make an effective gangster film. Instead, he made a film that was "magnificently photographed but with utterly hollow characters." (That's how a studio executive described *Heaven's Gate,* but the description suits *The Sicilian* just as well.)

The story is based on the true adventures of Salvatore Guiliano, who rose to fame in war-torn Sicily in the 1940s. He was a folk hero and Robin Hood figure who urged Sicilian peasants to rob land from the rich and settle it for themselves. He also killed, kidnapped, stole, and flirted with socialism and anarchy, urging Sicily to secede from Italy. The combined forces of the church, the Mafia, and the Italian government finally brought the reign of this "lord of the mountains" to an end.

The film stars French actor Christopher Lambert and a meaty role for John Turturro as Guiliano's aide-de-camp, the edgy Aspanu. It features exquisite photography and visual splendor but lumbers along disconnected to its plot and indifferent to its characters. The vendettas and Mafia intrigue get lost in the Sicilian dust, and Lambert becomes tiresome in prolonged close-ups of him pouting, musing, and sulking profoundly.

As critic Dave Kehr put it, it's a "sorry mishmash of loose plot threads, truncated scenes, impenetrable characters and clotted action." *Halliwell's Film Guide* notes, "Over-long and with a cast that lack authenticity as Sicilians, the movie rarely rises above incoherence." The most damning pan, though, came from Puzo, who said that Cimino turned his novel "into just a horrible movie. Everything in it is wrong, just everything. I've never been able to watch it all the way through."[14]

Mario Puzo, however, found a suitable collaborator one more time in Francis Ford Coppola, who finally agreed to create another Faustian portrait of a gangster named Corleone.

CHAPTER 10

New Age Dons and Wise Guys

> As far back as I can remember, I always wanted to be a gangster. To me, being a gangster was better than being president of the United States.
>
> —Henry Hill (Ray Liotta), *GoodFellas,* 1990

Coppola had spent the bulk of the 1970s and 1980s as the new DeMille of Hollywood. While trying to keep his art house studio American Zoetrope afloat, Coppola bounced between pictures as creative exercises and films that appeased his critics and financiers.

In 1979 Coppola went to the Philippines and made "the first $30 million surrealist movie,"[1] as he later described *Apocalypse Now*. The film excoriates human greed, aggression, and military hubris as much as the Vietnam War. It is a reflection of Coppola's brilliance and self-indulgence as a director and remains a mind-numbing journey into his art as well as the tangled, stifling jungles of Southeast Asia. The first half replicates Joseph Conrad's novel *Heart of Darkness,* and the second reflects the muddled vision of a strained genius.

The 1980s were rocky for Coppola, with some hits and many misses. *The Cotton Club* was supposed to be about the famous black cabaret during Harlem's Renaissance of the 1920s and 1930s. But that story was pushed to the background, and gangsters such as Dutch Schultz overpowered the story. Coppola's expensive romance fantasy *One from the Heart* was his *Heaven's Gate* and cost him dearly in dollars and industry esteem.

His artistic and blockbuster success with the *Godfather* sagas made it difficult for Coppola to match, surpass, or simply endure the endless comparisons. "For him *The Godfather* is at once his greatest accomplishment and his greatest curse," wrote Peter Bart. With each film, Coppola was expected to reach the zenith of his earlier work. If he made too commercial a film that aimed for the marketplace, he was criticized for being a sellout. If he made a small film that soothed him, he was called a burnout—or worse—a bore.

By the close of the decade, Coppola needed money to keep Zoetrope alive and needed to find his audience again. He told the *New York Times* that he accepted the offer to make another *Godfather* because again "they basically promised me carte blanche." More than ever, Coppola was under pressure to top himself or, at the very least, avoid embarrassing or dishonoring what had come before. By 1990, though, his audience was in a much different frame of mind.

Coppola, too, figured that Michael had indulged in some soul-searching over the years. He "is a man who wants to rehabilitate himself. Reflecting the mood in America . . . Michael wants to take stock of himself honestly." Coppola figured that by the decade's end, America was morally wounded and looking for redemption. In part, he was on target. The culture was making noise about remedies such as poet Robert Bly's *Iron John,* which had inspired a men's movement. This movement was one of many New Age approaches, as they were dubbed, that courted yuppies and corporate raiders and urged them to get in touch with their inner child—to reconnect with families and rediscover spirituality.

Pacino told Gene Siskel about Michael's journey back to virtue. "There's a thug in Michael, but he's uneasy with it. . . . He made that separation between him and his family when he was young . . . and as Part III begins it's important for him to get back to that place in his mind. . . . he's trying to achieve some kind of legitimacy, to leave a legacy that has a vision to it."

However, *The Godfather Part III* is the weakest of the Corleone trilogy because Coppola pushes the envelope. The sense of tragedy is so inflated to global proportions that the plot often appears contrived for grandeur's sake alone. In this final installment, Michael is made human again, but only so that he can be tortured like any other mortal by guilt. Michael tries to get out of the Mob instead of becoming its total master. He tries to "legitimatize" his fortune in order to be permitted to purchase controlling interest in the Vatican bank, Immobiliare. Doing so means severing ties with his former business associates—still deeply involved in illegal activities. He gives them enormous profits to stave off their appetite for greed, but they eventually demand a share in Immobiliare's financial windfall. Their avarice is nothing, though, compared to that of the European alliance of investors and Italian politicians connected to Immobiliare. Michael refers to them as "the true Mafia." At another time, he notes, "We're back with the Borgias!"

The conspirators end up killing the new reform-minded pope, who intends to clean up the corrupted financial arm of the church. They also target Michael for getting in their way. Puzo and Coppola borrowed from journalism about the Vatican's real-life scandals and speculated about the sudden death of John Paul I. Press stories reported on a Vatican banker who was mysteriously hanged from London Bridge while others faced charges in Italian courts.

Meanwhile, Michael's protégé, Sonny's illegitimate son, Vincent Mancini, is being groomed as his successor. Michael's son, Anthony, has chosen to become an opera singer, and his daughter, Mary, has become Vincent's forbidden lover (she's his first cousin). Michael finally makes Vincent choose between becoming the new godfather and coveting Mary. Vincent announces, "I want the power to preserve the family."

Vincent knows New York is up for grabs, and if the family doesn't get control of the rackets, "the Chinese and Colombians will." As Michael's last order, Vincent's name is changed from Mancini to Corleone. In Vincent, Coppola manages to create another Corleone to root for. Vincent combines old-fashioned notions about family loyalty, his father's taste for revenge, and Michael's shrewdness. He's also handsome, convincing, and likable, as any capable assassin can be. And he produces real tears when he says good-bye to Mary.

Although he invents a worthy successor, Coppola reduces Michael to an emotional wreck. At one point, he forlornly tells Kay, "Every night I dream about my wife and children and how I lost them." He ends up tearfully confessing his sins to the cardinal and soon-to-be dead pope. If emotional scars aren't enough, Coppola breaks Michael physically, having him succumb to diabetic comas and insulin seizures—one against

Coppola gives us a dashing, fresh-faced Corleone to root for and despise in *The Godfather Part III* with Vincent (Andy Garcia), Sonny's illegitimate son. Vincent carries on the family's quest for honor amid the dying and double-dealing. A *Godfather Part IV* could have Vincent working with a weakened American Mafia in a climate of rivalry from other criminal immigrant groups or worldwide syndicates.

the backdrop of a thunderstorm for added drama. As the future pope notes, "Your mind suffers and the body cries out."

Coppola's other unlikely contortion is the remarkable transformation of the Corleone women. Kay strong-arms Michael into giving up their son, Anthony, and letting him drop out of law school. In return, she lets Michael share in Mary's life. (The end of Part II showed Michael with tight-fisted control of his children, but somehow we're told that he later softened that grip.) Jeffrey Chown speculates that some of the appeal of the first two *Godfathers* was the precarious thrill men got from watching the women kept in their place—and their "feminine" solutions kept to themselves. "It is not surprising that boisterous movie audiences have cheered when Michael slams the door on Kay. She is a nagging conscience whose presence suggests there is a world where problems are not resolved with machine guns."[2]

But in a gangster film, she or whatever entity embodies such a conscience must be expunged. Audiences come to revel in the gangster's self-defeating solutions of violence and unchecked ambition (fantasies even women as mortals envision when enraged). Yet Coppola was never contemptuous of the traditional women he put on-screen. In fact, it almost seems as if he envied them for being able to stay in the kitchen and submerse themselves in the rituals of food, rather than be locked in the library with talk about vendettas, chiseling rackets, and who sleeps with the fishes.

For Part III, Coppola didn't suddenly become a feminist and decide to empower the women. Rather, he fulfills his goal of showing the family's ultimate corruption when even they contort power. In the first two films, Connie was an ethnic stereotype based on folklore and practice among Southern Italians, particularly among Sicilians, who have an old adage: a woman is like an egg, the more you beat her the better she gets. In Part III, Connie becomes an underboss. After hearing her plot revenge, Michael even comments, "Maybe they should fear *you*." It is she and one of Michael's aides who give Vincent the order to kill a rival.

Part III also includes the customary gala events and family and religious festivals as excuses for mayhem. Michael throws a lavish party after he earns the coveted Catholic layman's award—the Order of Saint Sebastian—in return for a $100 million endowment to church charities. (In 1991 the Gambino family only came up with a measly $1 million to have a children's cancer center built in their name.) An interesting character is the Gotti-like Joey Zaza, who's said to have graced the cover of *Time* as the best-dressed gangster in town. After Zaza storms out of the Mafia's commission meeting because he isn't shown respect, he complains to the press about its obsession with the Mafia and the defamation of the Italian people. As his grandfather Vito had done, Vincent (disguised as a mounted cop) uses Little Italy's annual festival as a noisy backdrop and shoots Zaza in the street.

Coppola creates a grandly exquisite opera as the backdrop for the profuse bloodletting and wrenching heartache in the finale of *The Godfather Part III*. Still, Coppola hoped an impression would resonate as loudly as the robust arias that Italian art has proven more resilient than Italy's exaggerated criminal element.

To provide the ethnic flavor that so marked the earlier sagas, the family travels to Sicily. There, Michael reminisces about Apollonia while courting Kay (whose husband is away) and taking her on a tour of his old haunts. A scripted scene had Kay and Michael make love but was never filmed. Pacino told Gene Siskel that he and Keaton argued that it "could have seemed gratuitous."

The flashbacks to favorite moments in Part I and Part II, though, seem manipulative. Rather than link the film with its superb predecessors, the flashbacks only underscore Part III's contrivances. Symbolic of the loss, now that everybody can say the word *Mafia,* the label has lost its sting—just like the Corleone mystique.

Coppola's pièce de résistance of the film, though, is a lavish opera in Palermo for the grand finale of gruesome executions. While tenors reach for vocal heights, hit men kill Immobiliare's Mafia backers along with assorted crooked Italian politicians. That list includes a corrupt archbishop, whom they murder inside the Vatican. Connie, too, orchestrates a murder, slowly poisoning the treacherous Don Altobello (Eli Wallach) with tainted cannolis. (He was her godfather.) Finally, posing as a clergyman, Michael's assassin stalks him inside the opera house and eventually wounds him but, more shockingly, kills Mary. Spilling emotional blood and displaying wrenching heartache, Michael drops to his knees in front of his daughter and watches her gulp her last breath. He had warned Vincent (and himself): "They'll come at what you love."

Pacino's performance was the most difficult, and he pulls it off with grace, conviction, and undressed emotion that never becomes cloying. What he accomplished in

Left, Pacino is shadowed by his successor Vincent (Garcia), who's anxious to be the new don and wield the family's still menacing power. But Pacino is the evolving gangster to watch as he tries to recapture his own former exuberance and create a legacy that reverses the sins of his Mafia career.

Part I was the remarkable transformation from being vulnerable to amoral—a natural for gangster characters. But Part III asks Pacino to reverse the order, and he earns every bit of his third Oscar nomination. But who else wanted to see the modern gangster prototype so "corrupted" besides Coppola?

Only our long memory of past Corleones and the superb performances of Pacino, Shire, and newcomer Andy Garcia make this one somewhat engaging. (De Niro, who had played the young Vito, was nearly cast as Vincent, which would have him playing Vito's grandson—a fascinating solution for continuity and family resemblance. However, he had another film commitment that would have postponed production too long.)

Although Coppola's sister Talia Shire long ago overcame charges of nepotism for her solid contributions as Connie, Coppola's daughter Sofia as Mary did not fare as well. She took a beating for her novice acting, being called "hopelessly amateurish" by the *Washington Post* and "ungainly affected by a 'Valley-Girl' accent" in *Variety*. Winona Ryder was originally cast but had to quit the film on doctor's orders for exhaustion. Madonna also fought hard for the role.

Coppola is nothing if not loyal and includes old friends and mentors in odd roles that often add much-needed wit: Roger Corman had posed as a senator in Part II, and Beat poet Gregory Corso and California politician Willie Brown sit in the commission meeting in Part III. Catherine Scorsese also appears in one of the Little Italy scenes. (Scorsese frequently put his mother in his films, in which she performed with spontaneity and grace.)

Another of the film's redeeming features is the parade of food as a Corleone staple. When Michael dies a decrepit old man, the symbolic orange drops out of his hand. (Oranges have been ever present throughout the trilogy to indicate the presence of evil. Bowls of oranges are seen in front of rival dons, and orange peels end up in Brando's gums as he plays the monster for his grandson.) In Part III Mary and Vincent make gnocchi, squeezing the pasta between their intertwined fingers—the dough becoming as sensual as their behavior. One of the most memorable lines from the original film was "Leave the gun. Take the cannolis." In Part III, the cannolis become poisoned and are used by family to kill family. But Connie's crime is anything but a droll use of Italian symbolism; it's executed with heartbreaking anguish and ruthless calculation like so many of the family's intimate murders. The corruption of Italian food to imply the ultimate disintegration of *la famiglia Corleone* is signature Coppola. The symbolism is pretentious, baroque, and memorable.

Overall, Part III earned mixed reviews. *Chicago Tribune* critic Dave Kehr roasted the film, noting it "feels like a weird satire of a '50s situation comedy, a sort of 'Godfather Knows Best.' " He concluded that it "leaves a final impression of exhaustion." The most unorthodox commentary came from Sammy "The Bull" Gravano. He's no film critic but is certainly a credible authority on realistic Italian gangsters. Although Gravano said he loved the first two *Godfathers*, he told Diane Sawyer that "the other one stunk."

However, as Gene Siskel points out, "Flaws and all . . . [it] is still a rich experience." His counterpart, Roger Ebert, also liked it, noting that it "evokes the same sense of wasted greatness, of misdirected genius." Perhaps Kay put it best when she tells Michael, "I think I preferred you when you were just a common Mafia hood."

While filming Part III in Sicily, Coppola filed for bankruptcy, according to the *New York Times*. He reportedly owed creditors as much as $7 million. But he had been promised $5 million to direct, write, and produce Part III—plus a 15 percent share of its gross, which would eventually put him back in the black. The *Godfather* trilogy to date has earned nearly $1 billion and still counting, with Coppola owning a piece of the profits.

But financial glut or penury has been a way of life for Coppola. More important, he seemed to be spent creatively. He told the *New York Times,* "I want my career to be in a place that gives me a lot of pleasure and satisfaction. . . . I'm very embarrassed about my career over the last 10 years. You know, an Italian family puts a lot of stock on not losing face, not making what we call *una brutta figura,* or bad showing."

In the decade ahead, he was haunted by persistent talk about a Part IV. Even Andy Garcia told David Letterman in May 1997 that he would be willing to take Vincent Corleone into the future. In the early 1990s, though, Coppola declared, "I really am not interested in gangsters." When asked to do the first sequel, he recalled, "I used to joke that the only way I'd do it was if they'd let me film *Abbot and Costello Meet the Godfather.*" Now, looking back at a trilogy and years devoted to the Corleones, Coppola noted, "I like the Italian part . . . but I always sort of resented that it took up so much of my life, and that it's about shooting people."

YUPPIES ON MEAN STREET

The same year *The Godfather Part III* was released, Scorsese gave us his gangster masterwork: *GoodFellas*. Scorsese, too, had had his share of triumphs and troubles in the years since *Mean Streets*. His musical *New York, New York* with De Niro and Liza Minnelli was a bust. Then he made what many critics call the best film of the 1970s with *Taxi Driver*—and the best film of the 1980s with *Raging Bull,* both starring De Niro.

Center, De Niro portrays Jimmy Conway, who mentors young Henry Hill *(left)* and Tommy DeVito in Scorsese's 1990 masterpiece *GoodFellas*. The boys grow up to become Jimmy's partners in crime but also his worst nightmares.

When Scorsese decided to return to the gangster genre with *GoodFellas,* his friend Marlon Brando asked him, "Why do you want to make a gangster film? You've done that." But Scorsese figured that "it was a project I could fall into," and it was like going home again.

GoodFellas is based on the true story of half-Irish, half-Sicilian Henry Hill, a Mafia associate who turned informant for the government and disappeared into its witness protection program. The story begins with Hill's childhood in a Brooklyn neighborhood where mobsters were princes. In a story largely explained in voice-over narration, Henry tells us, "At 13, I was making more money than most of the grown-ups in the neighborhood."

The young Henry is under the tutelage of Paulie Cicero, the local Mafia boss, who becomes more like a father to Henry. His real father is a miserable working stiff who beats him or ignores him. Scorsese uses freeze-frames in the opening sequence to show moments that have left a lifelong impression on young Henry: a frozen image of a belt flying over his head and a mailman's head being shoved onto a hot grill. The latter was Paulie's way of making sure that notes about Henry's truancy never made it home; nothing should interfere with his "apprenticeship" in the Mob. Once Henry is an adult, the story focuses on his close dealings with two legendary hoods, Jimmy Conway (De Niro) and Tommy DeVito (Joe Pesci), who work for Paulie. Paulie is depicted, notes writer Douglas Brode, as "one of those old-fashioned, anachronistic noble elder gangsters . . . [who] refuses to have anything to do with drug dealing." Drugs are what sabotage Henry's career as a wise guy.

For Jimmy, his ruin is his love of stealing, notes Henry (Ray Liotta). Jimmy orchestrates the heist of a Lufthansa plane carrying $6 million worth of cargo (the biggest score in criminal history). He turns over a portion to Paulie (Mob de riguer) but can't resist keeping the bulk for himself. "It made him sick to have to turn money over to the guys who stole it," Henry tells us. This greed forces Jimmy to kill his accomplices: Frankie Carbone is strung up in a freezer like a side of beef, Johnny Roastbeef and his new bride are found bloody and motionless in their hot pink Cadillac, and Frenchy and Joe Buddha come tumbling out of a dumpster.

Tommy's downfall, however, is rooted in his own sadism. When Billy Batts, an old-time mafioso, insults Tommy, mocking him about his youth as a shoe-shine boy, he loses his temper and stomps Batts to death. In a scene that opens the film and repeats later, Batts is somehow still alive and thumping around in a trunk while Jimmy, Tommy, and Henry drive to a remote location to bury his body. They stop at Tommy's house, where his mother (Catherine Scorsese) makes them a late-night snack. Then he takes one of her enormous butcher knives, telling her that they have wounded a deer that needs to be put out of its misery. Tommy opens the trunk and hacks Batts to death while spewing expletives at him for not dying the first time around.

Later, Tommy is told he's going to become a "made" man, the crowning moment in his career. It means taking a blood oath and formally entering a Mafia family. Instead, he's killed, as Henry speculates, for whacking Batts, who was already a "made" man and off-limits to Tommy to kill at the time without permission. It's the one ethnic holdover, explains Henry. Tommy's death was "between the Italians. . . . It's real greaseball shit." (Jimmy and Henry can never be "made" because of their Irish blood.)

Wedged in between these vignettes of brief, eye-popping violence, however, is the film's dizzying core: a roller-coaster look at the day-to-day excessive lifestyle of a group of wise guys and their families. They don't live the ethnic holism of the Corleones, with their sturdy links to Sicilian traditions. Instead, these hoods reflect the breakdown of the family order and the infiltration of yuppie nihilism. Henry and

Jimmy are products of "mixed" marriages, and Henry marries a Jewish girl named Karen (Lorraine Bracco), who turns into a Mafia princess. (The role earned Bracco an Oscar nomination.)

Karen was sucked in on her first serious date with Henry, impressed by the slick, good-looking wise guy with endless supplies of cash and impressive friends. "There was nothing like it. . . . You know, a twenty-one-year-old kid with such connections. . . . He was an exciting guy." He tells her his clout comes from being "in construction. . . . I'm a union delegate." Scorsese's camera stalks the couple as they arrive at the Copacabana and bypass the nobodies waiting in a long line outside the entrance. In one long, unedited shot, we bump along as Henry and Karen make their way through the kitchen, down winding hallways, past wedged-in patrons, around bustling waiters, and finally nestle into a ringside table. The shot is intoxicating in its totality and rewarding for its intimate view of power in action.

Almost as impressive to her is Henry's swift, brutal solution for the boy next door who tries to rape her. After Henry beats his face bloody with a gun, he hands it to Karen to hide. Rather than repulsing her, she admits, "It turned me on." Later, once absorbed into the lifestyle, she asks for shopping money by measuring in midair a space with her forefinger and thumb. She then rewards Henry for the one-inch wad of bills with impromptu fellatio in the kitchen.

"After a while, it all got to be normal," she tells us. "None of it seemed like crimes." The families vacation together and share holidays, christenings, and furnishings that fall off trucks. But she adds, "No outsiders, ever" were permitted, except for mistresses.

Oscar-nominated Lorraine Bracco portrays a feisty Karen Hill, who displays as much guts and personal greed in *GoodFellas* as her life partner—the adult Henry Hill (Ray Liotta), shown here shouting at her accusation of adultery.

"Friday night at the Copa was always for the girlfriends," Henry says. But Karen tries to scare Henry back into monogamy one morning, straddling him and pointing a gun in his face, waiting for him to wake up. Paulie has to remind Henry that divorce is out of the question. "We're not *animali.*"

Once Henry is pinched, however, despite a lifelong association with men whom he loved like family, he turns rat without a moment's hesitation. He explains that he figured Jimmy was planning to kill him (after killing all the others connected with the heist) and he had to choose between a code of honor or survival. "Your murderers come with smiles," Henry notes. "They come as your friends, the people who have cared for you all your life."

In the end, although he has avoided jail time, Henry's real punishment is to end up "an average nobody." He loses his lifestyle of fine restaurants, expensive clothes, immunity from cops, and $30,000 weekend gambling sprees. "We were treated like movie stars with muscle. We had it all, just for the asking. . . . [Now] I get to live the rest of my life like a schnook." The Mob had made him feel part of something special; he was a "somebody in a neighborhood of nobodies." And that's where his wild ride returns him.

The last quarter of the film is a masterpiece of shared perspective—the first virtual reality gangster film. Henry's final day as a wise guy is split between preparing ziti with meat sauce for his brother and preparing drugs for delivery to customers. A helicopter haunts him, as does the clock. When Henry is cooking, he turns and checks the time—the shot repeating itself in quick succession (pure Truffaut, says Scorsese). The cuts get quicker at the end of *GoodFellas,* with close-ups, fish-eye views, and frenetic voice-overs all adding to the viewer's understanding of Henry's increasing paranoia and disorientation (also the talented hand of longtime Scorsese collaborator, editor Thelma Schoonmaker).

Finally the music assaults the viewer, as the Rolling Stones, Cream, and the Who accompany Henry's spin out of control. Music in a Scorsese film is like another voice that conveys information. Tony Bennett sings "Rags to Riches" at the film's start and foretells the good life Henry and his associates have ahead. The songs of 1960s girl groups contrast their "pink" innocence with the wise guys' increasingly violent clashes. The film's closing song is a mocking, disgruntled version of "My Way" by the late Sid Vicious of the raunchy punk band the Sex Pistols.

Another aspect that adds to *GoodFellas'* palpable tension is the toxic interplay between De Niro and Pesci. They perform a brutal dance for control, always jockeying for power and searching for signs of imminent danger, and on occasion, a wisp of affection. In *Raging Bull,* De Niro's LaMotta was the tinderbox waiting to explode. In *GoodFellas,* Pesci is the short-fused psychotic waiting to unleash mayhem at an unsuspecting target. Pesci earned an Oscar (best supporting actor), for his manic character, who in one scene moves from chuckling jokester to cold-blooded killer in the time it takes to aim his gun. He has been trading comic quips with a stuttering bar boy named Spider while playing a friendly card game. Then, because the guys are teasing him about being soft, he plugs the boy full of holes.

The film garnered six nominations in all, including best picture and Scorsese as best director. Although De Niro was not nominated, his performance anchors the film. Liotta's Henry is well done, but he's merely our cocky eyewitness, and Tommy is like watching Fourth of July fireworks: eventually they run out of fuses. But De Niro's Jimmy Conway is the polished front man for the story's deeper cesspool. He's almost re-creating his courteous Lou Cipher (read Lucifer) from *Angel Heart.* Like that film's demon, Jimmy's sleek facade falls away, and his simmering paranoia finally bubbles to the surface. In the end, he shows himself to Henry (and to us) as another ruthless, cornered punk who kills to protect his turf. As Desson Howe of the *Washington Post* noticed, De Niro in *GoodFellas* "is at his seamless best, his face and body a virtuoso instrument of human gesture."

De Niro is the only son of two Greenwich Village artists who loved him but were preoccupied by their creative selves. A shy boy, his boyhood nickname was "Bobby Milk" because he was so thin, with skin as pale as milk.[3] Following his stint at the Actors Studio, he appeared in off-Broadway productions until De Palma and others gave him work in low-budget films in the late 1960s. De Niro didn't earn major recognition until he portrayed the slow-witted, dying baseball player in *Bang the Drum Slowly*—released the same year as *Mean Streets.* He grew up on Bleeker Street just a few blocks away from Scorsese, whom he remembered running into as a teenager at the same neighborhood dance hall. They hooked up again in the early 1970s and started talking about doing a film about the old neighborhood. Although De Niro earned an Oscar for his supporting role as the young Vito in *The Godfather Part II,* his star power didn't explode until his mesmerizing performance as Travis Bickle and then as Jake LaMotta in *Raging Bull,* which earned him an Oscar for best actor.

De Niro has carried on the tradition of Brando, although he is not fond of the comparison. Naturally and appropriately, he considers himself and his craft his own. (As LaMotta, though, De Niro delivers Brando's memorable speech about being a contender . . . instead of a bum.) The similarity, though, lies in De Niro's choice to play oblique roles that defy leading-man glamour. Like Brando, he also exerted a potent influence on the next generation of actors, including Sean Penn and Gary Oldman. As Scorsese puts it, "He isn't afraid to look unpleasant, to be mean, to be a person that nobody likes." With Scorsese, De Niro has made eight films, prompting filmmaker Michael Powell to observe, "They can almost be said to have invented each other. Martin's thoughts become Bob's actions. The dialogue becomes dense and taut, the looks and gestures are subliminal."[4]

Not only did the acting earn *GoodFellas* kudos, but its filmmaking techniques, for Pauline Kael, overtook the story. *Variety* called the film "simultaneously fascinating and repellent." It noted that the film was a return to *Mean Streets* but "from a more distanced, older, wiser and subtler perspective." Kathleen Murphy of *Film Comment* wrote that the film is "so surefooted, so teeming with authentic action, color, character, and risk, it literally takes your breath away."

Scorsese said the breakneck speed was intentional. "They've got to move fast. I was interested in breaking up all the traditional ways of shooting the picture. A guy comes in, sits down, exposition is given. So the hell with the exposition—do it on the voice-over, if need be at all." Realizing he had created a style that was being particularly revered by young filmmakers, Scorsese concedes, "[It's] sort of my version of MTV. . . . But even that's old-fashioned."

David Ehrenstein, in his book about Scorsese, notes a political edge to the film—one never purposely inserted but spilling onto the screen nonetheless. "*GoodFellas* will be recognized as less a gangster melodrama than an indictment of Reagan-Bush America, where brute force and conspicuous consumption have completely subsumed identity and ethics," wrote Ehrenstein. David Ansen of *Newsweek* agreed, writing that Scorsese's "wiseguys and their wives and mistresses are an upside-down parody of untrammeled consumerism."

"Yeah, the lifestyle reflects the times," Scorsese explained. One scene evens shows that lifestyle obliterating faith. When Henry first meets Karen's parents, he hides his crucifix by tucking it inside his shirt. Later, without a second thought, he gets married in a Jewish ceremony. Catholicism is a leftover piece of his childhood; it's no longer an integral piece of his identity.

David Denby, in his *New York* review, praised *GoodFellas* as "the greatest film ever made about the sensual and momentary lure of crime." Ebert dubbed *GoodFellas* the greatest gangster film ever and Scorsese "America's finest filmmaker" working today. Ebert gives Scorsese the mantle not because he presents individual tales of a punch-drunk boxer, a disturbed taxi driver, and a greedy wise guy, but because Scorsese's films are really "poems about guilt." Scorsese has mastered the gangster's artistic utility as a blunt revelation of social strain and cultural erosion. The film is like journalism, which more than any other source has always had strong alliances with the genre. Scorsese, though, prefers the phrase "*staged* documentary," which he said he aimed for with *GoodFellas*. In contrast, he once described Coppola's gangster tales—which he likes—as "epic poetry, like *Morte d'Arthur.* My stuff is like some guy on the street-corner talking."[5] By not aiming for allegory—merely carefully positioning his camera—Scorsese locates a meaningful one anyway.

MARRIED TO THE MOB

Scorsese said Karen Hill's inside view was, in part, inspired by actor-director John Cassavetes's film *Gloria* (1980), which starred his wife Gena Rowlands. Cassavetes was one of Scorsese's most revered mentors. *Gloria* is the story of a toughened, middle-aged moll who redeems her life by protecting the six-year-old son of a dead Mob accountant. The boy has possession of an incriminating ledger that the Mob wants back. Because Gloria was once the girlfriend of Mob boss Tarzini, she knows how gangsters think and how they kill. She goes on the run, killing, outsmarting, and negotiating with them until she eventually escapes with the boy. He's half Puerto Rican and stands in stark contrast to Gloria's cool blond veneer and seasoned outlook. The film is a superb character study and earned Rowlands an Oscar nomination. The film also offers a glimpse as to what might have happened to Poppy and all the other molls who populated the screen over the years. *Gloria* proves she intended to be left with a firm grip on a fat wad of cash and a safety deposit box full of jewels as a pension for her career in the Mob.

In the 1980s, John Huston created another superb female character living in the Mob universe: the Mafia princess Maerose Prizzi. In his black comedy *Prizzi's Honor,* Maerose is portrayed by Huston's daughter Anjelica (who netted an Academy Award). The main plot focuses on a hit man named Charley (Jack Nicholson) and his wife, Irene (Kathleen Turner)—a fellow assassin. The film is funny until Charley and Irene get contracts to kill each other, and one of them succeeds. But Maerose, as the don's daughter, steals the film. She had been outcast from the family after Charley broke off their engagement and she went into self-imposed exile—bringing dishonor to the family. But Maerose knows the codes and uses her inside track to get even with anyone who once snubbed her. She could be Connie if Connie had a Brooklyn accent and the profile of Nefertiti.

VIVA LAS VEGAS

Scorsese's 1995 film *Casino* is an unintentional diamond-studded sequel to *GoodFellas,* as several critics more or less unkindly dubbed it *GoodFellas Go Vegas* or *GoodFellas*

Lite. Casino stars the same duo of De Niro and Pesci in a familiar face-off: complex, smoldering gangster versus unmanageable, lunatic killer. But they have now mastered the dance, and it seems a parody, lacking all its former edginess and sense of threat. Worse yet, Scorsese seems intent on focusing on stylish technique—still dazzling as ever—but at the expense of fully developed characters and a coherent, well-paced story.

Las Vegas is the star of the film, which tracks its sad demise from Mob-controlled fun house to corporate sandlot. But the gaudy desert town we all know hardly whips up much emotional vexation or cultural fuss. The notion that Las Vegas is a metaphor for a crass, decaying America besieged by corporate takeovers and a loss of honor—even among mobsters—is well-worn turf.

As a backdrop to human suffering, the fraudulent desert oasis is ideal, as it was in *Leaving Las Vegas*. To be put at center stage while stock characters cheat, kill, and double-cross each other inside Las Vegas's decadent casinos, though, is uninspired and disappointing. In voice-over we're told that the town is set up to make money and that "the players don't stand a chance," which is hardly astounding news. When the multinational conglomerates take over, the players are still set up to lose. What's missing is the colorful presence of awesome mobsters and slick gamblers posing as "food and beverage" managers. Scorsese insinuates that something worse invades: Midwestern families with fat ankles, Hard Rock Café T-shirts, and cotton-candy appetites. "Today it works like Disneyworld," a voice-over tells us, like a sort of moving epitaph for Las Vegas. Scorsese, always the Catholic conscience, said, "Gaining Paradise and losing it, through pride and greed—it's the old-fashioned Old Testament story."

Imposed on the story of the town's transfer from mafiosi to corporate gangsters is a house-of-cards business arrangement between the Mob and genius gambler Sam "Ace" Rothstein. There's also a love triangle between Ace (De Niro); his wife, Ginger McKenna (Sharon Stone); and the Mafia enforcer Nicky Santoro (Pesci). Also complicating matters is her former pimp and lifelong leech, Lester Diamond (James Woods).

The story is based on Nicholas Pileggi's book, which tracks the real-life saga of Chicago gambler Frank "Lefty" Rosenthal. Pileggi also cowrote the screenplay with Scorsese, as he did with *GoodFellas*. In the film version, Ace, also known as "the Golden Jew," is hired by the Mob to manage the Tangiers Hotel's casino in secret while a puppet figurehead, Philip Green (Kevin Pollack), poses as the boss for press packets and the country club set. Although Ace longs to run the casino as a responsible entrepreneur, his weakness for Ginger, the Mob's greed, and Nicky's sadism and Napoleonic tendencies toward empire bring the whole plan to a bloody, sordid demise. In the end, Ginger and Ace fight over money and destroy their already battered souls (à la *War of the Roses*); she winds up a dead junkie, and he escapes a car bomb and returns to his knack for outsmarting the odds and winning bets. Nicky finally tests the Mob's patience with his bloody protection rackets and petty, risky thievery, which draw in the media along with the police and ultimately collapse their Las Vegas candy store. He ends up buried in one of the many holes he dug in the desert that waited for a fresh corpse.

Many critics pointed out the excessive use of voice-overs. "The film finally wears the viewer out," the *San Francisco Examiner* noted. The voice-over narrations go beyond fleshing out details and providing background. The device becomes abusive and overwhelms the viewer. It borders on schizophrenia, forcing the viewer to choose between another lengthy disclosure and Scorsese's dazzling visuals: cameras zooming in and out of intimate spaces, swirling around casino interiors awash in flashing lights, rolling dice, fluttering cards, and towering blonds; oblique angles, quick cuts, close-ups, and pan shots orchestrating glimpses of fascinating detail; overhead cameras panning aisles, stages, lounges, and the open desert until the entire picture becomes a three-hour flash card exercise.

In *GoodFellas,* such roller-coaster experiences were wedged between scenes in which a static camera captured explosive interactions between unpredictable characters. When the camera does linger on Ace in his revealing moments, he broods and we watch, he stews and we watch, and he lusts and we watch. The only time his character gets talkative is when he's off camera and we're supposed to be focusing on something else.

But not knowing Ace very well, we don't know why such a ruthless man and control freak would have such a weak spot for Ginger. He sincerely seems capable of loving her—or at least wanting really badly to try. Playing such an enigma may not inspire De Niro any longer. After personifying so many characters who can barely conceal their inner battles, perhaps De Niro feels we're quite familiar with such a character's conflicting motivations. And Rothstein is Jimmy Conway if Conway began dressing like a set of Crayola crayons. De Niro admitted part of his attraction to the part was the fabulous wardrobe Rothstein poses in—suit coats that glow with the vibrancy of toucan feathers and shiny shoes that sparkle under the blinding casino lights. "We had fifty-two changes for Bob, which was a lot," Scorsese noted.[6]

De Niro's controlled character in *GoodFellas* sucked you into the story by emanating a force field around himself. While Tommy ricocheted off the screen, and the boyish Henry seemed stupefied, Jimmy was aware, judgmental, and reactive. But such a cloaked strength is not enough to sustain a lead character unless he evolves or has a moment of revelation. As the *San Francisco Chronicle* pointed out, "Rothstein's passivity is a problem. He has everything he wants, so he has nothing to work for. Yet he has not Mafia power, so as his kingdom ebbs away he can do nothing. At the center of the film is a static protagonist." The only moments when Ace comes to life are those involving his domestic life. One scene in which he comforts his young daughter is naked and touching. Those involving his courtship and battles with Ginger are equally stunning.

The film's flawless feature, which nearly pulls it back from narrative purgatory, is Sharon Stone's performance as Ginger (earning her an Oscar nomination). She's brilliant as the brassy, hungry, unglued, doped-up hustler. She's cunning and myopic when it comes to keeping her eye on the sucker who will best do her bidding. But she can't see the sand for the desert when it comes to spotting her own weakness for the slimy Lester—a venal, utterly despicable character out of her past and obvious to everyone but her. The *Chronicle* wrote, "Stone takes this woman from sparkling confidence to dissolution and disintegration, hitting every bump and ditch along the way." The only enhancement that would have further enriched her character was to have allowed her the same voice-over control or perspective that the men enjoyed—as Karen was permitted in *GoodFellas*. Instead, Ginger remains their tool, viewed from a distance and never allowing us to get inside her skin. But this undermines the dialogue that tells us that she's a potent and vital player in this cycle of greed, power, and downfall. The film seems regressive for Scorsese, but at the same time, it's boldly progressive in creating such a full-blooded female character within a gangster story. Besides Stone, the only other interesting characters are Don Rickles's Billy Sherbert and Alan King's Andy Stone. Both show promise but never get enough screen time—despite the film's three-hour length—to make much of an impact.

Several Scorsese vignettes and sequences unraveling ministories work well. In one, Ace tricks a Japanese gambler into staying overnight and losing back the fortune he just won from the casino; Ace understands the nagging weakness of a gambler. One sequence deftly exploits Scorsese's stalking camera technique. The approach gives the viewer the feel of being on a piggyback ride behind the camera as it follows a pile of money. The cash is skimmed profits that are first collected from the casino tables, sorted in the backrooms, stuffed into bags, and ultimately sidetracked to the Mob in Kansas City. But Scorsese's usual prizefighter's control of violence—using nasty episodes for punctuation or quick jabs in the face to keep us connected to the action—is forfeited in favor of rubbing our noses in excess horror.

One scene demonstrates the Scorsese touch and then his tampering with it. After a man smarts off to Nicky, he acts on a berserk impulse and frantically stabs the man in the throat with a ballpoint pen. The violence is swift, brutal, and shocking to us and Ace. But then Scorsese lingers like he never has before. The man is gushing blood and has collapsed to the floor, moaning like a wounded animal, but Nicky keeps taunting and stabbing and kicking. The scene lingers longer so that Ace can finish his fat voice-over about Nicky being a relentless killer, which is plainly evident without the aside. (And as soon as Ace's voice-over is done, another by Nicky begins.)

The film's last part, however, in which the story is completely bruised by violence, just belabors the point already made. It begins to look less like Scorsese and more like De Palma, leaning on technical wizardry to pull off horror-style gore. Laurent Bouzereau, in his book *Ultraviolent Movies,* quotes a makeup artist at length describing the gizmos and gadgets used to create *Casino*'s finale of torture-style violence:

> We did a scene where a guy's head is crushed in a vice. We made an appliance that the actor wore on his face with an air bladder underneath so that the eyes could bulge out. We also did a fake head so that you could actually see it crush. . . . [Scorsese] was very enthusiastic about the effects we could create. . . . I don't think Marty had ever worked with something so elaborate. He really went for broke.[7]

The *Chronicle* noted, "Usually, violence in Scorsese's films has a quality of ironic distance, but here the violence is nasty and personal."

Further underscoring Scorsese's mood to "go for broke" is the film's musical accompaniment. Rather than providing supplemental context or massaging the moment, the music battles with the voice-overs for space. The music is also more ambitious in scope, stretching from rock 'n' roll to the baroque Bach. No doubt Bach's *Saint Matthew's Passion* is an awesome opening for the film, and even more attention-getting when followed by "Zooma Zooma" by Louis Prima. Scorsese said that the heady, biblically inspired piece by Bach was needed to evoke a sense "of an empire that had been lost." He added, "The destruction of [Las Vegas] has to have the grandeur of Lucifer being expelled from heaven for being too proud." The sweeping sentiment is a naked clue about what Scorsese saw as the tragic core of this story. It wasn't really in his usual league of intimate characters—but in their swank house of worship.

Scorsese remains an insightful, daring filmmaker, whose failures still soar above most Hollywood products because he aims so high to begin with. And he is probably not through with gangsters, as they never seem to leave him or us alone. In fact, during the five-year span between *GoodFellas* and *Casino,* an astonishing number of gangster films poured into the marketplace. Most of them were mediocre, but a few were gems, and some even managed to break new ground. Upstart and veteran filmmakers found gangsters still battling with Prohibition, killing to surf music, and haunting the mean streets we now call the hood.

CHAPTER 11

Boyz in the Hollywood Hood

> People want to get high. Real high and real fast and this is going to do it . . . and make us rich. . . . We gonna come off like the Mob!
>
> —Nino "the Untouchable" Brown (Wesley Snipes), *New Jack City,* 1991

The 1980s may have meant upward mobility for yuppies and a few wise guys, but for communities living in depressed urban areas—mostly black—the decade meant more desperate times than ever. The rich got richer, and the poor slid further behind. Many analysts compared the growing gap to the one that existed between the robber barons and the slum poor a century ago. But there was a major difference between then and now: the earlier immigrants would learn English and somewhat assimilate into American society. By minimizing their ethnicity, the newest immigrants hoped to mix into the fabled American melting pot.

But ambitious blacks at the turn of the century were segregated from the white population; the policy of "separate but equal" had been sanctioned by the United States Supreme Court. Even if not barred from entry, blacks couldn't possibly camouflage their ethnic and racial differences.

By midcentury, however, the formidable color barriers began to be breached. Following World War II, the hypocrisy of America's revulsion at the Holocaust's racial ugliness prompted several leaders to attack homegrown racism. The results included the Supreme Court's desegregation order (reversing its earlier judgment), Jackie Robinson's debut in major-league baseball, and mixing races within military fighting units, especially for the Vietnam War.

Just as "separate but equal" proved easy to compromise, the notion of forced integration could not alter centuries of prejudice. But in the early 1960s—along with the other challenges assaulting American society—Martin Luther King and other formidable activists began to challenge the remaining vestiges of official and unofficial racism. But change was slow and resistance fierce. As the 1960s raged on, black frustration prompted more confrontational leadership, including Malcolm X and the Black Panther Party. Malcolm X was a member of the Nation of Islam—an entity portrayed in the mainstream press as dangerously extreme. He had advocated that violence may be necessary to remedy racial inequality—if peaceful efforts went ignored. But in an era of assassinations of U.S. leaders of all stripes, Malcolm X became the victim of violence in 1965, reportedly killed by fellow Black Muslims caught up in an intense power struggle. (King was assassinated in 1968, the same year as Robert Kennedy.)

Urban rioting also plagued the late 1960s. The Watts section of Los Angeles became a war zone in 1965, and in the summer of 1967, widespread rioting erupted in the black neighborhoods of a dozen major cities. The violence was extensive enough to bring in the National Guard and the U.S. military and left the country and a generation scarred by the experience.

By the early 1970s, though, the Black Panther party suffered from the same fate as antiwar groups that increasingly preached militancy and counterrevolution: intense government harassment, arrests, and fractious infighting. Cofounder Bobby Seale went on trial with antiwar organizers in the infamous Chicago Seven trial. Seale, Tom Hayden, Abbie Hoffman, and the others had been arrested after the violent street demonstrations outside the Democratic National Convention in 1968. They were tried in 1970 as conspirators to incite violence. In a trial historians now consider draconian and an embarrassing artifact of the fractured times, the defendants were ultimately found not guilty, and the judge was accused of misconduct.

While the petty hoods and ruling mafiosi of Scorsese and Coppola gave moviegoers a cathartic outlet for Vietnam-era bloodshed, several black filmmakers debuted the black action hero and modern gangster who was purgative for some and a source of added worry for others.

BIRTH OF A NATION: WE SHALL OVERCOME

Black gangsters have been around as long as the genre. Yet they yielded as little influence over Hollywood as blacks did in other industries; they were virtually locked out of powerful regimes. For most of the twentieth century, black screen gangsters—like the larger black community—inhabited an "otherworld" that existed as a parallel universe to white America, already shadowed by an Underworld.

But that Underworld endorses the society it mimics. Film gangsters have traditionally been depicted as conservatives who must preserve the system they profit from. (As Don Barzini explained, "We're not communists.") Most white gangsters believe that whatever harm was done to their people in the slums, America is still the land of opportunity. Many often dream of becoming legitimate (*The Godfather Part III*) and of crossing over into legitimate society. But for black people, let alone black gangsters, that was hardly an option until recent times.

That scenario is all the more reason Oscar Micheaux remains an impressive figure in Hollywood's early history. Despite the odds against him, Micheaux worked throughout the silent era as a gifted entrepreneur who wrote, produced, and directed dozens of films. Of course, he was relegated to a segregated marketplace, using black casts and exploring black themes, which included "lynching, 'passing,' race purity, prostitution, gangland life, and he even made a jungle film."[1] During the same era of Sternberg's *Underworld,* Micheaux released his *Underworld*. His was a tale of a college-educated black man who avoids the pitfalls of the numbers racket and proves he's smarter than the criminal set.

By being based in Harlem and away from the power centers, though, Micheaux had trouble getting the financing to join the rush toward sound films. The transfer required intense investment in equipment and trained crews. After filing for bankruptcy in 1928, he joined forces with white partners, an act that essentially ended his astounding record of self-sufficient black cinema.[2]

With white scriptwriters and casting agents, black characters for the next several decades reflected the larger society's view of blacks as servants and scapegoats. Most roles reflected the "coon," "mammie," and "buck" image. The NAACP had been objecting to humiliation on-screen since the group formed in 1909, but with little impact.[3] (In 1915 objection turned into street demonstrations against Griffith's *Birth of a Nation.*)

Black crime films during the 1930s and 1940s included *Moon over Harlem, Straight from Heaven,* and *Gang War,* the latter involving gangsters battling over control of jukeboxes.[4] Eugene Rosow notes that in these films in particular, the gangster's Robin Hood appeal was exaggerated. After all, the audience for these films may have figured that ripping off the system wasn't necessarily a crime. The system was unjust anyway and, some argued, was a violation of the Constitution's assertion that all Americans are created equal.

Among white gangster films, *The Petrified Forest* included a black gangster as a member of Duke Mantee's gang. It was daring at the time, and a brief scene reveals its narrative promise. The black gangster saunters over to the rich couple's intimidated chauffeur and calls him "fellow brother." Then he mocks the chauffeur's profession, asking if he ever heard "about the big liberation." The gangster is shown self-destructing while the chauffeur keeps his job.

In the 1950s, when screen rebellion became box office magic, Sidney Poitier portrayed an angry young street punk in *The Blackboard Jungle* (1955). Poitier, though, soon became synonymous with the intelligent, stoic, and often righteous black men he portrayed and made him a major star. As the Black Power movement gained momentum, though, Poitier's poignant dignity seemed dated and much too passive for the new militancy. As Nelson George notes, "Sidney's films of the period . . . seemed too removed, way too precious a response to the street energy everybody, even we kids, were feeling."[5]

The crime films of the late 1960s, such as *The French Connection,* focused on the white cop's street struggle with the latest threats to social order. (During the same era, *Dirty Harry* and Charles Bronson's *Death Wish* sagas covered similar ground.) The black heroin addicts and street dealers were merely pawns on the battlefield between the NYPD and the Mob. Even the nuances of being a French importer who outwits both the police and Italian thugs were made more interesting in *The French Connection.* But there was an audience who wanted to see the view from inside the black community. Given the clout of black audiences, a new wave of films debuted to fill that void. (Black moviegoers regularly make up as much as one-third of the total audience, despite being only about one-eighth of the U.S. population.)

POWER TO THE BLACK CINEMA

Melvin Van Peebles didn't set out to be a pioneer when he made *Sweet Sweetback's Baadasssss Song* in 1971, but the film unlocked doors for both black filmmakers and independent films in general. The $500,000 production, in part financed with a $50,000 loan from Bill Cosby, in the end grossed $10 million, becoming one of the most successful independent productions in Hollywood history to that point.

The film is about a black stud (given the name Sweetback by a prostitute who introduced him to sex at age 10). For a living, he performs in sex shows in South Central L.A. until he's falsely charged with a crime and arrested one night. He's hauled down to the station, where he witnesses two white cops brutally beat a black militant named Moo Moo. Sweetback (Van Peebles) comes to Moo Moo's aid, and beats up the cops then flees. Sweetback is hunted by everyone from the LAPD to bloodhounds until he finally makes it across the border into Mexico. But he vows to return. The film concludes with this epilogue: "A Baadasssss Nigger is coming to collect some dues."

Van Peebles described the film as "a brother getting the Man's foot out of his ass." But he also wanted to make "a victorious film" with first-rate production values so that the door would stay open for other black filmmakers. "A film must be able to sustain itself as a viable commercial product or there is no power base. . . . That's the game people will listen to. So that's what I set out to do." Twenty years later, he told the *New York Times* that in 1971 the film had been labeled "preposterous, militant and downright un-American. . . . I had been inundated with death threats." But he credits Warner Brothers for sticking with the film throughout the controversy and remaining its distributor.

Before *Sweetback* Van Peebles had directed *Watermelon Man* within the Hollywood system. The film had been written by Herman Roucher, author of *The Summer of '42*. *Watermelon Man* is the story about a white suburbanite (Godfrey Cambridge in whiteface) who one day discovers he's black. It earned decent reviews but little box office clamor, and Van Peebles and Hollywood soured on each other. Before becoming a filmmaker, Van Peebles had lived in Mexico as a painter, in San Francisco as a photo-essayist, in Holland as a graduate student in astronomy, and in Paris as a journalist. After he learned that French cinema made filmmaking grants available to writers, he applied, completed his first film, and launched the career that finally brought him success.

Shortly after *Sweetback*'s debut, another practiced black filmmaker moved into the spotlight. Gordon Parks had already earned respect in Hollywood for writing, producing, and directing *The Learning Tree* in 1969. Parks had been the first black director to make a film for a major studio. However, his bittersweet autobiographical film about his childhood in 1920s Kansas wasn't a commercial success. Some critics speculate that Parks felt pressure to make his next effort more mainstream, and he was later criticized for helping fuel the trend that came to be called "blaxploitation" (films that exploit black themes for profit instead of art's sake).

That more commercial effort was *Shaft* (1971), a film right out of Hollywood tradition. With regard to genre history, the good-looking, laid-back private detective, John Shaft (Richard Roundtree)—dressed in turtlenecks and dress leather—is the black man's Bogart. Affable and shrewd, Shaft works both sides of the law to meet his needs. He's aware that he's operating in a white framework but maintains his worldview through self-assurance, intelligence, street instincts, and a healthy disdain for reckless danger. Under Park's directorship and a modest MGM budget, *Shaft* is a well-made formula film that puts Shaft in the middle of an Underworld war between the Mafia and black mobster Bumpy Jones (modeled on real Harlem gangster Bumpy Johnson).

Shaft enlists the help of black militants whom he knows from the old neighborhood in Harlem. However, he keeps a distance from their zealotry; after all, he has moved downtown to Greenwich Village. When the group's leader, Ben Bufort (Christopher St. John), accuses Shaft of thinking like a white man, Shaft tells Bufort it is he who isn't thinking at all and will wind up dead. Like Bogart's private dicks, Shaft is a loner and doesn't go in for causes—no matter what color sponsors them. Bumpy (Moses Dunn) hires Shaft to retrieve his daughter, who's been kidnapped by the Mafia. Bufort agrees to supply his trained "soldiers" because Bumpy's dirty money "can get a lot of brothers and sisters out of jail."

Richard Roundtree as "the black private dick that's the sex machine to all the chicks" in the 1971 hit *Shaft*. The story put Shaft between Harlem's crime boss and the ever-present Italian Mafia. Critics and fans alike called Shaft the "sepia Sam Spade," but sequels fell prey to blaxploitation absurdity.

Bufort and his handful of men, clad in guerrilla-like attire, infiltrate a top mafioso's fortress with the customary shoot-out and collect Bumpy's daughter unharmed. But the battle also promises to set off a larger war as soon as the Italians regroup. Shaft, his job done, calls his cop friend Vic Androzzi (Charles Cioffi), with whom he has a congenial but sparring relationship, and warns him, "Your case has just busted wide open." With a devilish smile, Shaft poses for his theme song, by Isaac Hayes, which closes the film: "Who's the black private dick that's the sex machine to all the chicks? / Shaft / Who is the man that would risk his neck for his brother man? / Shaft / Can ya dig it?"

Nelson George suggests Shaft as the "sepia Sam Spade" was a reflection of the director's state of mind; Parks had one foot in the bohemian Greenwich Village but remained connected "to the harsh heart of Harlem." Scholar Mark A. Reid is a bit more harsh, failing to see any "mythic black hero" in Shaft. Reid wrote, "Instead, like the doll-makers who painted Barbie's face brown, MGM merely created black-skinned replicas of white heroes of action films."[6] In any case, the film was highly successful at the box office with audiences of all colors but especially appealed to black youth hungry for a new screen likeness besides Jim Brown, who was more brawn than brains. The film also garnered favorable reviews from a few mainstream critics such as Roger Ebert. Isaac Hayes's title song earned him an Oscar, and his overall musical score was nominated as well.

The next generation in the family, Gordon Parks Jr., made his film debut a year later with a crime film that puts the spotlight on the gangster, not the law. His *Superfly* (1972) tells the tale of Youngblood Priest (Ron O'Neal) who deals in "superfly" quality cocaine and has 50 street peddlers working under him. But Priest wants to leave the rackets and needs one last score to net him $1 million to bankroll the rest of his life. A corrupt white deputy police commissioner, however, busts him (on a tip from Priest's old partner) and makes Priest work for him for chump change. Meanwhile, Priest's mentor Scatter, who got him started in the trade, gives him an incriminating file on the cop but is soon killed by cops who force Scatter to overdose. In the end, Priest uses the file to blackmail the top cop and hires Italian mobsters to hit him. Having beaten the system, Priest walks away unharmed to start a new life with his girlfriend.

Part of the film's appeal was Priest's veritable fashion parade of suede, leather, and assorted polyester eyesores from the 1970s. He also had an enormous customized Eldorado whose front grill looks like a vulgar grin coming up the street. George notes, "Where *Shaft* was a typical detective flick in blackface, *Superfly*'s cocaine dealer was a more romantic, conflicted figure whose slang and clothes cut deeper . . . into the black community's psyche." The film was a box office hit with black audiences, but the mainstream reviews—what few there were—were scathing. However, critics noted the invaluable contribution of the sweet, falsetto soul and political ear of musician Curtis Mayfield to the film's musical score. Mayfield performs the hit pop song "Pusher Man" in the film as well.

BLAXPLOITATION UNBECOMING

Music as another commentator on the action was not new to the genre but was of paramount importance in black crime films. At the time, music was one of the few fields in which blacks carried significant clout. While underscoring these movies, music also helped to provide a continuum of appeal to which blacks—and, increasingly, whites—could be drawn. Isaac Hayes, Curtis Mayfield, and other rhythm and blues or soul artists had a loyal following among white youth. For some critics, as the blaxploitation movies got more absurd, the music was often their only redeeming feature. For *Black Caesar* (1973) starring the ex-NFL football player Fred Williamson, George notes that the best thing about the film is the "amazing James Brown" score. George blames the film's mediocrity on "schlockmaster Larry Cohen," who wrote and directed the film. *Black Caesar* was originally intended by Cohen as a vehicle for Sammy Davis Jr. and was positioned to capitalize on the success of *The Godfather*.[7]

Perhaps because of the white production team, *Black Caesar* closely mimics the classic gangster format, but using a black character in the lead. The film starts with Tommy Gibbs (Williamson) earning his childhood credentials in crime and then tracks his meteoric rise, followed by his harrowing fall. The film opens with Tommy as a shoe-shine boy running petty errands for older white mobsters. One day he delivers a payoff to a white cop named McKinney (Art Lund), but the cop gets angry and claims that money is missing. He viciously beats the boy, leaving him with a limp for life, and locks him up for eight years. Once out, Tommy begins his career in various rackets, first doing work for an Italian mobster and then expanding turf and influence for himself. Tommy convinces his friend and business partner Joe "the Brain" Washington (Phillip Roye) that he intends to use some of the profits to better the community, but Tommy ultimately just pockets the profits. Joe eventually deserts Tommy and tries to build a legitimate life and private law practice. Another associate is a charlatan street preacher who ends up trying to live up to his sermons.

Tommy eventually gets his hands on detailed ledgers that implicate mobsters from Harlem to City Hall and uses the information as leverage and life insurance. After admiring his white associate's home, Tommy scrawls out a check on the spot to buy it—furnishings and clothes included. He then gives the home as a surprise to the associate's maid, who happens to be Tommy's mother. But like gangster moms from the genre's start, she calls her son "an ungrateful bum" and turns down his offer. He also has a grim encounter with his father, whom he nearly kills as payback for deserting the family long ago.

Soon Tommy decides Harlem belongs to a black gangster and not the Italians. He wages a war with them and enjoys a short-lived reign over the community. But he's growing increasingly corrupted by his own power and isolating himself from everyone he once cared about. He rapes Helen (Gloria Hendry), the woman he loves, and she finally runs off with Joe.

The cops blackmail Helen over Joe's criminal past and use her to help nail Tommy. While on a shopping spree to buy her a gift at Tiffany's, he's shot in the street by police. Despite a large hole in his gut, he jumps in a cab and heads for Harlem, settling the score with his would-be killers along the way. He gets to his office to find Joe and his white associate dead and McKinney holding a gun on him. But before shooting,

Echoing the theme of both the classic *Little Caesar*–style gangster and blaxploitation heroes, *Black Caesar* stars Fred Williamson *(center),* who proves, however, that the genre could adapt beyond the immigrant perspective and include America's longest-standing underdog: the African-American.

McKinney wants to humiliate Tommy by making him shine his shoes. Soon Tommy takes over the gun and the game. McKinney ends up with his face blackened and a bullet in his chest. After Tommy grabs the ledgers, he stumbles around his old Harlem neighborhood until a half-dozen boys beat him with sticks and leave him lying in garbage by an abandoned building.

The blaxploitation trend peaked in 1973 with this film and the slew of Williamson sequels such as *Hell up in Harlem* and *Boss Nigger.* Many of Williamson's efforts were made by American International Pictures, which had a history of bleeding a trend dry. (They made some of the worst gangster biopics of the late 1950s and launched another trifling trend with "beach and bikini" pictures.) The studio also distributed the sequel *Superfly T.N.T.,* directed by star Ron O'Neal, about the drug dealer's startling reform while living in Europe. Its writer, Alex Haley, would later became a household name for writing *Roots* and *The Autobiography of Malcolm X* (as told to Haley). But the black action films were increasingly being written and directed by white filmmakers who lacked genuine means of refreshing their themes. They also were increasingly making the themes and characters objects of scorn rather than honoring their uniqueness.

Although blaxploitation films from the start employed stereotypes, the first few had also infused the stories with a strong sense of black pride, humor, and a social sting unique to black America. Small gestures that had traditionally offered glimpses into a white character's background were used to reveal Shaft's worldview. One shot shows a taxi stop to pick him up and then zoom forward 20 feet to catch a white fare. Such moments were a refreshingly honest look at the man's daily hassles.

More important was the frankness with which Shaft and Priest wrestled control of racial epithets normally used against them. When Bumpy complains to Shaft that he can't go to the cops to get his daughter back, Shaft notes, "So you want me . . . spade detective?" Later he calls Bumpy a "cagey spook." Italian gangsters rarely acknowledge the outside world's labels for them of "wops" and "dagos"—let alone call each other such epithets. But black characters habitually verbally spar with each other using the "n" word with both humor and contempt. (It's as controversial within the black community as it's confusing to whites, who mistake the practice as pure self-denigration.) As Richard Pryor's brilliant, searing comedy album *This Nigger's Crazy* made clear, such name-calling often means seizing control of language once used to insult and turning it into a scathing, in-your-face tool.

Another perspective brought out in early and late blaxploitation films was the stress within the black community over more militant approaches to change. Shaft includes a scene in which the older, well-dressed gangster Bumpy meets Bufort, the young, dedicated revolutionary. Bufort accuses Bumpy of feeding off the miseries of his own people to make his fortune. "We all on the hustle," snarls Bumpy. "I sell broads and dope and numbers. You sell crap and blue skies—it's all the same game." A similar view of militants as preachy and dangerous is included in *Superfly* and other films of the period. More acute, loners like Shaft (who straddle white and black worlds) are often accused of being less black. (A character in *Superfly* even makes a crack about Priest's light skin color, casting doubt on his racial purity.)

The few white characters that appear in blaxploitation films are usually corrupt cops or Italian gangsters, with the latter obsessed with food. The Italians are also portrayed as being stupidly smug about their criminal power, leaving themselves vulnerable to black encroachment, particularly in Harlem.

Another resident character in these films is a woman, black or white, who becomes a trophy for the male leads—nearly always superstuds. Yet there frequently were interesting black women who were trusted allies and spoke their mind when they disliked how they were being treated. One woman, Pam Grier, took that concept and made a career out of it. Grier proved she could be black, beautiful, and a deadly aim with a double-barreled shotgun. She gave the blaxploitation period one of its best star attractions.

In *Coffy* (1973), Grier's character is a trained nurse who chucks her career to go on a killing spree of dope pushers, pimps, Italian mobsters, and crooked cops who ruined her family and ravaged the black community. Her last victim is her politician boyfriend, who tells her that he's changing things "for our people." But she finds out that he tells his white gangster partners that the rackets are color-blind: "Black, brown, or yellow—I'm in it for the green."

An advertisement for the film noted, "She is the 'Godmother' of them all." Grier made several films with the same basic plot and frequent outings of her breasts. But as George notes, she "became a cult figure who was even embraced by many feminists for her ball-breaking action flicks."[8] After *Coffy* came sequels *Foxy Brown, Friday Foster,* and the simply awful *Scream, Blacula, Scream*. But Grier mustered up enough dignity to make her persona memorable. As a woman, she was a convincing conscience to chastise black drug lords and pimps who worked for the Mob and wrought further harm on the black community. When a male character espouses the same minisermons in the black outlaw films, he appears effeminate or overbearing. Grier was also the master of her own sexuality—virtually absent from white women's roles of the same era. And she was streetwise enough to take care of herself without appearing sluttish or tough. White and black female action heroes (and gangsters) who populated later screens owe a large debt to Grier's trailblazing efforts. Like Grier's, John Shaft's two sequels, *Shaft's Big Score!* and *Shaft in Africa* showed the fatigue of the formula and tested the patience of their audiences.

GOOD TIMES—HARD TIMES

Although blaxploitation finally faded away, Hollywood had discovered the profits not only in appealing to black audiences but in inventing interesting characters that won over white audiences, as Shaft had done. Soon Hollywood began putting strong black characters in mostly white casts, finally vigorously integrating studio material aimed at the general marketplace. Bill Cosby had broken the color barrier on TV with *I Spy,* making him the first black actor to costar in a hit series. In the 1970s, TV launched black-cast, black-theme situation comedies such as *Good Times* and *Sanford and Son*. At the movies, Apollo Creed (Carl Weathers) became Rocky's nemesis. Richard Pryor and Gene Wilder got together for *Stir Crazy,* a film directed by Sidney Poitier. In this case, though, Pryor had the star power, being a major draw for hip white audiences along with the customary black support. In the 1980s, Danny Glover and Mel Gibson teamed up as buddy cops in the *Lethal Weapon* series. In fact, for some black entertainers, the 1980s were boon years. Eddie Murphy, Bill Cosby, and Oprah Winfrey became superstars dominating movies and television. They had the crossover power to draw customers and admirers from all pockets of society.

Noncelebrity blacks, meanwhile, were in nearly the same quagmire they had been a generation before. White America—despite the 1960s struggle—remained slow to eradicate the racism that had become learned behavior over generations. In the volatile economy of the 1980s, the white middle class felt squeezed, and its working class found itself increasingly put out of factories to accommodate downsizing or cheaper foreign labor. (Statistics, though, show that blacks were hardest hit in the

1980s, being unemployed at almost twice the rate of whites; economic conditions for blacks were at worse levels than in 1960—before the civil rights push.)

The 1980s witnessed a soaring deficit and a sense of social fatigue that left white America in no mood to concede more of its power to blacks or to the burgeoning Latino community—no matter how much the white middle-class conscience moaned. As Stallone and Schwarzenegger took over the screen, their cartoonlike superheroes suggested that the eighties were the decade of survival of the fittest. And that meant taking back control of America's image. Hollywood had spent its history fashioning that reflection as a lone white male who saves the day and rides off in the sunset. President Reagan endorsed Stallone's Rambo character as such a movie hero for modern times. But even in the debut film, he's referred to as a "killing machine" and a hair-trigger leftover of Vietnam anguish. If Rambo was a contemporary champion, it left a lot of people wondering what sort of crisis called for such a remedy.

Racism and xenophobia seemed reinvigorated, and a backlash against two decades of social strumming for change came into vogue. Our new TV star was a conservative young white male character named Alex P. Keaton who wanted to return to a kinder, gentler 1950s sensibility—before all the trouble started. But it wasn't the 1950s anymore, and black America in particular was tired of waiting for promises made long ago.

As the decade roared on, black America warned of intolerable crisis conditions wreaking havoc within their communities—still overwhelmingly poor, underemployed, and trapped in decayed urban areas. The younger generation within the hardest-hit neighborhoods were being swallowed up by increasingly meaner streets. One of the street's new weapons was a drug called crack cocaine, which cost less and delivered a greater (and more lethal) high. Its introduction into the ghettos by the mid-1980s ravaged the inner cities as badly as cholera or other diseases wiped out portions of the slum population at the turn of the century.

SPIKE AND THE GHETTO

A young black director named Spike Lee noticed his middle-class Brooklyn neighborhood was also changing for the worse. After attending NYU film school, he joined other distinguished alumni and began making daring films about subjects deep in his heart—and conscience. Lee's 1989 film *Do the Right Thing* took a provocative look at ghetto tensions during one hot summer day. In a mostly black Brooklyn neighborhood—entrenched Italians, resentful blacks, and newcomer Koreans clash in a final riot that leaves most of them worse off. Lee's screenplay was nominated for an Oscar, along with Danny Aiello as best supporting actor for his portrayal of the proud, bigoted, but conciliatory owner of a corner pizzeria. But the film produced a hailstorm of controversy from both white and black communities—mostly for having the audacity to suggest conditions were ripe for a repeat of the summer of 1967. Lee also exposed his own community's divisiveness, which exists as in any other. He had cut a large opening, though, through which other young black filmmakers could, and would, pass. They would bring their own observations and revelations—in particular about black gangsters, who were proliferating in the modern drug-infested ghetto.

GANGSTA OVERKILL

Another urban black voice, one that would soon fuse into film stories, was rap music. Rap combines preaching with rhythm and blues and first broke into mainstream music in the early 1980s. It also quickly separated the generations previously joined by rock 'n' roll and to a lesser degree defined a racial divide. Most rap music or hip-hop music—an evolved hybrid—addresses the timeless subjects of love, loss, hope, heartache, dreams, and personal confessions. But a renegade movement within the music genre captured an angrier, more confrontational approach. Again Spike Lee scattered influence for harder-edged groups such as Public Enemy by using its showdown tune "Fight the Power" as the musical backbeat for *Do the Right Thing*.

The group Public Enemy, as its name denotes, borrowed the image and nihilism of the gangster tradition, or as it's known in street idiom, gangsta. Such groups see themselves as cultural and social outlaws who put harrowing tales of life in the hood (or neighborhood) on vinyl. Groups named Capone-n-Noreaga, Black Caesar, Outkast, and Niggas with Attitude (NWA) are also a testament to gangsta rap's embrace of society's darker images.

Gangsta rap was soon condemned by established music reviewers along with community activists as a crude subculture product laced with vulgar messages about rape, torture, cop killing, and anarchy. Much of the brouhaha over rap lyrics, as with punk or heavy metal, is a battle over obscenity. These musical forms are permeated with the puerile fantasies of young males confused about manhood and obsessed with sex. Some lyrics focus on abusing women or in some way controlling them—a plight as old as history. But gangsta lyrics also seethe with an animus toward brutal police, the ravages of drugs, the false face of "brotherhood," and a fatalism that's downright chilling. As a reviewer noted of one album, gangsta rap is like "a house party crossed with a race riot."[9]

Many gangsta rappers are also gang members or at least claim to be to add to their mystique. More important, they may also be the best eyewitnesses to offer candid testimony as to what stink surrounds the escalating street carnage. Los Angeles–based rappers had warned of an impending altercation in South Central long before it erupted in 1992. (Chuck D of Public Enemy called rap "the black CNN.")

The impetus behind gangs, of course, hasn't changed in centuries. Gangs still offer bonds of brotherhood and feelings of empowerment to boys who think they can't find such benefits anywhere else. And most gang bangers still end up dead or in prison. The difference between today's gangs and those at the turn of the century is a matter of updated and deadlier weaponry—not end goals.

One rapper and former gang member known as Ice Cube (once of NWA), like several other rap artists, would soon be invited to star in a Hollywood movie.

MENACING MOVIES

One of the first major dramas to include a story about Los Angeles gangs (and a pounding gangsta rap score) was *Colors* in 1988. The movie's violence, along with the rhythmically hammering title song by rapper Ice-T, brought on howls of protest. *Colors*—a term that refers to bandannas and other clothing items that mark gang ranks—was directed by the former counterculture prince Dennis Hopper (of *Easy Rider* fame). The film starred Sean Penn and Robert Duvall as cops in a hopelessly deadlocked battle with L.A. gangs. Although the film peeks into the subculture and terror of gang mentality—rather than fit into the gangster genre—the story focuses on the cops' increasing frustration and their often brutal response.

However, in the early 1990s, three films debuted that electrified black cinema and reinvigorated the gangster genre: *New Jack City, Boyz N the Hood,* and *Menace II Soci-*

ety. Just as *Mean Streets* had done 20 years before, these films reintroduced the genre to the streets of America's slums cum ghetto cum hood, where the genre's best goods are derived. And just as *Little Caesar, The Public Enemy,* and *Scarface* were lumped together by critics and audiences alike, these films were compared and contrasted because of the shared "hood" theme, but also because all three directors were black. Each film, however, takes a unique perspective while paying homage not only to the legacy of black cinema but to the gangster genre's rich past.

New Jack City is the work of actor-director Mario Van Peebles, the son of *Sweetback*'s legendary creator, Melvin Van Peebles. The film unites the legend of a Harlem drug lord, gangsta rap fury, and flash filmmaking. It not only uses the genre's trusted conventions but borrows from the black action tradition, notably *Black Caesar.* "New jack swing" is a phrase coined by Barry Michael Cooper to describe at the time a bold new direction and attitude in black music, which took its cue from an increasingly dangerous urban milieu. Cooper frequently wrote about the street scene and looming drug culture for the *Village Voice* before being invited to add insights to a film script. Like Scorsese's comment about the loss of honor among Mafia thieves, Cooper notes, "In this day and age, [honor] is gone. . . . These are new jacks . . . they are the new breed of gangsters who will kill you in the blink of an eye and not think about it. . . . they have no sense of morality."[10]

The film tracks an ambitious drug dealer named Nino Brown (Wesley Snipes as a clone of legendary 1970s Harlem gangster Leroy "Nicky" Barnes, who's updated to crack lord). One of Brown's lieutenants, Gee Money Wells (Allen Payne), shows Nino a new drug that promises to transform them from neighborhood pushers to Harlem's crime rulers. As Keisha (Vanessa Williams), his female lieutenant and key assassin, notes, "[It] looks like cracked-off pieces of soap."

Following the classic formula, there's an equally determined coterie of cops who vow to destroy Nino's operation. But Nino proves his cunning and business acumen when he sees the potential of crack as a best-seller on the street and goes about building a criminal enterprise. "We gonna come off like the Mob," Nino proudly boasts. Part of his corporate-like expansion means creating a factory out of a mammoth apartment building, which gets made over with labs, high-tech computers, and military-style security. "If the tenants cooperate, they become loyal customers," Nino warns. "They don't, it'll be like Beirut. They'll become live-in hostages." He also gets rid of any spoilers or competition by sending Keisha and an aide to eliminate them. She relishes putting a gun to someone's head in broad daylight in front of horrified onlookers and pulling the trigger. She's a casual, skilled, and efficient killer.

The customary montage (accompanied by a revamped version of Stevie Wonder's "Livin' in the City") shows the takeover of the rundown building; tenants being shot, beaten, or ousted; close-ups of rolling glass vials full of cocaine nuggets; and Nino getting fitted for a custom-made suit.

Crack is flooding the streets and having the negative fallout of an epidemic, the police chief tells Detective Stone (Mario Van Peebles). Stone is told to go after Nino, but he wants to hire Scotty Appleton (Ice-T) and the white Nick Peretti (Judd Nelson), two cops on the fringe with spotty records and an intense dislike for each other. Appleton has dreadlocks and Peretti looks like a neobeatnik. The chief insists that the two are risky, but Stone insists, "I need some new jack cops to take down new jack gangsters. What you call a risk . . . it's our only shot."

Appleton, once assigned, goes one step further. He cleans up a crack addict named Pookie (Chris Rock), whom Nino once offered a job. After he's straight, and against the department's better judgment, Pookie goes undercover into Nino's operation, with a camera hidden in his belt buckle. As a nod to the black gangster heritage (and the reality of the street), Nino has another problem besides the cops: the Mafia.

Nino is enjoying the fruits of his labor, though, wearing electric blue suits and heavy gold chains and living in a lavish home, where he obsessively watches Pacino as *Scarface*. Tony Montana inspires Nino, and he too shouts about taking over the world. (In another nod to old gangster movies, while paddling on a raft in his swimming pool, he gives a wide grin and remarks, "This is some shit. . . . George Raft, James Cagney type shit.") On one occasion, he taunts his placid, upper-crust girlfriend, Selina, who like Elvira is unable to have children—and doesn't seem to like sex. Nino then beds down Gee Money's sluttish girlfriend, driving a further wedge between the two longtime friends. The final blow to their friendship, though, occurs when Gee Money makes a fatal business gaffe and allows Appleton to infiltrate the operation. He poses as a drug dealer who can circumvent Mob drug supplies.

Appleton has to take the risk after his protégé Pookie ends up dead in the factory after falling back into crack use. He had been stealing and using on the job until his manic behavior tipped off his employers that he was high on the product. (Most workers who handle the drug operate in the nude to eliminate employee smuggling.)

Once Pookie's cover is blown, the police raid the place. Nino's lieutenants splash gasoline around the factory and set its contents on fire. (Like the old incriminating ledgers, computer disks containing vital information are saved.) Later, at a meeting of his associates, Nino berates Gee Money for his sloppy checks of employees and then sticks a knife in another man's hand as a warning against any more screwups. This is business, and friendships don't matter much, Nino warns.

In fact, Nino sounds like a Corleone again when he tells his new associate Appleton that killing is "always business . . . never personal." As in the 1970s black outlaw films, a character is inserted who berates Nino about "committing genocide on your own people." With a chilly smugness, Nino asks the old man, "What can you offer them? Another 'I have a dream' speech?"

During a lavish wedding of one of Nino's "family" members, the Mafia send gunmen to kill him and his crew. Keisha gets annihilated trying to spray the Italians with an Uzi, but Nino escapes using a little girl as a human shield. Nino then retaliates and sends his men to a sidewalk café where Don Armeteo and his men are sipping espresso before being pumped full of bullets by drive-by shooters with AK-47s.

Just as Appleton and Gee Money are about to make their deal, one of Nino's men recognizes Appleton as a cop. A fierce shoot-out ensues, and Appleton and Peretti save each other's lives. Gee Money gets away only to be confronted by Nino. In a gripping scene, mixing affection, desperation, and tragedy, Nino hugs Gee Money then shoots him while he kneels in the street.

Nino goes on the run and hides in the neighborhood where the young kids protect him and the adults want him exterminated like a rat. Appleton finds Nino and beats him up on the street, finally aiming his gun but wrestling with pulling the trigger. He tells Nino his mother was killed by a junkie and he wants his revenge. But Appleton is talked into the legal solution, and Nino goes to trial. Nino, however, turns the witness stand into a bully pulpit to give his Tony Montana speech about the system being more culpable than him. "All of you who lobby against making drugs legal. Just like you did . . . during the Prohibition," he rants. "Ain't no Uzis made in Harlem. . . . Not one of us in here owns a poppy field. This thing is bigger than Nino Brown. This is the American way."

He points across the room at the man who gave him his start, a well-dressed business tycoon named Kareem Akbar—the natty, unghettoized black gangster who keeps out of the spotlight like a Mafia don. Once Nino gives him up, the prosecution cuts him a deal. This infuriates Appleton, who confronts Nino on the staircase. As they shout about injustice, the old man who once chastised Brown comes up the steps and shoots him. Nino sails through the open middle of the wrapping staircase and smashes down on the surface several floors below.

Before the credits roll, we get a 1932 *Scarface*-style disclaimer, as the epilogue reads: "Although this is a fictional story, there are Nino Browns in every major city in America. If we don't confront the problem realistically . . . without empty slogans and promises . . . then drugs will continue to destroy our country."

New Jack City, released by the veteran gangster shop Warner Brothers, was a box office smash, becoming the year's fourth highest grossing picture, according to Richard Corliss in his *Time* magazine review. Like Corliss, most critics gave *New Jack City* high marks for pizzazz but faulted the film's flattery of the drug lord's lifestyle and intoxicating clout. This is further aggravated by a stunning performance by Snipes as Nino, making him a well-dressed, smoldering figure of awe tinged with fear.

Newsweek called Nino's gang "super-Yuppie criminals. These are the new jacks: natty gangster Gekkos, with flashy sculpted hair, advanced computer systems, cellular phones and high-tech weapons. . . . Like Gekko . . . they believe that greed is good. . . . Crack is their junk-bond capital." *Variety* termed the film "a provocative, pulsating update on gangster pics." *Newsday* noted that "despite all your best defenses against the sordid glamour being depicted, it's exhilarating the way a good pulp thriller always is." *Newsday* also gives Snipes credit for "magnetism Pacino lacked as a drug kingpin."

If these reviews sound familiar, it's because the same basic summation has been said about popular gangster films since the genre's start. In her article "The New Ghetto Aesthetic," Jacquie Jones wrote, "It looms as little more than a Blackface *Scarface*."[11] In other words, *New Jack City* wasn't a black thing but a better-than-average gangster film. And its moral high ground is no more convincing than that of its predecessors. Any attempt to disclaim the gangster's attractiveness after spending two hours filming him like a rock star is ethically moribund. It was in 1931 and remains so 60 years later.

That aside, the film is well paced, with crisp, sincere performances and an intelligent script (sermons be damned). It often has the sound and appearance of an extended hip-hop video, with incessant attention to style, but skillfully rendered, never at the expense of substance. Janet Maslin lauded Francis Kenny's striking photography of Harlem's crumbling architecture to lend a sense of decay and to neatly balance the slick interior shots. The *Washington Post* called the factory's contrived interior "a nightmare commingling of IBM and Dante's 'Inferno.' "[12]

Producer Doug McHenry, speaking for himself and his partner George Jackson, said they've "always wanted to do a gangster film . . . [but] in a non-exploitation way." Jackson noted, "There are strong parallels between the Roaring Twenties and the Roaring Eighties . . . particularly in the emergence of the new American gangster." McHenry said the takeover of an apartment building is derived from tales of another notorious dead heroin dealer, Oakland's Felix Mitchell.[13]

Jackson and McHenry found actor-director Mario Van Pebbles, who had switched from acting (in his own TV series *Sonny Spoon*) to directing, having worked on several

Wiseguy episodes and the series *21 Jump Street.* Van Peebles hadn't been raised in the hood, though, but spent part of his childhood in Europe with his father and mother, a white German-born artist named Maria Marx. After attending the Ivy League Columbia University to study economics, he worked as a budget analyst for New York City's mayor Ed Koch. As a result, Van Peebles's views regarding cops and the system differ drastically from his father's. "I've worked for the government. . . . I've known some cops and some people in government who really care . . . but they're trying to do it within the system."[14]

For *New Jack City,* he said that he used the 1930s classic gangster films for inspiration, but for modern comparisons, he admitted he wanted the film to be more like De Palma's *The Untouchables* than De Palma's *Scarface.* Van Peebles wanted the cop to be as formidable as the gangster. Although Snipes's Nino Brown devours the screen, Ice-T, as the hungry cop who wants to avenge his mother's death, makes a convincing rival. When the finished film was screened for young test audiences, they gave Ice-T high marks and "rolled" with him, not the gangster. Usually, the gangster rules, because it is, after all, his turf—and genre. Tony Montana has been a longtime hero of hard-core rappers, and his best swaggering was aped in the film.[15] But having Appleton act on a personal obsession and vendetta more than out of duty is hardly a new strategy. Cagney was the only G-man who was convincing enough to beat the gangsters, mainly because he still acted and looked like one. In *New Jack City,* achieving this was not a matter of getting a screen persona to switch sides. It meant getting a real former gang member and hard-core rap artist to play a screen cop. The casting choice was as tricky for Ice-T as it was for the filmmakers. He had built a music career on lyrics that boil over with anticop sentiments. (In a few short years, his song "Cop Killer" would be controversial enough to get him dropped by his record company.) But his performance—vengeance motive aside—is riveting. The *Washington Times* critic noted, "The rap singer never varies from his expertly controlled impression of anger and sorrow." But the *Los Angeles Times* still found the story tipped in favor of the gangster, mostly owing to a "stunning" performance by Snipes—"an actor of tremendous resource and presence."

Stepping on the same turf as D. W. Griffith encountered nearly eight decades ago, the filmmakers said that real gangsters often drifted into camera range. "We would be filming a drug bust and there would be a drug bust going on down the block," said Cooper, who cowrote the script with Thomas Lee Wright. (Wright had been invited to cowrite a treatment and script for the third *Godfather,* in which he worked in the tale of Nicky Barnes.)

ANGELS IN THE HOOD

Whereas *New Jack City* added hip-hop to the classic gangster story, *Boyz N the Hood* tapped the late-1930s morality plays that used a gangster to warn young minds how not to become one. The story centers around three boys who grew up together in a tinderbox neighborhood in South Central Los Angeles. Tre (Cuba Gooding Jr.) is the survivor (and narrator), Ricky (Morris Chestnut) is the budding athlete with the chance to escape, and his half-brother Doughboy (Ice Cube) is already a gangster and still in grade school. Tre is raised by his demanding but loving father while his mother pursues her master's degree. The temporary-turned-permanent arrangement is also to help Tre learn how to be a man.

Cuba Gooding Jr. is one of the *Boyz N the Hood* trying to avoid the gangster life who painfully watches more homeboys die in the tough turf of South Central Los Angeles. John Singleton's screenplay and direction were nominated for Oscars, making the 23-year-old the youngest director ever nominated.

The first half hour of the film shows their childhood alliances and their basic characters. (Director John Singleton said that he wanted the opening scenes to portray the characters as Leone did in *Once upon a Time in America.*) Tre learns that his father, Furious Styles (Larry Fishburne), has strong opinions, plentiful advice, and lots of tough love. Styles tells his son not to become a father by accident, not to respect someone who doesn't respect you back, and not to be afraid to ask—stealing isn't necessary.

Ricky, his mother's favorite, is aware she has high hopes for him. Meanwhile, Doughboy settles for stealing and spends most of his teenage years in prison. The film picks up in 1991, after he has been released, and tracks the summer just after high school graduation. College looms in the fall for Tre, a football scholarship dangles in front of Ricky, and Doughboy has no plans whatsoever. He's rapidly becoming part of the battered landscape, which includes the incessant whirl of hovering helicopters looking for gang trouble. Doughboy spends his days with his homeboys on the front porch drinking malt liquor and getting high, a ready gun stuffed in his pants.

Tre and Ricky, like many neighborhood teenagers, congregate on Crenshaw Boulevard, an exaggerated malt shop for the 1990s with a deadly edge. As one girl puts it, "Can't we have one night where there ain't no fight and nobody gets shot?" One typical night finds Tre and Ricky strolling down the street, but Ricky isn't looking ahead and slams into a stranger—a hair-trigger gang banger. The scene turns ugly as the thug pulls out a gun and shoots warning shots in the air and flashes a macabre grin.

One day, as Tre and Ricky return home from a nearby party store—and part company in an alley—a car pulls up, and one of its passengers opens fire on Ricky. The shooter is the gang banger, who wants revenge for a shove in the street. In slow motion, Ricky stumbles as a bullet tears through his thigh. Then, as Tre turns toward the noise, he watches another bullet rip open his friend's chest. Within minutes, having heard the gunshots, Doughboy and his homeboys roar down the alley in a beat-up convertible. Unlike Tre, Doughboy's grief is laced with thoughts of vengeance. That night he plans retaliation, and Tre gets his father's gun and heads out the door to join them. But Furious stops him, mocking his mission, "Oh, you bad now, huh? You gotta

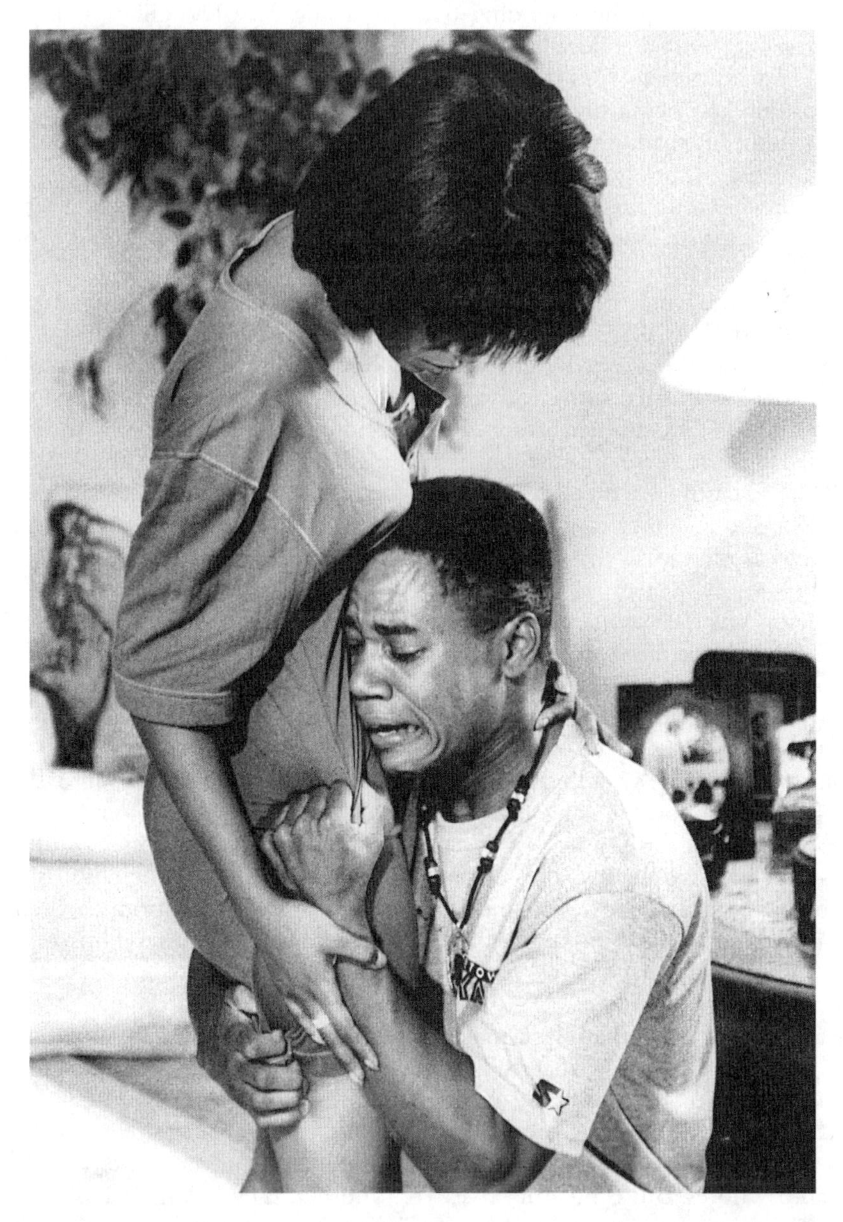

Tre (Cuba Gooding Jr.) clutches his girlfriend Brandi (Nia Long) in *Boyz N the Hood*. Tre is torn between the decent world, long represented by women in gangster films, and the codes of male pride and annihilating revenge that rule gang life in his battered neighborhood.

go shoot somebody?" Tre gives back the gun, quiets down, and goes to his room. But he eventually jumps out his bedroom window and joins the street cruise that looks more like a military convoy. Just as suddenly, Tre asks to be let out of the car.

But Doughboy and his gang—one of whom uses a wheelchair from a past street fight that left him crippled—eventually find their three victims munching on hamburgers at a take-out stand. They pull up swiftly and stealthily, then start blasting out the windows with ferocious noise, and leave two boys dead in the parking lot. The third is crawling along the ground until Doughboy finishes him off.

The next morning, Tre sits on his front stoop, watching the neighborhood under a naked sun, soaking up the pounding bass of passing cars. Doughboy is making his daily drug buy on the sidewalk; he's already clutching his morning bottle of malt liquor. He drifts over to Tre's stoop, where he sits down and talks about watching TV that morning and being disgusted at the reports of violence in foreign capitals but nothing about his brother's murder. He also admits he doesn't feel much better for his payback killing. "It just goes on and on," he admits.

The film ends with this epilogue: "The next day Doughboy saw his brother buried. Two weeks later he was murdered. In the fall Tre went to Morehouse College in Atlanta, Georgia, with Brandi across the way at Spelman College."

The film is the work of 23-year-old filmmaker John Singleton, who had graduated from the prestigious USC Film School and twice won the Jack Nicholson Writing Award. He had been signed right out of school by a powerhouse agent. He was noticed after a young executive forwarded his senior thesis, *Boyz N the Hood,* to Frank Price, the head of Columbia Pictures. Price decided to take a chance on the story and bankroll Singleton, who insisted on bringing his own material to the screen. Price said, "The last time I'd met someone that young with so much self-assurance was Steven Spielberg." Singleton idolized Spielberg, along with Coppola, noting, "*The Godfather* was the movie that changed my life. I consider it the quintessential American film."

Singleton was the youngest director ever to be nominated for an Academy Award, and his *Boyz N the Hood* screenplay was also up for an Oscar. Critics were generous with praise, as Roger Ebert described the film as "not simply a brilliant directorial debut, but an American film of enormous importance." It also became the most profitable movie of 1991.[16]

Enlisting the genre's tradition, Singleton brought gang members onto the set as advisors and cast former gang member Ice Cube in the film to lend realism. Ice Cube's performance as Doughboy is crusty and genuine and possesses an underlying pathos that draws sympathy to his character. But with its underlying emphasis not on gang mentality but on how to avoid it, *Boyz N the Hood* strays from the genre. The film's preaching is more in tune with the melodramatic gangster films of the late 1930s, which emphasized how the same conditions that create a gangster can also harden another boy's resolve.

Part of its sermon is that black males have to help raise their sons and take a firm hand. Many critics noted that Singleton could have gotten that message across without discrediting single black mothers, even Tre's. In his film, mothers are characterized either as forsaking their children while they pursue careers in the white world or as escaping responsibility through debilitating drug addiction that turns them into whores. But Singleton gives Tre's mother, Reva (Angela Bassett), a brief say when Furious nearly brags to her that Tre has become a man because of his hard work. She reminds him, "Don't think you're special. . . . you did what you're supposed to do."

BLACK GOODFELLAS

The last of the "hood" films that drew as much attention as accolades is *Menace II Society.* It was modeled after *GoodFellas,* which the filmmakers match with enthusiasm and candor. *Menace II Society* is by far the best of its ilk, as well as being one of the finest modern films about gangsters—black or white. It's a superb, brutally unsentimental portrait of thugs. Yet the story has a soul even when the gangsters lack one.

The film begins with a powder-keg clash between two cultures that's reminiscent of the spark that provokes the riot in *Do the Right Thing.* Two black youths saunter into a party store owned by a Korean couple who look jumpy and impatient. The boys become increasingly bugged by the assumption that they're going to steal something. When the Korean mumbles that he feels sorry for one of their mothers, the teen with the boyish face and tousled dreadlocks uncorks his rage. As quick as a movie cowboy, he pulls out a gun and puts a bullet into the man's head. Then he shoots the woman after making her hand over the surveillance video. He robs the register almost as an afterthought while his friend looks on in shock.

"This don't even make any sense," hollers the other youth, the stricken Caine (Tyrin Turner), the film's lead character and narrator. (The story is told through frequent voice-overs.) Caine clues us in about life in the hood, as he and his companion O'Dog (Larenz Tate) experience it. In voice-over, he says: "Went into the store just to get a beer, came out an accessory to murder and armed robbery. . . . It's funny like that in the hood. . . . You never knew what was going to happen or when. I knew it was gonna be a long summer."

As the credits roll, the screen fills with documentary footage of the 1965 Watts riots. Caine adds, "When the riot stopped, the drugs started." He casually explains the

Left, Caine (Tyrin Turner); *center,* the vicious O-Dog (Larenz Tate); and *right,* rapper MC Eiht as A-Wax in *Menace II Society* endure an old-fashioned park picnic, which puts them uncomfortably out of their element, leaving them bored and restless as ever.

Left, Caine (Tyrin Turner) passes his street lore and reliance on guns to another generation of ghetto youth in *Menace II Society*. The film by the twin 21-year-old Hughes brothers is an unflinching look at the cold-blooded meanness of today's urban gangster. Dubbed the black *GoodFellas,* the film purposely echoes Scorsese's film, along with De Palma's *Scarface*.

flashbacks that show his dismal childhood: a dope dealer for a dad, whom Caine watches kill a man during a card game; a heroin addict for a mother, whom Caine watches die from an overdose. His father's associate Pernell (Glenn Plummer) acts more like a father to Caine—except his advice focuses on "what being a hustler was all about."

The scene is brought back to Watts in 1993, shortly after the store killings. Caine is moping through his last day of high school, which he admits he only attended half the time. His boredom is relieved when his beeper goes off and reminds him he has drug business to tend to. When not with O'Dog and his other friends, Caine spends time with Ronnie (Jada Pinkett), a girl about his age but a young mother to the son of his mentor Pernell, now in prison. For Pernell's sake, Caine tries to take care of them but has his own feelings about Ronnie. He hides money in her house to help her out and plays video games with her son. He even bought the young Anthony a new Big Wheel when he saw the boy's was broken. Ronnie sees Caine's sweet side but is terrified of his teaching her boy any street lessons. She doesn't want Caine swearing around Anthony, which renders Caine nearly unable to finish a sentence. And she becomes enraged and terrified when she sees him teaching her son how to hold a gun, just the way Pernell taught him. When not with Ronnie or roaming the streets with his posse, he lives with his grandparents. But they seem disconnected from him and substitute Bible quotes for earthbound advice.

After his cousin Harold—a hustler with "a Beemer, a crib, and a fat pocket"—comes to visit, the two drop by a house party, where Caine introduces us to the rest of his friends. Sharif is trying to follow the strict discipline of a Black Muslim, and Stacey is headed for Kansas on a football scholarship. Later Harold and Caine cruise Crenshaw—a familiar habit for many youths. But its everyday, banal quality is shattered when a car pulls up next to them at a light. In a moment of unrestrained, abrupt horror, Harold is shot point-blank, and a bullet hits Caine in the shoulder. Both teens are thrown in the street, and the car jackers jump into Harold's BMW, clean his blood off the windshield so that they can see the road, and zoom off in their new status ride. A bloodied but breathing Caine is dragged off to the hospital by his frantic friends, who shout expletives at emergency room staff who look frayed from too many nights of bleeding boys in their care.

During Caine's hospital stay, he spends his time stewing about Harold being killed and "watching . . . gangster movies." Meanwhile, O'Dog seems to reveal a bit more sadism with each passing day. He gets a kick out of watching the Korean store videotape, and freeze-frames the part when the man's head seems to explode. The video makes Caine squirm, but he does little to stop O'Dog's antics. Another incident has O'Dog shooting a junkie in an alley because the guy wanted some cocaine so bad that he offered to perform oral sex for O'Dog. After O'Dog pumps several bullets into the junkie, he grabs his cheeseburger and offers it to his friends, chuckling and saying that it shouldn't go to waste.

After Caine is back home, street justice dictates that he has to avenge his cousin's death. He, O'Dog, and the rest of the crew take to the streets and hunt down their prey. At a food stand, they find their victims and summarily wipe them out. Later, alone in his room, Caine tells us: "I thought killing those fools would make me feel good. But it didn't really make me feel anything. I just knew I could kill somebody. If I had to, I could do it again."

The crew next gets a job stealing a car for a white guy who finds buyers for them. Caine ends up in jail, and police match his prints to those found on a beer bottle at

As Caine (Tyrin Turner, *left*) threatens car-jacking victim (Martin Davis, *right*) in *Menace II Society*, Davis's character reacts with astonishing resignation at an all too familiar occurrence in the hood.

the Korean store. They grill him, but because they have no other evidence, he's set free. Only momentarily forced to experience jail, which he finds disgusting, he quickly goes back to selling drugs. He buys $400 worth to process for street consumption, having learned from his father how to cook and cut up the hardened chunks into crack.

Sharif's father tries to save Tre, talking to him about surviving beyond the street and finding something to believe in. But Caine admits he loves "big money" and wouldn't look twice at a minimum wage job, which is all he's qualified to do. Caine soon ends up back in the hospital after being stopped and beaten up by cops. Ronnie comes to visit and to tell him that she's moving to Atlanta, where she's found a decent job. She invites Caine to come with her, but he balks. "Ain't nothing gonna change in Atlanta," he says. "I'm still gonna be black."

Friends throw a going-away party for Ronnie and say good-bye to Stacy and Sharif, who are headed for Kansas. But the party turns mean when one of their friends, Chauncy, starts manhandling Ronnie. Caine comes unglued and beats Chauncy with the butt of a gun. To add to his troubles, Tre gets a call from a girl who says he got her pregnant. He dismisses her claim and argues that the child is not his, but she delivers a crushing line: "You man enough to take a life but you ain't man enough to take care of one."

Caine goes with Ronnie to visit Pernell in prison and to say good-bye. But Caine is still bothered by doubts; he seems unable to leave the streets, the only place where he believes he has control. Pernell tells him to go with Ronnie with his blessing, and to take good care of his son Anthony. "Teach him that the way we grew up was bullshit." With that, Caine breaks down and cries.

Back home, the cousin of the pregnant girl shows up at Caine's house to demand that Tre do something to help her. Caine and O'Dog respond by savagely beating him up. His grandparents watch the attack in horror and finally kick Caine out of their lives. That seals his decision: he's going to Atlanta. He and his friends help Ronnie move things out of the house into a van. Meanwhile, blocks away, their beating victim plans his revenge.

In the last sequence, the cousin and his crew load guns while Ronnie and the boys load the van. As the action cuts to slow motion, the familiar street drama follows. A car comes rumbling up the street, with a masked gunman hanging out the window. He pokes an Uzi out of the darkness and starts shooting into Ronnie's front yard. A shot shows the car's wheels rolling by and then cuts to Anthony and his Big Wheel rolling down the sidewalk. Bullets rip through Sharif, and he falls over dead. Caine throws himself on top of Anthony to shield him, Ronnie screams in anguish, and O'Dog keeps frantically firing his weapon. After the assault is over, Stacey rolls Caine over to find Anthony unharmed but Caine gushing blood, convulsing, and barely alive. The scene finally draws a tear from the ruthless O'Dog as he watches another friend die. Caine speaks to us in one last voice-over: "I had done too much to turn back and I had done too much to go on. I guess in the end it all catches up with you. My grandpa asked me one time if I care whether I live or die. Yeah, I do. And now it's too late."

David Denby's review in *New York* called *Menace II Society* the most striking directorial debut in black cinema history. The film earned a standing ovation at the Cannes Film Festival in 1993 and was hailed by critics as the most disturbing and comprehensive hood film thus far. It also stirred up a storm of controversy like previous gangster sagas—black and white.

"*Menace II Society* has a manic energy and at times a lyricism that recall movies like *Mean Streets* and *Bonnie and Clyde*." But in one of the more scathing reviews, *Newsday* wrote, "It's an ugly film, almost an evil film, but whether that troubles you, whether it excites you, is also beside the point. The movie's amorality leaves you devoid of hope, and that's the point."

There's no doubt that the film's violence is undressed, graphic, and messy. When people are shot, they slobber, shake, and spit up. Witnessing the physical impact cuts deeper and more disturbingly into the psyche than the over-the-top killing in most action films. Films such as *Rambo* and *Die Hard* pile up higher body counts but attach little human misery to the deaths and rarely show their physical trauma. As such, they don't seem real—and rarely emotionally involve an audience.

Menace II Society is reminiscent of one of Scorsese "staged" documentaries, employing the same sleight of hand of a stunning filmmaker who knows how to both mesmerize and appall. In this case, the film is the work of two sets of hands—21-year-old filmmakers Allen and Albert Hughes, who are fraternal twins and partners in art. Allen works with the actors and their performances, and Albert handles directing's visual and technical side.

The Hughes brothers, born in Detroit, say that their mother, Aida Hughes, raised them with a firm hand and kept them away from gangs, despite a father who was never part of their household. Their mother, an Armenian, broke free of welfare when the boys were young, moved them to Pomona, California, and launched her own vocational rehabilitation business. She also gave her 12-year-old twins a video camera to keep them occupied. By age 19, they were professionals making inventive hip-hop videos for a living. But they wanted to evolve and expand into film—and not be "stuck in rap."

They say they borrowed *GoodFellas'* framework to structure the script and also borrowed some of Scorsese's editing treatments. They pay homage to Scorsese's long tracking shot at the Copacabana when their free-flowing camera follows Tre into a house party and gives the same impression of a perpetual, cloistered experience. Moreover, they wanted to match Scorsese's goal for *GoodFellas* of taking viewers on a harried, erratic roller coaster ride. It worked, as the *Washington Post* noted of *Menace* that it "doesn't build to a climax. It explodes unpredictably, out of the blue, and because you feel as if the thing could go off in your face at any second, you're never allowed to relax or let down your guard."

There are other filmmakers and films that the Hughes brothers admire, including Lee's *She's Gotta Have It* and Robert Townsend's *Hollywood Shuffle,* not to mention De Palma's *Scarface.* "We watched it a hundred times," Albert added. And they learned from Coppola not to "hesitate to kill off a starring character." One film that wasn't a role model, though, was *Boyz N the Hood,* which the Hughes brothers find lacking as a gangster film. "That had nothing to do with bad guys. . . . It had good guys going through this bad city, on their way to college," Allen said. His brother said that street gangsters mockingly called the film *Toys in the Hood.* As for *New Jack City,* they thought it had too much of "a comic book look" to it.

And although they interviewed gang members about street violence to lend *Menace* realism, they fought the studio about including recognizable L.A. gang colors. "We wanted to do something about a gangster lifestyle . . . not about being a gang member," or tie in too closely with gangsta rap, Albert said. "They wanted to make it into a rap film. Forget it."

Some of the film's characters could have been better defined, though. The brothers admit that Caine is a composite of several sources. "Caine is parts of everybody we know and parts of us," Allen said. "He's like the middle ground," and less violent and more sympathetic than the others. O'Dog occupies the extreme, as the more ruthless villain's villain. But Caine needed to be his own man to hold his own with the O'Dog character, nearly always infused in gangster stories with exceptionally tuned-up brutality. As the *Chicago Tribune* noted, "Caine's surroundings [are] as much a character as Caine." The *New York Times* described him as "opaque . . . more an unsettling symbol of a social malaise than a tragic figure." The *Times* also suggested that Jada Pinkett's Ronnie "is wonderfully strong, sassy and beautiful: In short, too smart to want someone like Caine to be her life companion." The strong, intuitive Ronnie was, in part, based on the brothers' mother and a symbol of hope.

Overwhelmed by their good reviews, the brothers were shocked at the reaction about the film's graphic violence, considering the films of the last decade. "People love seeing films about Italian gangsterism. But when you see black people with a gun, they start tripping."

MAKING ART COLOR-BLIND

In part, the "snatched from today's newspaper" feel of the hood films accentuates mainstream worries. Whenever the genre approximates journalism rather than history, it gets attacked. Added to the mix is the larger public's reaction to black films, a reaction that unfortunately contains an undercurrent of lingering racism. A renegade black thug scares white America far more than a Gotti-like mobster. A Gotti clone or a Pesci psycho is just as lethal, but he looks like someone they know. Most people also assume Mafia hit men only harm other mafiosi, and never aim at innocent people. That's not true today—if it ever was. Such a theory ignores the tremendous cost the Mafia adds to our everyday lives through their well-oiled machines that have infiltrated many sectors of our society. But organized crime is a scourge that doesn't make the nightly news quite as often as stories about crack babies, gang warfare, and deadly car-jackings.

Also aggravating the outrage were news reports of gang-related incidents at theater showings of the hood films. There were incidents surrounding *The Godfather Part III,* too, but the media and their consumers seize on the accounts that suit the more convenient stereotype.

Those stereotypes are precisely why black scholars and community leaders criticized the hood films as vociferously as some white critics, who hinted that such films are anarchistic. Black voices complained that the filmmakers were exploiting the problem of black-on-black violence without offering any solutions.

James P. Murray's influential 1973 book *To Find an Image: Black Films from Uncle Tom to Superfly* outlined three goals to which black cinema should aspire at that time: to correct white distortions, to reflect the black reality, and to create a positive image.[17] But preaching—whether espousing a black or white spin—undermines a gangster product, then and now. When, as an Italian American, Scorsese offers a look at the Mafia, we don't expect him to run a disclaimer at the end condemning the Mob. "With black cinema . . . they want you to teach instead of entertain," Allen Hughes remarked. "We don't consider ourselves black filmmakers. We consider ourselves filmmakers who are black. . . . We might tell black stories . . . but we're . . . filmmakers [first]."

Shortly after the three hood films were released, the real-life quagmire of American race relations couldn't appear to get any worse. Following the acquittal of four white

Los Angeles police officers who had been caught on videotape beating black motorist Rodney King, Los Angeles went up in flames. Such collateral damage hadn't been seen in the City of Angels since 1965. Within two years, the murder trial of football star and actor O. J. Simpson further aggravated tensions. He was accused of murdering his white wife, Nicole, and her friend Ronald Coleman. The national media frenzied over how race had colored people's perceptions of Simpson's guilt or innocence. And the circuslike trial and endless talk shows devoted to autopsying the trial left Americans as color conscience as ever. (A Gallup poll conducted in June 1997 reported that more than half of both whites and blacks questioned said "there will *always* be a problem" in the United States regarding race relations.)

The race card creates a problem for directors in depicting black gangsters and gang members, especially if they work within the genre. Gangster films are exaggerated public nightmares and are loaded with negative stereotypes. According to the movies, there isn't an honest cop left alive who doesn't want to thump heads and pocket overstuffed envelopes. Italian Americans rarely get a reprieve from their screen images as ice-picking, spaghetti-shoveling Mob soldiers, despite the real-life stories of Joe DiMaggio, Lee Iacocca, and Mario Cuomo. The black screen gangster will most likely continue to growl and pimp roll along to rap-driving, Uzi-spitting, gold-chained, baggy-panted barbarity—his lifestyle paid for by drugs and his fatherless childhood ravaged by poverty. He has become a myth, a stereotype, a legend. And he joins the genre's crowded roster of villains, who date back to the murdering, raping, stealing, thieving, drunken musketeers.

Only uplifting films in other genres, as well as success in the real world, will balance this movie image. Meanwhile, the black screen gangster—no more than the white—will not be tamed. He has roots in real life and in people's nightmares, and moving him off the screen won't get him out of the hood or their heads.

CHAPTER 12

Neo-noir and New Waves

We girls need new skills . . . 'cause by the time our boys are 21, they're in prison or disabled or dead. We're left alone to raise our kids.

—A female gang member, *Mi Vida Loca (My Crazy Life),* 1994

The early 1990s offered a veritable glut of gangster films. Despite what Coppola noted about the healing promise of the 1990s, nefarious gangsters came roaring out of Hollywood as if manufactured at a Ford assembly plant. Moreover, the dependable cast of white, black, Irish, Jewish, and Italian gangsters were being joined by a fresh crop of immigrants new to American soil—and the genre. That the 1990s didn't promise much roar didn't hamper the plots of gangster films; they merely returned to a tried-and-true era chock full of Hollywood-spun excitement and mayhem: Prohibition.

Miller's Crossing was one of the better but flawed neo-Prohibition tales premiering the same year as *GoodFellas* and *The Godfather Part III. Miller's Crossing* tells the tale of two crime kingpins vying for control: the low-key Irish mobster Leo O'Bannion (Albert Finney) and the cordial Italian sociopath Johnny Caspar (Jon Polito). But the starring role belongs to Leo's on-again, off-again confidant, friend, and underboss—the cagey Tom Reagan (Gabriel Byrne). In the end, Tom comes through for Leo after double-crossing double-crossers, sleeping with Leo's slinky, troublesome moll, and killing a rat or two himself. But Tom, a hopeless gambler and romantic—nagged by a sketchy moral canon—walks off and leaves the gangster life and the girl to Leo. For the viewer, it's often hard to connect with Tom because he keeps his doubting, scheming, and loving largely to himself.

This stylish period film is the product of the inventive Coen brothers: Joel the director, Ethan the producer. They earned their reputation with the 1984 neo-noir *Blood Simple,* about intimate killings. They also wrote the screenplay for *Miller's Crossing,* lacing it with sharp, fetching dialogue. After Caspar explains to Tom that he wants the double-dealing days of a character named Bernie stopped, Tom asks, "So, you wanna kill him?" Caspar grins and mutters, "For starters."

However, the characters often seem like moving portraits, revealing very little beyond their surface matte. Even the strong cast of supporting characters often seems to exist for the sake of visual relish. Steve Buscemi zips through scenes as a staccato-talking gangster who has little purpose outside comic relief. Another comic duo con-

Caught in a bloody gang war, Tom (Gabriel Byrne, *left*) wins the wary confidence of congenial but psychopathic Mob leader Johnny Caspar (Jon Polito) in *Miller's Crossing,* an acclaimed film by another brotherly filmmaking pair: director Joel Coen and producer Ethan Coen.

sists of the police chief and the mayor ("I voted for him six times!" Tom recalls of one election). They represent corrupt officialdom at moments too convenient to be anything but staged. The moll Verna, adroitly played by Marcia Gay Harden, promises to be a delight but remains a sultry enigma. That her character is underdeveloped is a shame considering that *Variety* recognized Harden for having "the verve and flintiness of a glory days Bette Davis or Barbara Stanwyck."

Because the film leans heavily on style, it offers some spectacular moments to showcase its best feature. When machine gunners come to Leo's palatial home to ambush him, despite being engrossed in a tenor's sweet version of "Danny Boy," he demonstrates why he's a formidable boss despite his gray hair. Once under attack, he proves as wily as ever, grabbing a machine gun and jumping out the window. As "the pipes . . . the pipes are calling," Leo sprays one black overcoat full of bullets and then kills another couple of thugs while standing barefoot in his silk robe in the middle of the road. As a car zooms passed him, he fearlessly lopes after it, his weapon vibrating and flickering until his would-be assassins crash and explode into a fireball. After the smoke clears, a smug Leo jams the cigar back into his teeth, rests the tommy gun at his side, and waits until "Danny Boy" comes to a bittersweet, falsetto end.

The scene is a stunning set piece of zestful violence and gangster bravura. Unfortunately, it stands alone. It's disconnected from the scenes that come before and after—entertaining like a music video in which the narrative is emotive and not meant to be taken literally. The film offers awesome period impressions and smart costuming, including a mysterious floating black fedora. But the Coen brothers "do not yet have . . . the ability to move beyond their handsome imagery to the human center of their material."[1]

Peter Travers of *Rolling Stone* called *Miller's Crossing* "a jewel of a gangster film." But Richard Alleva in *Commonweal* wrote, "The Coen brothers . . . have taken Hammett's excellent crime novel, exchanged its tense, logical action for gory special effects, dissolved its grimy urban poetry with overblown photography and forgettable sets, and substituted cheap ethnic stereotypes for Hammett's cruelly veracious characterizations." (Several critics noted the story's similarity to Dashiell Hammett's *The Glass Key,* which isn't credited, though, by the Coen brothers as the film's inspiration.)

The film contains several needling ethnic clichés. Caspar is shown in ironic scenes of affection with his plump son, whom he hugs and brutalizes almost simultaneously. After a particularly vicious smack, Caspar strokes the boy like a pet while telling Tom that life isn't complete without kids. The sentiment nearly insinuates that having children is animalistic for Italians and isolated from human impulses.

At the same time, the Irish characters are drained of Irishness, except for "Danny Boy" (which has universal appeal), and Byrne's brogue, which is real. The worst stereotyping is the venal Bernie Birnbaum, played by the able John Turturro. He's the quintessentially awful Jewish stereotype of a "kike," related more to Shakespeare's Shylock than to a gangster persona.

Prohibition continued to haunt films, including made-for-television products such as *Dillinger,* in which the gangster was gingerly portrayed by lightweight heartthrob Mark Harmon. The outlandish 1995 film *Dillinger and Capone* features Martin Sheen playing Dillinger as a grown-up Huck Finn. The film plays on the myth that an impostor was killed by G-men and Dillinger assumed a new identity. Years later he's found and reluctantly snared into service by a disintegrating Capone (F. Murray Abraham) who wants Dillinger to rob the Mob's "bank" and retrieve his hidden stash.

Other low-budget efforts further obsessed over Capone and his associates. *The Lost Capone* (1990) at least delved into the little-known tale of Al's brother Jimmy Capone, "the white sheep" of the family, who became a federal marshal. Jimmy's story would make an interesting film, but this one buries the story's uniqueness and lets Al (Eric Roberts) overcome the tale.

Even the big-budget films of the early 1990s seemed inordinately attached to superstar dead gangsters. *Bugsy* returned Warren Beatty to gangster turf, where we last watched him roll on the ground as a mortally wounded Clyde Barrow. In *Bugsy,* Beatty plays a contemporary of Barrow's, at least in the eyes of the law: Benjamin "Bugsy" Siegel—the psychotic, lovesick genius who invented Las Vegas.

The film's focus is his contorted love affair with superstar moll (and bit actress) Virginia Hill. Siegel's reckless nature and spasmodic brilliance is aptly captured by the seasoned Beatty, who was so convincing in his attraction to the ebullient Hill that he fell in love with the actress who embodied her. Annette Bening is superb as the stunning, tough-talking, self-preserving Hill, who embezzled $2 million of Mob money, which she later wisely returned. She was well known in the Mob world, having played bed partner to several top gangsters, none of whom she would rat on during her colorful performances before the congressional committees investigating organized crime. She was Siegel's soul mate—just as flashy, vain, and violent. She later committed suicide while living in Europe alone and broken. Siegel met his gangster fate earlier in a hail of bullets—his death serving as the film's climax. He was supposedly killed for building a casino in the desert at the cost of $6 million after promising his lifelong friends and partners Lucky Luciano and Meyer Lansky it would cost a trifling $1 million. As the film's epilogue notes, by 1991, the Flamingo had earned investors $100 billion, with little of the profits spent to commemorate the crazed visionary who made it possible.

The film's romance and the quirky scenes with Siegel's wife and kids soften its rougher edges and undermine its effectiveness as a gangster film. Director Barry Levinson *(Diner, Rain Man)* claims, however, that he and Beatty didn't set out to make a gangster piece. "Bugsy just happens to be a gangster," Levinson said. However, when Levinson was asked, "Are we supposed to like Bugsy or hate him?" his reply reiterated the genre's basic appeal: "We should be fascinated by him and appalled by him, and that's what shakes up our sensibilities."

Bugsy remains a compelling portrait of a myth, neatly tackling Hollywood's fascination with gangsters—and Siegel's fascination with Hollywood. As Douglas Brode noted, Bugsy's favorite films were the Warner Brothers gangster films, especially those starring his close friend George Raft.

Beatty's return as gangster star and film producer earned him another Oscar nomination. *Bugsy* was nominated for nine Oscars, including best picture, and won for art direction and costume design. *Variety* called the film an "intelligently conceived drama" and Beatty's performance a "gutsy playing" of a "fully realized, psychologically complex character." But *Variety* found Hill's character lacking, not the equal to Siegel that the filmmakers touted her to be. She "remains a one dimensional and annoying stick figure," *Variety* added. Fleshing out full-bodied female characters, though, even one as saucy as Hill, remains a nagging problem for Hollywood at large.

Another Prohibition tale using a female costar is *Billy Bathgate* (1991). The title comes from the lead character in E. L. Doctorow's novel of the same name. It's the story of a tough, Irish 15-year-old and Bronx gang member who becomes part of Dutch Schultz's inner circle. Billy (Loren Dean) is soon assigned to keep an eye on Schultz's offbeat socialite mistress, Drew Preston (Nicole Kidman). Schultz (Dustin Hoffman) becomes her patron after he has his henchman Irving (Steve Buscemi) kill her lover and his double-crossing enforcer, Mo Weinberg (Bruce Willis). Billy has a secret affair with her and later must choose between loyalties after Schultz orders her killed for witnessing Bo's murder. Billy saves her life and barely escapes with his own after Schultz is finally rubbed out by pal Lucky Luciano. Luciano had decided that Schultz was out of control when he vowed to gun down the high-profile Dewey, who was after Schultz for tax evasion.

Schultz's reign was nearly over by the story's setting of 1935; the story hints that he was growing more desperate in the face of ruin. But Hoffman—offering a mannered, one-note performance—revealed little metamorphosis of character. The book focused on Billy, but the film isn't able to subdue Schultz as a mythic figure, despite Hoffman's low-key effort. Part of the problem is that director Robert Benton (of *Bonnie and Clyde* screenwriting fame) gives Hoffman such ample screen time. Several key scenes revel in his lethal hold over underlings and his ignitable wrath at those who cross him. One scene tidily plays with Schultz's legend as he mentors Billy about the importance of gangs. Schultz says, "I hire from gangs. That's the training ground." Then he explains how he, born Arthur Flegenheimer, had his name changed by fellow gang members. They dubbed him Dutch Schultz when he showed the same grit as their most famous alumnus. The original Schultz was a legendary nineteenth-century gangster and "the toughest street fighter that ever lived."

Gene Siskel noted the film's lack of focus but lauded Benton's skill at infusing it with "a mature quietness." Siskel suggested that "a sadness pervades the material, which is rare for a gangster picture." But he calls Kidman's role little more than a "curio." Siskel wrote, "Almost by default, the most fascinating character . . . is Otto Berman, Dutch's long-suffering, paternal adviser. Veteran actor Steven Hill steals the movie with his world-weary voice and manner."

The film also demonstrates the problem of employing gangsters and then trying to keep them from arresting most of the attention. As Douglas Brode put it, "Watching *Billy Bathgate* is like watching *Bonnie and Clyde* by way of *Masterpiece Theatre*." And *Variety* noted, "this refined, intelligent drama about thugs appeals considerably to the head but has little impact in the gut, which is not exactly how it should be with gangster films."

YOUNG GUNS

With the increased traffic in the genre in the early 1990s, no longer were just veterans at work. It was the era of new-jack gangsters, gang life in the hood, and a younger generation of actors looking to cut their dramatic teeth on gangster roles.

Taking a hiatus from TV commercials, Michael Karbelnikoff debuted as a director with *Mobsters* (1991). It employed fresh faces but kept the Prohibition theme going. The film tells the supposedly true story of four friends from the New York slums who grew up to be Mob superstars. At the story's core is the friendship between Lucky Luciano (Christian Slater) and Meyer Lansky (Patrick Dempsey), with Bugsy Siegel (Richard Grieco) and Frank Costello (Costas Mandylor) playing minor roles. (In reality, Costello was 15 years older than Siegel and not his boyhood pal.)

Mobsters begins with the Italian-born Luciano's rough childhood on Mott Street, where he meets and befriends the others. It then tracks their rise, their challenge to the old Mafia bosses, and eventually their takeover of New York's Underworld. However, as the *Chicago Tribune* noted, "The film is ultimately boring. We have seen it all before: the don who gorges on pasta, the good-hearted chorine whose liaison with a Mafioso proves her undoing, the gleefully deranged hitman." And we've grown weary of such trite dialogue as, "When things are between Italians, one of the Italians ends up dead."

In the supporting cast is Anthony Quinn as Don Masseria and Nicholas Sadler as Mad Dog Coll, doing a dead-on impression of the giggling, sadistic thug Richard Widmark made famous in *Kiss of Death*. The story's underlying theme is contradictory, though. At one point, their mentor Arnold Rothstein (F. Murray Abraham) says to Luciano, "What's the secret of America? Money . . . money is everything!" Yet several times the film reiterates a flip-flopped view, as in the scene when Meyer tells Luciano, "This isn't about money. . . . It's about friendship." In the end, the young thugs kill off their enemies, sit down with Capone to map out Underworld territories, and cement their alliances. There's no tragedy, no degeneration, and no redemption. Ultimately, the film is more of a buddy picture than a gangster film.

An above-average offering during the busy year 1990 was *State of Grace,* which starred a new crop of actors but updated the Italian-Irish turf wars to modern day Hell's Kitchen. The neighborhood is in transition; once a haven for Irish gangs and tenements, it's now being remodeled as a yuppie enclave. The film tracks Terry Noonan (Sean Penn), who escaped the neighborhood a dozen years ago to become a cop in Boston. He has now been recruited by the New York police to infiltrate his old gang, manned by his childhood friend Jackie Flannery (Gary Oldman) and bossed by Jackie's older brother Frankie (Ed Harris). However, as the fight with the Italians gets more complex, Noonan is forced to choose sides, declare loyalties, and confuse his mission as a cop. Further complicating the picture is his rekindled romance with Jackie's sister Kate (Robin Wright), who moved uptown and away from the family violence. When she suspects Terry is just as corrupt as her brothers, he confesses, to prove that he's different, that he's a "fucking Judas cop." After Frankie has his own men murdered to please his Italian associates, including his brother Jackie, Terry goes on the offensive. He hands Frankie his badge and then waits for the showdown, which concludes the film.

Compounding Terry's troubles is an ambitious police lieutenant (John Turturro) who won't heed Terry's requests to abort the assignment. But it's unrealistic that an increasingly drunk, strung-out officer would be kept undercover. Also implausible is the cause given for Jackie's homicidal tendencies—a loss of the neighborhood's Irishness, which is never very well demonstrated. Creditable scenarios aren't always de riguer for gangster films because so much of the material deals in perceptions and myth. But if the film is selling street realism, as *State of Grace* is, then credibility matters a great deal.

A subtext, though, that was compelling and could have been further developed was the journalism-derived subplot. Turf wars between the Italians and Irish have broken out in contemporary times, especially after the Gambino family recruited the Irish street toughs known as the Westies. The scenes between the silk-shirted Italians (eating as usual) and the uncouth Irish punks are some of the film's most revealing moments.

The film's saving grace, though, is the skillful acting of Penn and Harris. Despite having a dangerous secret, conflicting loyalties, and a tough tryout as a returning homeboy, Penn is credible within the boundaries of his character's mental and physi-

Left, Sean Penn as undercover cop Terry Noonan, who returns to his boyhood turf of New York's Hell's Kitchen to infiltrate the gang of his ignitable best friend Jackie Flannery (Gary Oldman, *center*). Here the two flee a close call with Italian mafiosi angered over the Irish gang's bold, bloody assaults to defend its once-familiar turf.

cal turf. And Harris's boyish charm is deceiving, which only serves to heighten his surprising viciousness as a character. Only Jackie is conspicuously overplayed by Oldman. The English Oldman, who has meticulously mastered a street-worthy New York accent, too often torques up his anger to full throttle. This constant emotional pitch gets tedious and makes it difficult to explain Terry's fierce affection for him. Their relationship is a pale comparison to the offbeat bond that existed between crazy Johnny Boy and the more thoughtful Charlie in *Mean Streets*. De Niro let Johnny Boy erupt and then retreat, creating an unpredictable pattern that made him fascinating. Perhaps the strained comparison prompted critic Dave Kehr to call *State of Grace* "synthetic Scorsese."

In another failed comparison, director Phil Joanou mimics Coppola's striking use of contrast for the film's final shoot-out. Joanou juxtaposes shots of New York's Saint Patrick's Day parade up Fifth Avenue with shots of flesh-ripping bullet exchanges in an Irish pub in Hell's Kitchen. While Irish bagpipes blare on the street, blood splatters across the narrow strips of green crepe paper crisscrossing the pub's interior. But the pub, like the movie, has been devoid of Irish trappings. Without that context, Joanou's bagpipes don't carry the same emotional weight as Coppola's tarantella.

BY INDEPENDENT MEANS

A spate of independent filmmakers also tossed gangster films into the already glutted marketplace. William Reilly's *Men of Respect,* a Mafia saga starring John Turturro as a newly anointed Mafia don, fails to offer anything new, except for an ambitious wife who actually orchestrates her husband's bloody takeover. The film doesn't hide its inspiration, crediting Shakespeare's *Macbeth* for the origins of the story. The last time someone was that obvious about the oldest source behind a gangster saga was a British film called *Joe Macbeth* in 1955. Despite *Joe Macbeth*'s aim for timeless ambition, the *New York Times* panned the film for having "paraphrased the plot of Scottish intrigue into sophomoric precocity."[2] *Men of Respect* doesn't fare much better. It congeals decades of clichés, stock characters, slow-motion violence, and Shakespearean villains into one overwrought yarn, despite a first-rate cast with Dennis Farina, Peter Boyle, Stanley Tucci, and Rod Steiger as the implacable don who gets knifed to death.

Another independent filmmaker who has earned a strong reputation for his gritty underground crime tales—and both exulting and stinging praise from critics—is Abel Ferrara. His *Bad Lieutenant* (1993) earned first-rate attention for its voyeuristic view of a degrading demimonde inhabited by pushers, pimps, and rotten cops. The best kudos went to Harvey Keitel. He plays the thoroughly corrupt and despicable police lieutenant who degenerates until he chokes to death on his own evil, although a bullet actually ends his life. Because the downward spiral is so obvious early in the film, Keitel has to create the film's poignancy through sheer force of acting in a disturbingly raw performance. The cop's crisis of faith—as a lapsed Catholic—is nearly entirely delivered in stagnant silence except for Keitel's moaning, cursing, or snorting yet another lump of cocaine.

Richard Corliss called *Bad Lieutenant* "sulfur." He noted that two scenes are "indelibly repellent": the rape of a nun in a church using a crucifix and the lieutenant's humiliation of two young girls, with whom he uses his badge to force them to verbally participate in his masturbation outside their car. Corliss suggested that *Bad Lieutenant* is a "serious film about the gnawing of conscience and the thirst for redemption, but the tone is so dispassionately vile it may leave viewers shaken or sick." Other critics compared the film to *Mean Streets* and its view of a lapsed Catholic's nightmare for embracing guilt as greedily as sin. Unlike *Mean Streets*—despite the presence of Keitel in both films—there's little sense that *Bad Lieutenant* imparts anything meaningful outside of Keitel's artistic courage.

Ferrara first made a name for himself with *King of New York* (1990), which played at a theater in New York for nearly a year simply owing to stellar word of mouth. The film was an all-American production financed with Italian money. The film tells the tale of gangster Frank White (Christopher Walken), who after being released from prison wipes out competing Colombians, Italians, and a Chinatown gangster to regain his crown. He then announces, with a peculiar hint of sincerity, his desire to donate sizable profits from his empire toward community projects. His effort to be a modern Robin Hood (a poor neighborhood gets a hospital built with his drug money) never alters the man's essential sadism nor traces back to any illuminating moment of conscience. At the film's end, he and his multicultural band of killers and drug peddlers get killed as in any routine gangster film. Yet the stylish spectacle of gore and the ambiguity of White's motives made enough of an impression to prompt a cult following. Walken's flamboyant performance is nearly overshadowed, though, by his supporting cast, which includes Laurence Fishburne as his manic, hip-hop, Mad Hatter enforcer; Steve Buscemi; and Giancarlo Esposito; along with David Caruso and Wesley Snipes as revenge-seeking cops who behave and perish like gangsters.

Variety mentioned the "impressive . . . large scale setpieces, including a climax shot of bloodletting," in which White's two stunning femme fatale bodyguards are massacred. Quentin Tarantino, an unknown video clerk who would soon become Hollywood's wunderkind, declared, "As far as I'm concerned, *King of New York* is better than *GoodFellas*."

A telling moment, though, that smoothly links White to his gangster ancestors, especially Capone, occurs after White finds out he's become public enemy number one. He says, "This country spends $100 billion a year on getting high and that's not because of me. . . . I'm not your problem. I'm just a businessman."

THE MACHO BARRIO

While African-American filmmakers rushed to the forefront with several hood stories in the early 1990s, other minority filmmakers attempted to make inroads into the screen Underworld as well, most notably Latinos.

Latinos now comprise about 10 percent of the U.S. population, and that figure is growing at the fastest rate of any group. They're expected to overtake America's black population (now at 13 percent) within the next few decades. Despite that burgeoning number, Latinos are invisible in many industries, including Hollywood. Even the gangster genre has largely ignored the Latino gangster. When a Capone-like gangster named David Ramirez was brought down in Chicago in 1990, the case drew little national attention. The 28-year-old Ramirez was a multimillionaire who made his fortune as a cocaine dealer. Police said that at age 15 he was already employing "a cadre of elementary school children to peddle 'nickel' and 'dime' bags of marijuana" for him.[3]

But the Latino filmmaking community isn't particularly interested in bringing Ramirez's life to the screen. Latino filmmakers point out that Latinos are grossly underemployed in most Hollywood-related occupations, and when they're hired, the precious few roles are nearly always as gang bangers or street thugs on TV crime shows; more such roles wouldn't necessarily be welcome.

The most memorable Latino-themed story remains *West Side Story,* with its singing, dancing Puerto Rican street fighters. And as Italians complained for years about WASPs portraying cartoonlike Italians on-screen, so Latino roles are routinely given to Anglos who feign an accent and often adopt the most derisive mannerisms to approximate a Latino. Or prize roles are simply given to Anglo stars. Natalie Wood was darkened with makeup to portray Maria in *West Side Story,* and more recently Madonna outraged the Latino community by winning the coveted role of the legendary Argentinean Eva Peron, also known as Evita.

The secondary roles that do exist in crime series and gangster films portray Latinos as the all-purpose "outside" forces that prey on America's Underworld, still seen as largely dominated by black and Italian gangsters. It's intimated that Latino gangsters come from South and Central America: Mexico, Peru, Colombia, Bolivia, Guatemala, and Panama. In American gangster films, they're the only ones left on-screen with a heavy accent. But many of these Latino thugs aren't foreigners; they're American citizens who face our age-old prejudice against people who speak with an accent. It's reminiscent of the slum kids who held traces of their homelands in their voices but had decidedly American ideas about shortcuts to success. Like the Irish and Italian immigrants of a century ago, many Latino immigrants are at the bottom of America's social strata. And being similar to disadvantaged ethnic groups before them, many young men often find respect and power through gangs and organized crime or, in the modern parlance, by becoming gang bangers.

One Latino group, known as the Eighteenth Street Gang, is the largest and fastest-growing gang in the West, now absorbing many blacks, Asians, and Native Americans into its ranks.[4] This gang long ago surpassed the infamous black gangs—the Crips and Bloods—in sheer numbers and in dominance of the drug trade. Moreover, the turf wars between Latinos and blacks are increasingly responsible for the gang-related deaths in most major cities.

Latino gangs, however, renew an old problem for the media, which includes filmmakers. The generic term *Latino* does little to differentiate between American-born Latinos and Spanish-speaking immigrants by legal and illegal means. Reporters assumed Capone was a foreigner who could be more easily eradicated if the Deportation Act was enhanced. The same confused logic is often applied nowadays to the generic Latino gang banger.

Within recent years, a few Latino filmmakers have emerged to create Latino gangsters who are not only authentic but culturally complex. Luis Valdez set the stage with his 1980 film *Zoot Suit.* It probed the rich subculture of Latino Los Angeles in the late 1930s and early 1940s and starred the Mexican American actor Edward James Olmos. Olmos went on to fame with TV's *Miami Vice* and Oscar contention for his role in *Stand and Deliver.* He's also a well-respected activist within the Latino community and produced the acclaimed TV documentary *Lives in Hazard,* filmed in his native East L.A.

In 1992 Olmos made his directorial debut with *American Me,* a film about a ferocious Latino gangster named Santana from Olmos's East L.A. barrio. Olmos also cowrote and starred in the film. Its opening scenes revisit the Los Angeles Zoot Suit riots of 1943 when servicemen on leave attacked and raped Mexican Americans. (The police arrested the Latinos for rioting and ignored the marauding sailors.) Santana's boyhood is limited to gang life and juvenile detention centers, and he spends most of his adult life in Folsom State Prison. Despite being locked up, Santana (Olmos), constructs a criminal empire from within—what he calls the Mexican Mafia. The operation eventually carries over onto the street as inmates are released and Santana's influence spreads. As with crime films that dwell on the prison experience, the scenes are claustrophobic and clotted with exaggerated racism and unchecked brutality; the inmates vie for power amid a strict hierarchy. Olmos aimed for realism, spending three weeks filming inside Folsom, using guards and inmates as extras. The film was genuine enough regarding the Mexican Mafia to invite threats during production; a peace with street gangs, though, had been brokered to allow filming on their turf.

David Denby of *New York* noted that Olmos was trying to create a Mexican American *Godfather,* but the film's undertone of "reforming zeal just doesn't fit into the framework of the big, violent Hollywood movie he's making." *American Me*'s unrelenting scenes of gruesome prison rape are overtly sensational and overshadow the message underpinning the film: violence and machismo beget more violence. *Maclean's* noted, "The violence, which is both visceral and frequent, verges on exploitation. And the movie becomes a vicarious excursion into underworld exotica."

The violent episodes, unfortunately, are the most clearly defined moments in the story. The plot is muddled, and the characters are too broadly defined to grasp, leaving the film without an emotional core. Santana's cohorts and eventual assassins are portrayed by genre regulars William Forsythe and Pepe Serna, but they never unmask their interiors. Even Olmos's performance is too mysterious for its own good. Olmos's Santana embodies the gang's paramount belief that you can't show weakness or emotion. But that zipped-up, deadpan cool (similar to Olmos's monotone, whispering Lieutenant Castillo in *Miami Vice*) doesn't reveal much about Santana's inner torment. Even though we're led to believe he develops a social conscious reading the classics in prison, Olmos "can't give up the solemn macho fatalism that he's saying is a trap," Denby added. Finally, Santana returns to prison, and his enlightenment only serves to get him killed when his former underlings decide that he's gone soft.

Like genre mothers before her, Mama Santana (Vira Montes) remains fiercely loyal to her jailed son (Edward James Olmos, *right*), offering him religious advice but remaining fearful about his doomed path. Her still innocent six-year-old son Paulito *(center)* will soon follow in his brother's criminal footsteps.

Mexican Mafia boss Santana (Edward James Olmos) is arrested by police in the East Los Angeles barrio and sent back to prison, where he's spent most of his adult life. His return to prison forever spoils his chances to reform, as he attempted, and start life anew with Julie (Evelina Fernandez, *second from right*).

When the film isn't dwelling on prison life and kicks around the barrio, though, it offers some profound insights. During his brief stint on the "outside," modern fashions, fast-food stands, and youthful aggression assault Santana's confidence as if he just stepped off the boat. He's still wearing shoes that were in style in the late 1950s and has to be taught to perform functions as routine as how to drive. While aggressively taking on the Italians and black gangsters, he tries to divert young homeboys away from the gangster life. However, he's so emotionally crippled himself that he can't offer them much in the way of other examples. His one date as an adult male becomes a rape. The scene juxtaposes shots of Santana awkwardly trying to make love to a woman for the first time while a brutal prison rape occurs simultaneously. As the sodomy of the convict progresses, Santana's tenderness turns to terror, and he flips the woman over and violates her in the same manner; the filmmaking choice is almost as unsettling as the subject matter.

Despite Olmos's credentials and his sincere conviction, a smaller film by an Anglo—and a woman no less—presented a far more intimate and impressive effort. Allison Anders, a filmmaker from Kentucky, makes up for her lack of cultural links by tapping her firsthand experiences living in Echo Park, a "shabby, fashionable neighborhood where bohemia and barrio meet."[5] Anders herself is a "lavishly tattooed and pierced high-school dropout single mother of two who went from white-trash welfare to UCLA film school."[6]

Echo Park, located just east of downtown Los Angeles—once an exclusive hideaway for movie stars in the 1920s—is now a haven for gangs. Anders focuses, in particular, on female gang members and how their world is distinctive while shadowing and supporting the male-dominated environment. Anders's 1994 low-budget film, *Mi Vida Loca (My Crazy Life),* tells its three-part tale in near documentary style. She brings the same grit to these women that her highly acclaimed film *Gas Food Lodging* (1992) did for trailer park women.

Mi Vida Loca is told in episodic form, each "chapter" distinctly titled (with tattoo-like drawings) and featuring characters who communicate through frequent voice-overs. The main characters are the teenage homegirls Mousie (Seidy Lopez) and Mona (Angel Aviles), who's better known by her gang name, Sad Girl, tattooed across her knuckles. Early on they both have babies by Ernesto (Jacob Vargas), who wants both women but is more engrossed in his customized truck. He's also an experienced drug dealer.

Sad Girl and Mousie have been friends since childhood, when one arrived from Mexico unable to speak English and the other became her American sister. Armed with guns, the women have a showdown over Ernesto but can't bring themselves to kill each other. It's Ernesto who gets killed, by one of the many white middle-class junkies who come to the barrio to buy drugs. On occasion they've offered Ernesto CDs or sexual favors to pay for drugs. But Ernesto the businessman has rules: "I wouldn't fuck 'em . . . not white bitches. Not junkies."

Other female gang members include Whisper (Nelida Lopez, a gang member recruited to act in the film). Whisper tries to help Shadow (Arthur Esquer) take over his brother Ernesto's abandoned drug business. But she proves better at it than he is. Giggles (Marlo Marron), whom the girls consider wise because she has survived into her twenties, was the "first homegirl who ever got locked up." After the gang picks up Giggles from prison, she tells them that she's going to learn computers and get a job. The gang members are appalled and think she's gone soft. In turn, Giggles views them as the lost generation, lacking honor and adopting the machismo of the homeboys and their fatal pride.

Later, when the girls become enraged that proceeds from the sale of the customized truck are to be pocketed by the men rather than go to support Ernesto's children, Giggles calls a meeting of the female gang members. She proposes that they decide as a group what should be done and then negotiate with the boys.

Another subplot is about a lovesick young woman called La Blue Eyes (Magali Alvarado), who's in love with a gang member from a rival territory. He's known by the dashing title El Duran (Jesse Borrigo) and rumbles through the neighborhood in a shiny vintage car with adoring women draped around his shoulders. Before the film ends, the women expose El Duran for the street punk he is to save La Blue Eyes (who's headed for college). Although the women devise a complicated scheme to conquer El Duran, the men resort to the drive-by method and kill him because he has threatened to steal the prized truck.

After yet another funeral, Sad Girl tells us, "The homegirls have learned to pack weapons because our operation has become more complicated. . . . but we are safe and practical. Women don't use weapons to prove a point. Women use weapons for love." Shortly after El Duran's funeral, his death is avenged, this time by a menacing young woman with a gun. A third funeral closes the film, with the living gang members looking battered and shockworn for people so young.

The film's most superb moments are those showing the women coping with motherhood, economic crisis, and abandonment. They respond with appalling naïveté and promising determination. The irony of their entrenched dependence and stubborn loyalty to men who are often doomed isn't lost on the women. Yet they're struggling to stay true to their culture and survive it at the same time.

Anders's film also reflects a woman's take on the gang milieu. In one scene, while Whisper is directing Shadow on how to conduct a drug deal, the medium shot puts both characters in the frame but focuses on Whisper's frustrations as she silently watches Shadow fumble with the dealer's lifeline: the beeper. The direction favors Whisper's point of view and her internal contradictions. The point of view is startlingly fresh after decades of absorbing screen gangsters from strictly male perspectives. (Female gang membership also has its origins in the nineteenth century. A few notorious women were known even to male gangs because they filed their front teeth to sharp points and wore artificial brass fingernails as effective hidden weapons.)

Richard Corliss noted, "The film has too many slow spots, and its message is laid on with a trowel, but it has a kind of perverse Hollywood glamour." Maitland McDonagh in *Film Comment* offered more sweeping praise. "Anders's film not only defies glib characterization, it occasionally comes astonishingly close to poetry." She notes that by contrast, Taylor Hackford's "macho outpost of Latino gang movies," *Bound by Honor*—like *American Me*—is "hopelessly conventional." Hackford's, in particular, wrote McDonagh, "ends on a note of painfully artificial uplift, [but] as battered but never-broken childhood friends from the barrio turn their eyes to a brighter future, *Mi Vida Loca* finds triumph in getting through the day." Such an intimate view of the inner turmoil of gangsters or gang-related characters is why *Mi Vida Loca* is a better addition to the genre than the other Latino-themed efforts.

GROWING UP CAN BE MURDER

Although *Mi Vida Loca* explored gang life at the street level, it was also dubbed a "coming of age" film. A similar tag had been given to *Boyz N the Hood* as well as *Straight out of Brooklyn*. The latter was a film school project by 19-year-old writer-director Matty Rich in 1992, but the film emphasized destructive relationships rather than gang violence.

Such morality plays about gang life and impressionable youth were used for *A Bronx Tale* in 1993. It also returns us to an Italian American community. Robert De Niro, in his directorial debut, also portrays the hardworking, attentive father Lorenzo to the impressionable Calogero. The boy is torn between his father's straight-arrow example and the flashy lure of the local wise guys. The tale is based on an autobiographical one-man play by Chazz Palminteri, who portrays the story's gangster Sonny. He competes with Lorenzo for the boy's future but in the end becomes the boy's street mentor and guardian angel. "He's a hood with honor, one of those big-hearted movie bad guys, like James Cagney in *Angels with Dirty Faces*," wrote the *Chicago Tribune*'s Michael Wilmington.

Early in the story, the nine-year-old Calogero (named for his old-world grandfather) watches Sonny kill a man on the street in what seems like a tiff over a parking spot. After the police line up the usual suspects against the wall of the wise guys' hangout, the boy refuses to finger Sonny for the police and earns Sonny's gratitude and interest. Rather than become a Paulie to a Henry Hill, though, Sonny heeds Lorenzo's pleas not to mold the boy into a gangster. The era is similar to *GoodFellas*, and the music showers us with doo-wop and the a cappella harmonies of 1960—when "Mickey Mantle was like a God." (The music changes to Wilson Pickett and Cream as the late 1960s become the context.)

Sonny steers the boy away from the criminal life (aside from showing him how to gamble), in part because he regrets having wasted his own life as a feared thug—but an unloved man. He encourages Lorenzo to stay in school while attending his street-wise "University of Belmont Avenue."

The screenplay contributes a memorable line that could have been uttered by any gangster since the genre's start. When a priest asks young Calogero if he knows what the Fifth is, the boy explains that it means a person has the right not to incriminate himself on the witness stand. The priest, of course, was talking about the Fifth Commandment: thou shalt not kill.

When the teenage Calogero (portrayed by first-time actor Lillo Brancato) falls for a young girl from an encroaching black community, Sonny advises the boy to worry more about the girl's core values than her skin color. Given Calogero's coming of age coinciding with the powder keg racial politics of the late 1960s, the story equips him with a rebelliousness and wisdom to see past color and into the girl's heart. However, it's never clear where this sensibility comes from. Lorenzo doesn't believe that the races should mix, and Calogero grew up in the same community that nurtured his buddies, who go on a violent rampage with Molotov cocktails and assault blacks out of blind hatred. Calogero ends up enlightened; his buddies end up dead.

De Niro's direction was scrutinized for influences by Scorsese. De Niro, too, cleverly used nonactors in smaller parts that sparkle and encouraged a sense of spontaneity from them. But the film is much more wistful and optimistic than a Scorsese effort, leaving a warm glow and romantic tinge to the tough Bronx turf. The film's flaw, in fact, lies in its overarching sentimentality at the end, when De Niro belabors the point of Calogero's grief after Sonny is gunned down in a revenge killing. Their underlying bond is well understood. Therefore, the prolonged funeral scene, Joe Pesci's gratuitous character, and Lorenzo's predictable "let's go home" finisher are transparent and unnecessary.

WANTED: GANGSTERS OF ALL PERSUASIONS

For Asian-American gangsters, as Michael Cimino's *Year of the Dragon* demonstrated, it will probably take a filmmaker from that community or one with sincere interest to create complex, homegrown portraits. The FBI reports that Chinese and Vietnamese gangsters are increasingly muscling in on New York rackets, which were formerly controlled by the Gambino family, now in disarray after Gotti's downfall. Perhaps a budding filmmaker will note the narrative possibilities and give us a Japanese *Godfather* or an insightful look into the ever changing face of organized crime.

One ethnic group new to the American Underworld and to the Hollywood genre is the so-called Russian Mafia. Despite the name, the Mafia-like network is neither as organized as the original Italian group, nor exclusively Russian. The Russian Mafia is made up of citizens from several former Soviet republics along with East European countries previously under Soviet domination.

With the crumbling of the Soviet empire in the late 1980s and early 1990s, former Soviet criminals began coming out of the shadows. With exorbitant inflation, instant poverty (as socialist subsidies were abolished), and a mentality unaccustomed to trusting the "invisible hand" of marketplace control, conditions were ripe for a thriving black market and lethal, opportunistic criminals to prosper. They also came to America. The Brighton Beach section of Brooklyn, once the comic setting for a Neil Simon play, is now home for many former Soviet citizens. Because most of them are Russian, the area has been dubbed Little Odessa. Among the area's estimated 200,000 arrivals in recent years, roughly 2,000 of them have been pegged as hard-core criminals.[7] That includes the Godfather-like Vyacheslav Ivankov. Ivankov has been nabbed by the FBI, which claims he was the reigning boss of the Russian Mafia—a loosely organized network dealing in widespread extortion schemes and drug dealing. The FBI also notes that many innocent Russians and Eastern Europeans who settle in the United States, like immigrants before them, are distrustful of federal officials and local police. Their distrust makes them reluctant to inform against the remaining organized-crime figures within their communities.

Such Russian villains also began creeping into crime films, although so far they've been largely depicted as fodder for Tom Clancy–inspired action heroes. In 1993, however, *Romeo Is Bleeding* elevated a Russian gangster to costar. The film featured a multilayered performance by Gary Oldman as a corrupt police sergeant. But, more intriguing, it included a comic book version of a stiletto-heeled Russian assassin named Mona Demarkov (Lena Olin). She has frequently been used by the Italians for contracts, but now they want to whack her. After Oldman's character romances her, he does the dirty deed, but it takes him several tries and the length of the film.

A film that takes much better advantage of the new *vory v zakone* (Russian for "thieves in the law") is *Little Odessa* (1994). Written and directed by James Grey, the film is a dispassionate, bleak tale about a Russian American assassin named Joshua Shapiro, played by Tim Roth, another Englishman who has mastered American street speak. Joshua is ordered to return to his boyhood turf of Brighton Beach to do a hit. However, a local Russian crime boss, whose son Joshua killed, wants to avenge that murder. While in Little Odessa, Joshua visits his estranged family, including his impressionable younger brother Reuben (Edward Furlong) and his dying mother (Vanessa Redgrave). Joshua's father (Maximilian Schell), who helped harden him, still rejects him, and Joshua's old love Alla (Moira Kelly) rekindles in him an acceptance of affection. At the film's climax, though, everyone is killed but Joshua. With their deaths, his humanity gets snuffed out, leaving him a perfectly numbed killing machine. The film relies on brooding long shots and long silences. The effect is disappointing, considering the phenomenal cast and the stark settings begging for human voices. Perhaps Grey is making a point, but as in so many of the gangster films of the nineties, fatalism alone is not inherently profound nor the only honest ending.

CHAPTER 13

The Prince of Pulp and Royal Hoods

Normally both of your asses would be dead as fuckin' fried chicken. But you happened to pull this shit while I'm in a transitional period.

—Jules (Samuel L. Jackson), *Pulp Fiction,* 1994

Despite crowded screens, new accents, and fresh faces, the genre seemed spent again. It needed something or somebody to reinvent it, shake it up, or at the very least strip it down to its essentials and rediscover its basic appeal. That someone was Quentin Tarantino.

Tarantino was only two years old when his headstrong teenage mother moved them from their native Tennessee to a working-class section of Los Angeles to put herself through school. She instilled in him a love of learning, but he didn't share her views on schooling and dropped out after the ninth grade. At age 15, he was arrested for shoplifting a copy of Elmore Leonard's book *The Switch.* As punishment, his mother locked him in his room for the rest of the summer and forced him to read stacks of books. She also indulged his obsessive habit of movie marathons, and the two often saw as many as four films in an evening.

With a genius IQ and a voracious appetite for books, TV, and movies, Tarantino evolved into a self-taught cultural theorist with an encyclopedic memory. Although his mother married twice more, Tarantino credits Howard Hawks and his movie heroes for filling the void of not knowing his father. He credits *Rio Bravo,* in particular, for having taught him lessons about manhood, honor, and self-respect.

He studied acting for several years, with his most notable gig as an Elvis impersonator on an episode of *The Golden Girls*. But his main employment was as a minimum-wage clerk at an offbeat video shop in Manhattan Beach. There he honed his reputation as a cinephile and an expert on Hollywood genres and filmmaking trends. "I kind of fancied myself the Pauline Kael of the store," he recalled. Several of the clerks ended up in the film industry, but no one matched the success waiting for Tarantino. After six years of working as a self-proclaimed "movie geek," he moved to Hollywood and found work as a screenwriter—a sideline he had been honing since he was 16.

Unlike the generation of dazzling directors he admired, notably Brian De Palma and Sergio Leone, Tarantino couldn't afford formal training. "I didn't go to film school. I went to films," he says proudly. And once an agent put his script for *True Romance* into the hands of director Tony Scott (*Top Gun, Beverly Hills Cop II*), Tarantino's career was launched. For *True Romance,* he and his former writing partner Roger Avery envisioned "this big, flashy, show-offy first film" derived from every couple-on-the-run film they had ever digested: Penn's *Bonnie and Clyde,* Nicholas Ray's *They Live by Night,* and Jim McBride's *Breathless* (a 1983 remake of Godard's classic *A Bout de Souffle*). Tarantino explained, "We were going to try to be the Coen brothers, with him in Ethan's job and me in Joel's job."

Scott's film stars Christian Slater and Patricia Arquette as the criminal lovers Clarence and Alabama, with Dennis Hopper as Clarence's estranged father and Christopher Walken as the Sicilian drug lord who chases them. But Scott changed Tarantino's ending to give it more box office appeal. In the original script, Clarence dies in the final shoot-out, and Alabama goes on alone. Scott's feel-good ending shows the couple escaping and lolling on a peaceful beach with their young son, Elvis. Tarantino admits Scott "added a fairy-tale element to it." He had intended Alabama to be more like Pam Grier,[1] not "equal parts cutesy pie, best-buddy wish-fulfillment and wet dream," wrote a Tarantino biographer.[2]

True Romance and what would become *Natural Born Killers* began as one story. The theme reveals Tarantino's fascination with the bonds and stresses between partners—either as lovers or in later work as same-sex members of a gang. But the story eventually split into two. His second script, *Natural Born Killers,* features a more deadly couple who also indict the media as coconspirators. The focus on the couples as loners and outcasts from everyone but themselves largely isolates both films from the gangster genre.

In addition, once director Oliver Stone took control of *Natural Born Killers,* Mickey (Woody Harrelson) and Mallory (Juliette Lewis) became two sociopaths bent to suit his polemical aims. Stone's film shows the couple killing more than 50 people within a few weeks' time—their exploits tracked and broadcast by a perverse tabloid journalist named Wayne Gale (Robert Downey Jr.). Gale eventually abandons his pose of neutrality and joins in the savage mayhem. The film is a brilliant but stomach-turning diatribe on the media's perilous exploitation of real and invented violence: talk shows, commercials, news bulletins, along with gangster movies, including Stone's *Scarface.* He depicts the daily blended, blood-soaked cartoon being passively devoured by consumers and horribly mimicked by the disturbed, murderous lovebirds. He also suggests that our collective outrage is becoming dangerously deadened. Nearly echoing the sentiments of media scholar Neil Postman, Stone asserts that we are entertaining ourselves to death.

Stone uses a spectacular array of filmmaking techniques: animation, rear projection, unsettling angles, sickly green lighting, fish-eye lenses, a disconcerting mix of color and black-and-white film stock, and the discordant blend of rock anthems, pop-culture jingles, and blaring sirens. Stone called *Natural Born Killers* "a movie of images; it's a prism." Many critics called it sarcastic gore and accused Stone of perpetrating the very thing he was trying to expose. As David Ansen noted, "You leave it more battered than enlightened."

Tarantino complained, "Oliver basically took my script—which, as dark as it was, was also pretty playful—and he put this whole other serious agenda on it. I don't like to tell audiences what my movies are about, but Oliver has to get the big idea across and if one person doesn't get it, he thinks he's failed. I would rather the film never got made and that my script remained pure." (By request, Tarantino was given only original story credit, not screenplay credit, in Stone's film.) But Woody Harrelson suggested that the material added by Stone provided his character—and more so for Mallory—a scrap of motive at the root of the depravity. As Tarantino's success contin-

One of the genre's journeyman workhorses, Harvey Keitel portrays the honorable but capable thief and killer Mr. White in Quentin Tarantino's remarkable debut film *Reservoir Dogs.* Here Mr. White takes calculated aim with two guns at the cops chasing after him.

ued to unfold, he would be frequently lambasted for failing to explain the seeds of his characters' deviance—or their remarkable ability to show unscathed love and loyalty to each other.

Tarantino wanted total control with his next script, *Reservoir Dogs,* which meant directing it himself. To make that long shot a reality, Tarantino and his friend and producer Lawrence Bender formed a company called A Band Apart. The name came from the Godard film about a small band of social outcasts and wannabe gangsters (in turn derived from an American pulp novel). *Reservoir Dogs* became Tarantino's exceptional directorial debut.

The film—shot in stark tones by cinematographer Andrzej Sekula—gives a sheer black-and-white feel to a contemporary color film. Its story line is arranged in chapters, as in a book, with titles subdividing the tale of five professional criminals and one undercover cop. These characters are hired by a crusty gangster named Joe Cabot (the original *Dillinger,* Lawrence Tierney) to pull off a diamond heist. The job is coordinated by his top aide—his affable and fiercely loyal son Nice Guy Eddie (Chris Penn). *Reservoir Dogs* uses and abuses gangsters in a stripped-down style that both reveres the genre's traditions and fractures their nostalgic meanings. The film also made Tarantino the hottest name in town—and a boon to the exhausted gangster genre.

THE SAVORY BITE OF *RESERVOIR DOGS*

The film opens with the entire group assembled at a diner just finishing breakfast and talking about anything but their professions. Although Joe and Eddie know each of the thieves' identity, they know each other only by color-coded names assigned by Joe. As the scene opens, Mr. Brown (Quentin Tarantino) is explaining to his associates what Madonna really meant by her song "Like a Virgin." He insists that she's talking about having sex with a well-endowed man who brings her—a sexually active woman—something she hasn't experienced since her promiscuity began: pain. Later, the group starts needling Mr. Pink (Steve Buscemi), who refuses to leave his share of the tip. He argues that a tip shouldn't be automatic when the service is mediocre. Mr. Blonde sticks up for the plight of struggling waitresses; he was also the one who thought Madonna's song was about a woman feeling vulnerably in love despite her sexual maturity. His apparent sensitivity, however, later proves gruesomely misleading.

The scene abruptly shifts to a speeding car with Mr. White (Harvey Keitel) at the wheel, and a blood-soaked Mr. Orange (Tim Roth) wailing in the backseat. The story isn't told in chronological order, and the scene takes place after the gang's heist has been executed and things have gone terribly wrong. As the film progresses, flashbacks reveal the bloody shoot-outs following the bungled heist (but never the event itself). While the gang had been at the diamond wholesalers, we're told, Mr. Blonde (Michael Madsen) had shot several guards in cold blood, and Mr. Blue and Mr. Brown had been killed in the aftermath.

Once at the deserted warehouse where the thieves agreed to meet, Mr. Orange is hauled inside despite begging to go to a hospital. Mr. White, though, couldn't risk having him arrested there and perhaps ratting on the gang. But Mr. White feels compassion for the young man, who's in agonizing pain from a bullet in the stomach. He was shot by a woman whose car he and Mr. White were hijacking. In a reflex action, he returned fire and shot her in the face. Mr. White is now fussing over his bleeding colleague like a doting older brother, combing his hair and trying to soothe him.

The high-strung, bug-eyed Mr. Pink arrives—after having stashed the diamonds—and is ricocheting between anger and panic. He says that the cops were tipped off by a rat among them and insists that one of the colors is an undercover cop. The gang knew they had four minutes before the police could respond to the store's alarms. "In one minute there were 17 blue boys out there," Mr. Pink snarls. Paranoid and testing each other for cracks, Messrs. White and Pink spar until they're interrupted by Mr. Blonde, whom they quickly greet with shouts for acting like a trigger-happy madman during the heist. However, they decide that he isn't the undercover cop simply because he's too obvious a psychopath. Mr. Blonde watches their bickering with a chilling calm—like a rattlesnake at rest. He eventually unveils the "surprise" locked in his trunk: a uniformed cop whom he kidnapped at the scene.

Eddie arrives and joins the shouting match until he orders Messrs. White and Pink to go with him to get the diamonds and ditch some of the stolen cars. Mr. Orange has been passed out for a while, and the cop has been beaten and strapped to a chair. Once alone with them, Mr. Blonde cranks up the radio to K-Billy's Super Sounds of the Seventies (featuring the drained voice of Steven Wright) and begins doing a goofy dance to the Stealer's Wheel's hit "Stuck in the Middle with You." He flashes the cop a sneaky smirk, digs in his boot for a straight razor, dances a little more, then lunges at the cop. The camera pans away from the two men as we hear the cop's tormented howl. Mr. Blonde then dances around with the cop's ear dangling from his fingertips. He follows up by pouring gasoline on his victim, digs out a lighter, and puts his thumb to the flint roller. Suddenly Mr. Blonde's body starts jerking as bullets rip into his chest. The camera quickly moves from him to Mr. Orange, who's sitting up in a pool of his own blood and firing his gun. "Listen to me. . . . I'm a cop. . . . Freddy Newendyke," Mr. Orange tells the suffering cop. But Officer Nash already knew Mr.

Orange's real identity and kept his mouth shut despite being tortured. Freddy explains that their backup won't move in on the scene until they see Joe Cabot walk into the warehouse.

After the others return, Mr. Orange tries to explain Mr. Blonde's death. He swears Mr. Blonde was planning to kill the cop and him, ambush the rest of them, and make off with the diamonds. "I swear on my mother's eternal soul, that's what happened," Mr. Orange says, gasping from the floor. Eddie shoots and kills the cop, casually removing that irritant. Then he irately explains to Mr. Orange the intensity of Mr. Blonde's loyalty. We've been shown flashbacks in which Mr. Blonde, whose name is really Vic Vega, was released from prison after doing four years without turning state's evidence against Joe. We've also been shown Freddy preparing for his undercover role, for which he's told to act "like Marlon Brando. . . . To do this job you got to be a good actor." Then we saw his infiltration into the group using a protracted lie about a drug deal. It's cleverly filmed in a fluid scene that captures him rehearsing his monologue alone, then performing it in a surreal episode using the lie's imaginary participants, and then wrapping it up convincingly for the gang's amusement.

Joe eventually stomps into the warehouse and accuses Mr. Orange point-blank of being a member of the LAPD. Mr. White frantically argues, "He's a good kid. . . . I know this man; he wouldn't do that." Soon everyone but Mr. Pink is pointing a gun at someone else. A prolonged Mexican standoff ensues, each man waiting for the other to blink. In the end, Joe shoots Mr. Orange, Mr. White kills Joe, and Eddie shoots and wounds Mr. White, who quickly swings around and kills Eddie. Mr. Pink picks up the satchel of jewels and runs off. But the police bullhorn and sirens tell us that he's been nabbed outside. Meanwhile, Mr. White crawls over to Mr. Orange and gently wipes his brow. Whimpering like a child, Mr. Orange whispers, "I'm a cop. . . . I'm sorry." Mr. White starts moaning like a wounded animal and moves his gun toward Mr. Orange's cheek. The camera moves in on Mr. White's anguished face, and then we hear him firing his gun. The police barge in, another gunshot is heard, and Mr. White, too, drops out of camera range.

NATURAL BORN FILMMAKER

The film first premiered at the Sundance Film Festival. Tarantino had been invited to work on scenes at the Sundance facility—an opportunity given to struggling filmmakers who show promise. The film then caught the attention of Miramax. Miramax executive Harvey Weinstein recalled, "It was a blow-away movie. . . . Here is filmmaking the way we grew up with it as kids watching Bogart movies, yet it was an original voice, contemporary, not afraid to be politically incorrect, because it echoed the truth. It was like a wakeup call." But the distributor wanted the ear-slicing scene removed for greater box office potential. Despite being a first-time director, Tarantino refused. The film eventually found its audience, and the controversy surrounding its unvarnished brutalism enhanced its box office. Although the film was banned on video in Britain, it became a huge hit there, amassing a cult following who kept it playing continuously at select theaters for more than a year.

Mainstream American critics Siskel and Ebert gave *Reservoir Dogs* two thumbs down, abhorring its violence and calling the film "a stylish but empty crime film." The *Boston Globe* called it the "opposite of a male bonding movie; it's a male disintegration movie." The *Los Angeles Times* appreciated Tarantino's "undeniable skill" but thought the film was too "one-dimensional." The *Times* suggested that the director was too "in love with operatic violence. . . . The old gangster movies its creator idolizes were better at balancing things, at adding creditable emotional connection and regret to their dead-end proceedings."

Terrence Rafferty, in his *New Yorker* review, called the film "a theatre-of-cruelty exercise" and noted that "even when nothing violent is happening onscreen we're steeling ourselves for the next bout of gore." Rafferty believed that the film also lacked "the emotional weight and the sense of urgency that gave Peckinpah's films—and Scorsese's seventies films—their exploding-bullet power. . . . Tarantino has all he can do to maintain the movie's pulse." Although Vincent Canby in the *New York Times* echoed the shock comments of the others, he also lauded the film's "dazzling cinematic pyrotechnics" and Tarantino's awesome novice talent.

Despite the critics' obsession with the film's violence, it possesses a refreshing, economic display of gangster codes. *Reservoir Dogs* is a stripped-down morality play that doesn't waste our time with clichés; it goes beyond them to assault our expectations and reactions to what we *think* we're seeing. Tarantino argued that the film was "a total talkfest . . . a bunch of guys yakking at one another. And then once in a while there's a little bit of violence."

Corliss commented on the film's "verbal machismo" and suggested that Tarantino's style was influenced by the "existential gangster films of Jean-Pierre Melville; they talk all night about everything except what matters." In his review of *Reservoir Dogs,* he called the warehouse scenes one "long therapy session of bitchery and carnage. . . . the whole production reeks of *Glengarry Glen Ross* at gunpoint."

The talkfest, in part, is what drew such first-rate actors to the untested filmmaker in the first place. Once Harvey Keitel signed on to do the film—impressed by the script alone—it went from an amateur production to a minimal Hollywood product, attracting $1.5 million in financing. (It earned $22 million within a year.) Keitel was also named coproducer for his behind-the-scenes efforts to stir up investment interest and get other top-notch actors to audition.

Keitel said of the script, "When I read it . . . I just was very disturbed that here was . . . a new way of seeing these ancient themes of betrayal, camaraderie, trust, and redemption." Once Mr. Orange lies on his mother's soul, Paul A. Woods noted, "the movie is almost in a hysteria-pitch parallel to Scorsese's—cop or not, the boy's sin demands redemption or retribution, but there's no priest to confess to, only Larry. He might have died easy with the knowledge that he only did bad on behalf of the good guys. But, in his hood persona, Larry was his friend, and all it adds up to is another betrayal."

Keitel, whom Tarantino calls the father he never had, is an icon among young filmmakers, surpassing the likes of De Niro and Pacino as a journeyman actor who rarely gets his name above the title. Along with his stellar work with Scorsese, Keitel also was fresh from his Oscar-nominated performance as a no-nonsense gangster in *Bugsy.*

Tarantino nearly cast himself as Mr. Pink—the wired "Jiminy Cricket" character nervously riding the others about professional behavior.[3] Steve Buscemi won the role and made it so memorable that he's nearly been typecast. Michael Madsen believes he *has* been typecast. "For the rest of my life, I'm going to be known as Mr. Blonde." When he was approached to play the part of Mickey Knox in *Natural Born Killers,* he declined, not wanting to become "the Norman Bates of the nineties."[4] He said it was a Cagney performance that inspired the chilling Mr. Blonde. He gave him the same casual sadism that Cody Jarrett displayed in *White Heat*—gnawing on a piece of chicken while pumping a trunk full of lead.

Rounding out the cast were two gems from old Hollywood: Lawrence Tierney and Eddie Bunker. Tierney, now in his seventies, was ideal as the crusty, tough-talking veteran gangster. The *Chicago Tribune* called him "all jowls and growls." At one point, when someone asks what happened to Mr. Blue, he says, "Dead as Dillinger," poking fun at his most famous role. Bunker, who portrayed Mr. Blue, has a history as bold as any pulp thriller. He spent more than a dozen years in prison, where he became a prolific writer. He worked on a typewriter donated by the wife of *Casablanca* producer Hal Wallis, who had befriended Bunker. One of the novels, *Straight Time,* became a 1977 film starring Dustin Hoffman.

Tarantino tapped every heist film he ever saw, most notably Kubrick's *The Killing,* which played with time to show each accomplice's view of the heist. But Tarantino bravely dispenses with the crime itself. "I . . . focused on the psychodrama of the wounded, beaten guys holding an inquest on what went wrong." His next film would be something wilder, more daring, and would possibly direct Hollywood gangsters in a new direction.

PULP FICTION

Pulp Fiction, as its name implies, is a homage to the lurid, hard-boiled fiction once published in pulp paperbacks, which also inspired film noir. Like Tarantino's prior efforts, the film is episodic—more in tune with literary traditions than cinematic customs. The film comprises three stories, with a few characters floating in and out of each, most notably Vincent Vega (John Travolta), brother of *Reservoir Dogs'* Vic Vega.

Tarantino on the set of *Pulp Fiction*—his genre-jolting collection of cinematic short stories that puts likable but deadly hit men in black-comic vignettes along with other quirky characters. They all get messed up in gore and teasing send-ups of past screen characters and criminal predicaments.

The film opens with a lovey-dovey couple, Pumpkin (Tim Roth) and Honey Bunny (Amanda Plummer). They're in a standard family-style restaurant discussing the merits of knocking off liquor stores instead of gas stations—or perhaps restaurants full of patrons with wallets. They spontaneously decide to hold up the one where they just finished breakfast. As Honey Bunny brandishes a gun at the startled patrons, through a mouthful of expletives she orders them to cooperate or be blown away. After the manic couple jump-starts the film, the screen goes black, and the credits flicker by accompanied by the driving rhythms of Dick Dale's guitar and his branded surf sounds.

The first story shows Vincent and his fellow hit man Jules (Samuel L. Jackson) in a 1974 Chevy Nova tooling down what the script calls a "homeless-ridden street in Hollywood." Vincent and Jules are dressed in cheap black suits with thin black ties (as in *Reservoir Dogs*). Vincent, a white man with scraggly, unwashed hair, tells Jules about his lifestyle in Europe for the past few years, with quirky details about hash bars in Amsterdam and *les Big Macs* in France. Jules, in greasy Jheri curls and a scowl, is the more menacing of the two, but also the more reflective. On assignment for their boss, Marsellus Wallace, they've been instructed to recover a briefcase. Arriving a tad early for their scheduled "appointment," they stand in the hall like any two businessmen waiting for a meeting and discuss the sexual implications of massaging the feet of another man's wife. Marsellus has requested that Vincent entertain his wife, Mia, for an evening while he's in Florida. Vincent is anxious about the request because he's heard about a thug who was thrown off a balcony for giving Mia a foot massage.

Once inside apartment 49, Jules and Vincent find three terrified college-age men who feebly try to explain why they still have Marsellus's briefcase. In a booming,

Left, John Travolta as Vincent Vega and Samuel L. Jackson as Jules Winnfield—Tarantino's thought-provoking hired killers who bounce between contracted hits and breakfast banter. Jules provides a new ending for the gangster character, involving neither redemption nor ruin but early retirement.

authoritative voice, Jules chitchats about everything but his grim intentions. He asks them about their fast-food breakfast of Big Kahuna burgers and tells them what he's learned about French food. His unexpected chattiness makes them all the more frightened. When the ringleader, Brett (Frank Whaley), mutters an excuse for the screwup, Jules shoots his associate just as easily as he sucks down a strawful of Brett's soft drink. "Did I break your concentration?" Jules shouts at a trembling Brett. Jules's voice gets louder and the mood more macabre when he shoots Brett in the shoulder before putting the gun barrel against his cheek. He asks Brett if he reads the Bible, then launches into a thundering, fervent passage that he has memorized: Ezekiel 25:17.

> The path of the righteous man is beset on all sides by the inequities of the selfish and the tyranny of evil men. Blessed is he who, in the name of charity and good will, shepherds the weak through the valley of darkness, for he is truly his brother's keeper and the finder of lost children. And I will strike down upon thee with great vengeance and furious anger those who attempt to poison and destroy my brothers. And you will know my name is the Lord when I lay my vengeance upon thee.

Jules then shoots and kills Brett. The scene abruptly shifts to story number two. Butch Coolidge (Bruce Willis) is a white prizefighter pensively listening to the out-of-frame voice of Marsellus (Ving Rhames), an imposing, smooth-headed black man. (The script notes he "sounds like a cross between a gangster and a king.") Butch is being instructed on how he'll throw his next fight for money.

Vincent and Jules—wearing shorts and T-shirts—stroll into Marsellus's club. Later Vincent heads for Echo Park to visit his drug dealer. The affable entrepreneur Lance (Eric Stolz) lays out a sample of each of his heroin grades as if they were Mary Kay products. Vincent buys $300 worth of the most potent stuff, some of which he shoots up at Lance's before cruising over to the Wallaces' house in a blissful state of dopey solitude.

He lets himself in, as the note on the door instructs, and Mia (Uma Thurman) continues dressing and snorting cocaine before making her entrance. She's coquettish and mysterious, yet Vincent remains cordial and distanced. He takes her to the restaurant of her choice: Jackrabbit Slim's, a 1950s-style theme park of a diner with a bubbly Wurlitzer jukebox and a wait staff dressed like dead 1950s icons such as Marilyn Monroe and James Dean. A mock Ricky Nelson croons out one of his rollicking hits on a small bandstand, and Mia and Vincent take their seat in the cutout body of a vintage car. Their waiter, Buddy Holly (a comically gruff Steve Buscemi), takes their order and leaves them to their small talk. Mia tells of her one shot as an actress costarring in a TV pilot. Vincent asks why a foot massage can lead to a man's nasty fall. She questions him about the source of his gossip, then gives him a wry smile and remarks, "When you little scamps get together, you're worse than a sewing circle."

She pulls rank and forces a reluctant Vincent to enter the restaurant's twist contest with her, dancing to Chuck Berry's "You Never Can Tell." In the film's now famous showpiece, the shoeless couple do a slow, stylish twist that transcends into the frug, the pony, the swim, and a sly array of other faddish dances from a bygone era. They return to Mia's house with their trophy, still dancing and relishing their victory. While Vincent talks to himself about restraint in the bathroom, Mia finds heroin in his overcoat pocket and mistakes it for cocaine. Like a child who's found candy, she snorts a few lines and quickly convulses from the awful difference. When Vincent enters the room, he finds her unconscious on the floor with a bloody nose and bubbling foam erupting from her mouth. Panicked at the price of a Mia overdose, he scoops her up and drives to Lance's house. Lance and Vincent frantically argue about what to do until they finally opt for an untested adrenaline-to-the-heart injection Lance has stashed away. After an anxious exchange over who should do it, Vincent plunges the needle into Mia's chest (the film's most notorious scene); she rises up like a zombie, lunging across the floor while ogling the needle stuck in her chest and screaming like a banshee. Vincent drives the quiet, ghoulish-looking Mia home. They break their silence long enough to agree never to utter a word of the incident to Marsellus, who would surely kill them both.

The next scene reveals a little boy in a suburban living room. His mother brings in a uniformed soldier, a former POW from Vietnam, where the boy's father died. Captain Koons (Christopher Walken) has come to deliver a watch that belonged to Butch's father, and before him, his grandfather, who wore it through World War II, and before him, Butch's great grandfather, who safeguarded it through World War I. In an absurdist monologue, Koons explains to the wide-eyed boy how his father hid Butch's "birthright" on his body for five years in the POW camp. When Butch's father died, Koons "hid this uncomfortable hunk of metal up my ass for two years." Now home safe from the war, Koons tells the boy, "I give the watch to you."

Butch wakes up from his flashback in a locker room ready and dressed for the bout he's supposed to throw. Butch wins the fight and goes on the run instead, careening out of town in a taxi—its radio squawking about his performance, which accidentally killed his opponent. His cab driver, the sultry Esmarelda, befriends him and deposits him at an out-of-town motel room. Butch's doe-eyed, Betty Boopish girlfriend, Fabienne (Maria de Medeiros), is waiting for him there. She's sweet, innocent, and the tender spot for the otherwise rough, worn-out boxer. But he loses his temper with her when he finds out she didn't get all his prize possessions out of his apartment, especially his father's watch. He gently apologizes to her big, brown eyes, then zooms off in her car to fetch his watch. After sneaking back into his apartment and finding his watch, he notices a submachine gun laying on the kitchen counter. Then he hears a toilet flush. As Vincent Vega walks out of the bathroom with a copy of *Modesty Blaise* (1960s pulp fiction about a female James Bond), he locks eyes with Butch before being propelled backward by the force of the gunshots and crashing into the bathtub, bloody and dead. Stunned, Butch puts down the gun and flees the apartment.

Driving down the street, Butch stops at a red light and panics when he realizes that Marsellus is strolling across the pedestrian walk. They, too, lock eyes before Butch crashes into Marsellus and then is knocked out when he loses control of the car. Marsellus gains consciousness at the same time as Butch and starts shooting at him, sending pedestrians scattering and screaming. Butch runs and ducks into a dark, cluttered pawnshop with Marsellus in hot pursuit. He punches Marsellus out but is soon knocked out by a rifle butt belonging to the pawnshop clerk, Maynard. After Maynard phones his friend Zed, the two "hillbillies" (notes the script) put Marsellus and Butch in restraints customarily used for sexual bondage.

They bring in another character called The Gimp, wearing a studded leash and a leather mask. He's chained up next to Butch, and Marsellus is dragged off and savagely sodomized. Butch wrestles free and runs for the door. But he stops short, panged by his conscience when he realizes that no one deserves to be raped, not even Marsellus. He searches the shop, rejects a bat, then a chain saw, and finally picks up a sword and ambushes the hillbillies. Once untied, Marsellus exonerates Butch for his double cross, swears him to secrecy, and orders him out of town immediately. Butch steals Zed's chopper and fetches Fabienne, and they roar off to start a new life.

The final episode, called "The Bonnie Situation," turns back to the time when Jules was conducting his biblically inspired killing. As Jules and Vincent turn toward the still-breathing Marvin, the bathroom door bursts open and a fourth man starts blasting away with a shiny magnum. He misses with all shots—the bullets blowing holes in the wall behind Jules and Vincent. They exchange dumbfounded looks and then promptly kill their would-be assassin with swift, professional aplomb. In the car on the way to see Marsellus, with Marvin held hostage in the backseat, Jules is having an epiphany. He insists that the only reason they're alive is because of divine intervention. He's convinced he witnessed a miracle and vows to tell Marsellus that he's retiring. An agitated Vincent turns to ask Marvin what he thinks, waving his gun around just as the car hits a nasty bump. "Oh, man, I shot Marvin in the face," Vincent groans, looking over his shoulder and wincing. The camera stays on the two hit men in the front seat, but we're told not only that Marvin is dead but that his head has been blown off. We can see the blood and bits of bone and brain splattered around the inside of the car. Distraught but still thinking clearly, Jules remembers a friend in the area where they can stop for refuge and get themselves and the car off the streets.

Jules's friend Jimmie (Quentin Tarantino) is upset that they've brought Marvin to his house; Jimmie's wife is expected home in the next 90 minutes. He serves his uninvited guests gourmet coffee (tasty enough for Jules to compliment despite Marvin's mess all over him) and calls Marsellus for help. Marsellus agrees to send over a specialist known as The Wolf (Harvey Keitel). Wearing a tuxedo at 8:30 A.M. and oozing David Niven charm, The Wolf enters as if he's in an Underworld version of a Noel Coward play. With clipped efficiency, he promptly assesses the cleanup job and is sensitive to Jimmie's domestic plight—a divorce if Bonnie comes home to the mess.

Wiping up the exploded human remains, Jules and Vincent bicker as if they were Ricky and David sent out to clean the garage. Jimmie hoses the two down before donating some of his dorky mall-strolling clothes for them to wear (these are the shorts and T-shirts we saw them in earlier). After they dispose of the Chevy Nova and bid The Wolf good-bye, Jules and Vincent drop in on the nearest restaurant, where an anxious, cooing couple sits by the window.

Vincent offers him a strip of bacon, but Jules explains why he "don't dig on swine" and revisits his earnest plan to retire. "What is significant is I felt God's touch. God got involved," Jules says emphatically. After he has given Marsellus the briefcase, he plans to "walk the earth . . . like Caine in *Kung Fu.*" With *Modesty Blaise* in hand, a disgusted Vincent retreats to the bathroom. Seconds later Honey Bunny and Pumpkin pull out their guns and start robbing the till and the patrons, viciously taunting the frightened diners and the cornered manager and stashing wallets and watches in a plastic garbage bag. When Pumpkin comes on the unruffled Jules, he demands that Jules open the briefcase. Pumpkin promises to count to three and then shoot, so Jules agrees to open the case. Its contents make Pumpkin delirious (it glows in everyone's face but remains a mystery).

Jules quickly grabs Pumpkin's wrist and renders him defenseless while using his other hand to jam a .45 under Pumpkin's chin. The Mexican standoff leaves Honey Bunny shrieking and waving her gun at Jules. The stalemate drags on, with hostages holding their breath and Pumpkin and Honey Bunny gravely stunned by their rotten luck. Vincent suddenly emerges and holds a gun on Honey Bunny, further escalating the oppressive tension. Jules shouts at him to stay out of it. He has Pumpkin retrieve his wallet from the plastic bag. "I'm giving you that money so I don't hafta kill your ass," Jules tells Pumpkin, then asks, "You read the Bible?" He calmly recites the customary passage that usually serves as a prelude to a kill. But this time he pauses and explains that he now knows what it means. "The truth is you're weak. And I'm the tyranny of evil men. But I'm tryin'. I'm tryin' real hard to be a shepherd." He lowers the gun barrel, and Pumpkin and Honey Bunny grab their loot and scurry for the door. Backed by buzzing surf music and ever-present cool, Vincent and Jules saunter past the stupefied patrons, through the glass doors, and down the street until they disappear and the credits roll.

TARANTINO'S HOLLYWOOD HANGOVER

Pulp Fiction won the coveted Palme d'Or at the 1994 Cannes Film Festival. It was also nominated for an Academy Award as best picture but lost to the mammothly popular *Forrest Gump.* Tarantino and Avery won for best original screenplay, though, on Tarantino's 32d birthday. The film made Tarantino "the avatar of American hip," according to David Denby. Or as the *San Francisco Chronicle* put it, "Hollywood's newest anointed savior."

Typical of the gushing compliments *Pulp Fiction* earned was *Daily Variety*'s assertion that the film "blasts through such cobwebbed objections by virtue of its sheer exhilaration, and also because of the very self-consciousness with which it cranks up the stakes of its genre game-playing. It's small-time crime on an epic canvas, with low-life characters who take on iconographic dimensions before our eyes."

Robert Horton in *Film Comment* wrote, "I haven't seen many people use the word 'exquisite' to describe Tarantino's movies. But they should." Corliss, who was no fan of *Reservoir Dogs,* called *Pulp Fiction* a "vast, enthralling" film. He wrote, "Part of *Pulp Fiction*'s fun is that memorable weirdos keep popping up in the second and third hour."

Tarantino describes *Pulp Fiction* as "a cross between a rock 'n' roll spaghetti western and a blaxploitation movie." He intended to make a kind of crime anthology, he explained, borrowing familiar themes from the gangster genre and its many subgenres. "Part of the fun . . . if you're hip to movies [is] you're watching the boxing movie *Body and Soul* and then suddenly the characters turn a corner and they're in the middle of *Deliverance.*" When Vincent meets Butch, Tarantino suggests, "It's straight out of *On the Waterfront.* It's a true . . . movie star . . . moment." The Wolf is a "complete movie creation. . . . this movie star walks in, sprinkles some movie dust, and solves the problems." When Bruce Willis searches the pawnshop, Tarantino explains that Butch is looking for a movie hero to embody; he passes up the bat as in *Walking Tall,* then considers being a character out of *The Texas Chainsaw Massacre,* and finally settles for being a movie samurai. "I wanted to start off from these old chestnuts and go to the moon with them. . . . I want the audience's familiarity to be the source of their greatest surprise."

Considering the film's B movie references, black humor, and lurid overtones, the accolades shocked as many critics as they delighted. Although some reviews mentioned its cartoonlike violence, Tarantino points out that the film contains only about 2.5 minutes of actual violence out of its 153 minutes of screen time.[5] However, violence wedged between stretches of smart dialogue and darkly comic interludes disturbed viewers more than *Die Hard*'s higher body count. "Gangster films are a violent genre," Tarantino remarked. "If you make a swashbuckler, you expect to show people swordfighting. I'm dealing with the crime genre, and violence is part and parcel of it."

Tarantino was also aware that some critics viewed his work as a pastiche of cultural artifacts and filmmaking tricks. But Tarantino confidently contends that audiences were embracing his films not because they're clever rehashes but because they're something new. "I like the idea that I'm taking a genre that already exists and reinventing it, like Leone reinvented the whole Western genre. I think I've taken on an established genre . . . and made it challenging to myself and to my audience."

As David Ansen noted, "The miracle of Quentin Tarantino's *Pulp Fiction* is how, being composed of secondhand, debased parts, it succeeds in gleaming like something new. . . . When it works we, we call it postmodernism; when it doesn't, it's vampirism." The *Village Voice* declared Tarantino another disciple of Godard, "the inventor of movie postmodernism." Janet Maslin noted, "*Pulp Fiction* is the work of a film maker whose avid embrace of pop culture manifests itself in fresh, amazing ways. . . . [It] smacks of the secondhand. Yet these references are exuberantly playful, never pretentious. Despite his fascination with the familiar, this film itself is absolutely new." She placed Tarantino "in the front ranks of American film makers" for "a work of such depth, wit and blazing originality."

Richard Peña, director of the New York Film Festival, describes Tarantino as a "second-generation movie brat, whose range of influence now goes beyond old Hollywood and European *outre* cinema to include Hong Kong and a lot of other references, including television . . . whereas it wasn't at all with the earlier generation of people like Scorsese. And [Tarantino's] films are playful in a way that invites the audience to come play along."[6]

Tarantino has also turned musical accompaniment on its ear. He doesn't use music that parallels the on-screen action such as "Street Fighting Man" by the Rolling Stones, as Scorsese used. In *Reservoir Dogs,* Tarantino admitted, "I wanted to use the early, sugary, bubblegum stuff. . . . It gives the movie this weird, popsy personality, makes you laugh a little bit—though the bounciness of the song makes the scene more disturbing." *Pulp Fiction* featured an eclectic array of four decades of music from Chuck Berry to Maria McKee and the resurrection of Dick Dale's surf music. Tarantino views it as "rock 'n' roll Ennio Morricone music," referring to the composer who scored Leone's spaghetti westerns, along with *The Untouchables* and *State of Grace.*

ARE YOU WRITING FOR ME?

Tarantino even deftly recycles actors and plays with their pop-culture images. *Pulp Fiction*'s greatest surprise was Travolta. The film brought him a nomination for best actor and put him back in major-league roles, which are still coming his way. (He later starred in Elmore Leonard's best seller *Get Shorty* and John Woo's American action thrillers *Broken Arrow* and the 1997 summer hit *Face/Off.*)

Tarantino admits Travolta was an icon for him as a child, whether as the Brooklyn disco dancer that made Travolta a movie star or the pensive lead in De Palma's excellent *Blow Out.* In *Pulp Fiction* Travolta gets to poke fun at his glamour leads, or as the *Village Voice* noted, "Vega is a grown-up Vinnie Barbarino." Tarantino put his job on the line to make sure Travolta became Vincent. Producers, who were now dealing with an $8 million investment, reportedly wanted to cast Daniel Day Lewis.

Even Bruce Willis, a frequent target for critics, earned kudos for his scrappy but tenderhearted Butch. Like the others, Willis was anxious to work with Tarantino even though the whole movie was made for half the salary Willis received for the third *Die Hard.* (Most of *Pulp Fiction*'s major players were given points off the film's profits rather than fat salaries. Given the film's success, they've all earned tidy sums to date.)[7]

One reason actors want to work with Tarantino is his gift for writing smart, fluid dialogue. Ving Rhames, who played Marsellus, notes, "There's actor-talk, and there's people-talk. [Quentin] writes in a way that sounds like the way people talk. So there's no need for improvisation, because he does half of your work." Even Stanley Kauffmann, the veteran Hollywood critic and conservative culture watcher, noted that Tarantino's films are enriched with the "tap-dance, snaredrum rhythms of dialogue." It makes his often farcical stories irresistible and his offbeat characters likable.

The cameo roles in *Pulp Fiction* are rich with wit and self-reflexive movieness: Keitel is playing off his role as the disposer of corpses he portrayed in *The Assassin;* Walken is having fun with the grim POW moments from *The Deer Hunter,* the film that made him a star. As Woods writes, "We're being encouraged to laugh (with affection) at the way Hollywood portrays such ordeals of honour—not at honour itself."

Jackson, too, was nominated for an Oscar as best supporting actor, dominating nearly every scene in which he appears. As Janet Maslin noted, "Mr. Jackson, never better, shows off a vibrant intelligence and an avenging stare that bores holes through the screen." Jules was written by Tarantino with Jackson in mind, knowing he could deliver the biblical quote with mesmerizing punch—a type of thing Tarantino saw used in a kung fu movie. He said the quotation's meaning is central to the film. "What loyalty is to *Dogs,* redemption is to *Pulp Fiction,*" Tarantino said. Jackson noted, "The voice of redemption flows throughout the whole film. . . . Mia gets it when she comes back to life. . . . Butch gets it, Marsellus gets it, and I'm the person who actually voices it."

It's Jules, in fact, who offers a fresh option for the screen gangster. After he's confronted with his "moment of clarity," he grapples with the gangster's classic conundrum: continue to degenerate or seek redemption? Armed with past experience, we expect Jules to act one way or the other. He does neither and surprises us in a genre that has few untapped wonders left. Jules is the new thinking man's gangster. After seeing the light, he refuses to be the casual target of another man's bullet. Yet he realizes his limitations; he's a hit man by trade and is hardly a likely born-again crusader. He doesn't make Pumpkin and Honey Bunny give everyone back their valuables. Instead, he buys himself a clean conscience by buying Pumpkin's life for the $1,500 in his wallet. He knows he can't enlighten Pumpkin or stop another Jules-in-the-making, but he can take immediate action to wrestle back control of his own programmed-to-kill existence. The possibility of Jules's uncertain future remains fascinating. In contrast, Vincent Vega meets the classic gangster fate: he's killed by the same sword he uses for killing.

HOLLYWOOD'S UNDERWORLD AS A GLOBAL VILLAGE

Crime films still comprise nearly three-quarters of the world's movie products. Tarantino is among the first American filmmakers to comfortably embrace the blurring of international boundaries. He goes beyond French New Wave to find inspiration from previously untapped cultures for Hollywood products. He also brings tidbits buried in other mediums: TV, comic books, pop music, and even advertising.

"The thing about crime films, in particular, is that the *yakuza* movies they make in Japan, the triad movies they make in Hong Kong, the Italian Mafia movies, Jean-Pierre Melville's films in France . . . we're all telling the same stories," Tarantino noted. He cites a wide range of personal favorites from Japanese karate stars to Hong Kong's John Woo and Italy's Dario Argento, as well as the Mafia movies of Fernando Di Leo, whom Tarantino calls an Italian Don Siegel. "But we're all telling [these stories] differently, because we're all from different cultures, different nationalities, and that's what's really interesting to me, how different cultures attack the same story."

A prime example is the British use and embrace of the American gangster tradition. The British gangster favorite *The Long Good Friday* (1981), with Bob Hoskins as gangland boss Harold Shand, applied many of the stock conventions and characters. The film also includes American mafiosi who have come to London to make a deal with Shand but become leery of the sloppy gang war breaking out. The film's climax, though, keenly reveals a public nightmare unique to the British: the Irish Republican Army. The IRA is a force more threatening to their national psyche than the usual lot of predictable, greedy gangsters who are anything but anarchistic. Reminiscent of Michael Corleone's observation about Cuban revolutionaries, Hoskins's character finds out that political zealotry is a force he can't corrupt or subdue with any amount of gangster money or muscle.

As American gangster films once commented on America's public convulsions over Vietnam, so British gangster films continue to tap the gangster format to comment on their idle youth running amok. Kubrick's futuristic criminal meltdown, *A Clockwork Orange,* remains the nightmare vision about gang violence on either side of the Atlantic. Among the recent British entries is *The Young Americans* (1993), starring Harvey Keitel as an American federal agent in London tracking an American gangster who exploits British youth to carry out his London-based rackets. Another is *Trainspotting* (1996)—an uncommonly brutal film about working-class boys who take up drug trafficking instead of living on the dole (slang for the British welfare system.) The film is infested with crime film clichés, a heavy dose of Salvador Dali, and appallingly fresh anger.

HOODS AS HAMLET

While Tarantino contorts the genre, minority filmmakers add new voices, and foreign influences cross-pollinate products for global audiences, several veteran gangster creators continue to put out quality work. Aside from Scorsese's disappointing *Casino,* De Niro debuted as a subtle director, and Pacino and De Palma teamed up for another gangster duet. The 1993 film *Carlito's Way* was less theatrical than their previous union but much more layered in insights.

Like *The Godfather Part III, Carlito's Way* is about an aging gangster who wants to redeem himself and leave the life. The film also reiterated a common theme of gangster pictures in the 1990s: a takeover by a new breed of street punks who lack honor. "Ain't no more rackets our here. Just a bunch of cowboys ripping each other off," Carlito says. Pacino's uneven portrait of a brutal but sentimental Puerto Rican hood prompted some critics to note that he's so full of forlornness and passivity that he's almost dull. But the film's strength is De Palma's often hypnotic direction—or as Janet Maslin called it, the "swoop and soar" of his ever alert camera. Another perk is Sean Penn as Carlito's slimy defense attorney David Kleinfeld, who's a better gangster than most of the thugs he represents.

Some black filmmakers, too, arrived at the same redemptive theme after the initial burst of fatalistic hood films. Gangsta rap—the inspiring street theater and musical form behind many of the early hood films—began to burn out. Several of its star artists, such as Tupac Shakur, Snoop Doggy Dog, and Notorious B.I.G. have been killed or jailed. The 1993 film *Sugar Hill,* written by *New Jack City*'s Barry Michael

Cooper, showed Hollywood's hood now absorbing the gangster-as-Hamlet theme. *Sugar Hill* offered Wesley Snipes—the once sizzling Nino Brown—as a gangster who wants to quit. But first he must witness the destruction of nearly everything he covets or hopes to live for. It makes the old-fashioned ending of a swift bullet appear far more humane.

In 1997 the real Harlem hoodlum Bumpy Johnson, who had made his mark during the 1930s and inspired several blaxploitation characters, was given major screen time. Bumpy had served as one of the models for the character Bumpy Jones, who hassled John Shaft in 1971. The 1997 film *Hoodlum* featured actor Laurence Fishburne as the Harlem gangster and his 1930s turf battles with gangster superstars Dutch Schultz and Lucky Luciano. Although a flawed film, *Hoodlum* was a summer hit with younger audiences despite the Prohibition-era setting.

Hoodlum tracks Ellsworth "Bumpy" Johnson after he's released from Sing Sing prison and returns to Harlem and to the employ of Stephanie St. Clair (Cicely Tyson), the Martinique-born "queen" of the black-run "numbers" racket. However, when the infamous Dutch Schultz (Tim Roth) muscles in on her racket and she's jailed by corrupt officials, Bumpy takes on Schultz to save her criminal turf. Bumpy wages a bloody war with the sadistic Schultz before eventually forming an alliance with Mob chieftain Luciano (Andy Garcia), who puts an end to Schultz's reign of terror.

Bill Duke, the film's director, had previously created the stylish but derivative 1991 gangster tale *A Rage in Harlem*. As he did with that film, Duke forces a love story into *Hoodlum*'s mix, which only weakens its gangster pedigree. At the same time, Duke intensifies the use of raw violence, including Schultz's crude exhibition of the severed testicles of one of his victims. Such moments only undermine the film's reach for distinction and race-conscious high ground. In trying to be epic, running 142 minutes, it includes a *Godfather*-like reference to opera; an aria from *Tosca* is used for one sequence. That's unfortunate considering the rich reservoir of jazz that captivated the era and contributed to the acclaimed Harlem Renaissance. (Even the film's commercial soundtrack lets hip-hop influences dominate rather than remain true to the sweet, soulful sounds of 1930s Harlem.)

Hoodlum joins the genre's long tradition of mythologizing real-life gangsters to suit the ever-changing tastes and politics of audiences. For the 1990s, the filmmakers made Bumpy Johnson a proud, menacing black man who was able to live by his own rules, despite belonging to a segregated era. Their Bumpy may be a gangster, but he's also a well-spoken and thoughtful poet, elevated far above the usual Shakespearean or Robin Hood–style hoodlum until he's fast approaching a civil rights conscience. At one point, Bumpy says, "I'm a colored man and white folks left me crime." At another, he notes, "The numbers provide jobs for over 2,000 colored folks right here in Harlem alone. It's the only home-grown business we got."

The film's approach is reminiscent of the distorted presentations once reserved for white depression-era outlaws. However, it differs sharply from the complex and often revealing blaxploitation gangsters. Bumpy is presented not as another abuser of the black community but as a clever opportunist who merely seizes a ripe opportunity. The film's attitude toward Bumpy posits that becoming a gangster was the only "rewarding" outlet left for a gifted black man during the 1920s. That logic forsakes the talented Harlem artists and writers such as Langston Hughes who chose a pen instead of a gun to battle racism and to express powerful ideas. The excuse of being disadvantaged doesn't serve Bumpy any better than it did poor Italians who became mafiosi or marginalized Jewish youth who joined groups such as Detroit's notorious Purple Gang. Cagney's Tom Powers, Pacino's Michael Corleone, and Larenz Tate's

O'Dog are memorable because they explain how talented gangsters deftly exploit the social circumstances that favor them. However, they don't focus on making social excuses for such characters' gangster life. A gangster—regardless of his race, ethnicity, or creed—makes for a mesmerizing character, but his self-serving, shoot-'em-up solutions are rarely useful for a downtrodden community to find permanent uplift. Gangsters are businessmen who line their own pockets, not revolutionaries who want to better their people as a whole.

However, *Hoodlum* doesn't fail because of its politics; it falters because it expends most of its energy trying to look authentic rather than to be authentic. It's more a film about gangster films than about well-crafted gangster characters. Chris Vognar of the *Dallas Morning News* saw *Hoodlum* as a weak descendant of the blaxploitation film *Black Caesar*, the 1973 vehicle for Fred Williamson. Vognar concluded that *Hoodlum* was not nearly as "lean and ribald" as its predecessor. Moreover, Duke strains to infuse *Hoodlum* with the look of a classic gangster film, including gorgeous nightclubs, dapper costumes, cavernous mansions, and a Warner Brothers–style montage that advances time during a prolonged street war.

Newsday's John Anderson found fault with Chris Brancato's script, dubbing it "rococo" and noting that the "attempts to recreate the era through constant period references are ham-handed at best." Anderson adds, "*Hoodlum* would have been much better . . . had [Duke] expended less effort making a tortured demigod out of Bumpy and simply let him be a man."

The real Bumpy Johnson was a real hoodlum and rich material for a fresh gangster story if he had been honestly investigated. The beguiling "island" women such as Madame St. Clair, who enchanted and prospered in Harlem in the 1920s, are also untapped stories. But historical accuracy has never been the stuff of gangster films, and *Hoodlum*'s creators took considerable liberty with the facts. The real Bumpy, who spent a great deal of his adult life in several prisons, is promoted in the film from a Harlem numbers underboss to an equal player among Mafia chieftains. He's even invited to attend one of the Mafia's high-powered meetings for his opinion on the future of Harlem as a criminal marketplace. Moreover, Luciano did indeed wipe out Schultz, but not because Bumpy was able to pit one white man against another. Luciano and the Mafia commission had decided that Schultz had become a business liability after Schultz vowed to murder Thomas Dewey, which would have triggered a crackdown on New York's Underworld. The film also presents Dewey as the greedy recipient of frequent Mob payoffs, which isn't accurate considering Dewey eventually jailed the powerful Luciano and later had him deported.

Given the era and race relations at the time, these film moments are a stretch. Unfortunately, by contorting Bumpy so that he's in tune with current assumptions, the untapped saga of the real Bumpy Johnson is stripped of its uniqueness. His story would have had more bite and impact had it been presented against a realistic presentation of Harlem in the 1930s and the impenetrable race barriers that existed both in legitimate society *and* in the Underworld.

Further obscuring Bumpy's mere mortal status is the engaging Fishburne, who also served as one of *Hoodlum*'s producers. Besides his notable work in gangster films of the early 1990s, Fishburne earned a best actor Oscar nomination in 1993 for his compelling performance as Ike Turner in *What's Love Got to Do with It?* As a screen presence, Fishburne exudes a self-assured dignity and an underlying menace that are ideal for a gangster character. But as written, Bumpy's complexity is not so much unveiled as presented through overripe symbolism: a pious girlfriend, a love of chess, and a jovial but inept cousin for blatant contrast. Regardless of Fishburne's charisma, Bumpy isn't convincing as a vicious hoodlum in one scene and a caring romantic in the next. Furthermore, his spiritual reformation at the end of the film is as contrived as anything the Hays office recommended for Cagney's miscreants in the late 1930s.

However, if exaggeration for broad entertainment's sake was the film's goal, no better example comes out of *Hoodlum* than Roth's portrayal of Dutch Schultz. While Fishburne's Bumpy offers the inflated pose of a Harlem-bred Robin Hood, and Garcia's Luciano suggests a "cobra-like hypnotic power," as critic Michael Medved suggested, Roth's Schultz possesses a cartoonlike ferocity that chews up the scenery. It's almost as if each actor had worked with a different director, with Roth being paired with Roger Corman and told to have a ball. "I just wanted him to be funny and horrible and not too one-dimensional," Roth remarked.

Shakespearean-style tragedy, though, was restored to the gangster genre when the next Mafia saga was released: the 1996 film *Gotti*. It was also described as the rise and fall of *The Last of the Mohicans*–style gangsters. Gotti's real-life daughter Victoria described her father's downfall in those terms, implying he was an American hero who possessed honor and strong community ties. Considering the petty disturbances that broke out in the streets of Gotti's old Queens neighborhood after his conviction, she may have a point. Other observers saw the street demonstrations as a frightening testament to the enduring appeal of charismatic gangsters who portray themselves as community underdogs who make good.

The film *Gotti* stars Armand Assante and features William Forsythe as Sammy Gravano, the ambitious underboss turned rat. The screen Gotti warns that his career collapse is not the victory the federal government thinks it is. He notes at the film's conclusion, "OK, you humbled me . . . you gotta world-wide crime syndicate now. There's no rules, no parameters. . . . There's no feelings for this country. . . . five, ten years from now they're gonna wish there was American Cosa Nostra. . . . five, ten years from now they're gonna miss John Gotti." It's a perfunctory production that heavily favors a romanticized view of Gotti and makes Gravano the resident heavy. Yet the film was a ratings hit as a Home Box Office presentation and did well when released on video. Although Assante gives a capable performance in a mediocre film (he earned an Emmy for the role), it's curiosity about the real gangster behind the screen image that prompted people to tune in.

Another Mafia story, the 1997 film *Donnie Brasco*, not only proved the Mob's persistent appeal but demonstrated that skillful filmmaking can make a familiar subject sparkle again like something new. The film's most distinguishing feature is an exquisite Al Pacino, who remarkably finds one more subtle note to trumpet within a gangster character. He infuses Lefty Ruggiero—an aging and often pitiable small-time hood—with an element of grace and a jagged but honest sentiment. The film was directed by British director Mike Newell *(Enchanted April, Four Weddings and a Funeral),* an unlikely filmmaker for a gangster story. But his unfamiliarity with the genre is his greatest asset: he focuses on characterizations and spares us the predictable setups and affectations.

Lefty befriends an undercover agent Joseph Pistone, known to Lefty as Donnie Brasco—masterfully portrayed by genre newcomer Johnny Depp. Lefty mentors Donnie on Mafia codes, respect, and Mob survival. More important, Lefty lets the young man into his crusted-over heart. Pistone then tells his superiors, "I got him. I got my hooks in the guy." But the reverse also becomes gravely true as the agent sinks ever deeper into the gangster life. He can't stem the tide of feelings for Lefty nor shake off the wise-guy posturing he's increasingly absorbing. As Pistone tells his estranged wife, whom he's just roughed up, "I'm not becoming like them," as she accuses. "I am one of them."

Near the end of the film, after more than two years of undercover work, he's earned the trust and respect of his fellow hoods, including his volatile superior, Sonny Black. Black is deftly portrayed by Michael Madsen as another imposing rattler-at-rest. Donnie is finally ordered to perform his first professional hit. If done well, a proud Lefty will sponsor Donnie to become a "made" member of the Bonanno crime family: the last step in his total immersion into the Mob. Pistone's fellow agents, though, who are increasingly concerned for his state of mind (and also selfishly believe Pistone has spent his usefulness), swoop down on the murder scene just in time to stop Donnie from pulling the trigger. Even then, he doesn't want to "come out," perhaps skittish about his ability to be a civilian again. But he's also bothered by guilt because Lefty will be summarily killed when the truth is revealed. Lefty had vouched for Donnie, introducing him as a "friend of mine," which means a "connected" guy in Mob talk; it also means his sponsor is held accountable.

Donnie Brasco tells a familiar story of illusory trust and deadly betrayal. But the film doesn't settle for well-worn, surface assumptions; it moves in closer to capture more intimate, prickly moments. It presents the characters as a strained but loving father and son, with the petty irritations that often divide and unite them. Lefty criticizes Donnie for his mustache, his "rodeo" jeans, his youthful disdain for rules, his impatience with men he should respect. Yet when Lefty's junkie son lies comatose in a hospital, the petty, bullying, slow-witted hood also embarrassingly weeps and declares his love for his protégé.

Donnie can't help but perversely respect the aging hood's devotion to bosses and his dedication to duty. But the agent in him is also repulsed by Lefty's sacred regard for codes of silence and murderous rituals. Lefty had followed orders for 30 years and killed 26 men along the way. Fortunately, the film doesn't paint Donnie as a righteous crusader but as a flawed man tormented by his own demons and a threatened sense of duty. Depp's G-man exposes the dangers of wallowing in gangsterism — just as much a state of mind as a milieu.

Just before Donnie's cover was blown, he tried to offer Lefty an escape clause and a bag full of money without revealing his motive. But the agent finally grasps that Lefty is what he is; he would be unlikely to accept running away as a way to avoid the Mob's revenge. Once Lefty finds out the truth, he unflappably prepares for his marked death with forethought, candid silence, and few signs of cleansing remorse.

The work of the real Pistone, whose memoirs inspired the film, was responsible for 200 indictments and more than 100 convictions. A $500,000 contract on his life remains open. Pistone admits he was disturbed by ultimately having to betray the real Lefty. But he also knew that Lefty was capable of killing him if ever given the order. After Pistone had time to reflect, he noted that it was hard to feel permanent guilt for Lefty, who respected Mafia codes more than human life. But it took time to get there. The film leaves us with Pistone feeling drained and empty.

"*The Godfather* is a great movie, but it gives them too much credit. . . . Al Pacino as . . . [a] Corleone is eloquent, well-spoken, college-educated, a war hero," Pistone added, but "that's not the way it was." Ironically, Michael Corleone's creator, now the 56-year-old Pacino, is just as convincing and as distinguished as the lowlife Lefty. *Donnie Brasco* demonstrates that both Pacino and the genre have matured. The film strikes a balance between graphic violence, subtle emotion, and still-gripping tragedy. Janet Maslin called the film "crackling good," noting that Pacino "brings such color and pathos to a story that automatically invokes the breadth of his own career." And Depp she commended for moving through the film "with a brand-new hardboiled grace."

The staying power of Mafia characters and the men in blue who chase them is nearly unequaled among Hollywood topics. In 1997 they showed no signs of fading away. Mario Puzo's bloated novel *The Last Don* was transformed into a six-hour miniseries. Its success was evident when it topped the May ratings sweeps. Given network restrictions, the film had to pull in viewers without excessive profanity, ultraviolent graphics, and violated women—although all that was generously implied.

No doubt Sammy "The Bull" Gravano's story will eventually make its way to the big (or small) screen. The first step has already been taken, as Peter Maas has written Gravano's memoirs. The last time Maas helped a Mafia informant write a book, it ended up as *The Valachi Papers*, a 1972 film. Moreover, Gravano already proved his screen appeal when he gave Diane Sawyer and ABC's *Prime Time Live* a ratings winner with his spring 1997 appearance. And from that compelling interview, Gravano may prove to be the real embodiment of a Jules-type gangster. Gravano, who was personally responsible for 19 murders, claimed to be a redeemed man, having a type of epiphany in prison that went beyond cutting a deal to save his skin. Several federal agents and prosecutors who worked with him also contend that he seems a changed man. A peek inside his post-Mob life would make a fascinating movie. It could investigate the riddle: a man can leave the gangster life, but will the gangster leave the man? As Sawyer asked him, if he loses his temper one day living like a poor schnook, will he shout and get over it as most of us do? Or will he vow to whack somebody because a few bad habits die hard?

SHOOTING FOR SCREENS OF THE TWENTY-FIRST CENTURY

Video cameras have now put filmmaking possibilities into just about anyone's hands. Perhaps an enterprising filmmaker born and bred into our nation's most enduring hard-hit communities will soon pick up a camera instead of a gun and give us a renewed peek at the mean streets that still produce gangsters and public enemies. Furthermore, the interactive media world of cyberspace is still unfolding. The existence of Web sites devoted to Mob life, including the "Mafia Page," the "Unofficial Homepage of the New York Mafia," and even the satirical "John Gotti's Tribute Page,"[8] provides evidence of the Mob's enduring appeal as a media phenomenon. Also, there are dramas on CD-ROMs that enable users to get involved and attach different endings. Perhaps, as film increasingly mixes with computer technology, only the imagination will limit the choices for storytellers who still believe in the public's fascination with crime as entertainment and art.

Aside from those creative minds who haven't stumbled onto the genre yet, there are still the veteran players, practiced filmmakers, and rising stars who have much work left to do. Following *Pulp Fiction*, Tarantino had declared, "I don't want to be just the gun guy. . . . I want to make a western, a war film, a secret agent movie." Perhaps he forgot that they use guns, too, and lots of them. However, the boy wonder who didn't want to become "the gun guy" has made another crime film set for release in late 1997. Tarantino's film *Jackie Brown* is based on *Rum Punch*, a book by Elmore Leonard—the same author whose book *The Switch* Tarantino was caught stealing as a boy. The film will feature one of the reigning gangster movie stars, Robert De Niro, along with impressive genre talents such as Samuel L. Jackson and Pam Grier. Grier's career has been revived after the 1996 blaxploitation reunion film *Original Gangstas,* which also featured Fred Williamson, *Shaft*'s Richard Roundtree, and *Superfly*'s Ron O'Neal. Grier portrays the title character in *Jackie Brown*—a character whom the novel neatly describes as the accomplice to "a man who sells machine guns to bad guys."

The combined talents of Tarantino and actors well-versed in the screen Underworld promise to make the film memorable. On an even closer look, the film's basic premise about gangsters threatening to unravel the fabric of decent society promises to tap a topic that retains its currency and vicarious thrill for audiences. It's the same old story; it just keeps being told over and over again to suit the evolving times.

In fact, although technology advances and both fresh and familiar faces pop up onscreen and look through the camera's eye, the genre depends on one constant element: the gangster himself. And underneath his changing fashions of spats, fedoras, bandannas, and skinny black ties, we recognize his familiar rotten core. In fact, we count on him to remain unchanged, as so few things do except at the movies. There's a perverse satisfaction or warped comfort in his persistence; he's always there to remind us of our worst blight, our ugliest thoughts, and our most reprehensible greed. He's as timeless as some of the ingredients that combine to create him: poverty, ambition, homicide, and deceit. He remains the American dream turned on its head and enterprising youth run amok. He never grows up, gets wise, fully reforms, or says he's sorry.

Perhaps Martin Scorsese best sums up the permanence of the character, no matter how much his weaponry is upgraded or his rackets get a new product line. When Scorsese started out as a filmmaker, he dreamed of making a film that investigated the notorious street gangs that terrorized New York in the nineteenth century. He wanted to explore their violent street life, unchecked anger, desperation, ferocity, and lethal concepts of male camaraderie and neighborhood turf. Instead, he went on to make *Mean Streets* and *GoodFellas,* which looked at life in New York in the late twentieth century. His wise guys were no longer called Dead Rabbits or Five Pointers, and they no longer used bats for street fighting. Drive-by shootings and semiautomatic weapons had replaced hand-to-hand combat and rumbles using knives. But *Mean Streets* and *GoodFellas* ended up being about lowlifes living a violent street life; dealing with unchecked anger, desperation, and ferocity; and grappling with lethal concepts of male camaraderie and neighborhood affiliation. Not much had changed after all. In fact, *GoodFellas'* Tommy DeVito could trade places with Skinny the Rat from *The Regeneration* (1915) and the two characters would speak the same baneful language. They would share the same depravity, commit similarly gruesome crimes, and kill or be killed on the same grimy streets that are fated always to be mean.

As the future unfolds and a newly fashioned gangster menaces the screen Underworld—for those moviegoers among us who love to hate him—we too have a long memory and very high expectations. However, our demands haven't changed much more than his basic character: we still want the gangster to take us on that fast, forbidden ride into the darkness; to thrill and appall, shock and repulse, and always leave us feeling superior to him. And when his looting, scheming, and murdering is done, of course, we will expect him to sacrifice his life or his soul. If we've learned anything from the past 100 years, it's that crime doesn't pay, except in blood. But it's never our own, so keep shooting and keep the cameras rolling.

NOTES AND REFERENCES

Chapter 1

1. *Review of Reviews,* December 1908, 744–45, quoted in Garth Jowett, *Film: The Democratic Art* (Boston: Little, Brown, 1976), 44.
2. "The Ubiquitous Moving Picture," *American Magazine,* July 1913, 105, quoted in Jowett, *Film: The Democratic Art,* 42.
3. Jowett, *Film: The Democratic Art,* 45–46.
4. Lewis Jacobs, *The Rise of the American Film* (New York: Harcourt, Brace, 1939), 75.
5. Ibid., 153.
6. John Kobler, *Capone* (New York: Da Capo Press, 1971), 23.
7. Herbert Asbury, *The Gangs of New York* (New York: Alfred A. Knopf, 1928), introduction.
8. Charles Dickens, *American Notes and Pictures from Italy* (New York: Charles Scribner's Sons, 1898), 104–6.
9. Asbury, *Gangs of New York,* 40.
10. Ibid., see 114–16 for a comprehensive account of the street battle.
11. Ibid., 331.
12. Jack Warner with Dean Jennings, *My First Hundred Years in Hollywood* (New York: Random House, 1964), 35–36.
13. Adolph Zukor, *The Public Is Never Wrong* (New York: Putnam, 1953), 77.
14. John Drinkwater, *The Life and Adventures of Carl Laemmle* (New York: G. Putnam's Sons, 1931), quoted in Eugene Rosow, *Born to Lose: The Gangster Film in America* (New York: Oxford University Press, 1978), 63.
15. Terry Ramsaye, *A Million and One Nights* (New York: Simon and Schuster, 1926), 529.
16. Carlos Clarens, *Crime Movies* (London: W. W. Norton, 1980), 19.

Chapter 2

1. Francis Hackett, "Brotherly Love," *New Republic,* 20 March 1915, 185.
2. Frank Beaver, *On Film: A History of the Motion Picture.* (New York: McGraw-Hill; 1983), 86.
3. Richard Schickel, *D. W. Griffith: An American Life* (New York: Simon and Schuster, 1984), 177.
4. Tom Gunning, *D. W. Griffith and the Origins of American Narrative Film* (Urbana, Ill.: University of Illinois Press, 1991), 274.
5. Film intertitle, quoted in Scott Simmon, *The Films of D. W. Griffith* (New York: Cambridge University Press, 1993), 50.
6. Bill Severn, *The End of the Roaring Twenties: Prohibition and Repeal,* (New York: Julian Messner, 1969), 76–80.
7. Ibid., 101.
8. Ibid., 106–9 and 124–26.
9. William Edward Leuchtenburg, *The Perils of Prosperity* (Chicago: University of Chicago Press, 1958), 101.
10. Anthony Comstock, *Traps for the Young,* ed. Robert Bremner (Cambridge, Mass.: Belknap Press of Harvard University Press, 1967), 22.
11. Frederick Lewis Allen, *Only Yesterday* (New York: Harper and Brothers, 1931), 92.

12. Ibid., 93.
13. Jowett, *Film: The Democratic Art,* 123.
14. Clarens, *Crime Movies,* 31.
15. Richard Corliss, *Talking Pictures* (Newton-Abbott, England: David and Charles, 1975), 7.
16. Clarens, *Crime Movies,* 34.
17. Intertitle, quoted in Rosow, *Born to Lose,* 86.
18. Jacobs, *Rise of the American Film,* 408.
19. John McCarty, *Hollywood Gangland* (New York: St. Martin's Press, 1993), 26.
20. Ibid., 28–29.
21. Ephraim Katz, *The Film Encyclopedia* (New York: Perigee Books, Putnam, 1979), 1105.
22. David Thomson, *America in the Dark* (London: Hutchinson, 1977), 98.
23. Kobler, *Capone,* 25–26.
24. Cochran, Thomas Childs, *The Age of Enterprise: A Social History of Industrial America* (New York: Harper and Row, 1961), 157.
25. Quoted in Richard Campbell, *Sixty Minutes and the News* (Urbana, Ill.: University of Illinois Press, 1991), 137.
26. "The Vanderbilt Memorial," *The Nation,* 18 November 1869, quoted in Rosow, *Born to Lose,* 34.

Chapter 3

1. Raymond Moley, *The Hays Office* (New York: Bobbs-Merrill, 1945), 62.
2. Jacobs, *Rise of the American Film,* 409.
3. Ibid., 397.
4. Rosow, *Born to Lose,* 103.
5. Ibid., 118.
6. Clarens, *Crime Movies,* 85.
7. Charles Higham, *Warner Brothers* (New York: Charles Scribner's Sons, 1975), 89.
8. Gerald Peary, "Rico Rising: Little Caesar Takes Over the Screen," in *The Classic American Novel and the Movies,* ed. Gerald Peary and Roger Shatzkin (New York: Frederick Ungar Publishing Company, 1977), 286.
9. Francis Faragoh, *Little Caesar,* ed. Gerald Peary (Madison: University of Wisconsin Press, 1981), 25.
10. Richard Watts for *New York Herald Tribune,* 10 January 1931, in Stanley Kaufmann, *American Film Criticism* (New York: Liveright, 1972), 248.
11. John H. Lyle, *The Dry and Lawless Years* (Englewood Cliffs, N.J.: Prentice-Hall, 1960), 116.
12. Garth Jowett, "Bullets, Beer, and the Hays Office: Public Enemy," in *American History/American Film,* ed. John O'Connor and Martin Jackson (New York: Frederick Ungar, 1979), 60.
13. James Shelley Hamilton for *National Board of Review Magazine,* May 1931, in Kaufmann, *American Film Criticism,* 252.
14. Watts for *New York Herald Tribune,* 24 April 1931, in Kaufmann, *American Film Criticism,* 250–51.
15. Stanley J. Solomon, *Beyond Formula: American Film Genre* (New York: Harcourt Brace Jovanovich, 1976), 174.
16. Lincoln Kirstein for *Hound and Horn,* April/June 1932, quoted in Kaufmann, *American Film Criticism,* 263–64.
17. John Mosher for *New Yorker,* 28 May 1932, in Kaufmann, *American Film Criticism,* 261.
18. Clarens, *Crime Movies,* 86.
19. Rosow, *Born to Lose,* 209.
20. Clarens, *Crime Movies,* 93.

21. Rosow, *Born to Lose,* 210.
22. Kubec Glasmon, John Bright, and Harvey Thew, *The Public Enemy,* ed. Henry Cohen (Madison: University of Wisconsin Press, 1981), 19.
23. Rosow, *Born to Lose,* 104.
24. Jacques Becker, Jacques Rivette, and Francois Truffaut, "Howard Hawks," in *Interviews with Film Directors,* ed. Andrew Sarris (New York: Bobbs-Merrill, 1967), 190–91.
25. Corliss, *Talking Pictures,* 7.
26. Peary, "Rico Rising," in *Classic American Novel and the Movies,* ed. Peary and Shatzkin, 292.
27. Quoted in Clarens, *Crime Movies,* 61.
28. Molly Haskell, *From Reverence to Rape: The Treatment of Women in the Movies* (Chicago: University of Chicago Press, 1987), 91.
29. Jay Robert Nash, *The Motion Picture Guide* (Chicago: Cinebooks, 1986), 2760.
30. Gerald Mast, quoted in Richard A. Blake, *Screening America* (Mahwah, N.J.: Paulist Press, 1991), 148.
31. Rosow, *Born to Lose,* 115.
32. Corliss, *Talking Pictures,* 10.
33. Howard Hawks, quoted in Nash, *The Motion Picture Guide,* 2762.
34. Hamilton in Kaufmann, *American Film Criticism,* 252.
35. Blake, *Screening America,* 148.

Chapter 4

1. Jowett, "Bullets, Beer, and the Hays Office," in *American History/American Film,* ed. O'Connor and Jackson, 75.
2. Moley, *Hays Office,* 81.
3. Jowett, *Film: The Democratic Art,* 248.
4. Rosow, *Born to Lose,* 100–101.
5. Paré Lorentz, *Lorentz on Film: Movies, 1927–1941* (New York: Hopkinson and Blake, 1975), 59.
6. Will H. Hays, *President's Report to the Motion Picture Producers and Distributors' Association* (New York: 1932), 21.
7. Hank Messick, "Gigolos and Gorillas," in *Beauties and the Beast: The Mob in Show Business* (New York: David McKay, 1973), quoted in Rosow, *Born to Lose,* 151–52.
8. Rosow, *Born to Lose,* 151.
9. Moley, *Hays Office,* 71.
10. Breen, quoted in Moley, *Hays Office,* 100.
11. Moley, *Hays Office,* 103.
12. Breen as quoted in Moley, *Hays Office,* 98.
13. Graham Greene, *The Graham Greene Film Reader,* ed. David Parkinson (Manchester, England: Carcanet Press, 1993), 161.
14. Ibid., 19.
15. John Baxter, *The Gangster Film* (London: Tantivy Press, 1970), 9–10.
16. Ibid., 11.
17. Clarens, *Crime Movies,* 135–37.
18. Herbert Blumer, *Movies, Delinquency, and Crime* (New York: Macmillan, 1933), 70.
19. Ibid., 14–17.
20. Stuart Kaminsky, *American Film Genres* (Dayton, Ohio: Pflaum Publishing, 1974), 16.
21. Blumer, *Movies, Delinquency, and Crime,*16.
22. W. W. Charters, *Motion Pictures and Youth* (New York: Macmillan, 1933), 18.
23. Phyllis Blanchard, *Child and Society* (New York: Longmans, Green, 1928), 191–95.
24. Greene, *Film Reader,* 377.
25. Robert Warshow, *The Immediate Experience* (Garden City, N.Y.: Doubleday, 1962), 131.

Chapter 5

1. Allen Eyles, *Humphrey Bogart* (London: Sphere Books, 1990), 32.
2. James Robert Parish and Michael R. Pitts, *The Great Gangster Pictures* (Metuchen, N.J.: Scarecrow Press, 1976), 311.
3. Eyles, *Humphrey Bogart,* 34.
4. Jack Shadoian, *Dreams and Dead Ends: The American Gangster/Crime Film* (Cambridge: MIT Press, 1977), 69.
5. Ibid., 82.
6. Paul Kooistra, *Criminals as Heroes: Structure, Power, and Identity* (Bowling Green, Ohio: Bowling Green State University Popular Press, 1989), 119.
7. William Edward Leuchtenburg, *Franklin D. Roosevelt and the New Deal* (New York: Harper and Row, 1963), 22.
8. Kooistra, *Criminals as Heroes,* 147.
9. John Huston and W. R. Burnett, *High Sierra,* ed. George Gomery (Madison: University of Wisconsin Press, 1979), 18.
10. Kooistra, *Criminals as Heroes,* 128–29.
11. John Toland, *The Dillinger Days* (New York: Random House, 1963), 174–75.
12. Kooistra, *Criminals as Heroes,* 156.
13. Ibid., 120.
14. Ibid., 141.
15. Baxter, *Gangster Film,* 11.
16. Parish and Pitts, *Great Gangster Pictures,* 317.
17. Kooistra, *Criminals as Heroes,* 137.
18. Michael Wallis, *Pretty Boy* (New York: St. Martin's Press, 1992), 354.
19. Jacobs, *Rise of the American Film,* 507–8.
20. R. Barton Palmer, *Hollywood's Dark Cinema* (New York: Twayne Publishers, 1994), 39.
21. Palmer, *Hollywood's Dark Cinema,* 33–35.
22. Robert Sklar, *Movie-Made America: A Cultural History of American Movies* (New York: Random House, 1976), 253.
23. Clarens, *Crime Movies,* 192.
24. Palmer, *Hollywood's Dark Cinema,* 50.
25. Katz, *Film Encyclopedia,* 591.
26. Eyles, *Humphrey Bogart,* 114.
27. Foster Hirsch, *The Dark Side of the Screen: Film Noir* (New York: Da Capo Press, 1981), 60.
28. Abraham Polonsky, *Force of Evil: The Critical Edition* (Northridge, Calif.: Center for Telecommunications Studies, California State University, 1996), 34.
29. Polonsky, introduction to *Force of Evil,* 7–8.

Chapter 6

1. Shadoian, *Dreams and Dead Ends,* 191.
2. Ibid.
3. James L. Neibaur, *Tough Guy: The American Movie Macho* (Jefferson, N.C.: McFarland, 1989), 19.
4. Shadoian, *Dreams and Dead Ends,* 173.
5. Nathaniel Benchley, *Humphrey Bogart* (Boston: Little, Brown, 1975), 159–60.
6. Shadoian, *Dreams and Dead Ends,* 168.
7. Rosow, *Born to Lose,* 129.
8. Robert B. Ray, *A Certain Tendency of the Hollywood Cinema: 1930–1980* (Princeton, N.J.: Princeton University Press, 1985), 140–41.
9. Sklar, *Movie-Made America,* 129.
10. Jowett, *Film: The Democratic Art,* 407.
11. Clarens, *Crime Movies,* 189–90.

12. Baxter, *Gangster Film,* 10.
13. Parish and Pitts, *Great Gangster Pictures,* 318.
14. Ibid., 10.
15. Ibid., 317.
16. David Halberstam, *The Fifties* (New York: Ballantine Books, 1993), 191–92.
17. Ibid., 193.
18. Eyles, *Humphrey Bogart,* 146.
19. Peter Manso, *Brando: The Biography* (New York: Hyperion, 1994), 378.
20. Neibaur, *Tough Guy,* 172.
21. Ibid., 169.
22. David Downing, *Marlon Brando* (New York: Stein and Day, 1984), 56.

Chapter 7

1. Rosow, *Born to Lose,* 155.
2. David E. Ruth, *Inventing the Public Enemy* (Chicago: University of Chicago Press, 1996), 117.
3. Parish and Pitts, *Great Gangster Pictures,* 423.
4. Ibid., 383.
5. McCarty, *Hollywood Gangland,* 123.
6. Clarens, *Crime Movies,* 259.
7. Raymond Lee and B. C. Van Hecke, *Gangsters and Hoodlums* (New York: Castle Books, A. S. Barnes, 1971), 16.
8. Clarens, *Crime Movies,* 259.
9. Lawrence L. Murray, "Hollywood, Nihilism, and the Youth Culture of the Sixties: *Bonnie and Clyde,*" in *American History/American Film,* ed. John O'Connor and Martin Jackson (New York: Frederick Ungar, 1979), 246.
10. Page Cook, "Bonnie and Clyde," *Films in Review,* October 1967, 505.
11. Rev. Anthony Schillacci, "*Bonnie and Clyde:* A Catholic Comment," *Film Comment,* Summer 1968, 49.
12. Charles Thomas Samuels, "Bonnie and Clyde," in *Focus on Bonnie and Clyde,* ed. John G. Cawelti (Englewood Cliffs, N.J.: Prentice-Hall, 1973), 92.
13. Ibid., 92.
14. Laurent Bouzereau, *Ultraviolent Movies* (Secaucus, N.J.: Carol Publishing Group, 1996), 4.
15. Jean-Louis Comolli and Andre S. Labarthe, "Bonnie and Clyde: An Interview with Arthur Penn," in *Focus on Bonnie and Clyde,* ed. John G. Cawelti (Englewood Cliffs, N.J.: Prentice-Hall, 1973), 16–17.
16. Emma Parker and Nell Barrow Cowan, *The True Story of Bonnie and Clyde,* ed. Jan I. Fortune (New York: New American Library, 1968), 148.
17. Jim Hillier, "Arthur Penn," in *Focus on Bonnie and Clyde,* ed. John G. Cawelti (Englewood Cliffs, N.J.: Prentice-Hall, 1973), 11.
18. Samuels, "Bonnie and Clyde," 89.
19. Wallis, *Pretty Boy,* 345.
20. Murray, "*Bonnie and Clyde,*" 247.
21. Hillier, "Arthur Penn," 14.
22. Ibid.
23. Murray, "*Bonnie and Clyde,*" 241.
24. John G. Cawelti, ed., *Focus on Bonnie and Clyde* (Englewood Cliffs, N.J.: Prentice-Hall, 1973), 139.
25. Faye Dunaway with Betsy Sharkey, *Looking for Gatsby* (New York: Simon and Schuster, 1995), 122–23.
26. Robert Shelton, "Record Companies Are Plugging *Bonnie and Clyde,*" *New York Times,* 11 March 1968, 46.
27. Shelton, "*Bonnie and Clyde,*" 46.

28. Murray, "*Bonnie and Clyde,*" 249.
29. Ibid., 248.
30. James Childs, "Closet Outlaws," *Film Comment,* March-April 1973, 19–20.
31. Hillier, "Arthur Penn," 8–9.
32. Ibid., 11.
33. Ray, *Hollywood Cinema: 1930–1980,* 273–74.
34. Ibid., 274.
35. Ibid., 275.
36. Mark Thomas McGee, *Roger Corman: The Best of the Cheap Acts* (Jefferson, N.C.: McFarland, 1988), 95.
37. Douglas Brode, *Money, Women, and Guns* (New York: Carol Publishing Group, 1995), 74.

Chapter 8

1. David Ansen, "Martin Scorsese," *Interview,* January 1987, 50.
2. Haig Manoogian, *The Film Maker's Art* (New York: Basic Books, 1966), 29.
3. Les Keyser, *Martin Scorsese* (New York: Twayne Publishers, 1992), 12.
4. Ibid., 16.
5. Ibid.
6. Mary Pat Kelly, *Martin Scorsese: The First Decade* (Pleasantville, N.Y.: Redgrave, 1980), 14.
7. Keyser, *Martin Scorsese,* 30–31.
8. Mark Carducci, "Martin Scorsese," *Millimeter,* May 1975, 12.
9. Jeffrey Lyons, "*Boxcar Bertha,*" *Rock,* 25 September 1972, 8.
10. George Hickenlooper, *Reel Conversations* (Secaucus, N.J.: Carol Publishing Group, 1991), 18.
11. Ruth, *Inventing the Public Enemy,* 61.
12. Harlan Lebo, *The Godfather Legacy* (New York: Simon and Schuster, 1997), 2.
13. Richard Schickel and John Simon, *Film 67/68* (New York: Simon and Schuster, 1968), 529.
14. Lee Lourdeaux, *Italian and Irish Filmmakers in America* (Philadelphia: Temple University Press, 1990), 186.
15. Lebo, *Godfather Legacy,* 206.
16. Jeffrey Chown, *Hollywood Auteur* (New York: Praeger, 1988), 59.
17. Lebo, *Godfather Legacy,* 202.
18. John Hess, "*Godfather II:* A Deal Coppola Couldn't Refuse," in *Movies and Methods,* ed. Bill Nichols (Berkeley, Calif.: University of California Press, 1976), 83.
19. Manohla Dargis, "Dark Side of the Dream," *Sight and Sound,* August 1996, 17.
20. Quoted in Peter Biskind, *The Godfather Companion* (New York: HarperPerennial, 1990), 121.
21. Quoted in Michael Goodwin and Naomi Wise, *On the Edge: The Life and Times of Francis Coppola* (New York: William Morrow, 1989), 184.
22. Robert Johnson, *Francis Ford Coppola* (Boston: Twayne Publishers, 1977), 148.
23. Amy Taubin, "Blood and Pasta," *New Statesman and Society,* 9 November 1990, 13.
24. William S. Pechter, "*Godfather II,*" *Commentary,* March 1975, 79.
25. Lebo, *Godfather Legacy,* 191.

Chapter 9

1. Katz, *Film Encyclopedia,* 713.
2. Georgia A. Brown, "Obsession," *American Film,* December 1983, 32.
3. Bruce Weber, "Cool Head, Hot Images," *New York Times Magazine,* 21 May 1989, 116.
4. Katz, *Film Encyclopedia,* 330.
5. Joseph Gelmis, *The Film Director as Superstar* (London: Secker and Warburg, 1970), 29.

6. Frank Beaver, *Oliver Stone: Wakeup Cinema* (New York: Twayne Publishers, 1994), 58.
7. Bouzereau, *Ultraviolent Movies,* 66.
8. Ronald Koziol and Edward Baumann, "How Frank Nitti Met His Fate," *Chicago Tribune,* 29 June 1987, Tempo section.
9. Tom Mathews, "The Mob at the Movies," *Newsweek,* 22 June 1987, 64.
10. Laura Shapiro with Ray Sawhill, "The First Untouchable of Them All," *Newsweek,* 22 June 1987, 68.
11. Michael Wilmington, "Films That Went Splat," *Chicago Tribune,* 14 April 1996.
12. Beaver, *Oliver Stone: Wakeup Cinema,* 59.
13. Quoted in Brode, *Money, Women, and Guns,* 119.
14. John Blades, "One Man's Mafia," *Chicago Tribune,* 9 August 1996, Tempo section.

Chapter 10

1. Goodwin and Wise, *Francis Coppola,* 262.
2. Chown, *Hollywood Auteur,* 72.
3. Keith McKay, *Robert De Niro: The Hero behind the Masks* (New York: St. Martin's Press, 1986), 2.
4. Kelly, *Martin Scorsese: The First Decade,* 1.
5. Kathleen Murphy, "Made Men," *Film Comment,* September–October 1990, 28.
6. Martin Scorsese, interview by Ian Christie, *Sight and Sound,* January 1996; reprinted in the introduction to the published script of *Casino* by Nicholas Pileggi and Martin Scorsese (London: Faber and Faber, 1996).
7. Bouzereau, *Ultraviolent Movies,* 111–12.

Chapter 11

1. James R. Nesteby, *Black Images in American Films, 1896–1954* (Lanham, Md.: University Press of America, 1982), 75.
2. Jesse Algernon Rhines, *Black Film/White Money* (New Brunswick, N.J.: Rutgers University Press, 1996), 31.
3. Ibid., 32.
4. Rosow, *Born to Lose,* 279.
5. Nelson George, *Blackface* (New York: HarperCollins, 1994), 21.
6. Mark A. Reid, *Redefining Black Film* (Berkeley, Calif.: University of California Press, 1993), 84.
7. Darius James, *That's Blaxploitation!* (New York: St. Martin's Griffin, 1995), 32.
8. George, *Blackface,* 57.
9. Christopher John Farley, "Which Side You On?" *Time,* 19 September 1994, 76.
10. Paul D. Colford, "Barry Michael Cooper's *New Jack* Thing," *Newsday,* 14 June 1990, 4.
11. Jacquie Jones, "The New Ghetto Aesthetic," *Wide Angle,* July–October 1991, 35.
12. Hal Hinson, "*New Jack City*: Into the Raw Heat," *Washington Post,* 8 March 1991, D1.
13. David Mills, "The Ace behind *New Jack:* Mario Van Peebles, Director," *Washington Post,* 10 March 1991, G1.
14. David Klinghoffer, "As a Filmmaker, Mario Van Peebles Isn't His Father's Son," *The Washington Times,* 7 March 1991, E1.
15. Mills, "Mario Van Peebles," G1.
16. Janice C. Simpson, "Not Just One of the Boyz," *Time,* 23 March 1992, 60.
17. Quoted in George, *Blackface,* 56.

Chapter 12

1. Dave Kehr, "*Crossing* in Style Superb Engineering, But Where's the Human Side?" *Chicago Tribune,* 5 October 1990.

2. Parish and Pitts, *Great Gangster Pictures,* 214.
3. John Gorman, "Rags-to-Riches Tale Over for Drug Boss," *Chicago Tribune,* 11 November 1990.
4. V. Dion Haynes, "L.A. Anti-gang Plan," *Chicago Tribune,* 30 May 1997.
5. Maitland McDonagh, "Sad Girls," *Film Comment,* September–October 1994, 75.
6. McDonagh, "Sad Girls," 76.
7. Pierre Briancon, "Russian Mob Scene," *World Press Review,* October 1995, 28.

Chapter 13

1. Paul A. Woods, *King Pulp: The World of Quentin Tarantino* (New York: Thunder's Mouth Press, 1996).
2. Ibid., 113.
3. Ibid., 34, 36.
4. Jami Bernard, *Quentin Tarantino: The Man and His Movies* (New York: HarperPerennial, 1995), 151–52.
5. Woods, *Quentin Tarantino,* 16.
6. Bernard, *Quentin Tarantino,* 212.
7. Ibid., 107.
8. Teresa Wiltz, "Romancing the Mob," *Chicago Tribune,* 5 March 1987, Tempo section.

SELECTED BIBLIOGRAPHY

BOOKS

Allen, Frederick Lewis. *Only Yesterday.* New York: Harper and Brothers, 1931.

Alloway, Lawrence. *Violent America: The Movies, 1946–1964.* New York: Museum of Modern Art, 1971.

Asbury, Herbert. *The Gangs of New York.* New York: Alfred A. Knopf, 1928.

Bambara, Toni Cade. *Tales and Stories for Black Folks.* Garden City, N.Y.: Zenith Books, 1971.

Baxter, John. *Hollywood in the Thirties.* New York: A. S. Barnes, 1968.

———. *The Gangster Film.* London: Tantivy Press, 1970.

———. *Sixty Years of Hollywood.* Cranbury, N.J.: A. S. Barnes, 1973.

Beaver, Frank. *Dictionary of Film Terms.* New York: McGraw-Hill, 1983.

———. *On Film: A History of the Motion Picture.* New York: McGraw-Hill, 1983.

———. *Oliver Stone: Wakeup Cinema.* New York: Twayne Publishers, 1994.

Benchley, Nathaniel. *Humphrey Bogart.* Boston: Little, Brown, 1975.

Bergman, Andrew. *We're in the Money: Depression America and Its Films.* New York: New York University Press, 1971.

———. *James Cagney.* New York: Pyramid Publications, 1973.

Bergreen, Laurence. *Capone: The Man and the Era.* New York: Simon and Schuster, 1994.

Bernard, Jami. *Quentin Tarantino: The Man and His Movies.* New York: HarperPerennial, 1995.

Bing, Leon. *Do or Die.* New York: HarperCollins, 1991.

Biskind, Peter. *The Godfather Companion.* New York: HarperPerennial, 1990.

Blake, Richard A. *Screening America.* Mahwah, N.J.: Paulist Press, 1991.

Blanchard, Phyllis. *Child and Society.* New York: Longmans, Green, 1928.

Bliss, Michael. *Brian De Palma.* Metuchen, N.J.: Scarecrow Press, 1983.

———. *Martin Scorsese and Michael Cimino.* Metuchen, N.J.: Scarecrow Press, 1985.

Blumer, Herbert. *Movies, Delinquency, and Crime.* New York: Macmillan, 1933.

Bouzereau, Laurent. *The De Palma Cut.* New York: Dembner Books, 1988.

———. *Ultraviolent Movies.* Secaucus, N.J.: Carol Publishing Group, 1996.

Brode, Douglas, *Money, Women, and Guns.* New York: Carol Publishing Group, 1995.

Brown, Gene. *Movie Time.* New York: Macmillan, 1995.

Cagney, James. *Cagney by Cagney.* New York: Doubleday, 1976.

Campbell, Richard. *Sixty Minutes and the News.* Urbana, Ill.: University of Illinois Press, 1991.

Capra, Frank. *Frank Capra: The Name above the Title.* New York: Macmillan, 1971.

Cawelti, John G., ed. *Focus on Bonnie and Clyde.* Englewood Cliffs, N.J.: Prentice-Hall, 1973.

Charters, W. W. *Motion Pictures and Youth.* New York: Macmillan, 1933.

Chown, Jeffrey. *Hollywood Auteur: Francis Ford Coppola.* New York: Praeger, 1988.

Clarens, Carlos. *Crime Movies.* London: W. W. Norton, 1980.

Cochran, Thomas Childs. *The Age of Enterprise: A Social History of Industrial America.* New York: Harper and Row, 1961.

Coen, Joel, and Ethan Coen. *Barton Fink and Miller's Crossing.* London: Faber and Faber, 1991.

Comstock, Anthony. *Traps for the Young.* Edited by Robert Bremner. Cambridge, Mass.: Belknap Press of Harvard University Press, 1967.

Connelly, Marie Katheryn. *Martin Scorsese.* Jefferson, N.C.: McFarland, 1993.

Cook, Bruce. *The Beat Generation.* New York: Quill (William Morrow), 1994.

Corliss, Richard. *Talking Pictures.* New York: Overlook Press, 1974.

Cripps, Thomas. *Black Film as Genre.* Bloomington: Indiana University Press, 1978.

———. *Making Movies Black.* New York: Oxford University Press, 1993.
Crowther, Bosley. *The Great Films: Fifty Golden Years of Motion Pictures.* New York: Putnam, 1967.
Diawara, Manthia. *African Cinema: Politics and Culture.* Bloomington, Ind.: Indiana University Press, 1992.
———, ed. *Black American Cinema.* New York: Routledge, 1993.
Dickens, Charles. *American Notes and Pictures from Italy.* New York: Charles Scribner's Sons, 1898.
Downing, David. *Marlon Brando.* New York: Stein and Day, 1984.
Dunaway, Faye, with Betsy Sharkey. *Looking for Gatsby.* New York: Simon and Schuster, 1995.
Ebert, Roger. *Roger Ebert's Movie Home Companion.* Kansas City, Mo.: Andrews, McMeel and Parker, 1988.
Ehrenstein, David. *The Scorsese Picture.* New York: Carol Publishing Group, 1992.
Everson, William K. *The Bad Guys.* Secaucus, N.J.: Citadel Press, 1974.
Eyles, Allen. *Humphrey Bogart.* London: Sphere Books, 1990.
Faragoh, Francis. *Little Caesar.* Edited by Gerald Peary. Madison: University of Wisconsin Press, 1981.
Film Notes: The Silent Film. New York: Museum of Modern Art, 1949.
Freedland, Michael. *James Cagney.* London: W. H. Allen, 1974.
Gambino, Richard. *Blood of My Blood: The Dilemma of the Italian-Americans.* Garden City, N.Y.: Anchor Books, 1974.
Gelmis, Joseph, *The Film Director as Superstar.* London: Secker and Warburg, 1970.
George, Nelson. *Blackface.* New York: HarperCollins, 1994.
Goodwin, Michael, and Naomi Wise. *On the Edge: The Life and Times of Francis Coppola.* New York: William Morrow, 1989.
Greene, Graham. *Graham Greene on Film.* Edited by John Russell Taylor. New York: Simon and Schuster, 1972.
———. *The Graham Greene Film Reader.* Edited by David Parkinson. Manchester, England: Carcanet Press, 1993.
Guerrero, Ed. *Framing Blackness.* Philadelphia: Temple University Press, 1993.
Gunning, Tom. *D. W. Griffith and the Origins of American Narrative Film.* Urbana, Ill.: University of Illinois Press, 1991.
Hadley-Garcia, George. *Hispanic Hollywood.* New York: Carol Publishing Group, 1993.
Halberstam, David. *The Fifties.* New York: Ballantine Books, 1993.
Hammer, Richard. *Playboy's Illustrated History of Organized Crime.* Chicago: Playboy Press, 1975.
Harris, John. *The Family: A Social History of the Twentieth Century.* New York: Oxford University Press, 1991.
Haskell, Molly. *From Reverence to Rape: The Treatment of Women in the Movies.* Chicago: University of Chicago Press, 1987.
Hayden, Tom. *Reunion.* New York: Random House, 1988.
Hays, Will H. *Motion Pictures.* Garden City, N.Y.: Published for the American Institute of the City of New York by Doubleday, Doran, 1929.
———. *President's Report to the Motion Picture Producers and Distributors' Association.* New York: 1932.
———. *Memoirs.* New York: Doubleday, 1955.
Hecht, Ben. *A Child of the Century.* New York: Simon and Schuster, 1954.
Henderson, Robert M. *D. W. Griffith: The Years at Biograph.* New York: Farrar, 1970.
Hickenlooper, George. *Reel Conversations.* Secaucus, N.J.: Carol Publishing Group, 1991.
Higham, Charles. *Hollywood in the Forties.* New York: A. S. Barnes, 1968.
———. *Warner Brothers.* New York: Charles Scribner's Sons, 1975.
Hirsch, Foster. *The Dark Side of the Screen: Film Noir.* New York: Da Capo Press, 1981.
Huston, John, and W. R Burnett. *High Sierra.* Edited by George Gomery. Madison: University of Wisconsin Press, 1979.
Jacobs, Diane. *Hollywood Renaissance.* South Brunswick, N.J.: A. S. Barnes, 1977.
Jacobs, Lewis. *The Rise of the American Film.* New York: Harcourt, Brace, 1939.
Jakubowski, Maxim. *The Mammoth Book of Pulp Fiction.* New York: Carroll and Graf, 1996.

James, Darius. *That's Blaxploitation!* New York: St. Martin's Griffin, 1995.
Johnson, Robert. *Francis Ford Coppola.* Boston: Twayne Publishers, 1977.
Josephson, Matthew. *The Robber Barons.* New York: Harcourt, Brace, 1934.
Jowett, Garth. *Film: The Democratic Art.* Boston: Little, Brown, 1976.
Kael, Pauline. *Kiss Kiss Bang Bang.* New York: Little, Brown, 1968.
———. *Deeper into Movies.* New York: Bantam, 1973.
———. *Reeling.* New York: Warner Books, 1976.
———. *State of the Art.* New York: E. P. Dutton, 1985.
———. *5001 Nights at the Movies.* New York: Henry Holt, 1991.
———. *Going Steady.* New York: Marion Boyars Publishers, 1994.
Kaminsky, Stuart M. *American Film Genres.* Dayton, Ohio: Pflaum Publishing, 1974.
Karpf, Stephen Louis. *The Gangster Film: Emergence, Variation, and Decay of a Genre, 1930–1940.* New York: Arno Press, 1973.
Katz, Ephraim. *The Film Encyclopedia.* New York: Perigee Books, 1979.
Kauffmann, Stanley, with Bruce Henstell. *American Film Criticism.* New York: Liveright, 1972.
———. *A World on Film.* New York: Delta, 1967.
Kefauver, Estes. *Crime in America.* Garden City, N.Y.: Doubleday, 1951.
Kelly, Mary Pat. *Martin Scorsese: The First Decade.* Pleasantville, N.Y.: Redgrave, 1980.
———. *Martin Scorsese: A Journey.* New York: Thunder's Mouth Press, 1996.
Keyser, Les. *Martin Scorsese.* New York: Twayne Publishers, 1992.
Keyser, Les, and Barbara Keyser. *Hollywood and the Catholic Church: The Image of Roman Catholicism in American Movies.* Chicago: Loyola University Press, 1984.
Kobler, John. *Capone.* New York: Da Capo Press, 1971.
Kohn, George. *Dictionary of Culprits and Criminals.* Metuchen, N.J.: Scarecrow Press, 1986.
Kolker, Robert Phillip. *A Cinema of Loneliness: Penn, Kubrik, Coppola, Scorsese, Altman.* New York: Oxford University Press, 1988.
Kooistra, Paul. *Criminals as Heroes: Structure, Power, and Identity.* Bowling Green, Ohio: Bowling Green State University Popular Press, 1989.
Kracauer, Siegfried. *From Caligari to Hitler: A Psychological History of the German Film.* Princeton, N.J.: Princeton University Press, 1947.
———. *Theory of Film.* New York: Oxford University Press, 1980.
Langman, Larry, and Daniel Finn. *A Guide to American Silent Crime Films.* Westport, Conn.: Greenwood Press, 1994.
Lebo, Harlan. *The Godfather Legacy.* New York: Simon and Schuster, 1997.
Lee, Raymond, and B. C. Van Hecke. *Gangsters and Hoodlums.* New York: Castle Books, A. S. Barnes, 1971.
Leuchtenburg, William Edward. *The Perils of Prosperity.* Chicago: University of Chicago Press, 1958.
———. *Franklin D. Roosevelt and the New Deal.* New York: Harper and Row, 1963.
Loeb, Anthony, ed. *Filmmakers in Conversation.* Chicago: Columbia College Press, 1980.
Lorentz, Paré. *Lorentz on Film: Movies, 1927–1941.* New York: Hopkinson and Blake, 1975.
Lourdeaux, Lee. *Italian and Irish Filmmakers in America.* Philadelphia: Temple University Press, 1990.
Lyle, John H. *The Dry and Lawless Years.* Englewood Cliffs, N.J.: Prentice-Hall, 1960.
Man, Glenn. *Radical Visions: American Film Renaissance, 1967–1976.* Westport, Conn.: Greenwood Press, 1994.
Manoogian, Haig P. *The Film Maker's Art.* New York: Basic Books, 1966.
Manso, Peter. *Brando: The Biography.* New York: Hyperion, 1994.
Mardsen, Michael T., John G. Nachbar, and Sam. L. Grogg Jr. *Movies as Artifacts: Cultural Criticism of Popular Film.* Chicago: Nelson-Hall, 1982.
McArthur, Colin. *Underworld U.S.A.* New York: Viking Press, 1972.
McCarthy, Todd, and Charles Flynn. *King of the Bs: Working within the Hollywood System.* New York: E. P. Dutton, 1975.
McCarty, John. *Hollywood Gangland.* New York: St. Martin's Press, 1993.

McGee, Mark Thomas. *Roger Corman: The Best of the Cheap Acts.* Jefferson, N.C.: McFarland, 1988.
McKay, Keith. *Robert De Niro: The Hero behind the Masks.* New York: St. Martin's Press, 1986.
Messick, Hank, and Burt Goldblatt. *The Mobs and the Mafia.* New York: Ballantine, 1972.
Mills, C. Wright. *The Power Elite.* New York: Oxford University Press, 1956.
Moley, Raymond. *The Hays Office.* New York: Bobbs-Merrill, 1945.
Monaco, James. *The New Wave.* New York: Oxford University Press, 1976.
———. *How to Read a Film.* New York: Oxford University Press, 1977.
———. *American Film Now: The People, the Power, the Money, the Movies.* New York: Oxford University Press, 1979.
Murray, Edward. *The Film Classics.* New York: Frederick Ungar, 1978.
Murray, James T. *To Find an Image: Black Films from Uncle Tom to Superfly.* New York: Bobbs-Merrill, 1973.
Nash, Jay Robert. *Citizen Hoover.* Chicago: Nelson-Hall, 1972.
———. *Bloodletters and Badmen.* New York: M. Evans, 1973.
———. *Murder, America: Homicide in the United States from the Revolution to the Present.* New York: Simon and Schuster, 1980.
———. *Almanac of World Crime.* Garden City, N.Y.: Anchor Press, 1981.
———. *The Dillinger Dossier.* Highland Park, Ill.: December Press, 1983.
———. *Jay Robert Nash's Crime Chronology: A Worldwide Report, 1900–1983.* New York: Facts on File Publications, 1984.
———. *The Motion Picture Guide.* Chicago: Cinebooks, 1985.
———. *Dictionary of Crime: Criminal Justice, Criminology, and Law Enforcement.* New York: Paragon House, 1992.
Neibaur, James L. *Tough Guy: The American Movie Macho.* Jefferson, N.C.: McFarland, 1989.
Ness, Eliot, with Oscar Fraley. *The Untouchables.* New York: Julian Messner, 1957.
Nesteby, James R. *Black Images in American Films, 1896–1954.* Lanham, Md.: University Press of America, 1982.
New York Times Film Reviews, 1913–1990. New York: *New York Times*/Arno Press, 1970–1990.
Nichols, Bill, ed. *Movies and Methods.* Berkeley, Calif.: University of California Press, 1976.
O'Connor, John E., ed. *American History/American Film.* New York: Frederick Ungar, 1979.
Ottoson, Robert. *A Reference Guide to the American Film Noir: 1940–1958.* Metuchen, N.J.: Scarecrow Press, 1981.
Palmer, R. Barton. *Hollywood's Dark Cinema.* New York: Twayne Publishers, 1994.
Parish, James Robert, and Michael R. Pitts. *The Great Gangster Pictures.* Metuchen, N.J.: Scarecrow Press, 1976.
Parker, Emma, and Nell Barrow Cowan. *The True Story of Bonnie and Clyde.* Edited by Jan I. Fortune. New York: New American Library, 1968.
Peary, Gerald, and Roger Shatzkin, eds. *The Classic American Novel and the Movies.* New York: Frederick Ungar, 1977.
Pileggi, Nicholas, and Martin Scorsese. *Casino.* London: Faber and Faber, 1996.
Pistone, Joseph, with Richard Woodley. *Donnie Brasco.* New York: Penguin Books, 1989.
Polonsky, Abraham. *Force of Evil: The Critical Edition.* Northridge, Calif.: Center for Telecommunication Studies, California State University Press, 1996.
Puzo, Mario. *The Godfather.* New York: Putnam, 1969.
———. *The Godfather Papers.* Greenwich: Fawcett, 1972.
Pye, Michael, and Lynda Myles. *The Movie Brats: How the Film Generation Took Over Hollywood.* New York: Holt, Rinehart and Winston, 1979.
Ramsaye, Terry. *A Million and One Nights.* New York: Simon and Schuster, 1926.
Ray, Robert B. *A Certain Tendency of the Hollywood Cinema, 1930–1980.* Princeton, N.J.: Princeton University Press, 1985.
Reader, Keith. *Cultures on Celluloid.* London: Quartet Books, 1981.
Reid, Mark A. *Redefining Black Film.* Berkeley, Calif.: University of California Press, 1993.

Rhines, Jesse Algernon. *Black Film/White Money.* New Brunswick, N.J.: Rutgers University Press, 1996.
Riis, Jacob. *The Battle with the Slum.* New York: Macmillan, 1902.
———. *How the Other Half Lives.* New York: Dover Publications, 1971.
Rosow, Eugene. *Born to Lose: The Gangster Film in America.* New York: Oxford University Press, 1978.
Ruth, David E. *Inventing the Public Enemy.* Chicago: University of Chicago Press, 1996.
Samuels, Charles Thomas. *A Casebook on Film.* New York: Van Nostrand Reinhold, 1970.
Sante, Luc. *Low Life: Lures and Snares of Old New York.* New York: Vintage Books, Random House, 1991.
Sarris, Andrew. *The Films of Josef von Sternberg.* New York: Museum of Modern Art, 1966.
———. *The American Cinema: Directors and Directions 1929–1968.* New York. E. P. Dutton, 1968.
———, ed. *Interviews with Film Directors.* New York: Bobbs-Merrill, 1967.
Schatz, Thomas. *Hollywood Genres: Formulas, Filmmaking, and the Studio System.* Philadelphia: Temple University Press, 1981.
Schickel, Richard. *D. W. Griffith: An American Life.* New York: Simon and Schuster, 1984.
Schickel, Richard, and John Simon. *Film 67/68.* New York: Simon and Schuster, 1968.
Schulberg, Budd. *On the Waterfront.* Hollywood, Calif.: Samuel French, 1980.
Scorsese, Martin. *Scorsese on Scorsese.* Edited by David Thomson and Ian Christie. London: Faber and Faber, 1996.
Scorsese, Martin, and Nicholas Pileggi. *GoodFellas.* London: Faber and Faber, 1990.
Severn, Bill. *The End of the Roaring Twenties: Prohibition and Repeal.* New York: Julian Messner, 1969.
Shadoian, Jack. *Dreams and Dead Ends: The American Gangster/Crime Film.* Cambridge: MIT Press, 1977.
Simmon, Scott. *The Films of D. W. Griffith.* New York: Cambridge University Press, 1993.
Sinclair, Andrew. *Era of Excess: A Social History of the Prohibition Movement.* New York: Harper and Row, 1964.
Sklar, Robert. *Movie-Made America: A Cultural History of American Movies.* New York: Random House, 1976.
———. *City Boys: Cagney, Bogart, Garfield.* Princeton, N.J.: Princeton University Press, 1992.
Smith, Henry Nash. *Popular Culture in Industrial America.* New York: New York University Press, 1967.
Solomon, Stanley J. *Beyond Formula: American Film Genre.* New York: Harcourt Brace Jovanovich, 1976.
Stevens, Michael L. *Gangster Films.* Jefferson, N.C.: McFarland, 1996.
Talbot, Daniel, ed. *Film: An Anthology.* Berkeley: University of California Press, 1966.
Tarantino, Quentin. *Reservoir Dogs and True Romance.* New York: Grove Press, 1994.
———. *Pulp Fiction: A Quentin Tarantino Screenplay.* Hyperion, N.Y.: Miramax Books, 1994.
Theoharis, Athan. *The Boss: J. Edgar Hoover and the Great American Inquisition.* Philadelphia: Temple University Press, 1988.
Thew, Harvey. *The Public Enemy.* Edited by Henry Cohen. Madison: University of Wisconsin Press, 1981.
Thompson, Frank T. *William Wellman.* Metuchen, N.J.: Scarecrow Press, 1983.
Thomson, David. *American in the Dark.* London: Hutchinson, 1977.
———. *Overexposures: The Crisis in American Filmmaking.* New York: William Morrow, 1981.
Time-Life Books' editors. *Mafia.* Alexandria, Va.: Time-Life Books, 1993.
Toback, James. *Bugsy.* New York: Carol Publishing Group, 1991.
Toland, John. *The Dillinger Days.* New York: Random House, 1963.
Treherne, J. E. *The Strange History of Bonnie and Clyde.* New York: Stein and Day, 1984.
Von Gunden, Kenneth. *Postmodern Auteurs.* Jefferson, N.C.: McFarland, 1991.
Walker, John, ed. *Halliwell's Film Guide.* New York: HarperPerennial, 1991.

Wallis, Michael. *Pretty Boy*. New York: St. Martin's Press, 1992.
Warner, Jack, with Dean Jennings. *My First Hundred Years in Hollywood*. New York: Random House, 1964.
Warshow, Robert. *The Immediate Experience*. Garden City, N.Y.: Doubleday, 1962.
Webb, Michael, ed. *Hollywood: Legend and Reality*. Boston: Little, Brown in association with the Smithsonian Institution, 1986.
Weiss, Marion. *Martin Scorsese: A Guide to References and Resources*. Boston: G. K. Hall, 1987.
Whitehead, Don. *The FBI Story*. New York: Random House, 1956.
Wilson, John F. *Public Religion in American Culture*. Philadelphia: Temple University Press, 1979.
Wood, Robin. *Arthur Penn*. New York: Frederick A. Praeger, 1969.
Woods, Paul A. *King Pulp: The World of Quentin Tarantino*. New York: Thunder's Mouth Press, 1996.
Zuker, Joel. *Francis Ford Coppola: A Guide to the References and Resources*. Boston: G. K. Hall, 1984.
Zukor, Adolph. *The Public Is Never Wrong*. New York: Putnam, 1953.

ARTICLES

"Alexandre Grant Knows the Hits in Brighton Beach." *New Yorker*, 2 May 1994.
Alleva, Richard. "The Master Misses: Scorsese's *Casino*." *Commonweal*, 12 January 1996.
Ansen, David. "Martin Scorsese." *Interview*, January 1987.
———. "Movies in the Global Film Market: Action Speaks Louder than Words." *Newsweek*, 19 February 1996.
———. "Pulp, Passion, Petty Hoods." *Newsweek*, 26 October 1992.
———. "Growing Up Wise in the Bronx." *Newsweek*, 4 October 1993.
———. "The Redemption of Pulp." *Newsweek*, 10 October 1994.
Ansen, David, and Charles Fleming. "A Tough Guy Takes Cannes." *Newsweek*, 6 June 1994.
Arnold, Gary. "*Pulp* Carries Tarantino to the Top." *Washington Times*, 9 October 1994.
———. "Bleak Debut for Gray in *Odessa*." *Washington Times*, 14 July 1995.
Avery, William. "Film Reviews." *Films in Review*, November 1973.
Bart, Peter. "Hollywood and the Mob." *Gentlemen's Quarterly*, June 1997.
Bayles, Martha. "A Def Ear." *Forbes*, 22 May 1995.
Belton, John. "Ideology and Cinematography in Hollywood, 1930–1939." *Film Quarterly*, 22 March 1995.
Benson, Sheila. "Girl Gangs Get Their Colors." *Interview*, June 1994.
Berman, Eric. "What's New at the Dogg House?" *Interview*, December 1996.
"Black Film Directors: That Hollywood Shuffle." *Economist*, 30 March 1991.
"Black Hollywood." *Movieline*, December 1996.
Braudy, Leo. "The Sacraments of Genre: Coppola, De Palma, Scorsese." *Film Quarterly*, Spring 1986.
Braudy, Susan. "Francis Ford Coppola: A Profile." *Atlantic*, August 1976.
Briançon, Pierre. "Russian Mob Scene." *World Press Review*, October 1995. First published in *Libération*, 13 April 1995.
"Brighton Beach Goodfellas." *Vanity Fair*, January 1993.
Brown, Georgia. "Obsession." *American Film*, December 1983.
Butler, Robert W. "*Pulp Fiction* Rings True." *Kansas City Star*, 9 October 1994.
Carducci, Mark. "Martin Scorsese." *Millimeter*, May 1975.
Carr, Jay. "Acting It Up in *Reservoir Dogs*." *Boston Globe*, 23 October 1992.
Carroll, Jon. "Coppola: Bringing in the Next Godfather." *New York*, 11 November 1974.
Chappell, Kevin. "What's Wrong (and Right) about Black Music." *Ebony*, September 1995.
Childs, James. "Closet Outlaws." *Film Comment*, March–April 1973.
Chute, David. "*Scarface*." *Film Comment*, January–February 1984.
Collier, Aldore. "What's behind the Black-on-Black Violence at Movie Theaters." *Ebony*, October 1991.
Combs, Richard, "*Year of the Dragon*." *Monthly Film Bulletin* 53 (January 1986).
Cook, Page. "*Bonnie and Clyde*." *Films in Review*, October 1967.

Cooper, Arthur. "A Trough between *New Waves.*" *Newsweek,* 15 October 1973.
Corliss, Richard. Excerpts from his M.F.A. essay on censorship. *Film Comment,* Summer 1968.
———. "Shooting Up the Box Office." *Time,* 22 June 1987.
———. ". . . And Blood." *Film Comment,* September–October 1988.
———. "Boyz of New Black City." *Time,* 17 June 1991.
———. "Extra! Billy Bathgate Lives!" *Time,* 4 November 1991.
———. "Adding Kick to the Chic." *Time,* 16 November 1992.
———. "Saturday Night Fever." *Time.* 6 June 1994.
———. "The Little Movies That Could." *Time,* 12 September 1994.
———. "A Blast to the Heart." *Time,* 10 October 1994.
Cott, Jonathan. "Francis Coppola." *Rolling Stone,* 18 March 1982.
Cowie, Peter. "*The Godfather.*" *Focus on Film* 11 (Autumn 1972).
Curtis, Quentin. "Blood and Guts in the Diner." *Independent,* 23 October 1994.
Dargis, Manohla. "Dark Side of the Dream." *Sight and Sound,* August 1996.
De Curtis, Anthony. "Martin Scorsese." *Rolling Stone,* 1 November 1990.
Dempsey, Michael, and Udayan Gupta. "Hollywood's Color Problem." *American Film,* April 1982.
Denby, David. "*Mean Streets:* The Sweetness of Hell." *Sight and Sound,* Winter 1973–1974.
———. "Mr. Vice Guy." *New York,* 23 March 1992.
———. *"Menace II Society." New York,* 31 May 1993.
———. "Boy and the Hood." *New York,* 18 October 1993.
De Stefano, George. "Family Lies." *Film Comment,* July–August 1987.
Dicker, Ron. "Hollywood's Hottest Gun." *San Francisco Examiner,* 6 October 1994.
"*Dogs* at War with the Censors." *Scotsman,* 22 January 1993.
Doherty, Thomas, and Jacquie Jones. "Two Takes on *Boyz N the Hood.*" *Cineaste,* December 1991.
Douglas, Susan. "Nightmares of Depravity." *Progressive,* August 1995.
Dyson, Michael Eric. "Male Youth in African American Cinema." *Sight and Sound,* October 1992.
Edwards, Bob. "Critics Praise *Little Odessa* but Call Movie 'Bleak.' " *National Public Radio,* 9 August 1995. (Program transcript includes interview with James Gray, Maximillian Schell, and Tim Roth.)
Farber, Stephen. "Coppola and *The Godfather.*" *Sight and Sound,* Autumn 1972.
Farley, Christopher John. "Which Side You On?" *Time,* 19 September 1994.
———. "Open Heart, Open Arms." *Time,* 18 December 1995.
Gabrenya, Frank. "*Pulp* Director: Tarantino Spins Old Plot Lines into Dizzying Orbits." *Columbus Dispatch,* 12 October 1994.
Garner, Jack. "Turning Pulp Passions into *Pulp Fiction.*" *Gannett News Service,* 13 October 1994.
Giles, Jeff. "A *Menace* Has Hollywood Seeing Double." *Newsweek,* 19 July 1993.
———. "Straight out of Compton." *Newsweek,* 31 October 1994.
Glicksman, Marlaine. "Getting down to the Bone." *Film Comment,* September–October 1990.
Grobel, Lawrence. "*Playboy* Interview: Al Pacino." *Playboy,* December 1979.
Hackett, Francis. "Brotherly Love." *New Republic,* 20 March 1915.
Hartl, John. "Touted *Little Odessa* Is a Grim Gangster Flick." *Seattle Times,* 8 September 1995.
Haskell, Molly. "World of *The Godfather:* No Place for Women." *New York Times,* 23 March 1997.
Hatch, Robert. "Films." *Nation,* 25 November 1973.
Hess, John. "*Godfather II:* A Deal Coppola Couldn't Refuse." *Jump-Cut,* no. 7, (May–June 1975).
"Hollywood Blackout." *People Weekly,* 18 March 1996.
"In Defence of Movie Violence." *Scotsman,* 4 February 1993.
Jacobson, Harlan. "You Talkin' to Me?" *Film Comment,* September–October 1988.
———. "A Heap of 'Trash Culture' on Film." *USA Today,* 23 September 1994.
Jaehne, Karen. "*Casino.*" *Film Quarterly,* Spring 1996.
Jameson, Richard T. "Chasing the Hat." *Film Comment,* September–October 1990.
Johnson, Albert. "*Bonnie and Clyde.*" *Film Quarterly,* Winter 1967–1968.

Johnson, Brian D. "Latin Lovers and Losers." *Maclean's,* 23 March 1992.
Johnson, Malcolm. "*Little Odessa* Filled with Grim Heartbreak." *Hartford Courant,* 14 July 1995.
Johnston, Sheila. "Crimes and Misdemeanours." *Independent,* 18 December 1992.
Jones, Jacquie. "The New Ghetto Aesthetic." *Wide Angle,* July–October 1991.
Kael, Pauline. "Fathers and Sons." *New Yorker,* 23 December 1974.
Kauffmann, Stanley. "*Mean Streets.*" *New Republic,* 27 October 1973.
———. "*The Godfather Pt. II.*" *New Republic,* 18 January 1975.
———. "Body Count." *New Republic,* 29 October 1990.
———. "Billionaires and Lesser Folk." *New Republic,* September 1991.
———. "The Sorcerer's Apprentice." *New Republic,* 25 November 1991.
———. "Late Winter Roundup." *New Republic,* 30 March 1992.
———. "*Reservoir Dogs.*" *New Republic,* 23 November 1992.
Keefe, Barrie. "Haunting Friday." *Sight and Sound,* August 1996.
Klinghoffer, David. "No Bad Rap for Preachy *Boyz.*" *Washington Times,* 12 July 1991.
———. "As a Filmmaker, Mario Van Peebles Isn't His Father's Son." *Washington Times,* 7 March 1991.
Kort, Michele. "Filmmaker Allison Anders: Her Crazy Life." *Ms,* May–June 1994.
Koszarski, Richard. "The Youth of F. F. Coppola." *Films in Review,* November 1968.
Kroll, Jack. "De Niro as Capone: The Magnificent Obsessive." *Newsweek,* 22 June 1987.
Landau, Jon. "Films: *Mean Streets.*" *Rolling Stone,* 8 November 1973.
LaSalle, Mick. "Does Violent Art Reflect Life?" *San Francisco Chronicle,* 20 November 1994.
———. "Brooklyn Hit Man Stuck in *Odessa:* Trite Film Has Strong Cast, Directing. *San Francisco Chronicle,* 2 June 1995.
———. "Scorsese's *Casino* Comes Up Broke." *San Francisco Chronicle,* 22 November 1995.
Latimer, Jonathan P. "*The Godfather:* Metaphor and Microcosm." *Journal of Popular Film,* Spring 1973.
Leland, John, with Abigail Kuflik and Karen Springen. "Night of the Living Crackheads." *Newsweek,* 3 March 1991.
Leland, John, with Donna Foote. "A Bad Omen for Black Movies?" *Newsweek,* 29 July 1991.
Light, Alan. "Ice-T." *Rolling Stone,* 20 August 1992.
Lui, Melinda, and Gregory L. Vistica. "Searching for a Covert Victory over the Mob." *Newsweek,* 17 June 1986.
Lyons, Jeffrey. "*Boxcar Bertha.*" *Rock,* 25 September 1972.
MacBride, Joseph. "Coppola Inc." *American Film,* November 1975.
"The Making of *The Godfather.*" *Time,* 13 March 1972.
Malcolm, Derek. "Way to Make a Killing." *Guardian,* 4 February 1993.
Mathews, Tom. "The Mob at the Movies." *Newsweek,* 22 June 1987.
Mathews, Tom, with Michael Reese and Janet Huck. "*The Untouchables.*" *Newsweek,* 22 June 1987.
McDonagh, Maitland. "Sad Girls." *Film Comment,* September–October 1994.
"The Millennium: A Conversation with Quentin Tarantino." *Newsweek,* 26 December 1994.
Murphy, Kathleen. "Made Men." *Film Comment,* September–October 1990.
Murray, Steve. "The '50s Revised." *Atlanta Journal and Constitution,* 1 November 1994.
Norman, Neil. "Tarantino Facts behind the Fiction." *Evening Standard,* 6 October 1994.
Orth, Maureen. "Godfather of the Movies." *Newsweek,* 25 November 1974.
Painton, Priscilla. "When Life Imitates Art." *Time,* 25 March 1991.
Peachment, Chris. "Still Crazy after All These Years." *Sunday Times* (London), 22 November 1992.
Pechter, William S. "Keeping Up with the Corleones." *Commentary,* July 1972.
———. "*Godfather II.*" *Commentary,* March 1975.
Perlow, Maris. "Casting Director Thinks Gotti's 'A Natural.' " *New York Daily News,* 9 April 1992.
Phillips, Mike. "Chic and Beyond." *Sight and Sound,* August 1996.

Pinchbeck, Daniel. "Power to the Peebles." *Esquire,* May 1995.
Powell, Bill. "Murder in Moscow." *Newsweek,* 25 November 1996.
Pulver, Andrew. "The Movie Junkie." *Guardian,* 19 September 1994.
Quart, Leonard, and Albert Auster. "*The Godfather Part II.*" *Cineaste,* December 1974.
Rafferty, Terry. "Men Overboard." *New Yorker,* October 1992.
———. "*Casino.*" *New Yorker,* 4 December 1995.
Rosen, Marjorie. "Francis Ford Coppola." *Film Comment,* July–August 1974.
———. "Martin Scorsese Interview." *Film Comment,* March–April 1975.
Rosenbaum, Jonathan. "*The Godfather Part II.*" *Sight and Sound,* Summer 1975.
Samuels, Allison and David Gates. "Last Tango in Compton." *Newsweek,* 25 November 1996.
Schickel, Richard. "A Closed Circle." *Time,* 5 November 1973.
———. "A Fable of Mean Streets. *Time,* 11 October 1993.
———. "Travolta Fever." *Time,* 16 October 1995.
Schillaci, Rev. Anthony. "*Bonnie and Clyde:* A Catholic Comment." *Film Comment,* Summer 1968.
Schlesinger, Arthur, Jr. "*The Godfather* Plays on Our Secret Admiration for Men Who Get What They Want." *Vogue,* May 1972.
Schoemer, Karen. "The 'L' Is for Lucky." *Newsweek,* 5 June 1995.
Schrader, Paul. "Notes on Film Noir." *Film Comment,* Spring 1972.
Schruers, Fred. "Travolta." *Rolling Stone,* February 1996.
Scorsese, Martin. "Martin Scorsese's Guilty Pleasures." *Film Comment,* September–October 1978.
———. "Scorsese on De Niro." *Esquire* (British edition), May 1977.
Shapiro, Laura, with Ray Sawhill. "The First Untouchable of Them All." *Newsweek,* 22 June 1987.
Sherman, Paul. "Checking Tarantino References Leads to Video Store, Not Library." *Boston Herald,* 14 October 1994.
Shulgasser, Barbara. "Little to Recommend *Little Odessa.*" *San Francisco Examiner,* 2 June 1995.
Simpson, Janice C. "Not Just One of the Boyz." *Time,* 23 March 1992.
Sinclair, Ian. "Smart Guys." *Sight and Sound,* August 1996.
Smith, Gavin. "*Casino.*" *Film Comment,* January–February 1996.
Smith, Russell. "A Grim Picture of the Hood: *Menace II Society* Never Wavers from Its Violent Portrayal." *Dallas Morning News,* 26 May 1993.
Stamberg, Susan. "*Reservoir Dogs:* Low-Budget Crime Film Gains Notoriety." *National Public Radio* (program transcript), 9 November 1992.
Stark, Susan. "Talia." *Detroit News,* 28 May 1982.
Taubin, Amy, "Blood and Pasta." *New Statesman and Society,* 9 November 1990.
Thomson, David. "The Discreet Charm of *The Godfather.*" *Sight and Sound,* Spring 1978.
Travers, Peter. "*American Me.*" *Rolling Stone,* 2 April 1992.
Walinsky, Adam. "The Crisis of Public Order." *Atlantic Monthly,* July 1995.
Walker, Alexander. "Shooting the Dogs of Gore." *Evening Standard,* 5 November 1992.
Williams, Frank. "Rage against the Machine." *The Source: The Magazine of Hip-Hop Music, Culture, and Politics,* July 1997.
Wolfenstein, Martha, and Nathan Leites. "Crime Patterns in Today's Movies." *Films in Review,* March 1950.
Wood, James. "*Pulp Fiction:* 'You're Sayin' a Foot Massage Don't Mean Nothin', and I'm Sayin' It Does.' " *Guardian,* 19 November 1994.
Yates, John. "*Godfather* Saga: The Death of the Family." *Journal of Popular Film* 4, no. 2 (1975).
Zimmerman, Paul D. "*Godfather*: Triumph for Brando." *Newsweek,* 13 March 1972.
———. "Sons of the Godfather." *Newsweek,* 22 October 1973.
———. "Godfathers and Sons." *Newsweek,* 23 December 1974.

OTHER SOURCES

The following periodicals were used extensively for film reviews and background research:

Chicago Tribune
Los Angeles Times
New York Times
Newsday
Variety
Village Voice
Washington Post

Other multimedia sources used include the following:

American Film Institute Catalog: Feature Films 1921–1930. New York: R. R. Bowker, 1971.

The Beat Generation. CD collection from Rhino Records. 1992.

Biography video series. Arts and Entertainment Network.

Compton's Interactive Encyclopedia on CD-ROM. Compton's New Media, 1995.

Internet Movie Database (http://www.imdb.com).

Roger Ebert's On-line Archive Service. Chicago Sun-Times. "Roger Ebert on Movies" (http://www.suntimes.com/ebert).

USA Today: The '90s-Volume II on CD-ROM. Gannett Satellite Information Network, 1994.

Variety Movie Guide '96. London: Bath Press, 1995.

World Encyclopedia of Organized Crime on CD-ROM. Dallas: Zane Publishing and Crime Data Research News Service, 1995.

INDEX

THE AUTHOR

Marilyn Yaquinto is an award-winning writer and journalist who lives in Michigan. She cowrote the 1994 book *Sastun: My Apprenticeship with a Maya Healer.* The book chronicles the experiences of an American herbalist, Rosita Arvigo, and her work with renowned Maya healer and shaman Elijio Panti. Panti had been one of the inspirations for the shaman featured in the film *Medicine Man,* starring Sean Connery. As in the film, Arvigo and Panti worked closely with AIDS and cancer researchers to catalog and study the medicinal plants of the Central American rain forests. The book has also been featured on an episode of the ABC television show *Prime Time Live.* Ms. Yaquinto has also worked for several newspapers and publications, including the *Los Angeles Times.* She was included in the Pulitzer Prize awarded to the newspaper for its spot news reporting of the 1992 Los Angeles riots and the national response following the verdict in the Rodney King court case. Ms. Yaquinto has been a lecturer at the University of Michigan in Ann Arbor since 1993, focusing on courses that blend communication with cultural influences.

THE EDITOR

Frank E. Beaver, general editor of Twayne's Filmmakers Series, was born in Cleveland, North Carolina, in 1938. He was educated at the University of North Carolina at Chapel Hill (B.A., M.A.) and at the University of Michigan (Ph.D.). He has authored three books on the art and history of the motion picture as well as *Oliver Stone: Wakeup Cinema* (1993) and the *Dictionary of Film Terms* (1994), both published in Twayne's Filmmakers Series. For 20 years he has served as media commentator for National Public Radio stations WUOM, WVGR, and WFUM.